Christoph Heger

# An Approach for Guiding Developers to Performance and Scalability Solutions

**The Karlsruhe Series on Software Design and Quality**
**Volume 21**

Chair Software Design and Quality
Faculty of Computer Science
Karlsruhe Institute of Technology

and

Software Engineering Division
Research Center for Information Technology (FZI), Karlsruhe

Editor: Prof. Dr. Ralf Reussner

# An Approach for Guiding Developers to Performance and Scalability Solutions

by
Christoph Heger

KIT Scientific Publishing

Dissertation, Karlsruher Institut für Technologie
KIT-Fakultät für Informatik

Tag der mündlichen Prüfung: 15. Juli 2015
Gutachter: Prof. Dr. Ralf H. Reussner, Prof. Dr. Wilhelm Hasselbring

**Impressum**

KIT Scientific Publishing

Karlsruher Institut für Technologie (KIT)
KIT Scientific Publishing
Straße am Forum 2
D-76131 Karlsruhe

KIT Scientific Publishing is a registered trademark
of Karlsruhe Institute of Technology.
Reprint using the book cover is not allowed.

www.ksp.kit.edu



Print on Demand 2018 – Gedruckt auf FSC-zertifiziertem Papier

ISSN 1867-0067
ISBN 978-3-7315-0698-0
DOI: 10.5445/KSP/1000072059

# An Approach for Guiding Developers to Performance and Scalability Solutions

zur Erlangung des akademischen Grades eines

Doktors der Ingenieurwissenschaften

der Fakultät für Informatik
des Karlsruher Instituts für Technologie

genehmigte

Dissertation

von

Christoph Heger

aus Heidelberg, Deutschland

Tag der mündlichen Prüfung: 15. Juli 2015
Erster Gutachter: Prof. Dr. Ralf H. Reussner
Zweiter Gutachter: Prof. Dr. Wilhelm Hasselbring

# Abstract

The quality of enterprise software applications plays a crucial role for the satisfaction of the users and the economic success of the enterprises. Study results show a strong correlation between the performance of the software application and the revenue per user. Software applications with unsatisfying performance and scalability are perceived by its users as low in quality, as less interesting and less attractive, and cause frustration when preventing the users from attaining their goals. Software performance and scalability problems also lead to frustrated developers because the solution of these problems is a challenging task. Supporting developers with software performance experts becomes also difficult because of the decreasing number of performance experts caused by retirement and non-replacement with comparably skilled people. Hence, better approaches are required that expect less expertise in performance engineering from the developer compared to the state-of-the-art practice in solving performance problems.

Consequently, an approach to support developers in finding solutions for software performance and scalability problems should possess a set of properties: the approach should provide appropriate data representations for human computer interaction and possess a corpus of elicited performance expert knowledge. Furthermore, the approach should consider various implementation artifacts and provide a workflow that exceeds the sole identification of possible solutions. Existing design and performance model-based approaches focus on the architecture rather the implementation and support the software architect rather the developer. Existing measurement-based approaches are limited to a particular concern and do not provide a comprehensive workflow. Existing recommendation systems focus on functional aspects of the software application rather than on software performance and scalability.

This thesis proposes an approach for a recommendation system that enables developers who are novices in software performance engineering to solve software performance and scalability problems without the assistance of a software performance expert. The contribution of this thesis is the explicit consideration of the implementation level to recommend solutions for software performance and scalability problems. This includes a set of description languages for data representation and human computer interaction and a workflow to guide the developer through the solution process without the assistance of a software performance expert.

The validation of the approach includes an online survey and a case study. The results of the online survey, with respondents from industry and academia, show the validity of the assumptions and concepts of the contributions. The case study with three common software performance and scalability problems in using existing object-relational mapping frameworks for the Java programming language shows the feasibility of the approach.

# Zusammenfassung

Die Qualität von Software-Anwendungen ist ein entscheidender Faktor für die Zufriedenheit der Nutzer und den wirtschaftlichen Erfolg des Unternehmens. Studien zeigen eine starke Korrelation zwischen der Performance einer Software-Anwendung und dem erzielten Umsatz pro Nutzer. Software-Anwendungen mit unzureichenden Performance- und Skalierbarkeitseigenschaften werden von ihren Nutzern als wenig qualitativ, interessant und attraktiv wahrgenommen und verursachen dabei gleichermaßen Frustration sobald die Software-Anwendung ihre Nutzer daran hindert ihr Ziel zu erreichen. Performance- und Skalierbarkeitsprobleme in Software-Anwendungen führen aber auch zu frustrierten Entwicklern da das Lösen dieser Probleme als eine herausfordernde Aufgabe angesehen wird. Zusätzlich macht es die abnehmende Zahl an Performance-Experten durch Pensionierung und Nicht-Ersetzung mit vergleichbar qualifiziertem Personal schwierig, Entwickler bei der Lösung solcher Probleme zu unterstützen. Dadurch entsteht der Bedarf an besseren Werkzeugen die, im Vergleich zur Vergangenheit, nur wenig Expertise für Software Performance Engineering voraussetzen.

Entwickler beim Lösen von Performance- und Skalierbarkeitsproblemen zu unterstützen beinhaltet zahlreiche Probleme. Viele Performance- und Skalierbarkeitsprobleme von Software-Anwendungen können nicht durch Simulation gelöst werden, die Implementierung einer Software-Anwendung besteht aus heterogenen Artefakten, die Anwendung von Änderungen auf die Software-Anwendung birgt mehr Risiken als Änderungen von Entwurfs- und Performance-Modellen, die Durchführung von dynamischen Analysen durch Entwickler birgt das Risiko von Missverständnissen wenn diese Anfänger im Bereich Software Performance Engineering sind und Entwickler trauen Messungen mehr als Vorhersagen.

Ein Empfehlungssystem das Entwickler beim Finden von angemessenen Lösungen für Performance- und Skalierbarkeitsprobleme von Software-Anwendungen auf der Implementierungsebene einer Software-Anwendung unterstützt, sollte eine angemessene Datenrepräsentation für die Mensch-Maschine-Interaktion bereitstellen, einen Korpus an festgehaltenem Expertenwissen über Performance und Skalierbarkeit besitzen, verschiedene Implementierungsartefakte berücksichtigen und einen Arbeitsablauf bereitstellen, der über die alleinige Identifizierung möglicher Lösungen hinausgeht. Existierende Ansätze die auf Entwurfs- und Performance-Modellen basieren, konzentrieren sich auf die Architektur der Software-Anwendung und nicht auf die Implementierung und unterstützen den Software-Architekten und nicht den Entwickler. Existierende Ansätze die auf Messungen basieren sind auf bestimmte Belange konzentriert und bieten keinen umfassenden Arbeitsablauf. Existierende Empfehlungssysteme konzentrieren sich auf funktionale Aspekte der Software-Anwendung und nicht auf Performance und Skalierbarkeit.

Die vorliegende Dissertation präsentiert Vergil, einen Ansatz für ein Empfehlungssystem, das Entwicklern ermöglicht Performance und Skalierbarkeitsprobleme ohne einen assistierenden Performanceexperten zu lösen. Die Zielgruppe von Vergil sind Entwickler, die Anfänger im Bereich Software Performance Engineering sind. Die Beiträge der Dissertation sind das explizite Berücksichtigen der Implementierungsebene für das Empfehlen von Lösungen, Beschreibungssprachen für die Datenrepräsentation und die Mensch-Maschine-Interaktion, einen Arbeitsablauf zur Anleitung von Entwicklern durch den Lösungsprozess ohne einen assistierenden Performance-Experten und die Instanziierung des Ansatzes für drei häufige Probleme im Kontext der objekt-relationalen Abbildung. Hierzu werden Techniken aus der modellgetriebenen Software-Entwicklung eingesetzt wie die Metamodellierung, um heterogene Artefakte der Implementierung in Instanzen von Metamodellen zu überführen. Diese Modellinstanzen bilden die Grundlage für Vergil um mit Hilfe von Regeln Lösungsmöglichkeiten für ein Problem zu identifizieren. Die Regeln werden von Performance-Experten erstellt indem diese ihr Expertenwissen in einer Struktur aus Tests und Endpunkten festhalten. Die Tests nutzen dabei statische und dynamische Analysen wie auch Interaktionen mit Entwicklern, um die Anwendbarkeit eines Lösungskonzeptes zu ermitteln. Die Endpunkte instanziieren die anwendbaren Lösungskonzepte für das jeweilige Problem und die jeweilige Anwendung. Für die Instanziierung der Lösungskonzepte können die Endpunkte auf dieselben Datenquellen wie die Tests zurückgreifen. Vergil beschreibt die notwendigen Änderungen zur Implementierung einer Lösung mit einem Änderungsplan. Der Änderungsplan beschreibt welche Elemente der Implementierung betroffen sind und wie diese geändert werden sollten. Vergil ist reaktiv und erwartet eine Beschreibung des Performance- und Skalierbarkeitsproblems als Eingabe durch den Entwickler. Der Arbeitsablauf besteht aus fünf Aktivitäten und sieht neben der Rolle des Entwicklers auch die Rolle des Testers und des Entscheidungsträgers vor. Der Tester ist dafür verantwortlich dynamische Analysen durchzuführen um komplementäre Informationen über die Anwendung zu sammeln die von Vergil beim Entwickler nachgefragt werden. Hierbei beschreibt Vergil als Hilfestellung welche Metriken gemessen werden sollen, wo in der Software-Anwendung die Metriken gemessen werden sollen und welches operative Lastprofil simuliert werden soll. Der Entscheidungsträger ist außerdem dafür verantwortlich die Entscheidungskriterien zu definieren, zu priorisieren und festzulegen welche Eigenschaften der Lösungsalternativen für die Priorisierung der Lösungsalternativen benötigt werden. Vergil erstellt für den Entwickler eine Rangliste der Lösungsalternativen mit abnehmender Priorität als Entscheidungsunterstützung. Die Lösungsalternative mit der höchsten Priorität führt die Rangliste an. Neben der Identifizierung potentieller Lösungsmöglichkeiten und der Erstellung der Rangliste, schließt der Arbeitsablauf von Vergil die Identifizierung aller von der Implementierung einer Lösung betroffenen Elemente durch das Propagieren der initialen Änderungen, die Abschätzung des Implementierungsaufwandes einer Lösungsaltmöglichkeit, und die Evaluation der definierten Eigenschaften einer Lösungsalternative vor der Priorisierung mit ein. Die Änderungen werden mit Hilfe von Regeln propagiert und dem Änderungsplan entsprechende Änderungen hinzugefügt. Der Änderungsplan bildet dann die Grundlage für die Aufwandsschätzung der Implementierung einer Lösung. Vergil verwendet die vom Entscheidungsträger spezifizierten relevanten Eigenschaften, um dem Entwickler eine Hilfestellung zu geben welche Informationen der Entscheidungsträger zur Priorisierung über die Lösungsmöglichkeiten benötigt.

Die Validierung von Vergil beinhaltet eine Onlineumfrage und eine Fallstudie. Die Ergebnisse der Onlineumfrage mit 44 Umfrageteilnehmern aus Industrie und Wissenschaft zeigen die Gültigkeit der Annahmen sowie der Konzepte der Beiträge. Die meisten Umfrageteilnehmer gaben an, die Rolle des Entwicklers und/oder des Performance-Experten auszuüben und sich seit mehr als drei Jahren mit dem Lösen von Performance- und Skalierbarkeitsproblemen von Software-Anwendungen zu beschäftigen. Dabei gab die Mehrheit der Umfrageteilnehmer an, in der Industrie zu arbeiten und zwar bei einem Unternehmen mit 100 Mitarbeitern und mehr. Die Ergebnisse der Onlineumfrage bestätigen, dass Performance- und Skalierbarkeitsprobleme von Software-Anwendungen in einer allgemeineren Klassifikation klassifiziert und Lösungskonzepte auf Instanzen dieser Klassen angewendet werden können. Die Umfrageteilnehmer berichteten außerdem, dass sie sich häufig in Situationen mit einem Problem und mehreren Lösungsmöglichkeiten oder mehreren Problemen und mehreren Lösungsmöglichkeiten befunden haben. Die Umfrageteilnehmer stimmten auch der Aussage zu, dass die derzeit angebotene Unterstützung beim Lösen von Performance- und Skalierbarkeitsproblemen unzureichend ist. Die Fallstudie zeigt anhand drei häufig vorkommender Performance- und Skalierbarkeitsprobleme, die bei der Verwendung von Rahmenwerken für die objekt-relationale Abbildung im Kontext der Programmiersprache Java auftreten können, die Realisierbarkeit des Ansatzes. Die insgesamt acht erstellten Änderungshypothesen schlagen insgesamt 12 Lösungsmöglichkeiten für die drei Probleme vor. Die Ergebnisse der Fallstudie zeigen, dass Vergil die erwartete Ausgabe für eine gültige Eingabe liefert. Dabei wurde der Arbeitsablauf durchlaufen, der über das Identifizieren von Lösungsmöglichkeiten hinausgeht, um die angemessenste Lösungsmöglichkeit vorzuschlagen. Die empfohlenen Lösungsmöglichkeiten konnten dabei die Antwortzeit des betroffenen Dienstes um bis zu 98,7% verbessern, ohne dabei negative Auswirkungen auf andere Dienste zu verursachen. Von den vorgeschlagenen Änderungen betroffen sind dabei sowohl die Konfiguration der Java Persistence API aber auch die Implementierung und die Architektur der Software-Anwendung.

Die Ergebnisse der Dissertation zeigen, dass die Einschränkungen bestehender Ansätze überwunden werden können, um Entwickler bei der Lösung von Performance- und Skalierbarkeitsproblemen zu unterstützen, welche Anfänger im Bereich Software Performance Engineering sind. Techniken aus dem Bereich der modellgetriebenen Software-Entwicklung haben sich hierbei als praktisches Mittel erwiesen, um heterogene Artefakte der Implementierung zu berücksichtigen. Die Beiträge der Dissertation zeigen, dass sich Expertenwissen zum Lösen von Performance- und Skalierbarkeitsproblemen in Software-Anwendung in Regeln festhalten lässt. Die Ergebnisse sind auch ein Indikator dafür, dass es möglich ist die Konvergenz von mess-basierten und modell-basierten Methoden zum Lösen von Performance- und Skalierbarkeitsproblemen zu unterstützen.

Die sich ergebenden Vorteile sind unter anderen, dass die Arbeitslast für Performance-Experten dadurch reduziert werden kann, dass diese sich auf unbekannte Probleme konzentrieren und das neue Wissen in Regeln für Vergil festhalten, die einer Vielzahl an Entwicklern zur Verfügung gestellt werden. Entwickler können durch das Lösen von Problemen mit Hilfe von Vergil die Performance-orientierte Nutzung von APIs, Rahmenwerken und Bibliotheken erlernen. Die gesteigerte Qualität der Software-Anwendung kann dann wiederum die Attraktivität der Software-Anwendung für die Nutzer steigern.

# Danksagung

Auf meiner langen Reise habe ich die Unterstützung von sehr vielen wundervollen, aufrichtigen, inspirierenden und bemerkenswerten Menschen erhalten, die mit ihrer Förderung und ihrem Rat einen bedeutenden Teil dazu beigetragen haben, diese Doktorarbeit Realität werden zu lassen.

Allen voran möchte ich mich bei meinem Doktorvater Professor Dr. Ralf H. Reussner dafür bedanken, dass er mir diese Doktorarbeit ermöglicht hat und mich über den gesamten Bearbeitungszeitraum hinweg hervorragend betreut hat. Meinem Korreferenten Professor Dr. Wilhelm Hasselbring danke ich für die Übernahme des Korreferates und seinen Ideen und Hinweisen, die ihren Beitrag zu meiner Arbeit geleistet haben. Ich danke auch Dr. Wolfgang Theilmann für seine Unterstützung und Förderung bei der SAP SE, bei der ich während meiner Promotion war.

Bedanken möchte ich mich auch bei Dr.-Ing. Jens Happe, Dr.-Ing. Dennis Westermann und Roozbeh Farahbod, PhD, die durch ihr Engagement mein Promotionsprojekt erst ermöglicht haben. Ihre Erfahrungen, Einschätzungen und Ratschläge, sowie die Diskussionen und Anregungen haben einen bedeutenden Beitrag zum erfolgreichen Abschluss dieser Doktorarbeit geleistet.

Meinem Kollegen Alexander Wert gilt mein ganz besonderer Dank für eine einmalige und bemerkenswerte Zusammenarbeit. Als Kollege, Freund und Ratgeber hat er mich durch die Höhen und Tiefen der Promotionszeit begleitet. Viele Ideen sind in den Gesprächen und Diskussionen mit ihm entstanden. Ich danke auch meinen Kollegen am SDQ, FZI und der SAP SE für die produktiven und konstruktiven Diskussionen, die angenehme Arbeitsatmosphäre und die zahlreichen Ideen und Anregungen, die ich als Rückmeldung auf meine Arbeit erhalten habe. Einen bedeutenden Teil haben auch Studenten geleistet, die mich tatkräftig unterstutzt haben. Für diese Unterstützung bedanke ich mich in alphabetischer Reihenfolge bei Sven Kohlhaas, Edy Komgang Djomgang, Jonas Kunz, Oleg Löwen, Henning Muszynski und Till Neuber.

Dr. Robert Heinrich und Christian Nikels danke ich für das Korrekturlesen meiner Doktorarbeit und die Hinweise, die meine Arbeit verbessert haben.

Ein besonderer Dank geht an meine Familie, insbesondere an meine Eltern und Schwiegereltern, die mich auf meiner langen Reise immer unterstützt haben. Am allermeisten danke ich aber meiner Frau Isabel, die in den letzten Jahren auf vieles verzichten musste, als ich meine Zeit und Energie in die Doktorarbeit investiert habe. Ohne die Unterstützung und das Verständnis, das ich von ihr erhalten habe, und den Rückhalt und Zuspruch wäre diese Arbeit nicht möglich gewesen.

Karlsruhe, im Juli 2015 *Christoph Heger*

# Contents

# 1. Introduction

This thesis proposes Vergil, an approach to guide novice developers in solving software performance and scalability problems at the implementation level by recommending possible solutions. This chapter motivates and introduces Vergil and the contributions and goals of the thesis from a high-level perspective.

Section 1.1 motivates the development of Vergil and Section 1.2 gives the problem statement that is addressed by Vergil. Section 1.3 then describes the requirements for an approach to address the problem. Section 1.4 briefly outlines existing solutions and their limitations before Section 1.5 formulates the goal of this thesis. Section 1.6 introduces the challenges to attain the goal while Section 1.7 highlights the contributions of the thesis before Section 1.8 describes the conducted validation. Section 1.9 concludes the introduction with an outline of the remainder of the thesis.

## 1.1. Motivation

In the last decade, the usage of software applications for almost any concern became an essential part in the life of many people. Despite the functional aspects of the software applications that may also be provided by competitors, the quality of the software application plays a crucial role for the satisfaction of the users and the economic success of the company. Two important quality attributes of a software application are performance and scalability. Performance is “the degree to which a system or component accomplishes its designated functions within given constraints, such as speed, accuracy, or memory usage” (ISO/IEC/IEEE, 2010). Scalability is “[...] the ability of the system to sustain increasing workloads by making use of additional resources [...]” (Herbst et al., 2013) (this definition complies with the formal definition of scalability given in (M. D. Hill, 1990; Bondi, 2000)). A recently conducted survey (Compuware 2015) with 150 senior IT managers revealed that the large majority of 80% of the respondents reported that performance problems affect customer satisfaction. Furthermore, 39% of the respondents reported that developers have a significant responsibility for performance problems (Compuware 2015).

Software applications with unsatisfying performance and scalability quality attributes are perceived by its users to be of lower quality (Bouch et al., 2000), as less interesting (Ramsay et al., 1998), and as less attractive (Skadberg et al., 2004), causing frustration (Ceaparu et al., 2004) and higher blood pressure (Lazar et al., 2006) when the software application inhibits its users from attaining their goals.

Consequently, the performance and scalability of contemporary Web-based software applications become an important aspect in today's software development. While cloud computing provides theoretically unlimited resources, software applications with performance and scalability issues are unable to utilize the possible resources effectively to cope with varying workloads and usage profiles in order to provide a satisfying quality of service to its users. This has an influence on the total cost of ownership of the software application.

But, the total cost of ownership is only one aspect that is impacted by the application's performance and scalability quality attributes. Another aspect is the strong correlation between the performance of the application and the revenue per user. For example, Google reported that a 500 ms increase in response time results in a drop in revenue by 20% while Amazon reported that they increased their revenue by 1% for every 100 ms of response time improvement (Kohavi et al., 2007; Linden, 2006). This aspect can be generalized to other domains where the employees of the company are the users of the software application. A responsive application does not inhibit the workflow and pace of the employee compared to an application that suffers from performance and scalability problems and inhibits an employee to complete its task. The experienced frustration can reduce job satisfaction and increase blood volume pressure and muscle tension (Lazar et al., 2006). Study results show that employees can lose up to 50% of their productive time due to problems with software applications (Lazar et al., 2006).

Performance and scalability problems can not only lead to frustrated users of the software application but also to frustrated developers. Performance problems take longer to diagnose compared to functional issues (Chambers et al., 2015) and the solution of performance and scalability problems is the most challenging task (Jovic et al., 2011). Although the second most common cause for software performance and scalability problems is that developers misunderstand the usage of Application Programming Interfaces and the consequences with respect to performance and scalability (Jin et al., 2012), it is difficult for developers to learn how to use Application Programming Interfaces, frameworks, and libraries properly (Robillard, 2009). Supporting the developers with performance experts becomes difficult because the number of performance experts that are capable of managing performance during development is decreasing caused by retirement without being replaced with comparably skilled people (C. U. Smith, 2015). This causes the need for better tools requiring less performance expertise than in the past for performance engineering where performance efforts are focused on measurement and testing not prediction (C. U. Smith, 2015) because "[...] many developers *do not trust* or understand performance models[...]" (Woodside et al., 2007). The tools have to guide the developers in solving software performance and scalability problems in order to prevent that they spend a significant amount of time changing the implementation of the software application without seeing significant improvement caused by a random solution approach (Williams et al., 2002a).

To provide an approach to implement such a tool that supports novice developers in solving software performance and scalability problems of a software application requiring less performance expertise is the focus of this thesis.

## 1.2. Problem Statement

The central problem tackled by this thesis is to support developers in the task of finding appropriate solutions for performance and scalability problems at the implementation level of a software application not in design or performance models (Trubiani et al., 2011; Xu, 2010; Cortellessa et al., 2010c). This includes the identification of possible solutions, the identification of impacted elements, the implementation effort estimation, the evaluation of solution properties, the selection of the most appropriate solution among multiple alternatives, and the description of the implementation of the solution. This section refines the central problem into entailed problems that are tackled by this thesis.

- *Not all software performance and scalability problems are solvable with design models and performance models (P1)*: The modeling languages to create design models and performance models possess assumptions, simplifications, and limitations to keep the modeling effort feasible (Jain, 1991). The modeling languages also make by nature an abstraction from the real implementation of the software application. While design models and performance models provide the capabilities to identify solutions for software performance and scalability problems when designing the software architecture, they are not usable when implementation details are necessary for software performance and scalability problems that are not reflectable in the models and simulations (Trubiani et al., 2011).
- *The implementation of a software application consists of heterogeneous artifacts (P2)*: Design models and performance models are model instances of a metamodeling language such as UML, PCM, or QPN. In contrast, the implementation of a software application consists of heterogeneous artifacts, e.g., source code files, or configuration files where each may possess their own metamodeling language like the Java programming language for source code, and XML Schema Definition (XSD) for XML files. Despite the diversity, the heterogeneous artifacts have to be considered because they capture valuable information relevant for solution identification.
- *The application of changes to the implementation entails more risks than changes to design and performance models (P3)*: Intended changes to the implementation of the software application may cause other unintended changes recursively known as the Ripple Effect (Yau et al., 1978). In a worst case scenario, a developer applies the intended changes that are perceived as simple but the changes cause other unintended changes that ripple to parts of the software application that are impossible to change and the judged implementation effort is exceeded by orders of magnitude.

- *Novice developers can make unintentional mistakes when conducting dynamic analysis (P4)*: Dynamic analysis of the software application to study the behavior of the software application and to collect complementary information to identify solutions requires the execution of performance tests. Dynamic analysis is "the process of evaluating a system or component based on its behavior during execution" (ISO/IEC/IEEE, 2010). This requires the correct instrumentation of the software application to collect demanded information and a thorough execution of the performance test. Developers that are novices in software performance engineering may make unintentional mistakes "due to simple oversights, misconception, and lack of knowledge about performance evaluation techniques." (Jain, 1991).
- *Developers trust measurements more than predictions (P5)*: "[. . . ] [Performance] *models are approximate*, they leave out detail that may be important, and are difficult to validate" (Woodside et al., 2007) which might be a reason why "[. . . ] many developers *do not trust* or understand performance models [. . . ]" (Woodside et al., 2007). This prevailing opinion makes it difficult to convince developers of solution proposals by performance prediction.

## 1.3. Requirements

To support developers in the task of finding appropriate solutions for performance and scalability problems at the implementation level of a software application, an approach for a recommendation system of the type advisor should be developed that requires less performance expertise by guiding the developer in completing the task. We formulate the following requirements on an approach for a recommendation system that supports the developer in this task:

- *The approach should support appropriate data representations for human computer interaction (R1)*: Derived from design questions for recommendation systems (Mens et al., 2014), the approach should support appropriate data representations for human computer interaction. The developer should be able to describe the problem in the form of *what* is observed and *when* as input. While software performance and scalability problems often depend on the operational profile, complementary information from additional dynamic analysis are often necessary to identify possible solutions (P4), the approach should be able to describe what complementary information is required, where in the system the information is to be obtained, and when with respect to the applied operational profile in order to reduce the required performance expertise. To support the developer in integrating a solution into the application (P3), the approach should provide an implementation description on how to implement the solution in the particular application.

- *The approach should provide a corpus of elicited performance expert knowledge (R2)*: The approach should provide a corpus of elicited performance expert knowledge in the form of rules that include analysis and reasoning to identify possible solutions and to make recommendations. The rules should mimic the structured approach of a performance expert. A recommendation is the "provision that conveys advice or guidance." (ISO/IEC/IEEE, 2010).

- *The approach should consider various implementation artifacts (R3)*: The approach should consider various implementation artifacts (P1, P2) that are analyzed to identify possible solutions based on the elicited rules.

- *The approach should provide a workflow that exceeds the sole identification of possible solutions (R4)*: According to Merkert, 2014, developers have issues to select a solution for performance and scalability problems from a provided list. The approach should provide a workflow that exceeds the sole identification of possible solutions to recommend the most appropriate solution and to prevent a random solution approach. In contrast to recommending, for example, the next API method to use where the conclusion can be drawn from static analysis of the source code based on similarities (McCarey et al., 2005; Holmes et al., 2006; Lozano et al., 2011; Zhang et al., 2012), the assessment of solution proposals for software performance and scalability problems requires the evaluation of the performance impact with dynamic analyses (P4, P5). This requires the implementation of the solution, prototyping or simulation. Prototyping is "a hardware and software development technique in which a preliminary version of part or all of the hardware or software is developed to permit user feedback, determine feasibility, or investigate timing or other issues in support of the development process" (ISO/IEC/IEEE, 2010) and simulation is to employ "a model that behaves or operates like a given system when provided a set of controlled inputs." (ISO/IEC/IEEE, 2010). In the context of this thesis, prototyping refers only to the software aspect of the given definition.

## 1.4. Existing Solutions

The majority of current state-of-the-art solutions have the software architect as the intended user and support the task of finding an architectural design that satisfies quality attributes. Hereby, the provided cognitive support is focused on what to do in order that the architecture exhibits the desired quality attributes. The proposed information is often the recommendation of complete architectural design alternatives (A. Koziolek, 2013; Trubiani et al., 2011; Drago, 2012) or the proposal of concrete actions (Xu, 2010; Barber et al., 2002; Potena, 2013). The expected input is an initial architectural design model. The recommendations are derived by the application of rules (Xu, 2010; Barber et al., 2002; Bachmann et al., 2007; Kavimandan et al., 2009; Drago, 2012; Potena, 2013) or metaheuristics (Canfora et al., 2005; Aleti et al., 2009; A. Koziolek, 2013; Etemaadi et al., 2015; Grunske, 2006). Other approaches guide the software architect in exploring the design space through the employment of design space exploration techniques (Zheng et al., 2003; Bondarev et al., 2007; Ipek et al., 2008; Ardagna et al., 2014) to prevent unpromising parts of the design space. The output in many cases is a set of Pareto-optimal architectural design alternatives that satisfy the quality attributes. An issue of these approaches is not only that they do not support the developer but also that "[...] models are approximates [...]" (Woodside et al., 2007) and miss implementation specific details (Woodside et al., 2007) that are often responsible for many performance and scalability problems (Compuware 2015) due to the assumptions of the modeling language and the simplifications to keep the modeling effort feasible (Jain, 1991).

State-of-the-art solutions that explicitly consider the implementation-specific details of a software application are measurement-based and limited to find an appropriate configuration for middleware (Lengauer et al., 2014), recommending recovery actions to operators (Bodík et al., 2010), or to improve deployment architectures (Malek et al., 2004). Although, measurement-based performance evaluation is the most commonly used approach (C. U. Smith, 2015; Woodside et al., 2007), the field of measurement-based performance and scalability problem solution is not well addressed. Approaches are missing that provide support at the implementation level, e.g., how APIs are used to reuse existing functionality.

Many source code-based recommendation systems in software engineering support the developer in reusing unknown methods (Ye et al., 2005), recommend the next method of an API to use (McCarey et al., 2005), guide developers in using a framework or API (Bruch et al., 2006; Holmes et al., 2006; Duala-Ekoko et al., 2011; Mandelin et al., 2005; Zhang et al., 2012), correcting structural inconsistencies (Lozano et al., 2011; Castro et al., 2011), and other tasks (Čubranić et al., 2005; Lozano et al., 2015; Lozano et al., 2010). The expected input in many cases are source code fragments (Lozano et al., 2010; Duala-Ekoko et al., 2011), method calls (Dagenais et al., 2008; Zhang et al., 2012), or special queries (Xie et al., 2006; E. Hill et al., 2007). The output is often one or more methods (Bruch et al., 2009; E. Hill et al., 2007; Ashok et al., 2009; Ye et al., 2005; McCarey et al., 2005), or source code fragments (Mandelin et al., 2005; Duala-Ekoko et al., 2011; Cottrell et al., 2008; Holmes et al., 2006). Only (Cottrell et al., 2008; Duala-Ekoko et al., 2011) support the developer in integrating the code fragments into the source code of the particular application. While the existing recommendation systems support the developer in understanding and learning the usage APIs and frameworks, they do not have a special emphasis on the consequences for performance and scalability.

Obviously, no approach exists that supports developers in solving software performance and scalability problems and satisfies all requirements. Design model and performance model-based approaches focus on the architecture and not on the implementation and therefore do not satisfy requirements R1, R2, and R3. The approaches that focus on the implementation concentrate on a particular aspect and do not consider various implementation artifacts and do not provide a workflow for the developer and therefore do not satisfy requirements R1, R3 and R4. Recommendation systems consider various implementation artifacts as data source but focus on functional aspects of the software application rather than software performance and scalability and therefore do not satisfy requirements R1, R2, and R4.

## 1.5. Goal

Motivated by the impact of software performance and scalability problems on the satisfaction of users and the shortcomings of existing approaches, we formulate the goal of the thesis as follows:

> Development of an approach that satisfies the requirements and enables developers who are novices in software performance engineering to solve software performance and scalability problems without the assistance of a software performance expert.

If developers do not have a strong expertise in software performance engineering, they face a challenging and complex task when tasked with solving performance and scalability problems. Thereby, "*Software Performance Engineering (SPE) represents the entire collection of software engineering activities and related analyses used throughout the software development cycle, which are directed to meeting performance requirements*" (Woodside et al., 2007). To support developers in completing the task without the assistance of a software performance expert, a structured workflow that mimics the activities of software performance experts to solve a problem must hide the complexity behind higher-level techniques for reasoning and solution (Woodside et al., 2007) supported by tools that provide automation and encapsulate the necessary expert knowledge of possible solutions, selection of metrics, design of experiments, and analysis and interpretation of data.

## 1.6. Challenges

This section presents the challenges in developing an approach that satisfies the requirements and attains the goal.

- *Consideration of various implementation artifacts*: The explicit consideration of a software application's implementation entails the consideration of various heterogeneous implementation artifacts. The concrete instance of the implementation artifacts is unknown when the rules are developed that analyze the artifacts to identify possible solutions. The challenge targets requirement R3 and the hypothesis to overcome this challenge is:

  *Hypothesis (H1)*: Model-Driven Software Development (MDSD) techniques provide the facilities to consider various implementation artifacts to identify possible solutions.

- *Data representation for human computer interaction*: Vergil and the developer require means for human computer interaction to exchange information throughout the workflow. The data to represent includes the software performance and scalability problem, the required complementary information from dynamic analysis as well as the analysis results, the properties of solution proposals, implementation constraints, and the implementation of a solution at the implementation level tailored to the software application's implementation considering the propagation of changes. The challenge targets R1 and the hypothesis to overcome this challenge is:

  *Hypothesis (H2)*: Domain-specific description languages provide the required data representations.

- *Formalization of elicited rules from performance expert knowledge*: In order to support developers who are novices in software performance engineering with automation and tools that require less performance expertise, the knowledge of performance experts about changes for software performance and scalability problems, selecting metrics, performance evaluation techniques, workloads, designing experiments, analyzing and interpreting data must be formalized. The challenge targets R2 and the hypothesis to overcome this challenge is:

  *Hypothesis (H3)*: Solutions for software performance and scalability problems are identifiable with rules and static analysis, dynamic analysis and user interaction.

- *Definition of a workflow to guide developers*: In order to avoid a random solution approach the activities that are performed by performance experts have to be identified and transferred into activities of a workflow. The workflow then mimics the structured approach of performance experts and acts as guidance for novice developers. The challenge targets R4 and the hypothesis to overcome this challenge is:

*Hypothesis (H4)*: The activities in a workflow to guide novice developers are to identify possible solutions, to identify the impacted elements, to estimate the implementation effort, to evaluate the properties of solutions, and to prioritize solution alternatives.

- *Derivation of an implementation description*: Vergil requires a description of the implementation for each solution proposal at the implementation level tailored to the software application's implementation considering the possible propagation of changes, including the necessary changes and the impacted elements to support the review and discussion process as well as the actual implementation of the solution. The challenge targets R3 and R4. The hypothesis to overcome this challenge is:

  *Hypothesis (H5)*: Model-Driven Software Development techniques and rules enable the derivation of an implementation description.

## 1.7. Contributions

When comparing the state-of-the-art solutions with the problem statement, multiple insufficiencies of existing approaches become apparent in supporting the developer in the task of solving software performance and scalability problems in software applications. To provide sufficient support to the developer and to attain the formulated goal, the main scientific contributions of this thesis are:

- *Explicit consideration of the implementation level to recommend solutions for software performance and scalability problems*: Vergil's main corpus to provide recommendations are implementation artifacts with the source code of the software application as the most important data source. The elicited rules from performance expert knowledge start with a static analysis of relevant implementation artifacts. Complementary information is provided by dynamic analyses of the software application's implementation, design models, and performance models. Recommended solutions are provided as a change plan describing the necessary changes of the implementation in the form of what elements are impacted and how they must be changed.

- *Description languages for data representation and human computer interaction*: We propose description languages for data representation throughout the solution process and for the interaction between Vergil and the developer. The description languages describe the software performance and scalability problems and quality attribute requirements, decision criteria, the properties of solution proposals with respect to the decision criteria, constraints, and the change plan. Furthermore, the description languages support the conduction of dynamic analysis by describing what information to collect, where in the software application's implementation the data should be monitored, and when providing guidance in experiment design.
- *Workflow to guide the developer through the solution process without the assistance of a software performance expert*: Vergil considers a workflow that mimics the structured approach of performance experts to guide the developer through the solution process. The main activities of the workflow are the identification of possible solutions, the identification of impacted elements of the software application's implementation, the estimation of the implementation effort of solution proposals, the evaluation of solution properties with respect to the decision criteria, and the ranking of solution proposals by priority. To enable developers to solve software performance and scalability problems without the assistance of software performance experts, the workflow considers the additional role of a tester and a decision maker.
- *Instantiation of the approach for three common Java Persistence API (JPA) problems*: To validate Vergil, we instantiated Vergil for three common JPA problems, i.e., N+1 Selects, Excessive Dynamic Allocation, and Excessive Logging. All problems can occur when the consequences of using JPA methods and parameters on software performance and scalability are not understood. Thereby, learning to use JPA properly is difficult due to the complexity. We develop rules from accessible software performance expert knowledge that propose multiple solutions at different levels of the software application ranging from the

configuration of JPA to architectural changes of the employed software application.

## 1.8. Validation

The contributions of this thesis have been validated with a proof-of-concept case study by means of three common software performance and scalability problems that may occur in using existing frameworks for object-relational mapping. We used fault injection, an established research method in software engineering (Hsueh et al., 1997), to cause the software performance and scalability problems. Fault injection is "[...] the deliberate insertion of faults into an operational system to determine its response [...]" (Clark et al., 1995). Fault injection is most commonly used to validate critical software applications like aircraft flight control, nuclear reactor monitoring, business transaction processing, and others (Clark et al., 1995). Thereby, faults are injected into the software application under study to which Vergil is applied to solve the problems. We used reports from developers to inject the problems into a performant and scalable software application as research subject.

Furthermore, we conducted an online survey with 44 respondents from academia and industry to substantiate the validity of our assumptions and concepts of the contributions and to collect important information on how performance and scalability problems are solved in real-world scenarios.

## 1.9. Outline

The remainder of the thesis is structured as follows:

- Chapter 2 presents foundations that are relevant for this thesis. Section 2.1 introduces the software performance engineering approach including performance metrics, model-based performance analysis, and measurement-based performance analysis. Section 2.2 introduces the Palladio Component Model (PCM) that can be used for model-based performance analysis. Section 2.3 introduces the Java Persistence API (JPA) including relevant details for this thesis and the possible software performance and scalability problems addressed in the case study. Section 2.4 introduces relevant concepts of Model-Driven Software Development. Section 2.5 introduces the Java Model Parser and Printer (JaMoPP) including the JaMoPP Java metamodel. Section 2.6 introduces the Analytic Hierarchy Process (AHP) for decision making. Section 2.7 introduces the term enterprise application as it is considered in this thesis and Section 2.8 introduces the corresponding solution space for enterprise applications with respect to software performance and scalability problems. Section 2.9 introduces characteristics of the survey research instrument and relevant terms from survey methodology.

- Chapter 3 presents Vergil starting with an overview on Vergil in Section 3.1 and the presentation of the design decisions of Vergil as a recommendation system based on (Mens et al., 2014) in Section 3.2. Section 3.3 presents the approach of Vergil to satisfy the requirements and to attain the formulated goal while Section 3.4 introduces the considered roles of the developer, tester, decision maker, and performance expert. Section 3.5 describes the assigned responsibilities to each role.
- Chapter 4 introduces the description languages that Vergil uses for data representation through the workflow and for human computer interaction. Section 4.1 introduces the parameter specification and dimension language used to describe any parameter such as observations and requirements. Section 4.2 introduces the performance profile description language that builds upon the parameter specification language to describe the performance profile and collected data of dynamic analyses. Section 4.3 introduces the change plan description language used by Vergil to describe the implementation of solution proposals. Section 4.4 introduces the performance solution description language that describes decision criteria for prioritizing the solution proposals and the properties of solution proposals with respect to the decision criteria. Section 4.5 introduces the change hypothesis description language to create the rules for identifying solution proposals and to instantiate the change plans. Section 4.6 introduces the constraints description language to constrain changes to the software application's implementation.
- Chapter 5 describes the proposed workflow and the considered activities to guide the developer starting with an overview in Section 5.1. Sec-

tion 5.2 describes the creation of the decision criteria hierarchy required to prioritize the solution proposal to obtain the ranking. Section 5.3 describes the description of the software performance and scalability problem as input to Vergil. The workflow activities are then described in more detail in the consecutive sections. Section 5.4 describes the identification of possible solutions. Section 5.5 describes the identification of impacted elements of the implementation while Section 5.6 describes the implementation effort estimation based on the result. Section 5.7 describes the evaluation of solution properties with respect to the decision criteria. Section 5.8 describes the decision making support through a ranking of the solution proposals according to their priority.

- Chapter 6 introduces the created change hypothesis for the Java Persistence API that we have used to validate Vergil. Section 6.1 introduces the query hints change hypothesis, the mapping configuration change hypothesis, the shared cache change hypothesis, and the pagination change hypothesis for the N+1 Selects problem. Section 6.2 introduces the logging level change hypothesis for the excessive logging problem. Section 6.3 introduces the query hints change hypothesis, the mapping configuration change hypothesis, and the shared cache change hypothesis for the excessive data allocation problem. Section 6.4 discusses assumptions and limitations and Section 6.5 concludes the chapter with a summary.

- Chapter 7 presents the validation of Vergil starting with the validation design in Section 7.1. Section 7.2 presents the design, execution, and results of the online survey. Section 7.3 presents the proof-of-concept case study that we have conducted to validate the feasibility of Vergil. Section 7.4 presents the case study in which we assessed the evaluation of solution properties with simulation instead of measurement.

- Chapter 8 presents a discussion of related work. Section 8.1 presents documented software performance problem and solution knowledge most commonly in the form of software performance antipatterns. Section 8.2 presents approaches with a sole focus on software performance problem detection. Section 8.3 presents proposed recommendation systems in software engineering. Section 8.4 presents model-based performance solution approaches while Section 8.5 presents measurement-based performance solution approaches. Section 8.6

presents approaches from the field of self-adaptive resource allocation. Section 8.7 presents related work with respect to change description and change propagation.

- Chapter 9 concludes the thesis starting with a summary in Section 9.1. Section 9.2 justifies the scientific merit of the contributions before Section 9.3 describes the resulting benefits. Section 9.4 discusses our assumptions and presents limitations of Vergil while Section 9.5 discusses short-term and long-term future work.

# 2. Foundations

This chapter presents relevant foundations for this thesis and is structured as follows: Section 2.1 introduces the software performance engineering approach including, performance metrics, model-based performance analysis, and measurement-based performance analysis. Section 2.2 introduces the Palladio Component Model (PCM) used for model-based performance analysis. Section 2.3 introduces the Java Persistence API (JPA) including the possible software performance and scalability problems addressed in the case study. Section 2.4 introduces relevant concepts of Model-Driven Software Development this thesis builds upon. Section 2.5 introduces the Java Model Parser and Printer (JaMoPP) that provides the Ecore-based Java metamodel used as source code model. Section 2.6 introduces the Analytic Hierarchy Process (AHP) used for prioritizing criteria and solution proposals. Section 2.7 introduces the term enterprise application as it is considered in this thesis as software application and Section 2.8 introduces the corresponding solution space for enterprise applications with respect to software performance and scalability problems. Section 2.9 introduces characteristics of online surveys and relevant terms from survey methodology.

## 2.1. Software Performance Engineering

Software Performance Engineering (SPE) is a proactive approach for designing software applications that meet performance requirements using quantitative performance prediction techniques to identify potential designs, to compare design alternatives, and to make trade-off decisions prior to the implementation of the software application (C. U. Smith, 2015). This original scope of SPE was established in the 1980s by Connie Smith and has been revised by Woodside et al. in 2007 so that "*Software Performance Engineering (SPE) represents the entire collection of software engineering activities and related analyses used throughout the software development cycle, which are directed to meeting performance requirements*" (Woodside et al., 2007). Thereby, a performance requirement is "the measurable criterion that identifies a quality attribute of a function or how well a functional requirement must be accomplished." (ISO/IEC/IEEE, 2010).

Performance metrics and metric values are used to specify performance requirements. A metric is "a quantitative measure of the degree to which a system, component, or process possesses a given attribute" (ISO/IEC/IEEE, 2010). A metric value is "a metric output or an element that is from the range of a metric" (ISO/IEC/IEEE, 2010). Common performance metrics are response time, throughput, and resource utilization. Response time is "the elapsed time between the end of an inquiry or command to an interactive computer system and the beginning of the system's response" (ISO/IEC/IEEE, 2010). Throughput is "the amount of work that can be performed by a computer system or component in a given period of time" (ISO/IEC/IEEE, 2010). Resource utilization is "a ratio representing the amount of time a system or component is busy divided by the time it is available" (ISO/IEC/IEEE, 2010).

Whether a software application meets the performance requirements is analyzed with a performance analysis that is "a quantitative analysis of a [...] system (or software design) executing on a given hardware configuration with a given external workload applied to it" (ISO/IEC/IEEE, 2010). The workload is distinguished between a real workload and a synthetic workload. While the real workload is observed in operation when the end-users use the software application, e.g., the type and mix of requests sent to the software application, a synthetic workload is a model of the real workload that can be applied repeatedly and used for performance analysis studies (Jain, 1991). Two important aspects of a synthetic workload (henceforth referred to as workload) are its representativeness and timeliness. Representative means that the workload should match the real workload of the software application in terms of the arrival rate of user requests for an open workload (or number of end-users and think time for a closed workload), the resource demands to process the requests, and the resource usage profile. Timeliness means that the workload should include potential usage patterns of the end-users in a timely fashion (Jain, 1991). Performance analyses can be conducted either based on measurements where the software application is executed or based on performance models that are created as abstraction from the software application.

### 2.1.1. Model-based Performance Analysis

Model-based approaches for performance analysis predict performance metric values and can be grouped into approaches based on design models, performance models, and regression models. They are often used in designing a software application. Approaches based on design models use the UML metamodel or proprietary metamodels to describe the software application in terms of components, allocation, and behavior. Build in capabilities or extensions allow the specification of performance attributes and workload characteristics. Approaches building upon UML use the UML MARTE profile (Object Management Group, 2011b) for UML 2.1 to conduct performance analysis. Approaches based on proprietary metamodels propose their own metamodels to describe the software application and performance attributes. Examples are KLAPER (Grassi et al., 2005) and Palladio (Becker et al., 2009). To conduct the performance analysis, the model instances are transformed into performance models which are solved by simulation or numerical analysis (H. Koziolek, 2010). Popular performance models are Queueing Network (QN) and their extensions, stochastic Petri nets, stochastic process algebra, and simulation models (Balsamo et al., 2004).

Approaches based on regression models conduct performance analysis by predicting a random variable as a function of several predictor variables (Jain, 1991). Regression models are most commonly of the group of statistical models used for performance analysis (Jain, 1991). In performance analysis, the predicted value of the random variable is the metric value of a performance metric such as response time. Regression models are often created from the results of measurement-based experiments. Tools for systematic experiments to create regression models for performance analysis are proposed in literature, e.g., (D. J. Westermann, 2014).

### 2.1.2. Measurement-based Performance Analysis

Measurement-based performance analysis approaches can be active measurement approaches and passive measurement approaches. While passive measurement approaches monitor performance metrics during normal operation, active measurement approach use performance testing techniques and create the workload to monitor performance metrics (Menasce et al., 2002). The metric values for performance metrics are often called observations and the time span in which the observations are collected is called the observation period.

The observations are often collected by instrumenting the code of the software application. This technique adds additional code to the software application's implementation, e.g., at the beginning and the end of a method's body for monitoring the entry and exit timestamps to compute the method's response time. Different strategies exist to instrument a software application and are grouped into static, dynamic, and adaptive. Strategies that are referred to as static require that developers add the instrumentation code during development to create the observations at runtime or automatically add the instrumentation code during compilation. Dynamic strategies add the instrumentation code during class loading activities when the software application is executed. The benefit of dynamic strategies compared to static strategies is that the instrumentation is not an inherent part of the source code of the software application. Adaptive strategies extend dynamic strategies and allow to control the instrumentation at runtime in terms of what data is collected and where. The Adaptable Instrumentation and Monitoring (AIM) tool used in this thesis provides the adaptive instrumentation strategy. AIM uses the Instrumentation Description Model (IDM), a descriptive language, for the specification of what performance metric shall be measured and where in the software application.

The collection of performance metrics using code instrumentation techniques is an event-driven method. Observations are only created when the instrumentation code is part of the control flow and executed. In addition to the event-driven collection of observations for performance metrics such as response times, sampling is a common means to monitor resource utilization. Sampling collects information at fixed intervals and provides a good statistical summary of the observation period while it can miss occasionally occurring events. Further categories of data collection are tracing that extends event-driven techniques with additional information and indirect measurement where the desired performance metric has to be derived by other metrics (Lilja, 2005).

Performance measurements are stochastic in nature (Liu, 2009). Hence, important aspects of measurement-based performance analysis are the reproducibility of results of measurements, the repeatability of results of measurements, and the accuracy of measurements. The accuracy of measurement is "the closeness of the agreement between the result of a measurement and the true value of the measurand" (ISO/IEC/IEEE, 2010) where the measurand is the "particular quantity subject to measurement" (ISO/IEC/IEEE, 2010). For example, the accuracy of measurement can be influenced by the overhead caused by the execution of the instrumentation code. The repeatability of results of measurements is the "closeness of the agreement between the results of successive measurements of the same measurand carried out under the same conditions of measurement" (ISO/IEC/IEEE, 2010). The reproducibility of results of measurements is the "closeness of the agreement between the results of measurements of the same measurand carried out under changed conditions of measurements" (ISO/IEC/IEEE, 2010), e.g., when the performance test is conducted by a different tester. While variations in measurements cannot be avoided completely, controlling the test conditions is important to attain an acceptable level of reproducibility, repeatability, and accuracy of measurements. For example, Henry Liu proposes to neglect deviations in measurements as long as they are less than 5% (Liu, 2009).

## 2.2. Palladio Component Model

This section gives a brief introduction to the Palladio Component Model (PCM) (Becker et al., 2009) focusing on aspects that are relevant for this thesis. While a complete coverage of the PCM is not intended and relevant for the thesis, we refer the interested reader to (Reussner et al., 2011) for further details on the PCM.

The PCM is a metamodel to describe component-based software architectures with the possibility to specify performance attributes to make performance prediction by simulating instances of the PCM. The PCM metamodel consists of the component specification, assembly model, allocation model, and usage model to model different concerns of the software architecture. Figure 2.1 shows a the Palladio process with the roles and models. A PCM model instance can be used for performance analysis through model-to-model transformations and model-to-code transformations (Becker et al., 2007; Becker et al., 2009).

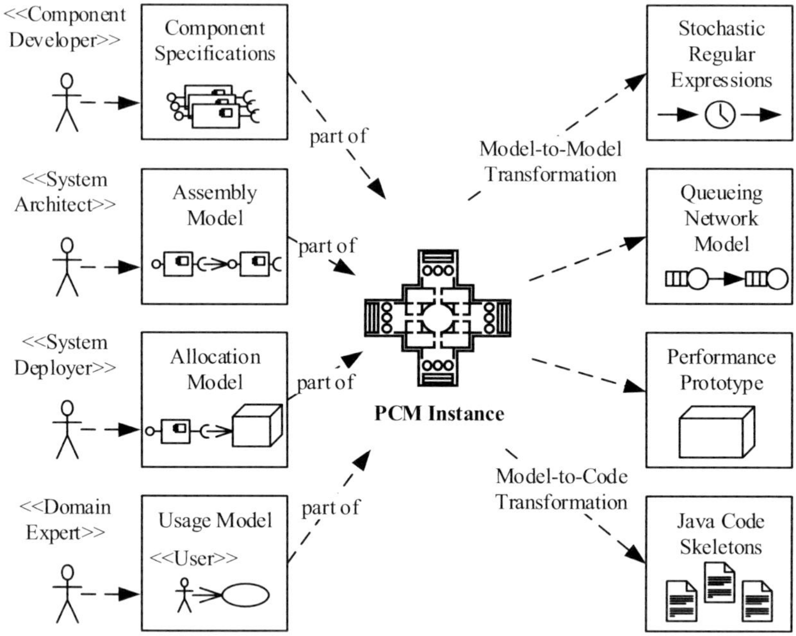


**Figure 2.1.:** Palladio overview (Becker et al., 2009)

The component specification allows an abstract description of the component and the component's behavior. A component is specified by provided and required interfaces that "[...] serve as a contract between a client requiring a service and a server providing the service" (Becker et al., 2007) and specify a set of services. In PCM, interfaces are first-class entities that are neither requiring nor providing. PCM distinguishes between the provided role and required role of an interface and the relation to a component. When a component provides an interface, the provided interface has the provided role. When a component requires an interface, the required interface has the required role. The assembly model allows to connect a required role of a component with a matching provided role of another component. Resource Demanding Service Effect Specifications (RDSEFFs) specify the behavior of a provided service of a component for performance analysis. A RDSEFF specifies call sequences of required services, resource usage, transition probabilities, loop iterations, and parameter dependencies. The allocation model allows the specification of resource environments and provided resources (i.e., active resources, passive resources, and linking resources) and to allocate components from the assembly model instance to the resources. The usage model allows the specification of workloads and usage scenarios and is important for performance analysis (Becker et al., 2007).

The RDSEFF metamodel includes actions to model the performance relevant behavior of a provided service. The actions that are relevant in this thesis are internal action, external call action, and branch action. An internal action allows the modelling of component-internal computations and utilizes the resources the component is allocated to through the specification of demands that can be specified as distribution functions, e.g., response time distribution. External call actions model the execution of a required service and are associated with the service signature of the required service. A branch action models branches in the control flow behavior and consists of two or more branch transitions that have specified branch probabilities. Start actions and stop actions model the beginning and ending of a modeled resource demanding behavior (Becker et al., 2007).

To conduct performance analysis and to obtain performance metrics, a simulator takes a model instance of the PCM as input and transforms the model instance into simulation code including the creation of simulated resources and workload drivers for the specified workload and usage scenario. The generated simulation code simulates the performance relevant behavior and sensors collect the execution times during the simulation. The specified resource demands are used by the simulator to utilize the simulated resources (Becker et al., 2007).

## 2.3. Java Persistence API

The Java Persistence API (JPA) allows Java developers to manage relational data in Java applications through object-relational mapping and consists of the Java Persistence API, the query language, the Java Persistence Criteria API, and object-relational mapping metadata. JPA addresses the paradigm mismatch between the object model and the relational database model by automatically transforming the data between the objects in a Java application and the tables in a relational database. Popular implementations of JPA are EclipseLink (The Eclipse Foundation, 2015), Hibernate (Red Hat, Inc., 2015b), and OpenJPA (The Apache Software Foundation, 2013). The JPA specification defines the interfaces that are to be implemented and delegates certain details to the implementation. For example, query hints to configure the query are foreseen by the specification but the available query hints depend significantly on the implementation. EclipseLink offers 65 query hints (The Eclipse Foundation, 2013a) whereas Hibernate offers only 12 unique and non-deprecated hints (Red Hat, Inc., 2015a).

The primary artifact of JPA is an entity, i.e., a lightweight persistent domain object in the form of a top-level Java class annotated with the entity annotation (Java Persistence 2.1 Expert Group, 2013). The properties of an entity are given by the instance variables of the class that represent the persistent state of the entity and are only accessible by clients through getter and setter methods or other business methods. The naming of getter and setter methods is defined by convention and starts with the get or set following the name of the property, e.g., for a property *property* there is a getter method *getProperty* and a setter method *setProperty*. Any entity class has to define a primary key that can also be inherited in an entity hierarchy were the primary key is defined once in the root of the entity hierarchy. Entities can have one-to-one, one-to-many, many-to-one, or many-to-many relationships to other entities. Relationships are modeled by applying the corresponding relationship modeling annotation to the persistent property of the referencing entity. JPA supports the eager fetch strategy and lazy fetch strategy for relationships. The eager fetch strategy requires that the associated entity has to be fetched eagerly with the referencing entity while the lazy strategy points out that the associated entity should be fetched when it is first accessed (Java Persistence 2.1 Expert Group, 2013).

The Entity Manager API "[...] is used to create and remove persistent entity instances, to find persistent entities by primary key, and to query over persistent entities" (Java Persistence 2.1 Expert Group, 2013) that are defined by a persistence unit. "A persistence unit defines the set of all classes that are related or grouped by the application, and which must be colocated in their mapping to a single database" (Java Persistence 2.1 Expert Group, 2013). A persistence unit is defined in the persistence.xml configuration file and may include also properties that are used to configure the persistence unit and the entity manager factory (Java Persistence 2.1 Expert Group, 2013).

Entity graphs can be used to define paths and boundaries for an operation or query and can be used as query hint in the form of a fetch graph or load graph for queries or find operations. Entity graphs can be constructed dynamically with the entity graph API, i.e., entity graph, attribute node, and subgraph interfaces, or statically through annotations, i.e., named entity graph, named attribute node, and named subgraph annotations. Fetch graphs and load graphs differ in their semantics. The specified persistent properties in an entity graph used as fetch graph are fetched eagerly and the not specified persistent properties are fetched lazily. The load graph semantic differs from the fetch graph semantic in the way that the not specified persistent properties are fetched according to the specified or default fetch strategy (Java Persistence 2.1 Expert Group, 2013).

The Query API supports parameter binding and pagination control and is used to execute queries that are formulated in the Java persistence query language. The Java persistence query language is a string-based query language that is used to define static queries expressed through metadata annotations (i.e., named queries) and dynamic queries. The Criteria API provides an alternative approach to the string-based approach of the query language "[...] through the construction of object-based query definition objects [...]" (Java Persistence 2.1 Expert Group, 2013). Queries are executed using the getResultList and getSingleResult methods of the Query API. Queries can be further configured through the application of query hints. Available query hints depend on the used JPA implementation (Java Persistence 2.1 Expert Group, 2013).

Root entities are objects "[...] from which the other types [entities] are reached by navigation" (Java Persistence 2.1 Expert Group, 2013). The concept of navigation over relationships is used for various concerns in JPA including the formulation of queries, entity graphs, and query hints. The navigation is expressed by a path expression. A path expression consists of "An identification variable followed by the navigation operator (.) and a state field or association field [. . . ]" (Java Persistence 2.1 Expert Group, 2013). The identification variable corresponds to a root entity (Java Persistence 2.1 Expert Group, 2013).

JPA supports first-level caching of entity instances for the persistence context and second-level caching of entity instances for the persistence unit. "A persistence context is a set of managed entity instances in which for any persistent entity identity there is a unique entity instance" (Java Persistence 2.1 Expert Group, 2013). The entity manager manages the entities of a persistence context. Entity instances cached in the persistence context cache are not shared among persistence contexts (Java Persistence 2.1 Expert Group, 2013).

Proposing JPA-implementation-specific solutions can affect the portability of an application (e.g., the usage of implementation-specific Java Persistence Query Language (JPQL) extensions). This is not the case for query hints which have to be silently ignored if provided hints are not supported (Java Persistence 2.1 Expert Group, 2013). The usage of database-specific native SQL queries which is also supported by the JPA specification limits the portability of an application. The changes that are proposed by the change hypotheses do not affect the portability of an application such as query hints or can be easily replaced by the correspondence of another implementation, e.g., the batch fetch annotation in EclipseLink with the batch size annotation in Hibernate.

Common problems that occur when JPA is used without considering the consequences on software performance and scalability are:

- *Excessive Database Queries*: This problem is also most commonly known as the N+1 Selects problem (Haines, 2014; Brekken et al., 2008; Winand, 2012a) and defines an antipattern where excessive database queries cause high response times. In its simplest form, a single query reads a set of $n$ entity instances from the database. While the entity to which the entity instances belong defines a relationship to another entity, accessing the relationship causes $n$ queries to read the associated entity instances from the database for the $n$ referencing entity instances. A common cause for this problem is that the fetch strategies for relationships, either explicitly specified or defaults, are used without understanding their consequences. Although, the appropriateness of fetch strategies for relationships significantly depends on the usage profile (Haines, 2014).

- *Excessive Logging*: This problem refers to a simple oversight when moving a software application from development and testing to operation (Grabner, 2012). "Excessive logging adversely affects the performance of the application as well as causes scalability issues." (Hunt et al., 2012). The logging level of the persistence unit is configured to provide excessive logging information that may be necessary for debugging and testing but inappropriate for operation. Individual requests that are processed by the application involving JPA causes a significant amount of log entries that may include complete SQL statements and bound parameters.
- *Excessive Dynamic Allocation*: This problem refers to the antipattern where a large amount of objects are unnecessarily created and destroyed during the execution of the application (C. Smith et al., 2003). A common cause for this problem in the context of JPA is that associated entity instances are fetch eagerly unnecessarily because they are never or only seldom accessed. This can cause high response times because the entity instances must be read from the database and can lead to temporary pauses of the application where no requests are processed due to the execution of the Java garbage collection.

## 2.4. Model-Driven Software Development

Vergil makes use of Model-Driven Software Development (MDSD) techniques to attain the formulated goal. MDSD is a software development approach that considers models and source code as first-class entities. Some of the goals of MDSD is to increase the development speed through automation by creating runnable code from formal models and to improve manageability of complexity through abstraction (Stahl et al., 2006).

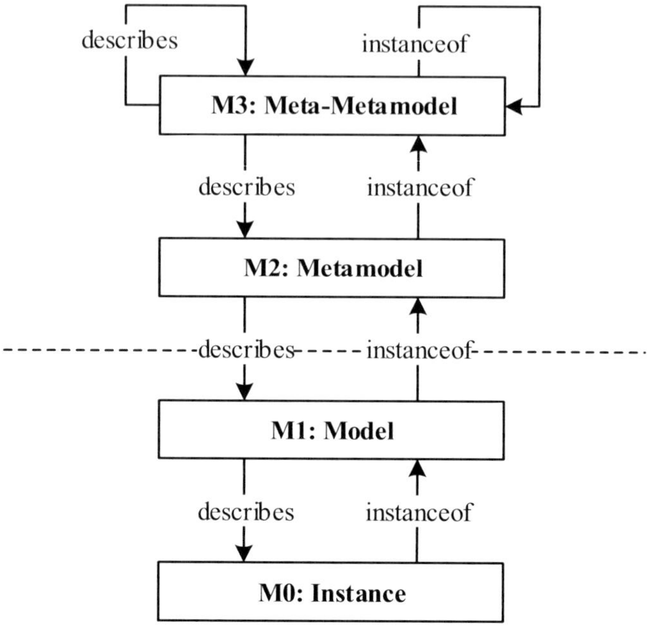


**Figure 2.2.:** Metalevels (Stahl et al., 2006)

An important aspect of MDSD is metamodeling. A "[. . . ] metamodel defines the *abstract syntax* and the *static semantics* of a modeling language [. . . ]" (Stahl et al., 2006) and is used to construct domain-specific modeling languages. Vergil uses metamodeling to construct the proposed description languages employed for data representation and human computer interaction (see Chapter 4) and to consider heterogeneous implementation artifacts for the identification of possible solutions. Any model is an instance of a metamodel. Programming languages like Java or modeling languages like UML have a metamodel. The metamodel itself is defined by a metamodeling language that is described by a meta-metamodel. Figure 2.2 shows four different metalevels and their relationships as published by (Stahl et al., 2006).

While software developers are most commonly familiar with metalevels M0 and M1, we use an object-oriented analogy for the description. In object-oriented programming, models are used to describe classes. Instances of the classes are created at runtime in the form of objects. In MDSD, the models describing the classes are defined in M1 and the instances of the classes are created in M0. This familiarity to software developers is also indicated by the dashed line which is a border that non-MDSD software developers do not pass. In M2, the metamodels of the modeling languages are defined that allow the creation of the models used in M1 while the meta-metamodels that provide the means to define the metamodels are defined in M3. The Unified Modeling Language (UML) is a popular example for a metamodel used to create models for the design of software applications. The Object Management Group (OMG) provides a meta-metamodel in the form of the Meta Object Facility (MOF) standard (Object Management Group, 2014b). The number of metalevels is not fixed and ranges most commonly from at least two to less than or equal to four metalevels (Object Management Group, 2014b). Vergil makes use of the meta-metamodel, metamodel, and instance level. Vergil uses the Ecore metamodel of the Eclipse Modeling Framework (EMF) (Eclipse 2015) as meta-metamodel to implement the metamodels of the proposed description languages.

## 2.5. Java Model Parser and Printer

The Java Language Specification (JLS) (Gosling et al., 2005) does not publish a formal metamodel for Java. The Java Model Parser and Printer (JaMoPP) uses metamodeling based on the Ecore metamodeling language to define a metamodel for Java. This allows that the programming language Java can be handled like other models. The JaMoPP Java metamodel complies with the Java 5 language specification and contains all Java elements, e.g., classifiers, members, statements, imports, types, modifiers, variables, literals, and expressions. In total, the JaMoPP Java metamodel defines 80 abstract and 153 concrete classes. Figure 2.3 shows 7 of the 18 packages, i.e., classifiers, types, members, annotations, references, parameters, and types, containing the defined elements of the metamodel that are most relevant for the model instance excerpts in the remainder of the thesis (Heidenreich et al., 2009; Heidenreich et al., 2010).

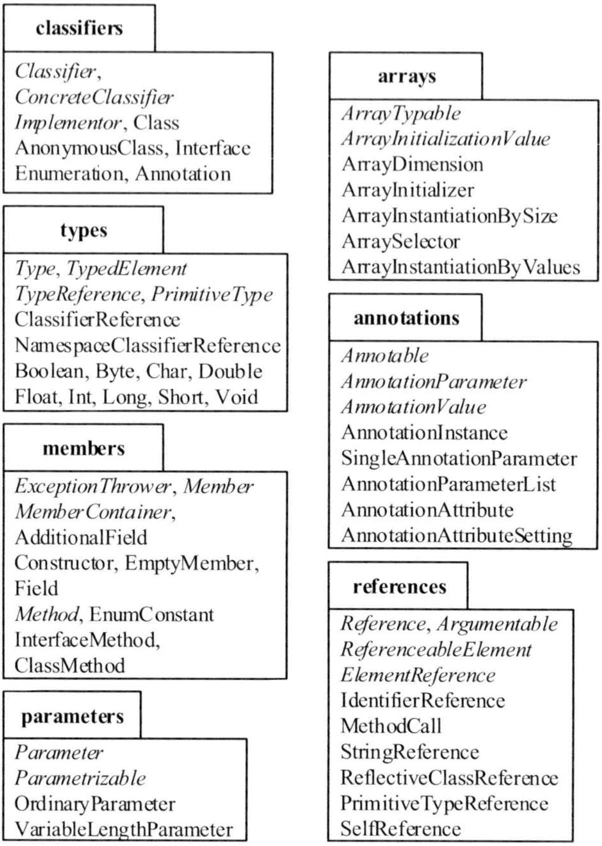


**Figure 2.3.:** JaMoPP Java metamodel excerpt (Heidenreich et al., 2009)

JaMoPP contains a parser to create a model instance from Java source code and a printer to create Java source code from a model instance. The parser takes Java source code as input and creates an Abstract Syntax Tree (AST). The AST is a model with unresolved cross-references between model elements. Resolving the cross-references creates the JaMoPP Java model instance. The printer de-resolves the cross-references between model elements in the JaMoPP Java model to create the AST. The parser then prints the source code based on the AST (Heidenreich et al., 2009; Heidenreich et al., 2010).

Vergil uses the JaMoPP Java model instance as source code model instance to describe the implementation of the software application. The proposed changes of a solution are described with respect to the JaMoPP Java model instance. Applying the changes to model elements in the model instance allows to generate the corresponding Java source code.

## 2.6. Analytic Hierarchy Process

Decision science offers well-established techniques and methodologies that are practically used in many disciplines to support decision making, e.g., economics, operation research, and software engineering. According to (Ngo-The et al., 2005), the Analytic Hierarchy Process (AHP) (Saaty, 2005) is the most common decision making technique in requirements engineering and is often used as sophisticated method to prioritize requirements (Berander et al., 2005). In (Zhu et al., 2005), AHP is used to select an architecture from a set of alternatives. We consider the AHP as an established decision making technique in software engineering. In general, AHP is a goal-oriented decision making method that models the decision problem with a criteria hierarchy. The criteria hierarchy has the goal as root, following the top-level or primary criteria. The primary criteria can be refined into secondary criteria that can be refined into tertiary criteria and so forth. Each leaf criterion is connected with each alternative. Pairwise comparisons of criteria (of the same level and with the same parent criterion) are used to determine the priority of each criterion. This requires $n(n-1)/2$ pairwise comparisons for $n$ criteria. When the priorities among the criteria in the hierarchy are established, the alternatives are pairwise compared for each criterion. This requires $n(m(m-1)/2)$ pairwise comparisons for $m$ alternatives and $n$ criteria. The prioritization effort grows quadratically with the amount of criteria and alternatives.

AHP employs a ratio scale to prioritize criteria and alternatives. The decision maker uses a priority of 1 to 9 to specify the importance of one criterion (alternative) over another criterion (alternative) in a pairwise comparison. While 1 represents equal importance as it is the case when both criteria (alternative) contribute equally to the goal, 9 represents extreme importance of one criterion (alternative) over another criterion (alternative) as it is the case when one criterion (alternative) is favored with the highest possible order of affirmation (Saaty, 2005). The reciprocal of the specified importance is used for the inferior criterion (alternative). The ratio scale has the benefit that it is quantifiable how much more important one criterion (alternative) is than another which is impossible with the ordinal scale (Berander et al., 2005). AHP allows to identify judgment error through a consistency check based on the redundancy of the pairwise comparisons by calculating a consistency ratio.

Experiences with the application of AHP in the requirements engineering discipline are as follows (Berander et al., 2005): Studies in the requirements engineering discipline showed that a large number of requirements renders AHP unsuitable (Lehtola et al., 2004; Maiden et al., 1998). Nevertheless, solutions to reduce the pairwise comparison effort have been proposed that are able to reduce the pairwise comparison effort by as much as seventy five percent (Karlsson et al., 1997). A side effect of reducing the redundancy in the pairwise comparisons is the reduced ability to identify inconsistency (Karlsson et al., 1998).

## 2.7. Enterprise Application

In this thesis, the term software application refers to a component-based enterprise application. “Enterprise applications are about the display, manipulation, and storage of large amounts of often complex data and the support of automation of business processes with that data” (M. Fowler, 2002). They are “[...] different from embedded systems, control systems, telecoms, or desktop productivity software” (M. Fowler, 2002). Enterprise applications often have to deal with a significant amount of concurrent data access especially in the case of Web-based applications that are accessed over the Internet by end-users and they often have to integrate with other enterprise applications (M. Fowler, 2002). An example for an enterprise application in a business to customer scenario is a Web-based e-commerce application. Such enterprise applications must be capable of handling a large amount of end-users (M. Fowler, 2002).

Enterprise application architectures often consist of a presentation layer, domain layer, and data source layer. The presentation layer is responsible for displaying information to end-users and to transform end-user commands into actions for the domain and data source. The domain layer is responsible for executing the business logic such as validating data, manipulating data, and executing data source logic. The data source layer is often a database that is responsible for storing persistent data (M. Fowler, 2002).

Important quality attributes of enterprise applications with respect to performance are response time, responsiveness, and throughput as well as the capacity of the enterprise application and the scalability (M. Fowler, 2002).

The target layer of Vergil is the domain layer. While the presentation layer and data source layer are in general also important for performance and scalability, they are out of scope of this thesis.

## 2.8. Solution Space

The solution of software performance and scalability problems may require changes at different levels of a software application. Cheng (Cheng, 2008) outlines five levels of a software application at which developers may have to implement changes to solve software performance and scalability problems, i.e., hardware resources, software configuration, source code, software architecture, and business process.

The application of changes at the software configuration level is an effective and cost-efficient way. Components of software applications are often configured through configuration files, e.g., cache size, resource pool size, logging level, or activation or deactivation of features. The configuration files are often changeable even for software applications in productive usage. When the software application is scalable then adding more hardware resources can solve any software performance and scalability problem (Cheng, 2008). This principle is used in self-adaptive systems to solve performance problems, e.g., (Huber et al., 2012).

When software configuration changes and additional hardware resources are unable to solve software performance and scalability problems then changes to the source code are necessary, e.g., how APIs are used. When performance and scalability problems cannot be solved with code changes, architectural changes are necessary (e.g., redesign of interfaces, changes in the business logic, changes in the defined components, component assembly, or component allocation). If at the end, no solution potential can be identified in the application, the business process must be considered to solve the performance and scalability problems (Cheng, 2008).

Table 2.1 summarizes the solution levels, i.e., hardware resources, software configuration, software implementation, software architecture, and business process and provides examples of potential modeling languages for each level.

In the remainder of this thesis, Vergil applies changes at the software configuration level, software implementation level, and software architecture level in the context of the JPA case study.

**Table 2.1.:** Solution space of software applications

| Application level | Modeling language examples |
|---|---|
| Business process | BPMN (Object Management Group, 2011a) |
| Software architecture | PCM (Reussner et al., 2011),<br>KLAPER (Grassi et al., 2005),<br>UML Profile for MARTE<br>(Object Management Group, 2011b) |
| Software implementation | JaMoPP Java metamodel<br>(Heidenreich et al., 2009) |
| Software configuration | XSD (W3C, 2012a; W3C, 2012b) |
| Hardware resources | PCM,<br>KLAPER,<br>UML Profile for MARTE |

## 2.9. Online Survey

This section describes foundations relevant for the conducted survey including characteristics of the online survey as research instrument, aspects of designing surveys, and aspects of designing survey question.

Online surveys are a contemporary form of self-administered questionnaires where respondents visit a Web-based questionnaire and provide their responses. Compared to interviews, the absence of the interviewer can have a positive effect on the measurement error (de Leeuw, 2007). The absence of the interviewer mitigates the risk that the interviewer influences the question-answer process, e.g., with what the interviewer says (de Leeuw, 2007). The respondent is dependent on the formulated questions and the given instructions in the questionnaire (de Leeuw, 2007). This gives the respondent a better feeling of anonymity that mitigates the risk that respondents present themselves in a positive light (de Leeuw, 2007). This also makes question design an important aspect in designing the questionnaire.

Online surveys involve the risk that respondents are distracted, e.g., many applications or browser tabs are open at one time, and that respondents can quickly terminate the online survey at any time, e.g., by closing the browser tab (de Leeuw, 2007). Online surveys also involve the risk that respondents cannot be convinced about the trustworthiness of the online survey (de Leeuw, 2007). Internet misuses, e.g., SPAM, make users distrustful of email invitations that invite them to participate in an online survey by clicking a link in the email (de Leeuw, 2007). Personalization, prenotifications, and reminders have shown that they can have a positive impact to convince respondents (de Leeuw, 2007). The missing personal contact to respondents in online surveys, makes it difficult to detect and clarify the reason for nonresponse (de Leeuw, 2007). Another risk entailed in online surveys is that respondents select response options early in the list without reading the provided list entirely (de Leeuw, 2007). Attention has to be given to the visual design of the online survey that has to encourage respondents to read all response options. The amount of time the respondent has to find to complete the survey is especially important for online surveys (de Leeuw, 2007). The online survey should be completed in less than 15 minutes since 10-15 minutes are already considered as critical (de Leeuw, 2007).

According to (de Leeuw, 2007), there are no mature information available about the impact of online surveys on measurement error. The few available comparisons of online surveys with other data collection methods give mixed results.

The design of the survey is an important aspect for the validity of the results. The goal of proper survey design is to minimize coverage error, sampling error, nonresponse error and measurement error that can affect survey results (de Leeuw et al., 2007; Lohr, 2007). Note, the aspects of proper survey design described in this section are taken from (de Leeuw et al., 2007; Lohr, 2007). De Leeuw describes the error types as follows: Coverage error occurs when potential respondents of the target population have a probability of zero to be selected to participate in the survey. Sampling error occurs when not all potential respondents of the target population are surveyed. Nonresponse error occurs when selected respondents of the target population do not respond and the responses of these respondents differ from others and are relevant for the survey. Measurement error occurs when the answer of a respondent is inaccurate and departs from the true answer or the measurement (de Leeuw et al., 2007; Lohr, 2007).

Nonresponse error is distinguished between unit nonresponse and item nonresponse (de Leeuw et al., 2007). Unit nonresponse occurs when we are unable to obtain any question response from eligible respondents due to noncontact or refusal (de Leeuw et al., 2007). Item nonresponse occurs when some questions are answered completely and others are not (de Leeuw et al., 2007). According to (de Leeuw et al., 2007), it is unproblematic and does not bias the conclusion when nonresponse is completely at random.

Another important aspect is the design of the survey questions in particular that the measurements are valid and reliable. Fowler and Cosenza describe the validity and reliability of measurements as follows: Valid measurements are responses that correspond to the true value of the metric that is measured. Reliable measurements are responses to the same question that do not change over time when the true value of the respondent for the question has not changed. Measurements are also reliable when two respondents share the same true value and both provide the same answer to the same question (F. Fowler et al., 2007).

# 3. Vergil

This chapter gives an overview on Vergil and introduces the provided guidance, the concept to satisfy the requirements, and the different roles and their responsibilities.

The chapter is structured as follows: Section 3.1 gives a short overview on the provided guidance and interaction. Section 3.2 describes design considerations of Vergil based on design alternatives proposed in literature. Section 3.3 presents the approach to satisfy the requirements. Section 3.4 introduces the four different roles that are used in the remainder to distinguish responsibilities and Section 3.5 describes the responsibilities of each role.

## 3.1. Overview

Vergil provides recommendations upon request from the developer. Involved in the workflow are the role of the developer, tester, and decision maker. Figure 3.1 shows an idealized sequence as overview on the provided guidance by Vergil and parts of the interaction with the developer, tester, and decision maker in the form of a UML sequence diagram. Note, not all possible interactions are included in this overview. The performance expert provides elicited expert knowledge in form of rules to Vergil. To request recommendations, the developer provides the problem description as input that is then analyzed by Vergil. Vergil uses the rules of the performance expert to identify possible solutions. Vergil requests the decision criteria from the decision maker in order to create the proposals and to guide the developer in evaluating the properties of solution proposals with respect to the decision criteria in the remainder of the workflow. Thereafter, Vergil identifies all impacted elements within the software application's implementation to determine the scope of change propagation. The tester conducts necessary tests and provides the evaluation results to assess the properties of solution proposals. Vergil requests the priorities for the criteria and the solution proposals from decision maker in order to rank the solution proposals and to recommend a solution to the developer.

## 3.2. Design

Vergil is an approach to build a reactive recommendation system that supports the developer in solving software performance and scalability problems. In the following, we briefly outline the characteristics of Vergil based on the design alternative considerations proposed in (Mens et al., 2014).

### 3.2.1. Intent

The intent of a recommendation system is concerned with the purpose such as who is using the system, what task is supported by the system, what support is provided, and what information is produced to support the task (Mens et al., 2014):

**Intended user** The intended audience of Vergil are developers who are novices to software performance or are only less trained in the respected topics, e.g., solving software performance and scalability problems, performance and scalability aware usage of frameworks, components, and services.

**Supported task** Vergil supports the task of finding appropriate solutions to software performance and scalability problems at different levels of a software application (see Section 2.8). This includes the identification of possible solutions, the identification of impacted elements, the implementation effort estimation, the evaluation of solution properties, and the selection of the most appropriate solution proposal when alternatives exist.

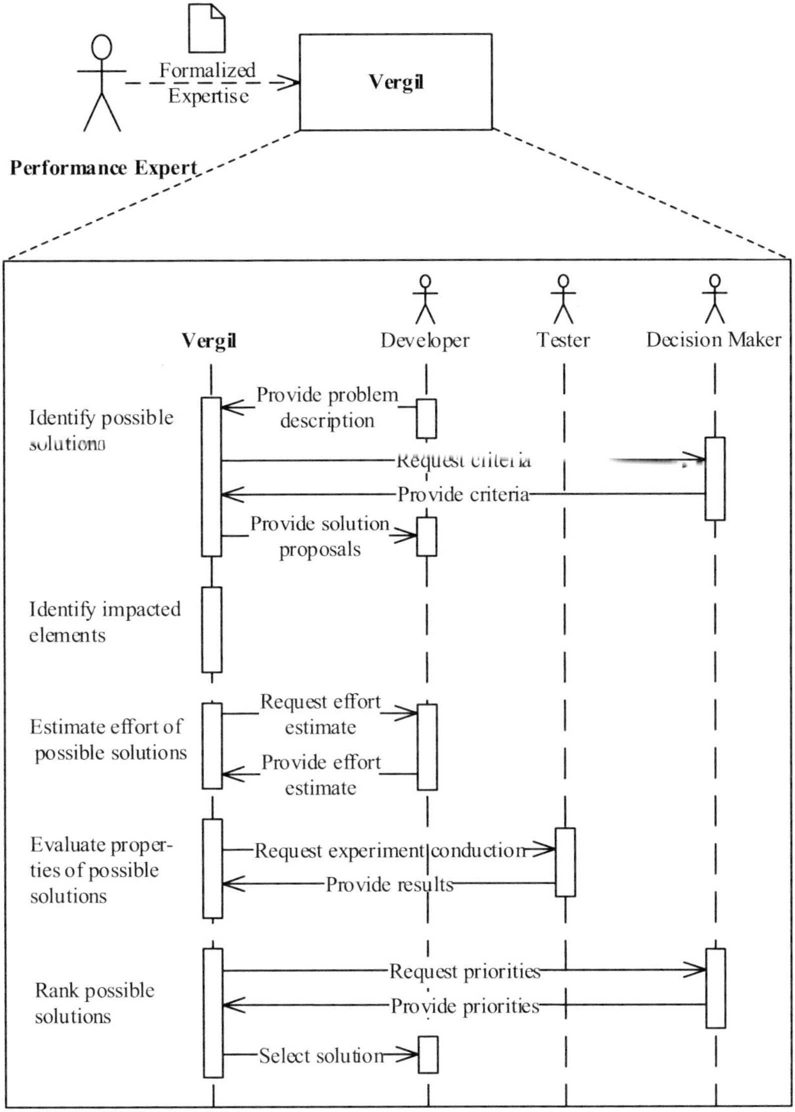


**Figure 3.1.:** Overview of provided guidance and interaction

**Cognitive support** Following the distinction about the five questions a recommendation system can help answering (Mens et al., 2014), Vergil provides answers *how* a software performance and scalability problem can be solved and *what* information is required to successfully complete this task.

**Proposed information** Vergil proposes concrete changes advising what needs to be changed and how. Depending on the changes, the changes can be applied automatically or require the developer to apply the changes manually.

### 3.2.2. Human Computer Interaction

The concern of human computer interaction is how the system can be implemented, what kind of system it is, and the expected input from the developer (Mens et al., 2014):

- *Type of system*: Vergil can be implemented as standalone application, as a plugin for popular integrated development environments, e.g., Eclipse, or integrated in software performance and scalability problem detection tools such as DynamicSpotter (Wert et al., 2013; Wert et al., 2014). However, a complete implementation of Vergil is future work and practitioner interviews may have to be conducted to determine the most appropriate type of system.
- *Type of recommendation system*: Recommendation systems in software engineering are distinguished between the categories finder, advisor, and validator (Mens et al., 2014). Vergil is an advisor due to the fact that Vergil advices possible solutions in the form of concrete changes.
- *User involvement*: Vergil requires involvement of the developer and other roles, i.e., decision maker, and tester, to provide required input data and to rank the solution proposals. The degree to which the input has to be provided manually depends on the availability of adapters to interact with other tools, e.g., performance monitoring tools. The developer provides the required data in the expected data representation through the description languages. Developers can modify solution proposals in terms of revising the proposed changes and they can add

custom solution proposals. The decision maker provides decision criteria and priorities for the decision criteria and for the solution proposals with respect to the decision criteria. The tester provides required complementary information from dynamic analysis for the prioritization.

### 3.2.3. Corpus

The corpus of a Vergil is concerned with what data sources are required that Vergil can provide its recommendations (Mens et al., 2014):

- *Implementation artifacts*: The main corpus of Vergil are implementation artifacts most important the source code of the software application where the developer has to solve the problem. The implementation artifacts typically also include configuration files. The implementation artifacts have to be identical with the version of the implementation artifacts when the software performance and scalability problems occur, e.g., the same source code revision. Implementation artifacts can also include existing design-models.
- *Complementary information*: The occurrence of software performance and scalability problems often depends on the operational profile. Therefore, Vergil needs additional complementary information from dynamic analysis when the software application is executed in a representative test environment and when a representative operational profile is applied. The complementary information includes execution traces, resource utilization, timing behaviors and others.
- *Correlated information*: Vergil correlates the data collected from static analysis, dynamic analysis, and user interaction to test whether potential solution proposals are applicable in a particular case and to determine the changes included in each solution proposal.

### 3.2.4. General and Detailed Input/Output

The concern of the input and output is to refine the human computer interaction by defining the interaction between the developer and Vergil. This includes what Vergil expects from the developer and what Vergil explicitly requests from the developer (Mens et al., 2014):

- *Input mechanism*: Vergil relies on the input of the developer or a complementary tool to get a description of the problem for which solution proposals are requested.
- *Nature of input*: Vergil takes non-code artifacts as input in the form of a problem description. The problem description can contain references to code elements in the source code model instance, e.g., method calls. The artifacts are data representations created with the developed description languages (see Section 4).
- *Type of input*: In addition to the implementation artifacts and the problem description, Vergil requests additional data to validate that solution proposals are applicable and to instantiate solution proposals for the particular context of the software application.
- *Response trigger*: Vergil is triggered by the developer and provides solution proposals upon explicit request only. This means that Vergil is non-intrusive.
- *Nature of output*: Vergil presents solution proposals in the form of performance solution artifacts described with the performance solution description language. The solution artifacts describe their properties with respect to the defined decision criteria and contain a change plan describing the implementation.
- *Type of output*: The change plan contains change types and references to implementation artifacts. The change plan describes what element must be changed and how.
- *Multiplicity of Output*: Often, several solution proposals exist to solve a problem. Vergil ranks the solution proposals by priority when multiple proposals exist to lower the burden for the developer to select the most appropriate solution.

### 3.2.5. Method

The method of Vergil concerns the design choices of how recommendations for the developer are achieved (Mens et al., 2014).

- *Data selection*: The granularity of data as well as what data is required is determined by performance experts when they design and develop the tests contained in the rules. For example, this can be call frequencies of methods, passed method parameters, timing behavior, and others.
- *Type of analysis*: Vergil employs static and dynamic analysis techniques. The static analyses operate on multiple models that describe the implementation artifacts of the software application such as the source code and configuration files. Dynamic analyses use tests like performance tests where the software application is executed and instrumentation of the source code to collect data.
- *Data requirements*: Vergil is designed for modern object-oriented programming languages such as Java or C#. This includes that API based-programming concepts are used and that the software application is designed using a component-based architecture. Vergil focuses on the application logic of enterprise applications. These requirements are commonly supported by current enterprise software applications in industry.
- *Data representation*: The relevant data is represented by the developed description languages that can describe raw or aggregated data and are used for further processing.
- *Analysis technique*: The employed analysis technique uses rules that identify relevant solution proposals from the data. Vergil uses rules developed by performance experts that include tests to analyse the data and to request additional data.
- *Filtering*: To avoid irrelevant and not applicable solution proposals, Vergil uses the tests defined by performance experts for filtering. Only when relevant tests are passed and a so called end point of the rule is reached, Vergil creates the particular solution proposal. The collected results of evaluating the properties of solution proposals are used to enable the decision maker to prioritize the solution proposals with

respect to the criteria. Vergil uses the prioritization to rank the solution proposals in order to present the most appropriate solution proposals at the top.

## 3.3. Approach

This section introduces the concept of Vergil to satisfy the requirements described in Section 1.3. Vergil focuses on implementation artifacts of a software application and uses model instances of different metamodels to describe the implementation artifacts that are extracted from the implementation artifacts that they describe to satisfy requirement R3.

The models provide different viewpoints on and information about the software application. The usage of Model-Driven Software Development (MDSD) techniques by parsing implementation artifacts into model instances of metamodels unifies the different application levels for solution identification. Various model instances on different application levels provide a holistic viewpoint on the software application, e.g., models describing the configuration of particular components, the source code, the component-based architecture, hardware resources and component allocation, or business processes for mapping business processes to the software application. Trace links between heterogeneous models that are assumed to be given, allow the identification of the same entity in different metamodel instances and the navigation between them. For example, the PCM allows to describe the resource environment (hardware resources level), the component allocation to hardware resources, and the component assembly (software architecture level). The JaMoPP Java metamodel allows to describe the complete Java source code of the implementation. This allows to employ different levels of detail and to use various viewpoints of the software application to identify solutions while providing the possibility to select among different evaluation techniques. The trace links provide the means to propagate changes between the models.

Vergil uses a series of goal-oriented activities to provide a workflow (Section 5) as guidance for the developer to satisfy requirement R4. The workflow activities use the model instances for static analyses and reasoning to guide developers through the solution process. The workflow includes activities to identify possible solutions, to identify all impacted elements, to estimate the implementation effort of solution proposals, to evaluate the properties of solution proposals with respect to constraints and decision criteria, e.g., project budget, time, development resources and high-level strategies (Cheng, 2008), and to rank the solution proposals by priority. The activities serve the need to collect information about solutions in order to select a solution that is to be implemented at the end.

In order to enable the human computer interaction with developers, testers and decision makers, Vergil uses a set of description languages (Chapter 4) to exchange information as well as to manage the collected data throughout the workflow activities to satisfy requirement R1. The performance profile (Section 4.2) describes observations (e.g., timing behavior, throughput or resource utilization) of the software application, the information where the observations originate from (e.g., service, or resource) and the applied operational profile when the observations have been made. Constraints (Section 4.6) describe changes that cannot be implemented, e.g., changes to a third party interface, component, or service, changes to a legacy system, or are not going to be implemented due to high-level strategies. Performance solution artifacts (Section 4.4) contain the change plan and describe the solution's properties with respect to defined decision criteria. Vergil uses change impact propagation techniques from the domain of software evolution and maintenance to create a change plan that describes the implementation of a solution based on the impacted elements and how they must be changed. This supports developers in understanding the consequences of the changes. The initial changes in the change plan are created by a change hypothesis. Propagation rules are then applied to assist developers with understanding how the solution is to be implemented and the consequences of changes by identifying the impacted elements and determining how they are affected; respectively how they must be changed (Lehnert et al., 2013).

Vergil uses rules with elicited performance expert knowledge called change hypotheses (Section 4.5) embodying solution knowledge to identify potential solutions for performance and scalability problems as well as data analyses and reasoning to satisfy R2. This includes a description of the dynamic analysis to conduct for the collection of complementary information, what metrics to analyze, where in the system the information to take, what evaluation technique is recommended and which operational profile and workload to apply. The test profile describes the information as guidance for the tester (Section 4.2).

The main data source of Vergil for complementary information about the behavior of the software application are measurements. The measurement environment to conduct performance tests and to collect complementary information includes a workload generator to simulate user interaction with the software application and instrumentation and monitoring tools to collect data. When measurements are not feasible, Vergil considers simulation as an alternative. To evaluate the properties of a solution proposal with respect to performance and scalability of the software application, the changes must be implemented at the model level for simulation or at the implementation level for measurement.

## 3.4. Roles

This section describes the five roles considered by Vergil. The roles are not individuals and individuals can switch between various roles throughout the day. The four roles are:

- *Performance Expert*: The performance expert has a profound knowledge about performance problems and solutions. Therefore, the performance expert has the overall responsibility for developing the change hypotheses. This includes identifying required tests and analyses, selecting metrics, evaluation techniques (e.g., simulation or measurement), and workloads, designing experiments as well as providing the logic for analyzing and interpreting data. The development also includes the logic for creating the appropriate test profiles and change plans. The performance expert does not participate in the workflow activities. This is a distinctive point compared to the Software Performance Engineering (SPE) process (C. U. Smith, 2007; C. U. Smith, 2015).
- *Decision Maker*: The decision maker is responsible for assessing the properties of solution proposals, specifying decision criteria, and prioritizing decision criteria and solution proposals with respect to the decision criteria. Ideally, this role is taken by a group of representatives from all interested parties (e.g., developer, software architect, project manager, customer, and user) or may be taken by a project manager or a software architect in small projects.

- *Tester*: The tester is responsible for conducting experiments and to collect required data according to the provided test profile. This includes setting up and executing tests, maintaining the measurement environment, recovering from errors, evaluating test execution and logging results (Kruchten, 2003).

- *Developer*: The developer is the target audience of Vergil and responsible for solving the software performance and scalability problem. This includes the description of the problem as input to Vergil, implementing and unit testing changes, and building an executable system for the tester.

## 3.5. Responsibilities

This section describes the responsibilities of each role which are further refined in the context of the workflow activities (see Section 5):

- *Performance Expert*: The performance expert embodies knowledge in change hypotheses to support developers in solving the software performance and scalability problem of the software application. The creation of a change hypothesis is illustrated in the use case model in Figure 3.2 (UML notation). A change hypothesis includes problem and solution knowledge. This includes the development of necessary tests and data analyses as well as the changes to apply when all tests are passed. A change hypothesis also includes a systematic approach to performance evaluation. Inexperienced developers are often missing a proper performance evaluation methodology entailing the risk to make unintentional mistakes caused by oversights, misconceptions and lack of knowledge about performance evaluation techniques (Jain, 1991). To mitigate the given risk of mistakes, the performance expert designs the evaluation experiments to collect additional data beforehand describing *what* (metric) is to be analyzed, *where* (instrumentation) in the system the information is to be taken, *how* (evaluation technique) the information is to be obtained and *when* (operational profile) resulting in a test profile to provide recommendations for the tester to implement and execute the required tests. The information is analyzed to reason if the conditions for the changes (embodied in a change hypothesis) are satisfied and to assess the properties of changes.

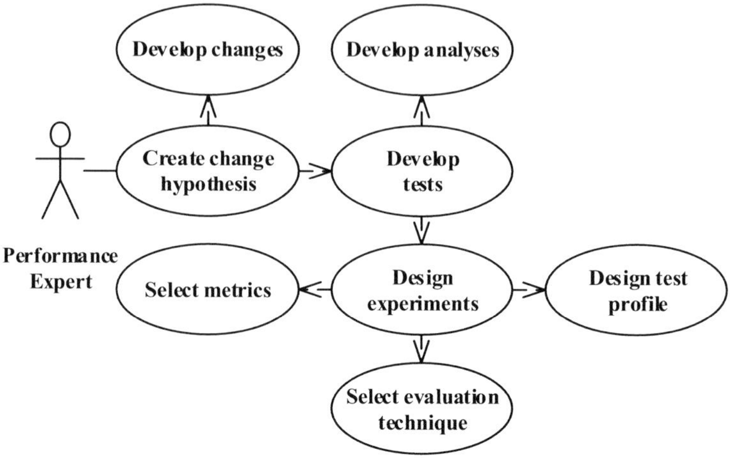


**Figure 3.2.:** Responsibilities of the performance expert

The effort of building the knowledge base of change hypotheses can be distributed among various projects and performance experts. If the knowledge base is continuously maintained, the knowledge in the knowledge base can become, at a certain point in time, more comprehensive as the knowledge of an individual performance expert. Domain knowledge that is independent of technology can be reused in a broad range of projects. Component-specific knowledge can be reused in projects where components are obtained from a marketplace or reused from another project. In the case of freely available or bought components obtained from a marketplace, component providers could deliver developed components with component-specific problem and solution knowledge ensuring that development organizations correctly consume, integrate, configure, and use the services offered by such components. Development organizations, that make components specifically for applications, might not be able to gain a high benefit of the problem solution knowledge for such components until the components are reused in other projects too. Nevertheless, the problem and solution knowledge can be supportive in different life cycle phases of a particular application (e.g., development, maintenance).

- *Tester*: The tester conducts experiments to collect required data from the application as shown in the use case model in Figure 3.3. The most appropriate evaluation technique is given as recommendation in the test profile provided by Vergil. The tester selects the type of test, evaluation technique, operational profile, workload, and instrumentation according to the test profile. The tester sets up the experiment, maintains the measurement environment and evaluates the test execution to ensure construct and internal validity of the results. After conducting the test, the tester collects the results and provides the results to Vergil. In dependence of available test automation, conducting the tests might be covered to a large degree by Vergil through adapters mitigating manual effort.

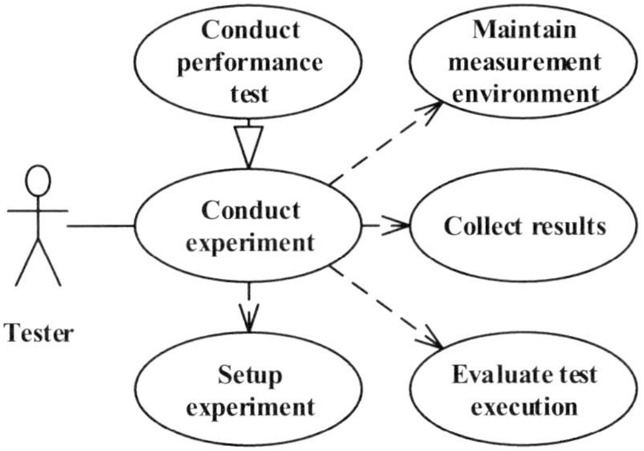


**Figure 3.3.:** Responsibilities of the tester

- *Developer*: The developer creates a performance profile to describe Vergil what the performance problem is and where the root cause is located in the software application. The developer interacts with Vergil to review proposed solutions, to review and revise change plans of solution proposals, and to add own solution proposals as shown in the use case model in Figure 3.4. The developer uses the relevant properties of solution proposals as guidance to collect the data for solution prioritization. The developer provides additional data upon request by Vergil.

Depending on the changes, Vergil may apply changes automatically or in collaboration with the developer through interaction and generation of code stubs. The developer is responsible for validating the changes. This includes unit testing modified components and ensuring that functionality has not been broken and integrating the components into an executable system for tests. In dependence on available build automation, building an executable system might be also covered by Vergil. Vergil supports the developer in estimating the implementation effort of changes with the help of a change plan describing impacted elements and how they must be changed.

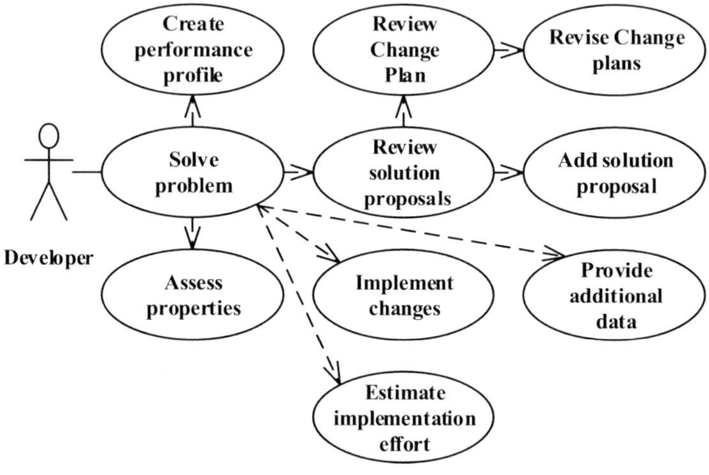


**Figure 3.4.:** Responsibilities of the developer

- *Decision Maker*: The decision maker specifies decision criteria (e.g., with respect to quality attributes, schedule, budget, or impacted system parts) and prioritizes the decision criteria with respect to the goal and the solution proposals with respect to the decision criteria as shown in the use case model in Figure 3.5. The decision maker selects the solution proposals for which the properties is to be assessed and validated. Performance metrics (e.g., response time, throughput, and resource utilization) are obtained with simulation or measurement. The properties of each solution with respect to other criteria are to be determined by the developer or the decision maker. The decision maker also specifies constraints to constraint certain elements of the application for changes.

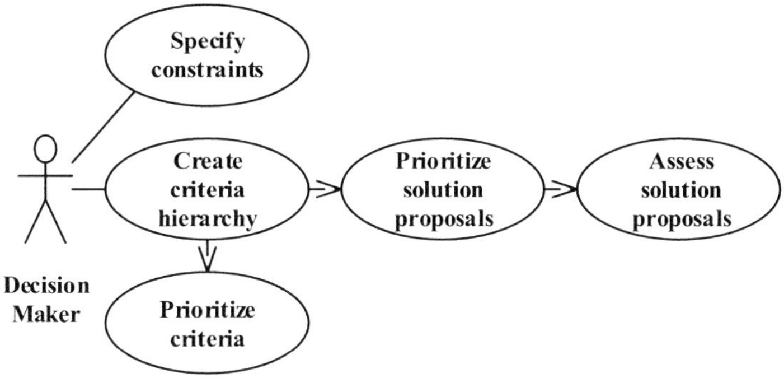


**Figure 3.5 :** Responsibilities of the decision maker

# 4. Description Languages

This chapter introduces the set of description languages of Vergil to satisfy requirement R1 and that are used for human computer interaction and as data representation throughput the workflow. We describe the requirements for each description language, present the abstract syntax in the form of UML class diagrams and explain the informal semantic of the defined model elements.

The chapter is structured as follows. Section 4.1 introduces the parameter dimension and specification language that is used as foundation for the definition of dimensions, e.g., performance metrics, and the specification of observations and requirements for defined dimensions. The parameter dimension and specification language is used in the context of other description languages for this purpose. Section 4.2 introduces the performance profile language that describes the performance of a software application. The performance profile language is used to describe the symptoms and the root cause of performance and scalability problems in a trace-like structure with observations and requirements for performance metrics that are associated with elements of the software application represented by model entities, e.g., methods. The test profile, a specialization of the performance profile language, is used to describe the dynamic analysis in terms of what observations are to obtain, where in the software application and which performance evaluation technique to use. Section 4.3 introduces the change plan language that describes the implementation of a solution without prescribing the developer in how the changes are concretely implemented. The change plan language lists the impacted elements of the software application that are to be changed and how the impacted elements must be changed in order to implement the solution. The resulting change plan instance is also the foundation for the developer to estimate the implementation effort. Section 4.4 introduces the performance solution language that describes a solution in terms of the decision criteria and the solution's properties with respect to defined decision criteria. Each solution has a change plan instance describing the implementation of the solution. Section 4.5 introduces the change hypothesis language that structures the elicited knowledge in a decision tree-like structure. Section 4.6 introduces the constraints language that enables the decision maker to specify constraints in terms of constrained changes for elements of the software application, e.g., third-party interfaces, or legacy components.

## 4.1. Parameter Dimension and Specification

In order to guide developers in solving performance and scalability problems, information is to be exchanged between various workflow activities, and between Vergil, developers, tester, and decision makers. This section introduces the parameter dimension and specification language that has exactly the aforementioned purpose.

### 4.1.1. Requirements

This section lists the requirements for the parameter dimension and specification language and evaluates existing solutions.

- *The parameter dimension and specification language should generically describe dimensions and observations (PDS-R1)*: Conducting performance evaluation experiments often includes data for various performance metrics. Common performance metrics are response time, throughput, and resource utilization (Jain, 1991). Considering other quality attributes, e.g., reliability, security, or availability, additional parameters with quantitative and qualitative data are added. Vergil requires a generic means to describe dimensions and observations. Dimensions can be performance metrics defined by the performance expert and metrics defined by the decision maker. Especially in the case of metrics defined by the decision maker, the kind of metric depends often on the concrete case and is seldom known at the time when a description language is defined. Consequently, the need for a generic description of a dimension and observations for that dimension arises.

- *The parameter dimension and specification language should generically describe requirements for dimensions (PDS-R2)*: A performance and scalability problem is often representative for an unsatisfied expected or contracted level of quality of service. Quality of service requirements for performance are often formalized in service level agreements as mean values and percentile values for performance metrics, e.g., response time, throughput(Frølund et al., 1998). A performance and scalability problem can be considered as solved, when a solution enables the application to satisfy the specified requirements. Consequently, the parameter dimension and specification language should be able to specify requirements for defined parameters.
- *The parameter dimension and specification language should describe the employed evaluation technique for observations (PDS-R3)*: Performance evaluation experiments can be conducted with analytical modeling, simulation and measurement (Jain, 1991). Vergil considers measurement as main and simulation as alternative performance evaluation technique since analytical modeling is often unfeasible in practice. Which performance evaluation technique to choose is often case specific. Each evaluation technique has a certain accuracy. The accuracy of a simulation depends on the level of detail in the model, the calibration with previous measurements and the performed analysis, e.g., a different usage model of the application is to be analyzed or a different workload is to be tested. The accuracy of measurement depends on the instrumentation of the application and how invasive the instrumentation is. A change in a performance metric must be larger than the accuracy of the evaluation technique to be considerable (Cheng, 2008). For example, when the accuracy of the evaluation technique is 30% it cannot be said for sure that a performance improvement of 10% really leads to an improvement. Consequently, Vergil needs the information which performance evaluation technique has been used to obtain the observation and if available information about the accuracy.

In literature, different domain-specific description languages have been proposed to formalize performance metrics and measurement. The Structured Metrics Meta-Model (SMM) (Object Management Group, 2012) is a meta-model for the definition of measures and measurement results for the domain of model-based measurement (i.e., simulation). SMM uses the term measures as a substitute for metrics. Frey et al. extended SMM by additional metamodel constructs and tool support in the SMM example implementation called Measurement Architecture for Model-Based Analysis (MAMBA) (Frey et al., 2011). The implementation of SMM by MAMBA uses the Ecore metamodeling language. The SMM is designed to be a common interchange format between tools of various vendors. While SMM satisfies requirement PDS-R1 and PDS-R2, requirement PDS-R3 remains unsatisfied.

Westermann et al. designed the experiment specification language to describe and automate software performance evaluation experiments. Part of the experiment specification language is the specification of parameters. Westermann et al. distinguish between input (parameters that can be controlled) and output (parameters that can be observed) parameters as part of the measurement environment specification. The purpose of the parameters is also to enable the performance analyst to define metrics. Concrete metrics are not part of the experiment specification language. The performance analyst can express metrics through the names of parameters, e.g., CPU utilization. Additional semantics for a parameter are to be specified in a description attribute of a parameter, e.g., what possible values are (D. Westermann et al., 2013; D. J. Westermann, 2014). The different objectives of the experiment specification language, and the rudimentary description of parameters render the experiment specification language insufficient for the needs of Vergil. The experiment specification language does not satisfy any defined requirement.

The Quality of service Modeling Language (QML) (Frølund et al., 1998) is a description language designed to define QoS specifications for component-based systems. QML enables the specification of custom QoS categories that can be associated with component interface definitions. Noorshams et al. implemented QML using the Ecore metamodeling language (Noorshams et al., 2010) and extended the metamodel with additional concepts to support multiple objective software architecture optimization. QML satisfies requirement PDS-R2 while requirement PDS-R1 and PDS-R3 remain unsatisfied.

### 4.1.2. Abstract Syntax

To address the specific needs of Vergil, we have developed the parameter dimension and specification language upon the Ecore metamodel-based QML implementation (Noorshams et al., 2010). Note, when we refer to QML in the remainder, we refer to the Ecore metamodel-based implementation (Noorshams et al., 2010). The parameter dimension and specification language has the goal to provide a generic means to describe dimensions and observations (PDS-R1), requirements for defined dimensions (PDS-R2) and the evaluation technique of observations (PDS-R3). The implementation of the parameter dimension and specification language is based on the Ecore metamodeling language.

#### 4.1.2.1. Parameter Dimension

The part of the parameter dimension and specification language describing a dimension is a modified version the QML metamodel part describing a contract type. We changed the enumeration of the relation semantics into higher is better, lower is better, and nominal is better which are the three utility function classes a performance metric can be classified into according to Jain, 1991. The higher is better semantic applies for metrics where higher values of such metrics are preferred, e.g., in the case of throughput. The lower is better semantic applies for metrics where lower values of such metrics are preferred, e.g., in the case of response time. The nominal is better semantics applies for metrics where high and low values of such metrics are undesirable. Consequently, a particular value in the middle is typically considered as preferred, e.g., in the case of CPU utilization. Very high resource utilization often results in high response times whereas very low resource utilization means that provisioned system resources are not being used (Jain, 1991). The part of the parameter dimension and specification language for defining the specification of a dimension is shown in Figure 4.1 in the form of a UML class diagram.

The parameter dimension and specification language allows to specify the definition of one dimensional dimensions. A dimension has a name, e.g., response time, and can have an associated unit of measurement. A unit of measurement is a "particular quantity defined and adopted by convention, with which other quantities of the same kind are compared in order to express their magnitude relative to that quantity." (ISO/IEC/IEEE, 2010). A unit has a name, e.g., seconds, processed transactions/second, or percentage. A dimension has a certain type and can have a certain relation semantics. The relation semantic describes which values are preferred. Possible semantics

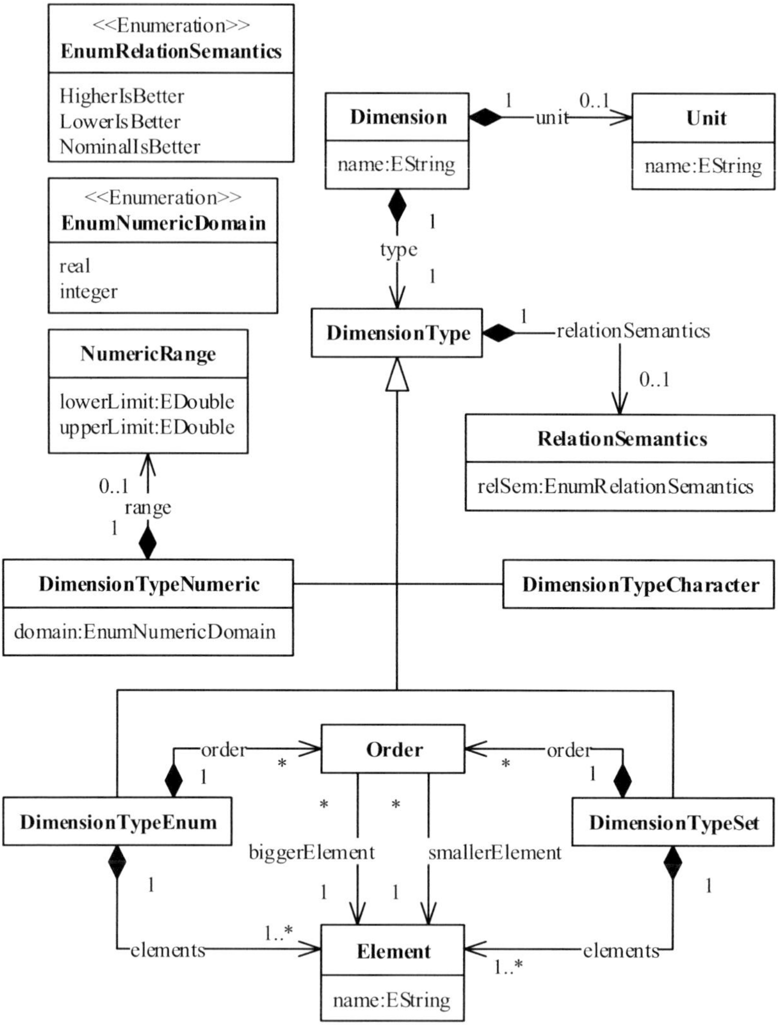


**Figure 4.1.:** Dimension definition (based on (Noorshams et al., 2010))

are higher is better, lower is better, and nominal is better. A dimension type is specialized into a numeric dimension type for a numeric dimension, enum dimension type for an enumeration of elements, dimension type set for a set of elements, and dimension type character for strings. Quantitative metrics, e.g., response time, throughput and utilization, are examples for a numeric dimension. Qualitative (nominal) metrics, e.g., a rating scale for priority that is measured in low, mid, and high as symbolic values are examples for an enumeration dimension. The possible values of a dimension of type enum and set are specified as element. Both dimensions can have one or more elements. An element has a name representing the value. The elements can be ordered using the order entity. An order entity references two elements, one element as the bigger element and another element as the smaller element, e.g., low is less than mid and mid is less than high. The difference between a dimension of type enum and a dimension of type set is, that an observation and requirement for a dimension of type set can be a set of values. An observation and requirement for a dimension of type enum can only be a value that is part of the specified enumeration of elements.

#### 4.1.2.2. Example

This section provides examples for defining common performance metrics, i.e., response time, throughput, resource utilization, and a priority rating scale.

- *Response Time*: Figure 4.2a shows the definition of the response time dimension in the form of a UML class diagram. The name of the dimension is response time. The associated unit of measurement is milliseconds. The dimension is a numeric dimension of real numbers. The domain of the dimension type is accordingly set to real. The relation semantics are set to lower is better since lower response time values are preferred. The range of the dimension has a lower limit set to 0 since negative response time values are invalid. If desired, there can be different response time dimensions defined to satisfy a certain purpose differing in the specified unit of measurement, e.g., nanoseconds, milliseconds, seconds.

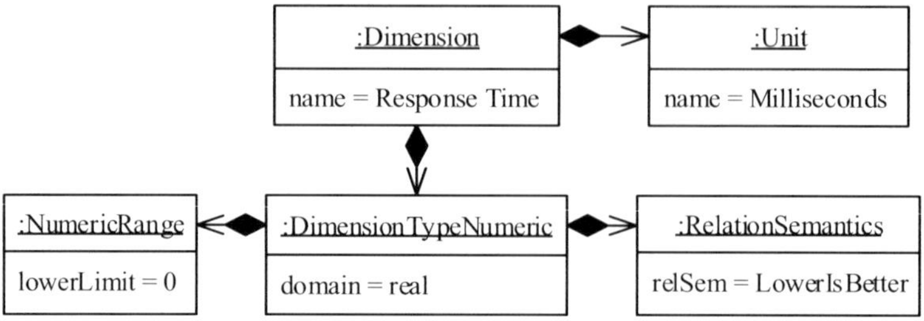


**(a)** Response time

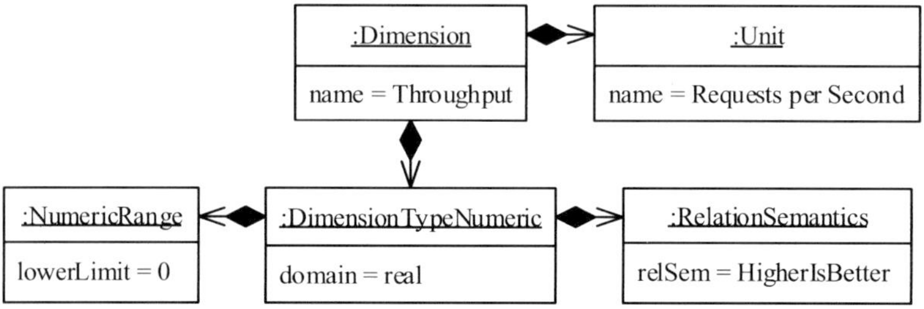


**(b)** Throughput

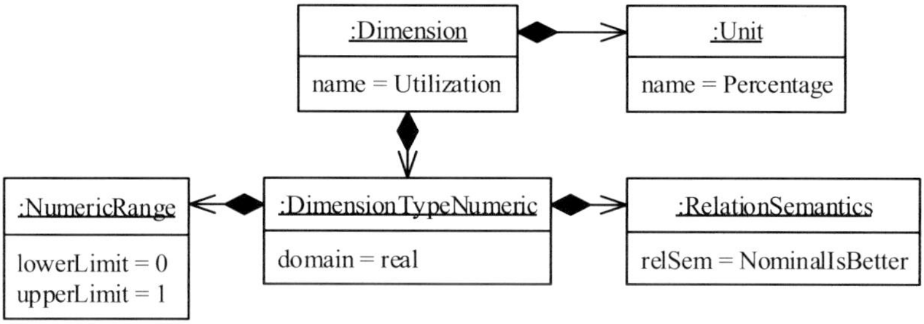


**(c)** Utilization

**Figure 4.2.:** Dimension examples

- *Throughput*: Figure 4.2b shows the definition of the throughput dimension in the form of a UML class diagram. In difference to the response time dimension, the name of the dimension is throughput and the unit of measurement of the throughput dimension is requests per second. The relation semantics is set to higher is better since higher throughput is preferred. The domain of real numbers as well as the lower limit of the numeric range remains the same. Other throughput dimensions can have other units of measurement, e.g., transactions per second, batch jobs per hour.

- *Utilization*: Figure 4.2c shows the definition of the utilization dimension in the form of a UML class diagram. The name of the dimension is set to utilization. The unit of measurement is accordingly set to percentage. Percentage has a defined interval, i.e., $[0,100]$, which is often given as $[0,1]$. The numeric range of the domain is accordingly limited to 0, as lower limit, and 1, as upper limit. A preferred value of resource utilization is often somewhere in the range of 50% to 70%. Low utilization is often undesired because provisioned resources are less used. High utilization often causes high response times which is also undesired (Jain, 1991). The relation semantic is accordingly set to nominal is better.

- *Rating Scale*: The response time, throughput, and utilization dimension use almost the same entities of the parameter dimension and specification language for the specification of the dimension. Figure 4.3 shows the definition of a priority rating scale dimension with an enumeration of possible values, i.e., low, mid, and high. The dimension has the name priority and the type enum. The enumeration enumerates the valid values of the dimension. There is an element for each value with the name attribute set to the corresponding value. The values are ordered in the form that low is less than mid, and mid is less than high with respect to the priority semantic of the dimension. Something that has a high priority is often preferred to something that has a medium or low priority. Analogously for something with a medium priority compared to something with a low priority. The relation semantic is accordingly set to higher is better.

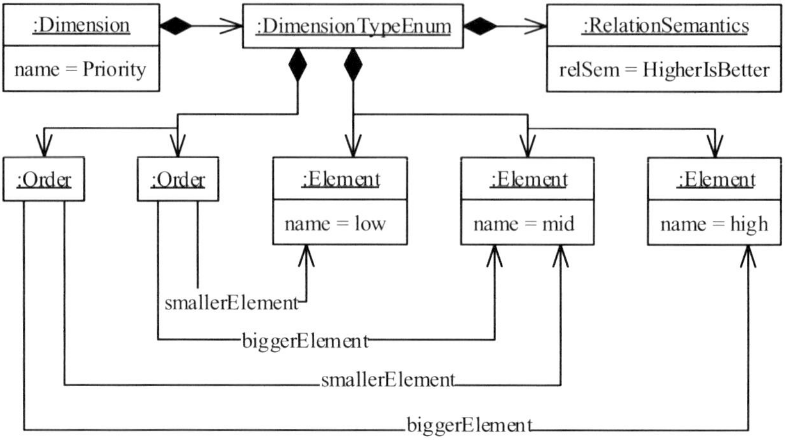


**Figure 4.3.:** Dimension priority example

#### 4.1.2.3. Parameter Specification

The second part of the parameter dimension and specification language is the definition of parameters. The parameter dimension and specification language enables the generic specification of parameters for defined dimensions. A parameter is the generic means to describe a value for a dimension. The second part of the parameter dimension and specification language is a modified version of the QML contract metamodel (Noorshams et al., 2010). Metamodel elements are renamed to fit the domain-specific needs of Vergil. The simple QML contract element is renamed into parameter specification. The generalization of the simple QML contract into generic QML contract is discarded. The QML contract type containing the dimensions is renamed into dimension repository. The criterion element is renamed into parameter. The relation between criterion and refined QML contract is removed. The specialization of criterion into objective and constraint is replaced with the specialization of parameter into observation and requirement. The evaluation aspect element is renamed into parameter value. The aspect requirement element is renamed into value literal. The specialization of aspect requirement into restriction and goal is discarded. The necessary semantic is given by the parameter specializations observation and requirement and the relation semantics of the dimension. The specialization of the original evaluation aspect into deterministic evaluation aspect and stochastic evaluation aspect are renamed into deterministic value and stochastic value. The specialization of deterministic evaluation aspect into value is discarded since parameter value has a value literal to represent the actual value of the parameter. The specialization of the original stochastic evaluation aspect into frequency is replaced with the interval estimator for confidence intervals. Two additional specializations are added for the point estimator, i.e., max and min.

Figure 4.4 shows the resulting parameter definition part of the parameter dimension and specification language. A parameter specification references the dimension repository. The dimension repository provides a set of dimensions. A parameter specification contains parameters and a parameter can be specialized into an observation or requirement. An observation specifies what has been actually observed. The evaluation technique that was used to obtain the observation can be specified in the attribute evalTech. The possible evaluation techniques are provided by the evaluation technique enumeration. Thereby, measurement and simulation are the considered evaluation techniques. A requirement specifies the value that is required for the parameter. The relation semantic of the dimension is used to determine if the observed value for the parameter satisfies the requirement. A parameter has one or more parameter values. A parameter value can be specialized into a deterministic value and a stochastic value. A stochastic value can be specialized further into point estimator and interval estimator. In the case of the interval estimator, the confidence level of the confidence interval is specified. The point estimator has a set of specializations, i.e., min, mean, max, percentile, and variance. In the case of percentile, the concrete percentile is specified. Percentiles are common and preferred means in industry to describe the performance of an application (Kopp, 2012a; Hirschauer, 2012). The specializations of the generic parameter value give the value a concrete type and semantic. Additional specializations can be added if needed. A parameter value has an associated value literal specifying the actual value. The value literal is specialized into set literal, enum literal, numeric literal, and string literal according to the possible types of a dimension. In the case of the numeric literal and string literal, the actual value is specified in the value attribute. In the case of the enum literal, the actual value is an element that is part of the enumeration defined in the dimension of the parameter. In the case of the set literal, the actual value can be a set of elements of the defined elements in the dimension of the parameter.

figure[t]

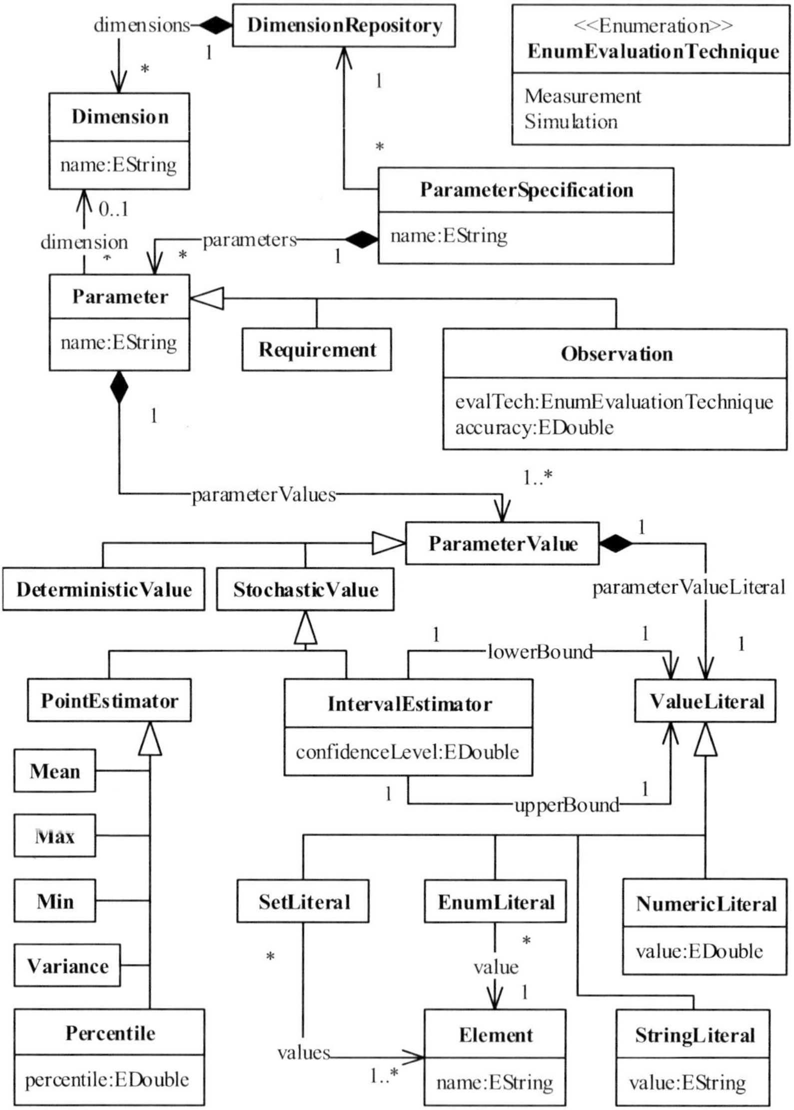


**Figure 4.4.:** Parameter definition (based on (Noorshams et al., 2010))

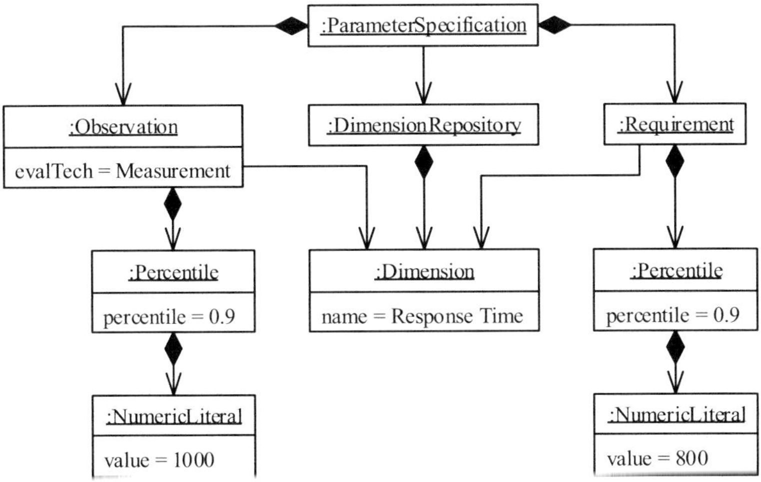


**Figure 4.5.:** Parameter definition example

Here is the aforementioned difference in the semantic between dimension type enum and dimension type set of the dimension definition evident.

#### 4.1.2.4. Example

Figure 4.5 shows the parameter specification specifying an observation and a requirement for the response time dimension (cf. Figure 4.2a). in the form of a UML class diagram. Both parameters have the response time dimension as dimension. The observation parameter defines a percentile value of 1000 for the 90% percentile. The specified evaluation technique for the observation is measurement. The requirement parameter defines a value for the 90% percentile given by percentile. The numeric literal specifies the value of 800 that is required for the percentile.

## 4.2. Performance Profile

This section describes the performance profile language. The purpose of the performance profile language is to describe the performance and scalability of applications based on observations and to describe what additional observations are to be obtained by the tester or automated tools, e.g., application performance monitoring tools, as complementary information. We have published an early version of the performance profile language in (Heger et al., 2014b).

### 4.2.1. Requirements

This section introduces the requirements for the performance profile language. The requirements are:

- *The performance profile language should generically describe the software performance and scalability problems of a software application based on observations (PP-R1)*: Software performance and scalability problems are often observed at system boundaries in terms of high response times, low throughput, and high resource utilization. The isolated root cause of software performance and scalability problems is often nested deep in the software application, e.g., a call to the database, or a call to an API method. There can also be a set of root causes along the call tree inside the application that contribute to the problem. Consequently, the software performance and scalability problem should be described in a trace-like structure. The performance profile language should describe *what* performance metrics are observed, *where* in the software application, *how* the performance has been evaluated and *when* (operational profile).
- *The performance profile language should generically describe the required observations and experiments to conduct for dynamic analysis of the software application (PP-R2)*: Vergil often needs complementary information from dynamic analysis to test change hypotheses and to identify possible solutions. To ensure a proper performance evaluation methodology mitigating the risk to make unintentional mistakes

caused by oversights, misconceptions and lack of knowledge about performance evaluation techniques (Jain, 1991), the performance profile language should describe *what* metric is to be analyzed, *where* in the system, *how* the observation is to be obtained (evaluation technique), and *when* (operational profile).

### 4.2.2. Abstract Syntax

Figure 4.6 shows the performance profile language in the form of a UML class diagram. A performance profile contains performance aspects. A performance aspect has an associated operational profile describing the *when*. The operational profile references a load testing script by its name. The load testing script describes the scenario in which the observation has been made and the scenario for which the requirement is specified. The usage profile of the application is part of the load script. The operational profile has a workload and a workload specifies the duration of the observation period in seconds after all simulated users are started and before any user is stopped by the load generator. The workload is specialized into open workload and closed workload. The open workload includes the specification of the inter-arrival time between two requests issued to the system. The unit of measurement is seconds. The closed workload specifies the number of users that interact with the system, the ramp up interval for starting simulated users, the ramp down interval for stopping simulated users, and the minimum and maximum think time of users. The attribute values are measured in seconds. Different workloads are used to distinguish between observations when a set of performance profiles are used to describe the scalability of the application or when observations are made under different operational profile conditions, e.g., to control monitoring overhead. A performance aspect can have a reference to the impacted element in form of the EObject in the source code model instance describing *where* the observations belong to, and one or more parameter specifications describing *what* has been observed. When the scope of a performance aspect cannot be limited to a single element, no impacted element is specified. In this case, Vergil concludes a system wide scope, e.g., CPU utilization. An individual performance aspect uses multiple impacted elements when the method element in the source code model is not enough as identifier, e.g., in scenarios with replicated components. In such scenarios, a reference to the component instance is allowed as additional impacted element. Each observation in any parameter specification (see Section 4.1.2.3) describes the *how* by specifying the evaluation technique. The parameter specification (see Section 4.1) describes the actual observation, requirement and dimension. Section 7.3.9 shows examples for the performance profile.

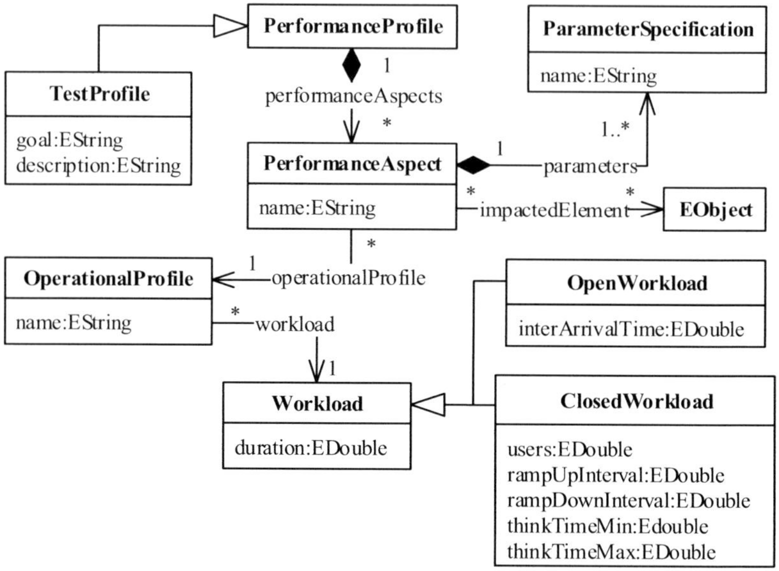


**Figure 4.6.:** Performance profile definition

#### 4.2.2.1. Distributed Application Scenarios

In the case of distributed application scenarios where instances of the same component are deployed on the same or different application servers, Vergil currently relies on other models to describe the performance with the performance profile language. The performance profile references elements of the deployment model of PCM to describe the component instance. The performance profile references elements of the source code model to describe performance aspects of the implementation of components (as it is the case in a non-distributed application scenario), e.g., performance aspects of individual methods. If necessary, Vergil can be extended by developing a metamodel that takes over the responsibility of describing the deployment and resource environment of applications. The metamodel that is to be developed can be technology specific, e.g., for Enterprise Java Beans technology, in order to include technology-specific information that can be used to identify possible solutions.

#### 4.2.2.2. Performance and Scalability Problems

The performance profile language enables the description of performance in terms of performance metrics, observations and requirements for elements of the software application. The performance profile language describes software performance and scalability problems in a trace-like structure. Starting at the system boundaries where problems are often observed as high response times or low throughput, the root cause of the problem is often located deep inside the software application. For example, a service has high response times exceeding the specified requirement of the quality of service contract. The high response time symptom can be traced down method by method in the call tree of the service to the execution of a database call. The performance profile has at least a performance aspect for the called method of the service which is given by the respective method element of the source code model instance as impacted element, and a performance aspect for the database call as root cause. The database call is also referenced as impacted element.

The performance profile language also enables the description of the scalability of a software application with respect to the operational profile. The performance profile language describes scalability with a set of performance aspects that have different workload specifications.

#### 4.2.2.3. Test Profile

Vergil uses the performance profile also as test profile to communicate what information is needed from dynamic analysis of the software application and how the experiment should be conducted. The test profile is a specialization of the performance profile and describes *what* metric is to be analyzed, *where* in the software application, *how* the observation is to be obtained (evaluation technique), and *when* (operational profile). The type of the parameter value and the dimension of the observation specify what is to be measured. The evaluation technique specified in the observation describes how the value is to be obtained. The impacted element of the performance aspect specifies where in the system the value is to be measured. The operational profile specifies the usage scenario to use when the value is measured. The tester and monitoring tools (with the required adapters) can consume the performance profile created by Vergil, execute the dynamic analysis and collect the results. The test profile serves as template for the creation of the performance profile describing the results. The result for a requested observation is then added to the performance profile with a specialization of the value literal. The performance profile is given back as result to Vergil. Vergil can then analyze and interpret the data. Section 6 shows examples for the test profile.

## 4.3. Change Plan

This section describes the change plan language that has the purpose to describe the changes of the software application to implement a solution without prescribing the developer in how the changes are concretely implemented. The change plan has the goal to describe *what* elements of the sofware application are impacted by changes, and *how* the impacted elements must be changed. Consequently, the change plan references elements of model instances. The change plan can describe changes on all solution levels of the solution space when metamodel-specific change types are defined. We have published an earlier version of the change plan (in former times referred to as work plan) in (Heger et al., 2014a; Heger et al., 2014b).

### 4.3.1. Requirements

This section describes the requirements for the change plan language. The requirements are:

- *The change plan language should describe the elements of a software application that are impacted by changes (CP-R1)*: Vergil uses implementation artifacts of the software application to identify solutions.

Solving performance and scalability problems in a software application with an existing code base often requires changes that are to be applied to the implementation of the application. Changes applied to an element of the implementation can propagate changes to other elements. This process is known in literature as *Ripple Effect* (Yau et al., 1978). In worse cases, simple changes can propagate through the implementation of a software application and cause architectural changes. The elements that are to be changed to implement a solution can influence the decision maker in prioritizing solution proposals. While Vergil uses different levels of abstraction that are given by different metamodel instances and solutions can be found on different application levels, the change plan language should describe impacted elements of heterogeneous models.

- *The change plan language should describe the necessary types of changes (CP-R2)*: Many solution implementation descriptions are generic and describe a concept in natural language, e.g., in software performance antipattern definitions (C. Smith et al., 2003; Dudney et al., 2003). Developers have to transfer the generic solution concept into a concrete solution for each individual problem. Vergil supports developers in implementing the changes of a solution by tailoring the implementation description to each individual case. Consequently, the necessary types of changes should be described by the change plan language.
- *The change plan language should provide a foundation for estimating the effort for implementing the changes (CP-R3)*: Project schedule, budget, and development resources are often considered when the decision maker prioritizes solution proposals. The impacted elements and the necessary types of changes have to be suitable to act as foundation for estimating the implementation effort.

The change plan language is based on the taxonomy of change types by Lehnert et al. and the application of the taxonomy in the context of software evolution to analyze the impact of changes in heterogeneous models (Lehnert et al., 2012; Lehnert et al., 2013) and the concept of metamodel-dependent and metamodel-independent changes (Burger, 2014). The change plan language also includes concepts of the Karlsruhe Architectural Maintainability Prediction (KAMP) approach (Rostami et al., 2015). KAMP uses work activities to create a work plan where developers assign an effort estimation to each work activity in the plan. A work plan is a hierarchical structured collection of work activities. The work activities are stepwise refined into smaller activities. Two assumptions of KAMP are that (1) change efforts must take into account all artifacts of software development and operation, e.g., testing, deployment, and (2) estimating the change effort with small specific tasks is easier than with coarse grained tasks (Heger et al., 2014a).

### 4.3.2. Abstract Syntax

Figure 4.7 shows an excerpt of the metamodel of the change plan language in the form of a UML class diagram omitting the metamodel-dependent change types. The change plan element is a container for a set of change elements. A change plan can have any number of change elements where a certain change belongs always to a particular change plan. The change element includes a description attribute to provide additional information and an effort attribute to capture the effort estimate. The ancestor of a change identifies the change instance from which the change descends from when propagated.

A change is specialized into an atomic change and a complex change. An atomic change is a single change specialized into metamodel-dependent change types to update, delete, and add instances of metamodel elements to an instance of the metamodel, e.g., an instance of the JaMoPP Java metamodel describing the source code. Metamodel-dependent atomic changes inherit the attributes of the metamodel element to describe what attributes change. A complex change (e.g., move, split, swap, or higher semantic changes) is a set of changes that is refined by an ordered series of other changes until expressed by a series of atomic changes creating a hierarchy in the change plan.

A change references the impacted element in a model instance through a reference element. The reference element is specialized into a changed element reference, new element reference and unchanged element reference. The reference specializations define the expected state of the impacted element. Therefore, the changed element reference has a particular change as target and describes that the change expects the impacted element in the state after applying the referenced target change. This implicitly models dependencies between the changes and allows to derive an order. The new element reference describes the creation of a new instance of a metamodel element of a certain type in a particular model instance. This allows other changes to reference the newly created element instance. The unchanged element reference expects the impacted element to be unchanged and references the particular element in the corresponding model instance. An impacted element can be referenced by any number of changes.

While the set of metamodel-dependent atomic changes is large, the metamodel excerpt in Figure 4.7 includes the add identifier reference change for the identifier reference element of the JaMoPP Java metamodel as an example. Section A.2 provides a list of metamodel-dependent changes used in the case study. The identifier reference element includes the next attribute that models the separator "." and the target attribute for the identifier element. The add identifier reference change inherits the attributes. Section 6 and Section 7.3 include examples of change plan instances.

### 4.3.3. Semantic Lifting

The change types in the change plan language are atomic and metamodel-dependent describing changes at the model instance level of heterogeneous metamodels. A metamodel-depended extension of the change plan language can be developed to declare change types with higher semantics for the particular metamodels. The process of deriving complex change types from a series of atomic change types with higher semantic is called semantic lifting (Kehrer et al., 2011). A fixed set of atomic changes is insufficient for Vergil. In the context of Vergil, semantic lifting has to define the valid types of changes that define a particular complex change without prescribing the concrete number of instances of a type. For example, the complex change type *Split* is expressed with atomic change types *Add* and *Delete*. When an interface in the source code model is to be splitted, the number of methods that are to be moved to another interface is always case specific. Consequently, the needs and requirements of a specific case have to be taken into account. A pair of *Add* and *Delete* changes are to be present in the change plan for the developer. The number of *Add* and *Delete* change pairs cannot be foreseen to support individual cases, when complex changes are defined in the metamodel-dependent change plan language extension. As a result, enhancing the change plan language with metamodel-dependent change types that have a higher semantic, constraints must be defined to ensure that complex change types are refined only with valid atomic and other complex change types without prescribing the number of occurrences, e.g., such a constraint ensures that a change type instance of *Split* is refined by one or more change type instances of *Move*. The constraints can be defined with the Object Constraint Language (OCL) (Object Management Group, 2014a).

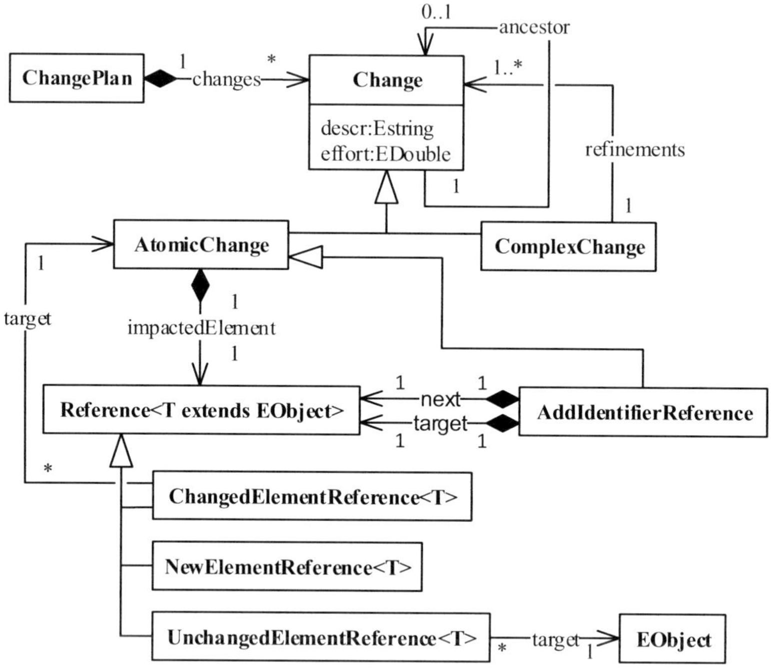


**Figure 4.7.:** Change Plan definition

## 4.4. Performance Solution

The goal of the performance solution description language is to describe a solution in terms of its properties with respect to decision criteria and its implementation with respect to the changes that are to be applied to the software application.

### 4.4.1. Requirements

This section describes the requirements for the performance solution language. The requirements are:

- *The performance solution language should generically describe the properties of a solution with respect to decision criteria (PS-R1)*: Selecting a solution among alternatives is often a multiple criteria decision problem. Various decision criteria, e.g., impact on performance, maintainability, extensibility, project schedule, budget or development resources, are to be considered by the decision maker in prioritizing solution proposals in order to select the most appropriate solution for each individual case. Each solution proposal can have different properties for the defined decision criteria. Consequently, the performance solution language should describe the different properties of a solution for the defined decision criteria.
- *The performance solution language should generically describe the implementation of a solution (PS-R2)*: A performance solution can require changes on the hardware resource level, software configuration level, software implementation level, and software architecture level. The required changes on each level are tailored from a generic solution pattern to the individual application to support the decision maker in prioritizing solution proposals and the developer in implementing the changes. Consequently, a performance solution language should describe *how* the solution is to be implemented and *what* elements of the application are to be changed.

The conceptional idea to describe solutions with respect to decision criteria and to establish a decision criteria hierarchy originates from the Analytic Hierarchy Process (AHP) (Saaty, 2005) that is commonly used in multiple criteria decision analysis. In the AHP, the decision maker defines the goal and the criteria hierarchy. The criteria hierarchy contains primary criteria, secondary sub criteria, tertiary sub criteria, and so forth.

## 4.4.2. Abstract Syntax

Figure 4.8 shows the performance solution language in the form of a UML class diagram. A solution contains a decision criteria hierarchy for the decision model. The top-level criteria are referenced by the criteria hierarchy element. Each criterion has a name attribute that defines the semantic, e.g., performance, effort. A criterion can have an impacted element. The impacted element is an associated element in a model instance to which the criterion refers to, e.g., if the criterion is the response time of a certain method call, the impacted element would be the source code model element of that method call. The impacted element can be any model element. A criterion has a priority and the parameter specification gives the concrete priority value. The priority of each criterion defines the importance of the particular criterion among other criteria in the hierarchy. The parameter specification contains the dimension (see Section 4.1) and the value for that dimension as priority given by the decision maker. A criterion can have sub criteria to build the criteria hierarchy. For example, taking performance as top-level criterion, the sub criterion (second-level) can be the response time of a transaction (see Section 7.3.7). The criteria hierarchy is then referenced in each performance solution model instance in the context of a particular application scenario. A solution has properties and a property is associated to a criterion in the criteria hierarchy (cf. Saaty, 2005). A property specifies the particular property value of the solution for the associated criterion, e.g., the observed response time for a transaction. The parameter specification gives the property value. A property can have an associated operational profile to specify the usage scenario in which the observation should be obtained. The specification of the operational profile is especially important for a performance metric, e.g., response time, throughput, resource utilization. A solution has changes describing what elements of the application are to be changed and how each element is to be changed in order to implement the solution. The associated change plan contains the changes. A solution has priorities for each leaf criterion in the decision criteria hierarchy. The parameter specification gives the concrete priority value. Section 7.3.12 shows an example of describing a solution.

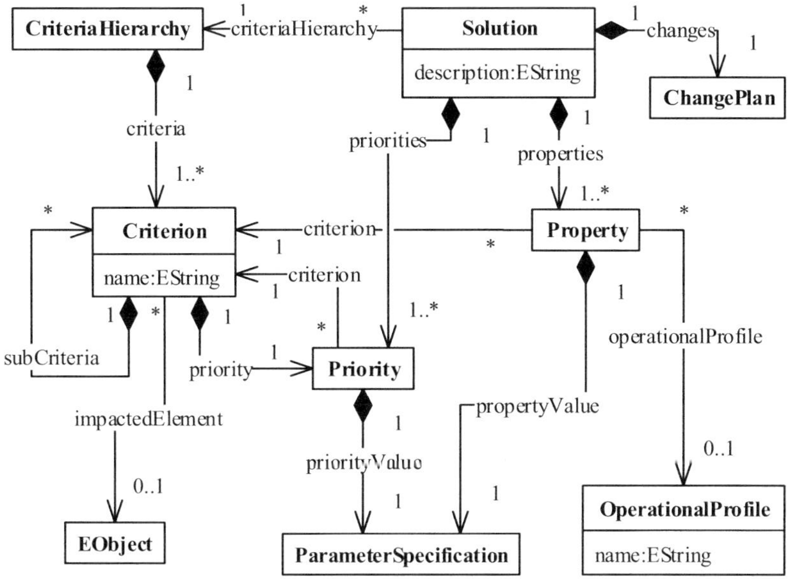


**Figure 4.8.:** Solution definition

# 4.5. Change Hypothesis

The purpose of the change hypothesis language is the description of solution knowledge of performance experts to solve performance and scalability problems. A change hypothesis describes analyses, tests and changes that performance experts do in a very generic way. We published an early version of the change hypothesis language in (Heger et al., 2014b).

## 4.5.1. Requirements

This section describes the requirements for the change hypothesis language. The requirements are:

- *The change hypothesis language should generically describe the analysis procedure in a decision tree-like structure (CP-R1)*: Performance experts typically execute tests, analyze the results, and draw a conclusion in an iterative process to come up with changes. Performance experts usually have a hypothesis of what can solve the problem. The procedure of testing the hypothesis often resembles a decision tree. Consequently, the change hypothesis language should describe the solution knowledge in a decision tree-like structure.

- *The change hypothesis language should include the analyses to obtain required information for decision making (CP-R2)*: Performance experts analyze the structure of the application, study the behavior of the application with performance tests, and talk to developers to gather information. To mitigate the risk of unintentional mistakes caused by oversights, misconceptions and lack of knowledge about the analyses that are to be conducted, the change hypothesis language should include the logic to perform the analyses automatically, to request observations from dynamic analyses and to ask the questions to obtain the required information.

### 4.5.2. Abstract Syntax

Figure 4.9 shows the change hypothesis language in the form of a UML class diagram. A change hypothesis has a root node where the test of the change hypothesis begins. A node has any number of analyses that are specialized into static analysis, dynamic analysis, and user interaction. A static analysis investigates available model instances and uses structural information given by the model instances, e.g., performance profile, source code model, or Palladio Component Model. A dynamic analysis studies the behavior of the software application at runtime by means of experiment-driven evaluations, e.g., timing behavior, resource utilization, control flow, or data flow. Therefore, the logic that is contained in a dynamic analysis creates a test profile to request the required observations. The tester is responsible for conducting the dynamic analysis and to provide the observations. A user interaction asks questions to the developer to obtain the required information. These questions typically address information that are not obtainable from the available resources or are not obtainable automatically, e.g., where particular parameter values can be provided. This typically includes information that are easily derived by humans but require an exhaustive and complex analysis because special cases have to be considered when done automatically. A node is specialized into a test and an end point (Rokach et al., 2008). An end point is a leaf in the tree structure. An end point node has the logic to formulate the changes as result of the change hypothesis. The changes are given as change plan (see Section 4.3). A test node has one or more nodes as next nodes. The logic in each test node determines which of the possible next nodes have to be executed. Section 6 shows examples for the change hypothesis language.

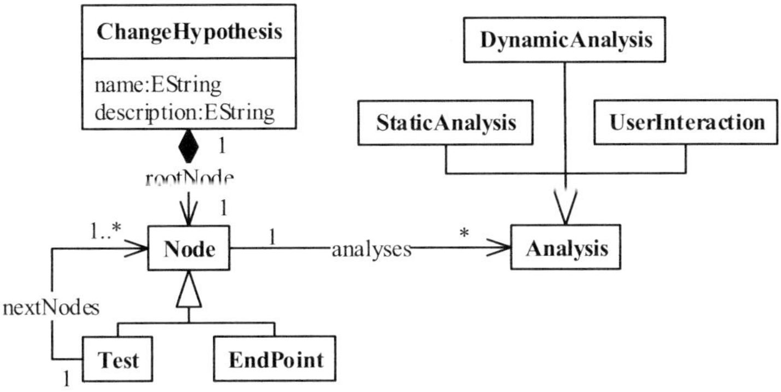


**Figure 4.9.:** Change hypothesis definition

## 4.6. Constraints

The purpose of the constraints language is to enable decision makers to specify which parts of a software application they are not willing to change or that cannot be changed. The goal of the constraints language is the description of constraints with respect to changing the application in terms of preferences for change types. Arcelli and Cortellessa already raised the concern to consider change constraints to support the selection of the most appropriate solution (Arcelli et al., 2013a). We already published the rudimentary idea of preference-based constraints expression in (Heger et al., 2014b).

### 4.6.1. Requirements

This section describes the requirements for the constraint language. The requirements are:

- *The constraints language should generically describe constrained changes for a software application (C-R1)*: In component-based software architectures, there are often components bought from a marketplace, consumed from a component repository with freely available components or reused from other projects. Changes to the API and the internals of the components are often undesired or impossible. Enterprise applications are often integrated with other enterprise applications and there are also often legacy systems involved that cannot be changed. The constraints language should describe undesired changes by specifying the undesired change type for the particular element of the application and a preference for that particular change.
- *The constraints language should generically describe preferences for constrained changes (C-R2)*: There are often different preferences for change types. A binary specification of exclusion for particular change types for a certain element of the application is often to coarse grained. Consequently, the constraints language should express different preferences for change types.

### 4.6.2. Abstract Syntax

Figure 4.10 shows the constraints language in the form of a UML class diagram. The constraints element is a container for all defined constraint elements. Any number of constraint elements can be defined. A constraint refers to the impacted element in a model instance for which changes are constrained. A constraint can contain any number of constrained change elements. The change element is the change element in the change plan language (see Section 4.3). Each constraint comes with a preference rating given by the referenced parameter specification. The rating scale is defined in the dimension. The specified constraints are used to warn the developer and decision maker when the changes in the change plan do not satisfy the specified constraints. The preference rating can be considered in decision making (see Section 5.8) for prioritizing the solutions with respect to their conformity to the specified constraints.

The granularity of specified change types depends on the objectives of the decision maker. For example, when any kind of change to a particular element is undesired, the super type of all change types is to be used. The definition of higher semantic changes in the metamodel-dependent part of the change plan language can provide a better resolution for the decision maker to clarify the objectives of the specified constraints. For example, when a certain refactoring is to be excluded that is a series of complex changes (without semantic lifting), the decision maker has to use the generic change super type that also renders other specialized change types as undesired. Alternatively, the decision maker has to identify which complex changes and atomic changes of the change plan language are part of a complex change that is to be excluded. The decision maker can then specify the identified change types of the change plan language as constrained. Section 7.3.8 gives a constraints definition example.

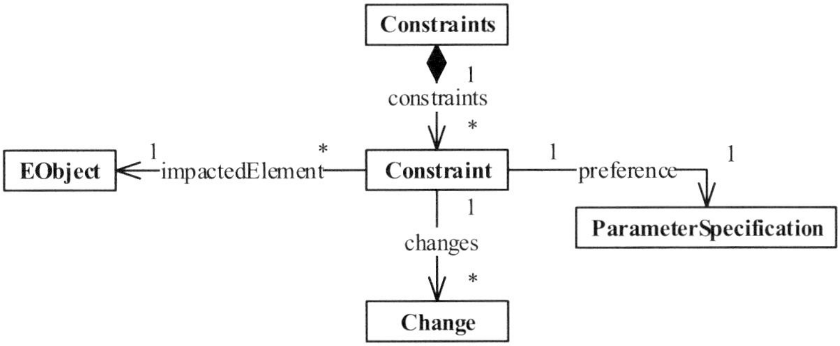


**Figure 4.10.:** Constraints definition

# 5. Developer Guidance

This chapter introduces the workflow of Vergil that exceeds the sole identification of possible solutions to support the developer in selecting the most appropriate solution proposal to satisfy requirement R4. Note, parts of the developer guidance have already been published in (Heger et al., 2014a; Heger et al., 2014b).

The chapter is structured as follows: Section 5.1 gives an overview on the workflow activities and their concerns. Section 5.2 describes the creation of the criteria hierarchy as input from the decision maker before Section 5.3 describes the description of the performance and scalability problem as input from the developer. Thereafter, the workflow activities are described in detail. Section 5.4 describes the identification of possible solutions, Section 5.5 describes the identification of impacted elements, Section 5.6 describes the effort estimation for solution proposals, Section 5.7 describes the evaluation of the properties of solution proposals with respect to the decision criteria, and Section 5.8 describes the ranking of the solution proposals by prioritization.

## 5.1. Workflow Overview

We performed a conceptual analysis of the guidance problem to identify the essential workflow activities and compared the results with the recommendations of Williams and Smith (Williams et al., 2002a) as well as Cheng (Cheng, 2008) that provide recommendations for a proper approach on solving software performance and scalability problems. The core activity of the workflow of Vergil is to identify potential solutions for the problem. Additionally, to provide a holistic workflow, the workflow includes further activities to collect data with the goal to rank the solution proposals according to defined decision criteria. The data that is collected throughout the workflow answers questions such as:

- What is the software performance and/or scalability problem?
- What are the criteria that drive the decision about the solution?
- What are the possible solutions?
- What are the efforts of a possible solution (e.g., including efforts for coding and testing of changes, or distribution of the software)?
- What are the properties of a possible solution (e.g., including properties such as the impact on performance, maintainability, sustainability, or any side effects like performance degradation of another service)?

The data that is collected depends significantly on the decision criteria and therefore also the properties of the solution proposals that have to be determined. An exception is the performance impact. The performance impact of a solution proposal as property has to be quantified in any case.

The prerequisite of the workflow is that the developer describes the software performance and scalability problem with the performance profile description language and that the decision maker describes the decision criteria hierarchy and the associated solution properties with the performance solution description language. The description of the performance problem often has to interplay with the patterns that are recognized by the defined change hypothesis. To ensure that the problems are described such that the appropriate change hypotheses recognize their own applicability to the problem is the responsibility of the implementation of Vergil. For example, when the change hypotheses match particular dimensions in the performance profile, the implementation has to ensure that only such dimensions are used to describe the problem. Because the change hypotheses are available to Vergil, the relevant dimensions can be determined and provided to the developer as dimension possibilities when describing the problem. The description of the decision criteria hierarchy has to include all relevant decision criteria that are important for the goal of solving the software performance and scalability problem. The criteria hierarchy is a tree where the leaf criteria define the relevant properties of the solution proposals and against which criteria the solution proposals are prioritized. For this reason, the decision maker has to specify the properties of solution proposals that have to be determined for this purpose. This includes the creation of the parameter specification to specify the required parameters. For example, considering the response time criterion for a particular service, the parameter specification specifies that the 90% percentile value of the response time has to be measured for all solution proposals in order to prioritize the solution proposals with respect to the response time criterion. The data is then used by the workflow activities to provide guidance.

The workflow of Vergil defines five main activities (see Figure 5.1) to guide the developer from a software performance and scalability problem to a solution without the assistance of a performance expert in each particular problem case:

- *Identify possible solutions*: The available set of change hypotheses is tested to identify possible solutions. Testing of a change hypotheses often requires additional data that are either determined automatically through static analysis, or requested with a dynamic analysis of the software application through conducting experiments, or requested through questions to the developer. To guide the experiment that is to be conducted, Vergil provides a test profile describing what data to obtain, where in the system the data to measure, and when with respect to the operational profile to apply. This test profile also acts as template to guide how the resulting data is to be described as performance profile that is given back to Vergil. The result of the workflow activity is a set of solution proposals described by the performance solution description language containing the created change plan of the corresponding end point of the change hypothesis. The change plan contains the description of the initial changes that are necessary to implement the solution. The description of the decision criteria hierarchy and the relevant properties are also part of the solution description. Section 5.4 describes the identification of possible solutions activity in more detail.
- *Identify impacted elements*: The created change plans with initial changes are used as input to identify all impacted elements in the available model instances (depending on the available propagation rules). For this reason, change propagation rules are applied to determine whether a change propagates to another element and how this particular element has to be changed. Therefore, an additional change is created in the change plan to describe how the element has to be changed. The result of the activity is the set of completed change plans describing the changes to implement the solution proposal. Section 5.5 describes the identification of the impacted elements in more detail.

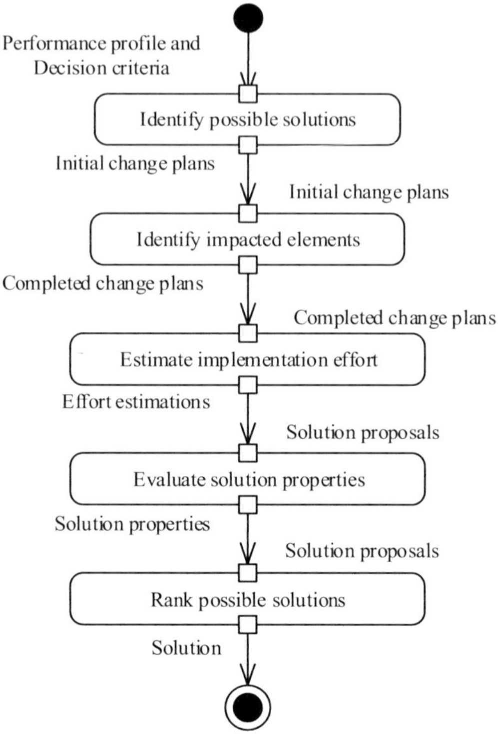


**Figure 5.1.:** Workflow overview

- *Estimate implementation effort*: The completed change plans are used to assess the implementation efforts for the application of the changes as well as additional efforts for testing, deployment, or distribution of the software application. For example, the criticality of the changes can determine the required effort for testing (Cheng, 2008). The workflow defines the implementation effort estimation as individual activity because the implementation effort and the performance impact are considered as the fundamental properties of a solution for decision making (Williams et al., 2002a; Cheng, 2008). The result of the estimate implementation effort activity is the individual effort estimate for each change plan. Section 5.6 describes the estimation of the implementation effort in more detail.

- *Evaluate solution properties*: The specified properties of the decision maker are the input to evaluate the properties of the solution proposals. Vergil uses the description of the properties and the parameters to create a test profile as guidance. For properties that require dynamic analyses (e.g., timing behavior of the software application in the case of each solution proposal), the test profile again acts as guidance for the tester on what needs to be measured, where in the system and when. For other properties like maintainability or sustainability, the developer has to assess the solution proposals and to provide the assessment result. In all cases, the test profile again acts as template to describe how Vergil expects the description of the results. In this activity, the performance impact of each solution proposal has to be evaluated at minimum to assess the possible performance improvement (Cheng, 2008). The result of the evaluate solution properties activity are the concrete parameter values for the properties. Section 5.7 describes the evaluation of the solution properties in more detail.
- *Rank possible solutions*: The solution proposals with the collected data are the input to rank the solution proposals based on the total priority of each solution. Therefore, the decision maker has to prioritize the criteria in the criteria hierarchy in pairwise comparisons on how important each criterion is to attain the goal compared to another criterion. The decision maker then uses the determined property values to prioritize the solution proposals with respect to the criteria in the decision criteria hierarchy in pairwise comparisons on how much a solution contributes to the goal compared to another solution proposal. The reasons for the necessity of the ranking are described in literature (Williams et al., 2002a; Cheng, 2008). For example, the solution proposal that achieves the best performance may use unfamiliar technologies, negatively impact the performance of other services, or the maintainability of the application (Williams et al., 2002a). The totaled priority of each solution proposal determines the rank of the solution proposal with the highest priority ranked at the top. The result of the rank possible solution activities is the ranking of the solution proposals. This supports the selection of the solution that is used to solve the software performance and scalability problem. Section 5.8 describes the ranking of the solution proposals in more detail.

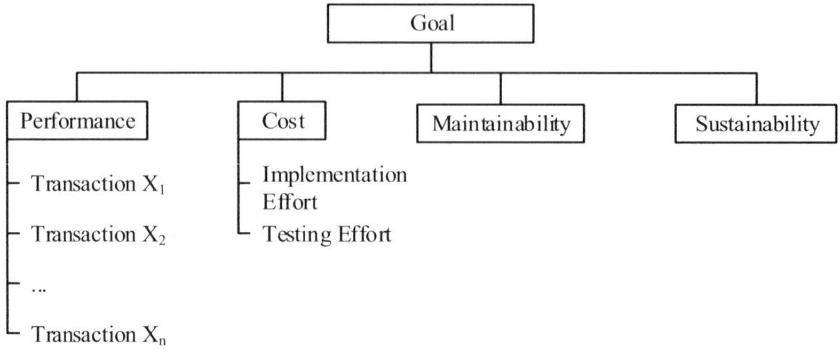


**Figure 5.2.:** Example of a decision model

The quantification of the current state, the test of which rules are applicable, the application of the applicable rules, the evaluation of the changes with respect to performance improvement and costs, and a ranking of the possible solutions are also applied in (Xu, 2008) and partly in (T.-H. Chen et al., 2014).

## 5.2. Creation of Criteria Hierarchy

The decision maker describes the decision criteria hierarchy with the solution description language (see Section 4.4). The decision maker defines the goal of the decision, e.g., select the most appropriate solution alternative and refines the goal into criteria that are important for goal attainment, e.g., performance, cost, maintainability. The primary criteria can be refined as necessary to suit the particular context and conditions e.g., performance is refined into the different transactions of the software application.

Figure 5.2 shows an example decision criteria hierarchy based on the criteria examples that we have collected from respondents in the collected data of the online survey (see Section 7.2.7). The *Goal* is refined into the primary criteria *Performance*, *Cost*, *Maintainability*, and *Sustainability*. Maintainability and sustainability seem to be an important concern of a solution by the respondents of our survey. Especially with respect to sustainability, a solution can solve the root cause of the problem or mitigate the symptom of the problem. A solution with superior performance that is hard to maintain may not be in favor of the decision maker. We refined *Performance* into the different transactions of the software application, i.e, *Transaction* $X_1$, *Transaction* $X_2$, ..., *Transaction* $X_n$ (omitting a further refinement of each transaction into particular performance metrics for simplicity). Improving the performance of a particular transaction that suffers from a software performance and scalability problem can worsen the performance of other transactions. Since not all transaction may have the same priority with respect to the performance criteria, the decision maker has to prioritize them. For example, a business critical transaction like purchasing products is certainly more important than a seldom used administrative transaction. Consequently, the importance of the various transactions should be considered in decision making. We refined *Cost* into the secondary criteria *Implementation Effort* and *Testing Effort.* A solution alternative with superior performance that requires an exceptional effort to implement the solution with potentially unfamiliar technologies may also not be in the favor of the decision maker. The more parts of the software application are impacted by changes of the solution or the more critical the impacted parts are the more testing effort can be necessary (Cheng, 2008). Other criteria that we have not included in the decision model are, for example, the documentation effort, hardware costs, and other potential risks. The decision model and the included criteria are thought to be an orientation for the decision maker to create the individual decision model.

## 5.3. Description of Performance and Scalability Problem

The developer describes the problem with the performance profile description language. The developer describes the current state of the problem such as the response time of the affected service as well as the root cause, e.g., the number of SQL statements. The developer also describes the objectives in form of quality requirements such as the desired response time of the affected service (Williams et al., 2002a; Cheng, 2008). The quality requirements serve as performance objectives and can be utilized during decision making to measure goal attainment for each solution proposal. The determination whether a solution proposal achieves the desired quality is part of the evaluation of solution properties activity. The defined performance aspects describing the problem are analyzed by the nodes of the change hypotheses to test their applicability. The interplay of the change hypotheses and the problem description has to be ensured by the implementation of Vergil. Section 7.3.9 shows a performance profile excerpt describing the response time of a Servlet method and the number of SQL queries that are used to read the objects from the database.

Important for the guidance throughout the workflow is that the performance profile contains a description of the operational profile that has been used to obtain the parameter values of each performance aspect. Vergil uses the referenced operational profiles of particular performance aspects when test profiles are created by using the association between dimensions and operational profiles. In cases where only one operational profile has been used to obtain all observations, no distinction is necessary and Vergil will use the same operational profile in the test profiles. This includes that Vergil may adjusts the workload parameters appropriately for the experiment. The association between the observed values and the operational profile is also necessary to ensure that the same usage profile is applied to the application to avoid misleading analysis results.

## 5.4. Identification of Possible Solutions

An important part of providing guidance to solve software performance and scalability problems is to identify possible solutions. In the context of Vergil, solution knowledge is provided as change hypotheses that encapsulate elicited performance expert knowledge about conditions that must be satisfied, analysis that have to be conducted, and changes that are to be applied to solve the problem. Because not every change hypothesis may be applicable in a particular problem case, they have to be tested. The goal of the identification of possible solutions is accordingly:

> *Identify potential solutions for the software performance and scalability problem.*

The idea to attain this goal is that Vergil tests change hypotheses to identify possible solutions. This includes that change hypotheses have been developed by performance experts and are available to Vergil. A similar concept has been used by Miller et al. to isolate the root cause of performance problems (Miller et al., 1995).

## 5.4.1. Activities

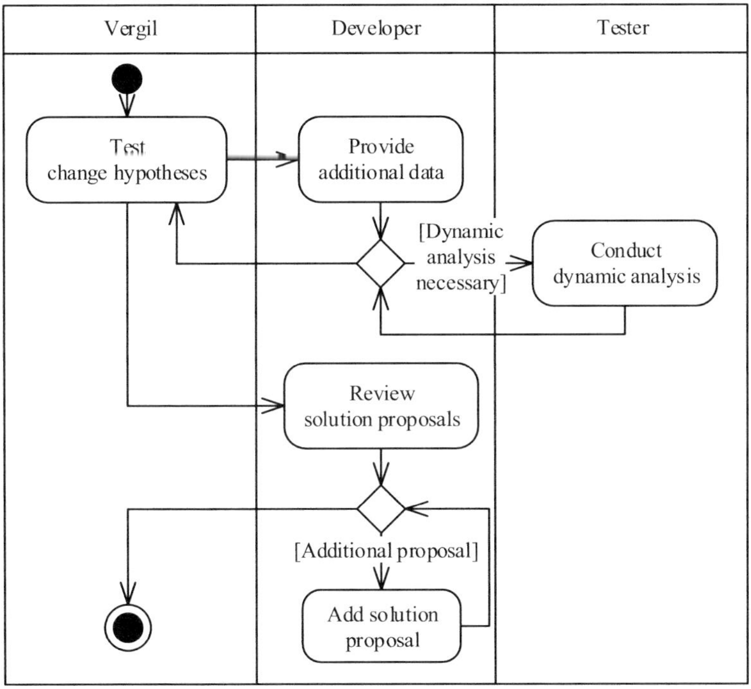


**Figure 5.3.:** Identification of possible solution activities

Figure 5.3 shows the activities of the *Identify possible solutions* activity. Vergil tests the change hypotheses by executing the nodes of the change hypotheses. When additional data is required by a change hypothesis' node, the developer provides the requested data. In the cases where additional dynamic analyses have to be conducted to determine the requested data, e.g., by studying a particular behavioral aspect of the application, the tester conducts the necessary analyses. When the change hypotheses testing is completed, the developer reviews the solution proposals and can contribute additional solution proposals that have not been proposed by the change hypotheses.

## 5.4.2. Test of Change Hypotheses

Algorithm 1 shows the change hypotheses test algorithm that is a depth-first-search on the nodes of the change hypothesis. The input to the test algorithm is the set of all change hypothesis $\mathscr{C}$, and the set of all models $\mathscr{M}$. The blackboard $\mathscr{B}$ is used for exchanging data between nodes. The algorithm requires that neither $\mathscr{C}$ nor $\mathscr{M}$ is empty. When $\mathscr{C}$ is empty, no change hypotheses are provided that are to be tested. When $\mathscr{M}$ is empty, no models are provided that can be analyzed by the nodes in the change hypotheses. The test algorithm executes the depth-first-search for each change hypothesis $c$ in the set of change hypotheses $\mathscr{C}$. The processing of the change hypothesis starts with the root node. The logic of the root node is executed by calling the do method and providing $\mathscr{B}$ and $\mathscr{M}$ as input. Analysis results are persisted in $\mathscr{B}$ to be used by the following nodes. Any node knows its successors and makes the decision what succeeding nodes are to be processed. The list of nodes to be processed is retrieved from the root node through the getNextNodes method. The test algorithm then processes the nodes in the next nodes list until the list is empty. The node that is processed next is always the current head of the list. The next node is pulled and removed from the list and executed by calling the do method providing the $\mathscr{B}$ with the analysis results of other nodes, and $\mathscr{M}$. When the processing of the node finished, the test algorithm checks the type of the node. When the node is an end point, no succeeding nodes are valid and a solution returned by the node is expected. The solution is obtained from the node and added to the set of solutions $\mathscr{S}$. When the node is not an end point, the succeeding nodes are obtained and added to the beginning of the next nodes list. After all relevant nodes have

**Algorithm 1** Test of change hypotheses

$\mathscr{C} \leftarrow$ Set of change hypotheses as input
$\mathscr{S} \leftarrow \emptyset$ // Set of solution proposals as output
$\mathscr{B} \leftarrow \emptyset$ // Blackboard for data exchange between nodes
$\mathscr{M} \leftarrow$ Set of model instances as input
**Require:** $\mathscr{C} \neq \emptyset$
**Require:** $\mathscr{M} \neq \emptyset$
  **for all** $c \in \mathscr{C}$ **do**
    Node rootNode = $c$.getRootNode()
    rootNode.do($\mathscr{B}, \mathscr{M}$)
    List<Node> nextNodes = rootNode.getNextNodes()
    **while** $nextNodes \neq \emptyset$ **do**
      Node nextNode = nextNodes.getAndRemoveHead()
      nextNode.do($\mathscr{B}, \mathscr{M}$)
      **if** $nextNode.getType() = EndPoint$ **then**
        $\mathscr{S}$.addSolution(nextNode.getSolution())
      **else**
        nextNodes.addNodes(nextNode.getNextNodes())
      **end if**
    **end while**
    $\mathscr{B} \leftarrow \emptyset$
  **end for**
  **return** $\mathscr{S}$

been processed and the solutions are added to $\mathscr{S}$, the test algorithm resets $\mathscr{B}$ and continues with the next change hypothesis until all $c \in \mathscr{C}$ have been processed.

We use a depth-first-search instead of a breadth-first-search because we assume that it is more beneficial when interaction with the developer is necessary. Algorithm 1 does not cover the combination of change hypotheses due to the fact that we assume an iterative application. In each iteration, the most appropriate solution is selected and has to be evaluated before the next iteration can begin which may require a complete solution implementation. In such cases, testing all possible combinations of solutions may require a unfeasible high effort. Hence, reducing the effort by selecting the most appropriate solution in every iteration entails the potential risk to miss combinations of solutions that may result in a larger performance improvement at the end. However, in each iteration, the applicability of each change hypothesis is tested again. Thereby, a change hypothesis may be applied multiple times or even discarded by another change hypothesis in a later iteration.

Advanced test algorithms may include the application of machine learning techniques. However, we consider machine learning techniques as difficult due to the required training set. A potentially large collection of problems and applications to create an appropriate training set is required for generalization. This may be possible when the cases to which Vergil is applied to are documented in a way that they can be used as training sets. Based on this training set, a new algorithm can be developed. We consider the employment of evolutionary algorithms also as difficult due to the possible high manual testing effort involved for each candidate of each generation. When automation is available to a large degree, the situation might be different and the application of such algorithms to determine solutions consisting out of multiple change hypotheses can be feasible.

An argument for the iterative approach is that software performance and scalability problems can hide other problems (Wert et al., 2013; Wert et al., 2014). In such cases, multiple problems have to be solved subsequently where the decision maker has to make a decision in each iteration.

### 5.4.3. Data Collection

During the test of a change hypothesis, additional data about the software application is often required to make decisions about the applicability and to continue the processing of a hypothesis' nodes. When the processed node of the change hypothesis is a static analysis, Vergil obtains the required data autonomously from the available models. In cases, where required models are not available, the processing of the node terminates. When a node is a user interaction, Vergil prompts the developer and the developer provides the required data through answering the questions (Chambers et al., 2015; Bachmann et al., 2007). When a node is a dynamic analysis, Vergil creates the test profile that describes what complementary data is requested. The test profile serves as means to communicate with the developer or available tool adapters. The tester is then responsible for conducting the dynamic analysis to obtain the requested data. The dynamic analysis to collect the data for the tests of change hypotheses are different to the performance evaluation experiments described in Section 5.7. The difference relies in the aim of the experiment. While the aim of the experiments in the context of a change hypothesis' analysis is to study a particular aspect of the behavior of the software application, the aim of the performance evaluation experiments is to collect performance metrics as defined in the decision criteria hierarchy (see Section 5.2). When an adapter for the measurement environment is available, the adapter is responsible for translating the test profile into an instrumentation description for the monitoring tool, controlling the measurement environment (e.g., restart the application server, reset the database, etc.), and to translate the monitoring results back into a performance profile that is given back to Vergil. In such an automated scenario, a challenge is to design the experiment. In some cases, it may not be possible to obtain all required data at once within a single experiment. In contrast, when a tester conducts the experiment, the tester can design the experiment appropriately based on the particular knowledge about the software application. However, in experiments that are not interested in performance metrics where monitoring overhead is crucial, a high monitoring overhead may be negligible because it does not disturb the relevant information. The type of data that is requested by a test profile can be distinguished between raw data, already aggregated data, and pre-analyzed data.

- *Request of raw data*: When raw data is requested, the aggregation of data is part of the analysis in the context of a change hypothesis' node. A benefit of requesting raw data is that potential aggregation flaws are avoided and more information about the data is available. For example, requesting the entry and exit timestamps of a method execution allows to analyze the number of measurements that may be necessary to assess the application of statistical hypothesis tests. A drawback of requesting raw data is that the performance profile may contain a very large number of parameter specifications to describe the results (see Section 7.3.9.2 and Section 7.3.11.2).

- *Request of aggregated data*: Requesting aggregated data on the other hand, requires the tester or the measurement environment adapter to determine what raw data needs to be monitored to obtain the requested aggregated results. Requesting aggregated data also means reducing guidance on how the data is obtained. For example, in contrast to requesting the entry and exit timestamps of a method, the mean value of the response time is requested. The mean value does not describe how many samples have been used. A potential solution can be to recommend a minimum number of samples and to request the aggregated data as well as information about the samples, e.g., the number of samples that have been aggregated.

- *Request of pre-analyzed data*: The highest degree of delegating responsibility is the request of pre-analyzed data. The tester or measurement environment adapter then has the responsibility to execute an appropriate analysis including the test of potential preconditions. Requesting pre-analyzed data may require experienced and well-trained testers. For example, the large number of parameter specifications in the resulting performance profile of the case study (see Section 7.3.9.2 and Section 7.3.11.2) is caused by the getter and setter methods of the Java Persistence API entities. This large number can be avoided by requesting pre-analyzed data. For this example, the test profile can request the specification whether a getter or setter method is executed in the context of a particular method. The performance profile then contains only one performance aspect and parameter specification for each getter and setter method. However, a specification of a context is currently not supported by the performance profile description language. This can be part of future work to improve the description languages with the gained experience. Based on our current experience, requesting pre-analyzed data can significantly reduce the complexity of the analysis that is to be included into a test node.

### 5.4.4. Addition of Custom Solutions

Vergil can only test change hypotheses that have been created and provided by performance experts. The solution of software performance and scalability problems can nevertheless depend on the creativity and experience of the developer. Developers may develop their own solution proposals based on their creativity or through the right trigger based on a solution proposal of Vergil. In both cases, developers have to be able to contribute their solution proposals to the set of solution proposals determined by Vergil that are then processed analogously in the remainder of the workflow. Therefore, developers can provide their solution proposals to Vergil. Such solution proposals may include "quick-and-dirty" solutions. The integral part of providing a solution proposal is the change plan that contains the initial changes. The provided solution proposals can also be assessed by performance experts in order to develop new change hypotheses.

## 5.5. Identification of Impacted Elements

When a change to a software application is applied, the intended change can have other unintended changes as consequence which is known in literature as the *Ripple Effect* (Yau et al., 1978). Investigating the consequences of an intended change with a change impact analysis (Arnold et al., 1996) is an important aspect when a software application is to be changed as shown by the number of proposed approaches (Lehnert, 2011). Knowing which elements are to be changed enables developers to judge the required amount of implementation effort to implement a given change. The analysis can also help to identify the necessary test cases that have to be executed to ensure that the implementation of the change has not broken the functionality of the software application (Lehnert et al., 2013). Solving software performance and scalability problems often requires changes in different implementation artifacts and at different application levels. This entails the same risks as the software maintenance discipline is concerned with. In light of the similarities, the two goals of the *Identify Impacted Elements* activity is as follows:

> *(1) Support the developer in assessing the consequences of an intended change by determining all elements that are impacted and (2) support the developer in implementing the solution by deriving a change plan as implementation description.*

The idea to attain the goals is to use rules to propagate changes in heterogeneous models (Lehnert et al., 2013). The rules determine whether a change propagates to a certain element and when a change propagates how the impacted element has to be changed in order to complete the change plans. Note, parts of the preliminary idea to the identification of impacted elements have already been published in (Heger et al., 2014a).

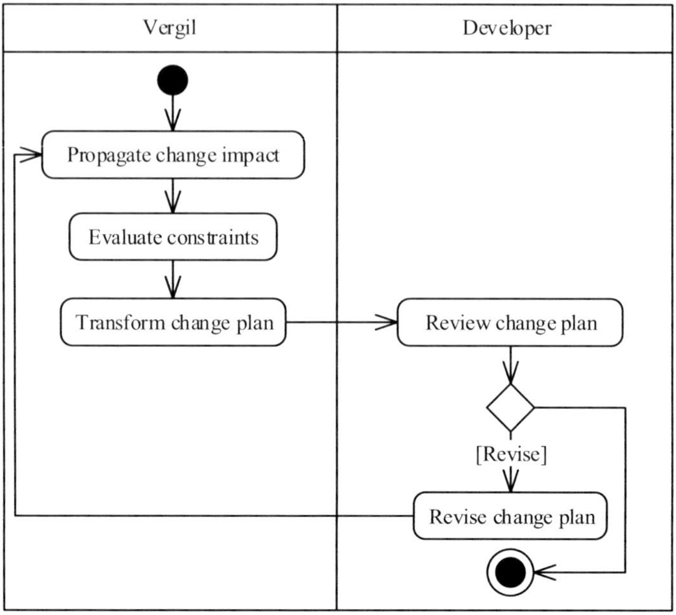


**Figure 5.4.:** Impact analysis activities

### 5.5.1. Activities

Figure 5.4 shows the tasks in the *Identify Impacted Elements* activity in the form of a UML activity diagram. Vergil completes the change planes by propagating the change impact within and between model instances. Vergil evaluates the compliance of the change types and impacted elements in the change plan with the constraints specified with the constraints description language (see Section 4.6). Vergil supports the developer in reviewing the changes by transforming the change plan into a convenient and intuitive visualized presentation, i.e., a list, as shown in Figure 5.5. Conflicting changes can be highlighted with an exclamation mark to attract the attention of the Developer during the review as shown in Figure 5.5. The developer reviews the completed change plan and can revise the change plan as necessary. A revision can be desired when the developer is able to improve the change

**Algorithm 2** Change impact propagation

```
  ℛ ← Set of propagation rules as input
  𝒫 ← Set of change plans as input and output
  ℳ ← Set of model instances as input
Require: ℛ ≠ ∅
Require: 𝒫 ≠ ∅
Require: ℳ ≠ ∅
  for all p ∈ 𝒫 do
    List<Change> unprocessedChanges = p.getAllChanges()
    while unprocessedChanges ≠ ∅ do
      Change c = unprocessedChanges.getAndRemoveFirst()
      for all r ∈ ℛ do
        List<Change> progatedChanges = r.propagate(c,ℳ)
        if propagatedChanges ≠ ∅ then
          unprocessedChanges.addAll(progatedChanges)
        end if
      end for
    end while
  end for
```

plan based on experience, domain, or design knowledge. When a revision of the change plan occurs, Vergil evaluates the impact of the changes in the change plan again. Changes applied to the change plan can have side effects because the propagation rules take the type of change into consideration. When the activities are completed, the change plan provides a description of the implementation of a solution that is also used in the remainder of the workflow as foundation to estimate the implementation effort and for decision making.

### 5.5.2. Impact Propagation

Any end point of a change hypothesis creates a change plan with the changes that are to be applied to solve the software performance and scalability problem. An end point does not consider potential propagation of changes. This concern is subject of the change impact propagation. Algorithm 2 shows the change impact propagation algorithm that executes the propagation rules to identify all impacted elements and to complete the change plans. The algorithm is based on the recursive change propagation algorithm of (Lehnert et al., 2013). We use the change instance instead of the tuple and delegate the responsibility of checking whether a change has already been propagated to the propagation rules. The input to the algorithm is a set of propagation rules $\mathscr{R}$, a set of change plans from the solution proposals $\mathscr{P}$, and the set of models $\mathscr{M}$. The algorithm requires that no set is empty. When $\mathscr{R}$ is empty, no rules are available to apply. When $\mathscr{P}$ is empty, no changes exist to apply the rules to. When $\mathscr{M}$ is empty, no models are available to identify the elements where the changes may propagate to. The algorithm propagates the changes for each change plan $c$ individually. The initial list of unprocessed changes contains all change elements from the change plan $p \in \mathscr{P}$. The propagation rules are then executed until the list of unprocessed changes is empty. In each iteration, the first change $c$ is taken and removed from the list of unprocessed changes. The algorithm then executes each propagation rule $r$ by calling the propagate method of the rule and providing the change $c$. When the rule propagated any changes, the rule returns a list of the created change elements in the change plan. The returned changes are added to the list of unprocessed changes. The algorithm terminates when all change plans have been processed.

### 5.5.3. Propagation Rules

This section presents the concept of propagation rules with an example. A propagation rule encapsulates the knowledge whether a particular change type propagates to a particular element type and how. A propagation rule also includes the analysis whether the processed change has already been propagated by analyzing the change plan. Hereby, the ancestor relation of changes is of particular interest. Algorithm 3 shows the propagation rule for updating the parameter list of a method to add an ordinary parameter to a method in the JaMoPP Java metamodel instance of the source code. This rule is used in the case study (see Section 7.3.9.5). The aim of the rule is to propagate the update parametrizable change to an interface method when the affected method is an implementation of an interface method. The input for the algorithm is the particular change instance to be processed $c$ and the set of model instances $\mathscr{M}$ (including the change plan) used for analysis purposes. The output of the algorithm is a set of propagated changes $\mathscr{O}$. The

**Algorithm 3** Update parametrizable change propagation

```
c ← Change instance as input
𝓜 ← Set of model instances as input
𝒪 ← Set of propagated changes as output
Require: c ≠ null
Require: 𝓜 ≠ ∅
  if typeOf(c) == UpdateParametrizable then
    EObject e = c.getImpactedElement()
    if typeOf(e) == ClassMethod then
      ClassMethod m_c = (ClassMethod) e
      Class clazz = getClassOfMember(m_c)
      List<Interface> interfaces = getImplementedInterfaces(clazz)
      for all i ∈ interfaces do
        if definesMethod(i, m_c) then
          InterfaceMethod m_i = getMethodDefinition(i,m_c)
          if not hasPropagatedChange(m_i, c) then
            UpdateParametrizable c_p = createPropagatedChange(c)
            c_p.setImpactedElement(m_i)
            c_p.setAncestor(c)
            𝒪.add(c_p)
          end if
        end if
      end for
    end if
  end if
```

algorithm requires that neither the change $c$ nor the set of models $\mathcal{M}$ is empty. The algorithm validates the applicability of the propagation rule by a set of checks. The change $c$ has to be an update parametrizable change. When this is the case, the impacted element is determined where the parameter should be added to. For this reason, the JaMoPP Java source code model instance is analyzed. The returned impacted element $e$ has to be a class method $m_c$. When this condition is also satisfied, the impacted element is casted to a class method and the class is determined that has the class method $m_c$ as member. Thereafter, the interfaces that the class *clazz* implements is obtained. Each interface $i$ is then analyzed whether the interface defines method $m_c$. In the case that the interface $i$ defines method $m_c$, the existence of the propagation result is checked. When the propagated update parametrizable change already exits, the conclusion is drawn that the change has already been propagated. Otherwise, a new update parametrizable change $c_p$ is created by copying the relevant values of the existing change $c$ to the update parametrizable change $c_p$. This includes the creation of referenced elements that have to be newly created. The interface method $m_i$ is set as impacted element and the ancestor relationship between the original change $c$ and the propagated change $c_p$ is set by setting $c$ as the ancestor of $c_p$. Finally, the created change is added to the set $\mathscr{O}$.

Vergil may request additional data to limit propagation in order to avoid an optimistic change set through user interaction similar to the user interaction of a change hypothesis. For example, in the conducted Java Persistence API case study, method parameters are propagated from calling method to calling method along the call tree. The method in which the parameter values can be provided cannot be determined automatically. In such cases, the developer has to provide the information in which method the parameter values can be provided to stop the propagation appropriately.

### 5.5.4. Constraints Evaluation

There are different possibilities how Vergil can deal with solution proposals that require changes that do not comply with defined constraints. A simple approach is to discard solution proposals that do not comply with all constraints. This approach entails the risk that all solution proposals are discarded, because no solution proposal complies with the specified constraints. This risk might be mitigated by enabling the developer to define how the implementation of Vergil reacts on constraints violation. This means that the discarding of solution proposals can be made optional. Another approach is to keep all solution proposals until the developer explicitly discards a solution proposal prior to solution prioritization. This approach includes that Vergil draws the attention of the developer to constraint violation. The reaction of constraint violation is then the responsibility of the developer or decision maker. A further approach is to include constraint compliance as decision criteria in the decision criteria hierarchy. The desired approach to constraint violation is subjective and may depend on the individual developer and context. However,

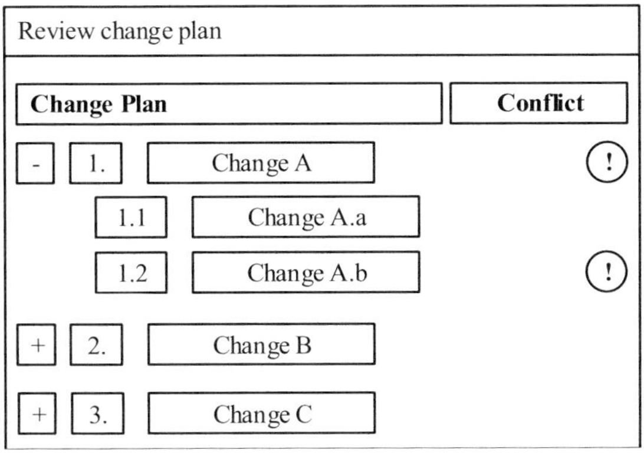


**Figure 5.5.:** Change plan visualization for review

we got the feedback from practitioners that discarding solution proposals before presenting them to developers may the least practicable approach due to the reason that specified constraints may have to be violated in order to solve the problem.

Algorithm 4 shows the algorithm to identify the changes in a change plan that impact a constraint element. The input for the algorithm are the change plan $\mathscr{P}$ and the constraints model $\mathscr{C}$. The algorithm requires that neither $\mathscr{P}$ nor $\mathscr{C}$ is null. Each constraint of the constraints model is processed individually. The impacted element $e$ is obtained from the processed constraint $c$ as well as the constraint change types. Each constraint change type is then processed individually. When the change plan $\mathscr{P}$ contains a change for the constraint element $e$ then a list of all affected changes of the change plan is obtained. The affected changes are then added to the set of identified changes $\mathscr{V}$ that is processed during the visualization of the change plan. The identification whether a change complies with a defined constraint is the most complex task. When a change of the same change type for the constraint element $e$ exists, the identification is simple. The identification is more complex when a violation has to be concluded. For example, when a change super type is used to constrain a potential change to an element, the logic has to draw the conclusion that a specialization of the change type is also affected by the constraint. Therefore, inheritance relationships between change types have to be analyzed as well as the relationships between constraint and impacted model elements.

**Algorithm 4** Validate constraints compliance

$\mathscr{P} \leftarrow$ Change plan as input
$\mathscr{C} \leftarrow$ Constrains model instance as input
$\mathscr{V} \leftarrow \emptyset$ // Set of violations as output
**Require:** $\mathscr{P} \neq$ null
**Require:** $\mathscr{C} \neq$ null
**for all** $Constraint\ c \in \mathscr{C}$ **do**
  EObject $e$ = $c$.getImpactedElement()
  List<Change> constraintChangeTypes = $c$.getChanges()
  **for all** $Change\ constraintChangeType \in constraintChangeTypes$ **do**
    **if not** $containsChange(constraintChangeType, e, \mathscr{P})$ **then**
      List<Change> affectedChanges = getAffectedChanges(constraintChangeType,$e$,$\mathscr{P}$)
      **for all** $Change\ affectedChange \in affectedChanges$ **do**
        $\mathscr{V}$.add(affectedChange, $c$)
      **end for**
    **end if**
  **end for**
**end for**
**return** $\mathscr{V}$

## 5.6. Estimation of Implementation Effort

The implementation effort of solutions is often considered in decision making as reported by the respondents of our conducted survey (see Section 7.2.7) and others (Xu, 2008; Cheng, 2008; Williams et al., 2002a). Note, we published the implementation effort estimation in the context of Vergil already in (Heger et al., 2014a). The implementation effort depends on various factors and can vary between individual developers, e.g., the familiarity with the technology, the amount and type of changes, development experience and practice. While most software development projects suffer from effort and/or schedule overruns (Moløkken et al., 2003), the goal of the *Estimate Implementation Effort* activity is as follows:

*Support the developer in estimating the implementation effort for solution proposals.*

The idea to attain that goal is to transform the change plan of each solution proposal into a convenient format for the developer and that the developer estimates the implementation effort based on the changes listed in the change plan and also determines additional efforts such as for testing or deployment.

### 5.6.1. Activities

Figure 5.6 shows the tasks in the *Estimate Implementation Effort* activity in the form of a UML activity diagram. Vergil supports the developer in estimating the implementation effort of solutions by transforming the *Change Plan* of each solution into a convenient and intuitive visualized presentation, i.e., a hierarchical list. We follow the concept of estimating the implementation effort based on the description of the necessary changes similar to the approach presented in (Rostami et al., 2015) to estimate the software evolution effort. Figure 5.7 shows the list-based visualization of change plans. Any change in the change plan is enumerated individual. The refinement of complex changes is visualized as hierarchy of changes based on the refinement relation (see Section 4.3). The developer can expand complex changes to list the refinement and study the details, and collapse complex changes to hide details when the details are unnecessary. The changes are enumerated according to the ancestor and implicit dependency relation. The effort estimation can be assigned to each change in the change plan by entering the value in the corresponding field next to the particular change.

### 5.6.2. Estimation Methods

The methods to estimate the implementation effort are categorized into expert judgment (Hughes, 1996; Boehm, 1984), formal models (e.g., COCOMO (Boehm et al., 1995), function point analysis (Albrecht, 1979)), and combinations of both (Jørgensen, 2007). Expert judgment-based effort estimation solicits the opinion of one or more developers that are experienced with the development of software applications with a similar size and complexity.

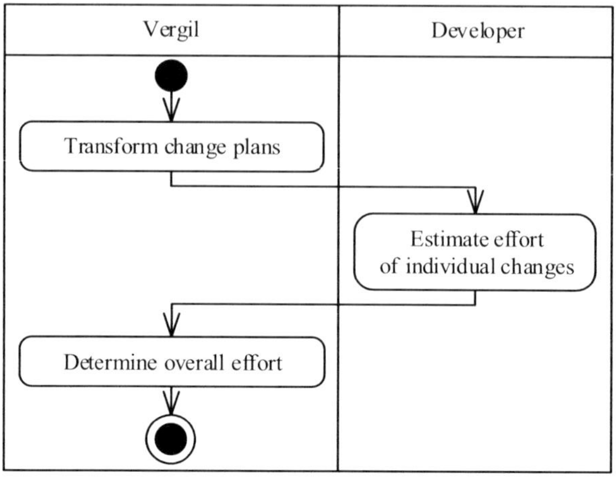


**Figure 5.6.:** Effort estimation activities

Developers should be involved in the actual development to have more reliable estimates (Hughes, 1996). Expert judgment is suggested to be the most frequently used estimation method in development projects (Jørgensen, 2004; Hughes, 1996) with a higher estimation accuracy on average compared to formal models (Jørgensen, 2007). The studies in (Jørgensen et al., 2008) show that it is important to use the most competent and highly skilled developers (e.g., senior developers) and to give them the right information to increase the accuracy of the effort estimation.

### 5.6.3. Estimation Approach

The developer can estimate the effort in a top-down approach or in a bottom-up approach. In the bottom-up approach, the developer estimates the implementation effort on the finest granularity (Rostami et al., 2015), i.e., the atomic changes that are the leafs in the hierarchy. Vergil totals the estimates to derive the total implementation effort estimate. The developer specifies the estimation in absolute numbers such as staff hours in order to determine whether a solution requires more effort than others and to quantify how much more effort is required. When more than one developer is solicited, methods like

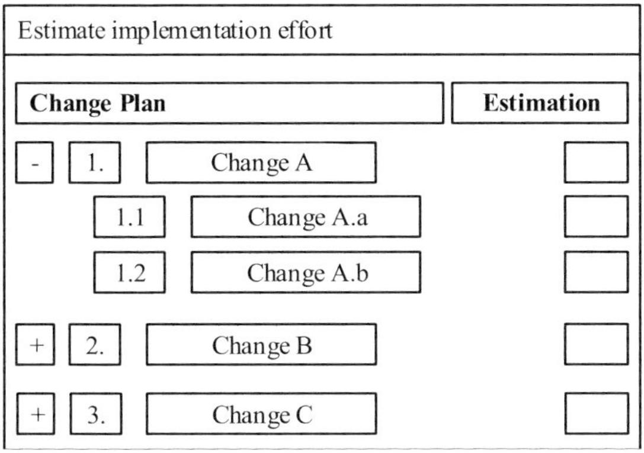


**Figure 5.7.:** Change plan visualization for effort estimation

the Delphi technique (Dalkey et al., 1969; Linstone et al., 1975) can be used to find an expert consensus (Boehm, 1984). In the context of the Delphi technique, each developer completes the effort estimation individually and anonymously. A more simplistic approach is to aggregate the estimations to the average effort estimation when a thorough effort estimation assessment is not necessary.

## 5.7. Evaluation of Solution Properties

One of the essential activities in solving software performance and scalability problems is to assess the performance impact of solution proposals (Cheng, 2008; Williams et al., 2002a; Xu, 2008; Trubiani et al., 2011). This is necessary for decision making in order to assess whether a solution proposal is able so solve the problem in a particular case as well as to compare the achievements of a solution proposal with others. The collection of data for performance metrics used as decision criteria is of particular interest. The goal of the performance evaluation activity is as follows:

> *Evaluation of the properties of each solution proposal with respect to the defined decision criteria.*

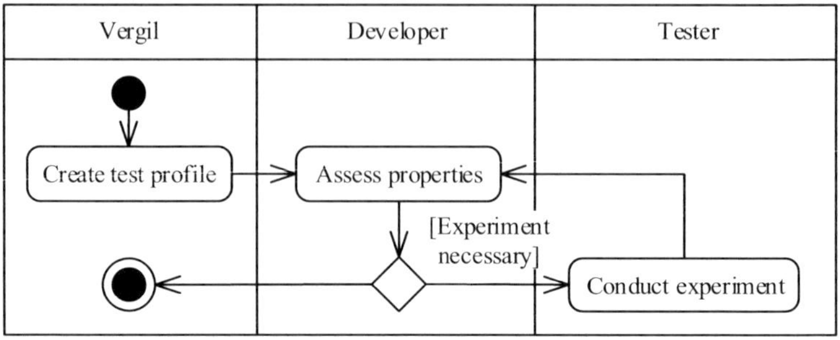


**Figure 5.8.:** Performance evaluation activities

The idea to attain that goal is to support the developer with a test profile that describes which properties of the solution proposals are relevant and what parameters of the properties have to be determined for decision making.

### 5.7.1. Activities

Vergil creates a test profile based on the decision maker's specified properties and parameters that are part of the decision criteria hierarchy to guide the developer in what data has to be determined. The developer assess the properties of each solution proposal and when additional experiments are necessary such as performance test to quantify the performance improvement of a solution proposal, the tester conducts the necessary experiments.

### 5.7.2. Evaluation Means

Vergil considers the employment of different performance evaluation means to evaluate the performance impact of solution proposals prior to the prioritization for decision making. This typically includes the evaluation of potential side effects of changes. The means of choice depends on various factors and can vary from solution proposal to solution proposal as well as from case to case without considering the subjective opinion of individuals. In general, the selection of the most appropriate performance evaluation means is influenced by the granularity of the changes and the desired accuracy of the results. Arguments in favor of model-based performance evaluation are when the complexity of changes prevents the automatic application to the implementation and when they can be applied automatically to models due to the chosen level of abstraction. Further arguments for models are when the operational profile cannot be simulated anymore due to physical or economic reasons, e.g., the simulation of millions of users. Arguments in favor of performance measurements with the implementation are when the granularity of the changes to evaluate is fine such that they cannot be reflected in performance models. Further arguments for measurement-based performance evaluation are when interaction effects have to be analyzed that are not considerable in performance models, e.g., due to the capabilities of the modeling language or the infeasible high modeling effort. Another argument that has to be considered and may lead the decision is the implementation effort of the changes of solution proposals. There are indications that additional prototyping and measurement efforts can be considered to be feasible in practice (Cheng, 2008) supported by the fact that developers have more trust in measurement (Woodside et al., 2007). When the implementation of the changes may only be a question of minutes and additional effort such as testing and deployment does not add a significant overhead, performance evaluation with the implementation may the means of choice. In the following, we give examples for what different evaluation means have already been utilized:

- *Simulation of performance models*: In (A. Koziolek et al., 2011; A. Koziolek, 2013), Palladio Component Model (PCM) instances are used to evaluate component selections, server processing rates, and component allocations. In (Huber et al., 2011), PCM instances are used to evaluate the changes in user workloads and resource configuration. In (Trubiani et al., 2011), PCM instances are used to evaluate changes to common software performance antipattern, e.g., mirroring of components, sizing of resource pools. In (Gooijer et al., 2012), PCM instances are used to evaluate changes in component replication, number of CPU cores, and component allocation.

- *Solving of analytical models*: In (Kounev et al., 2011a), QPNs are used for capacity planning. In (Xu, 2008), Layered Queueing Networks are used to evaluate changes for software bottlenecks and long path performance problems, e.g., addition of resources or batching of operations. In (X. Chen et al., 2014), QNs are used to predict response time, throughput and CPU utilization for different numbers of CPU cores and network interfaces. Martinec et al. showed the inaccuracy of existing models for JMS middleware and proposed a new QPN model in (Martinec et al., 2014). Libič et al. report on the limitations of analytical models in predicting frequency and type of Java garbage collections (Libič et al., 2014).

- *Performance prediction with statistical models*: In (D. J. Westermann, 2014), statistical models are used to predict the performance of Web pages for different numbers and kinds of user interface elements. In (Vuduc et al., 2004), statistical models are used to evaluate which implementation is best suited for the input with respect to performance.

- *Performance measurement with prototype implementations*: In (T.-H. Chen et al., 2014), measurements with a prototype are used to evaluate the performance improvement of batching database queries. Peiris et al. used prototyping to collect performance metrics of a batching algorithm (Peiris et al., 2014a). We use prototyping and measurements in our Java Persistence API case study (see Section 7.3) to evaluate the pagination solution proposal.

- *Performance measurement with implemented solution*: In (Lengauer et al., 2014), measurements are used to evaluate changes of the Java memory management configuration. We used measurements in our Java Persistence API case study to evaluate the proposed changes (see Section 7.3). In (Wert et al., 2013), measurements are used to evaluate infrastructure changes, component replacement, and database lock mechanism granularity. In (Horikawa, 2011), measurements have been used to evaluate lock mechanism to solve scalability bottleneck problems. In (T.-H. Chen et al., 2014), measurements are used to evaluate changes applied to annotations in Java source code. Tools that support the collection of measurements are, for example, presented in (Wert et al., 2015c; Eichelberger et al., 2014; van Hoorn et al., 2012).

According to (Jain, 1991), the criteria for the selection of a performance evaluation technique are, among others, the time required to get results (models are assumed to be available), the desired level of accuracy, the suitability for trade-off evaluation, and the costs.

Analytical modeling requires many assumptions and simplifications that can make results less accurate and is often also not feasible in practice. Simulations can usually provide more details while requiring less assumptions than analytical modeling and are often closer to reality. Measurements can give the most accurate results but depend significantly on the design and execution of the experiment (Jain, 1991).

### 5.7.3. Implementation of Changes

The proposed changes often give an overview on how the solutions can be implemented with respect to the particular implementation of a software application. This means that there may exist a small or large degree of freedom of how the solution is concretely implemented. For example, our conducted Java Persistence API case study shows that the implementation of changing a relationship or a persistence unit configuration property does not allow much degree of freedom on how the changes are implemented concretely. In contrast, the pagination solution proposal offers the highest degree of freedom and requires design decisions of the developer. The case study results also highlight that the changes may have to be applied differently as proposed due to differences between specification and implementation of components. Therefore, the generated change plans are proposals outlining what needs to be changed and how but not how the changes are implemented concretely. Guidelines and best-practices that are individual project specific are not reflected in change hypotheses until they are created for this specific project. We consider that developers will review and potentially revise changes in any case when the changes have been applied automatically in front of any performance evaluation effort. This typically includes to validate that all test cases are successfully passed and the functionality is not broken because this may cause incomparable results.

We distinguish between automated and semi-automated implementation of changes. When changes are applied automatically, developers revise the changes and apply the required modifications. When changes are applied semi-automatically, we consider that at least code stubs can be generated to support the developer in implementing the solution proposal. However, in any case the developer decides how the changes are implemented for performance evaluation as we, for example, deviated from the change plan for the pagination solution proposal to use prototyping of the changes to evaluate the performance (see Section 7.3.9.5).

### 5.7.4. Design of Experiment

Each solution proposal has to be evaluated in isolation under the same experiment conditions. This is crucial to the assessment of solution proposals based on their characteristics. The performance metrics have also to be measured for the case with the software performance and scalability problem in place. The important aspects of the performance evaluation experiment are that the tester has to ensure that the actual measurement complies with the indented measurement as well as that no other changes as the changes to be evaluated are applied. This means in particular that only the solution proposal is varied to mitigate the risk that a bias is introduced. This concerns address basic experimentation aspects that have to be carefully planned (Runeson et al., 2012). This includes that the tester resets the measurement environment used to conduct the experiment to an initial state that is identical in each experiment run, e.g., reset of database content that has changed during the last experiment run.

What the tester has to measure with the experiment and what operational profile to apply is defined by the decision maker in the decision criteria hierarchy. Therefore, we assume that the tester is aware of and follows established software performance evaluation methodologies (Georges et al., 2007; Jain, 1991; Weyuker et al., 2000). When this is not the case Vergil can be extended with additional analysis to mitigate the risk of potential performance evaluation flaws. The analysis that must be developed has to automatically determine an appropriate workload parameter through a calibration run. The results of the calibration run are analyzed by Vergil to update workload parameter appropriately or validates the values, e.g., duration, ramp up interval.

## 5.8. Ranking of Solutions

When the developer has to select the most appropriate solution and response time is the only criterion then the decision is easy. The developer selects the solution alternative with the best response time. If there is only one solution possible, there is no decision necessary. The decision is not that easy in real industrial software projects. There are often trade-off decisions necessary while the "optimal" solution to a software performance and scalability problem does often not exist. The decision becomes more complex and can already be difficult to make when only a couple of solution alternatives and decision criteria are involved. In industry, the association scenarios between problems and solutions that occur most often are one-to-many and many-to-many scenarios (see Section 7.2.7). The best performance might not be that important when other aspects (e.g., implementation effort, maintainability, and sustainability) are also considered. To support the developer, the decision maker has to prioritize each solution alternative for each leaf decision criterion. Otherwise, the selection of the solution is a random choice. The goal of the *Rank Solutions* activity is as follows:

> *Support the developer in selecting the most appropriate solution when a variety of solution choices exist.*

The idea to attain this goal is to utilize the Analytic Hierarchy Process (AHP) in Vergil to support the developer in selecting the most appropriate solution. This includes that the decision maker prioritizes criteria and solution proposals. The AHP has been used in software engineering for various concerns such as prioritizing requirements (Karlsson et al., 1997), design solutions (Hatvani et al., 2010), and architecture design alternatives (Zhu et al., 2005; Svahnberg et al., 2002; Al-Naeem et al., 2005).

### 5.8.1. Activities

Figure 5.9 shows the activities that are to be executed in order to rank the solution alternatives. The decision maker prioritizes the decision criteria in the hierarchy with respect to the goal and Vergil checks the consistency of the judgments. When the inconsistency exceeds a recommended threshold, the decision maker revises the judgments to improve consistency. After an

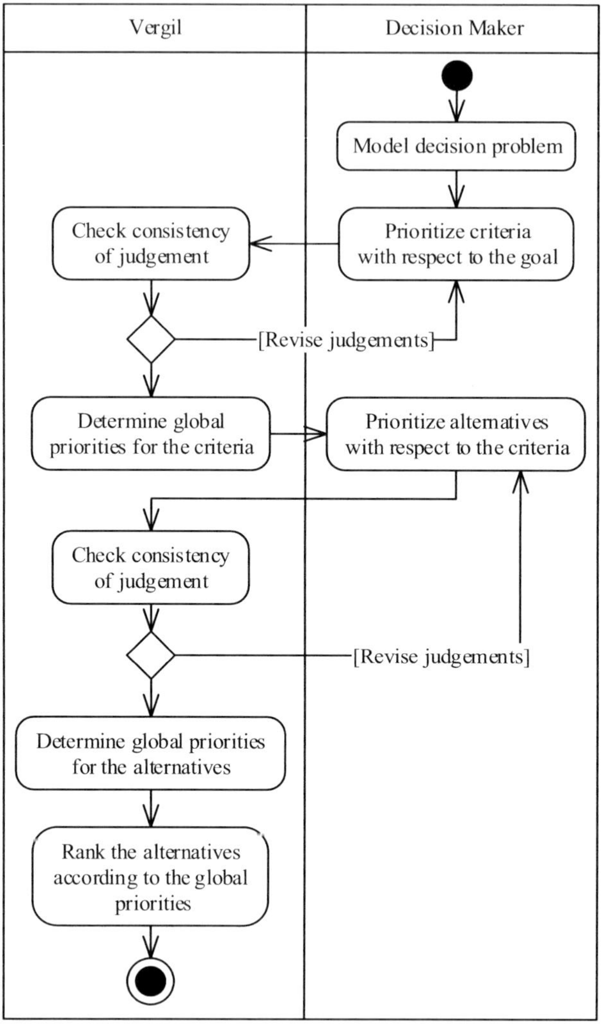


**Figure 5.9.:** Decision making activities

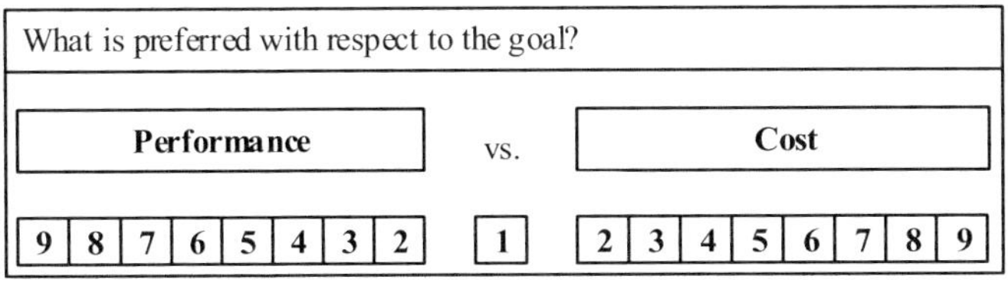


**Figure 5.10.:** Criteria prioritization dialogue

appropriate consistency is achieved, Vergil determines the global priorities of the decision criteria in the hierarchy. Thereafter, the decision maker prioritizes the solution proposals with respect to the criteria. Vergil checks the consistency of the judgments and asks the decision maker to revise the judgments when the consistency is not satisfying enough. When a satisfying consistency is achieved, Vergil determines the global priorities for the solution proposals. Vergil then ranks the solution proposals based on the totaled priority of each solution proposal and visualizes the ranking results and the achieved priority of each solution proposal with respect to the criteria.

#### 5.8.1.1. Prioritization of Criteria

In the *Prioritize criteria with respect to the goal*, the decision maker does pairwise comparisons to prioritize the criteria. Vergil supports this task by compiling the pairwise comparisons from the decision hierarchy. For the pairwise comparisons, Vergil prompts the decision maker to specify which of the two criteria is preferred with respect to the goal. Figure 5.10 shows an example for this dialogue for the comparison of the criterion *Performance* versus the criterion *Cost*. The employed scale is the ratio scale of AHP (Saaty, 2005). Vergil computes the reciprocal automatically after the decision maker specified the priority for the favored criterion in each comparison.

#### 5.8.1.2. Validation of Consistency

In the *Check consistency of judgment* activity, Vergil calculates the Consistency Index (CI) (Saaty, 2005). The CI equals 0 only when the judgments are consistent. Slight inconsistencies are tolerable when $\frac{CI}{RI} < 0.1$ where the Random Index (RI) is the consistency index when the judgments are completely at random (Saaty, 2005). RI can be calculated with simulations. A table with computed RI values for a matrix with a size of up to 10 by 10 can be found in (Saaty, 2008, p. 83). Saaty recommends that the CR should be less than 5% for a 3 by 3 matrix, less than 9% for a 4 by 4 matrix and less than 10% for a larger matrix (Saaty, 2008). Consistency can be improved by revising the judgments. According to (Saaty, 2005), increasing consistency becomes difficult when there are more than about seven criteria compared.

#### 5.8.1.3. Determination of Global Priorities

In the *Determine global priorities for the criteria* activity, Vergil calculates the global priorities for each criterion in the hierarchy. The decision maker specifies the local priority of the criteria for each group at each level with the judgments in the pairwise comparisons. The global priorities of the subcriteria show the importance of a particular subcriteria with respect to the goal.

#### 5.8.1.4. Prioritization of Solution

In the *Prioritize alternatives with respect to the criteria* activity, the decision maker judges the priorities of the solution alternatives with respect to the criteria in pairwise comparisons. Vergil supports this activity by compiling the necessary comparisons and by prompting the decision maker with a dialogue similar to the dialogue as shown in Figure 5.10. The decision maker specifies which alternative is in favor over another for each criterion and how much more by selecting the appropriate value. Vergil assigns the reciprocal value to the unfavored solution alternative automatically. The change plan of each solution alternative supports the decision maker in judging the priorities with respect to the *Maintainability* and *Sustainability* criteria. The implementation effort estimation of the developer serves the decision maker in judging the priorities of the solution alternatives with respect to the *Implementation Effort* criterion. The testing effort estimation for functional and non-functional tests of the tester support the decision maker with respect to the *Testing Effort* criterion. Performance evaluation results obtained by the tester support the decision maker in judging the priorities with respect to performance criteria.

#### 5.8.1.5. Determination of Global Priorities

In the *Determine global priorities for the alternatives* activity, Vergil determines the global priorities for the solution alternatives. This is equal to deriving the global priorities for the criteria. The global priorities of the solution alternatives show how much a solution alternative contributes to the goal with respect to the criteria.

#### 5.8.1.6. Ranking of Alternatives

Finally, in the *Rank the alternatives according to the global priorities* activity, the global priorities of each solution alternative with respect to each criterion are totaled. The solution alternatives are then ranked in accordance to their total priority. Vergil provides a graphical visualization of the results in form of bars and stacked bars similar to the visualization techniques of a Value Chart (Carenini et al., 2004) and a Table Lens (Rao et al., 1994) for the leaf criteria as shown in Figure 5.11. Value charts have already been utilized in (A. Koziolek, 2013) to support decision making on choosing a software architecture candidate when various alternatives exist. The lengths of the bars correspond to the priority of the particular solution alternative for the criteria. The rank of the solution alternatives correspond to their totaled priority. Alternatively, the graphical visualization of results of the solution alternatives with respect to two specific criteria can also be achieved with Pareto diagrams.

### 5.8.2. Effort for Criteria Prioritization

The prioritization of the criteria among the hierarchy can also be reused when the priorities are stable for many problems throughout a project or when the priorities are given due to strategic reasons by the management of an organization. Consequently, it is not necessary to establish the priorities among the criteria in the hierarchy from the beginning for every problem.

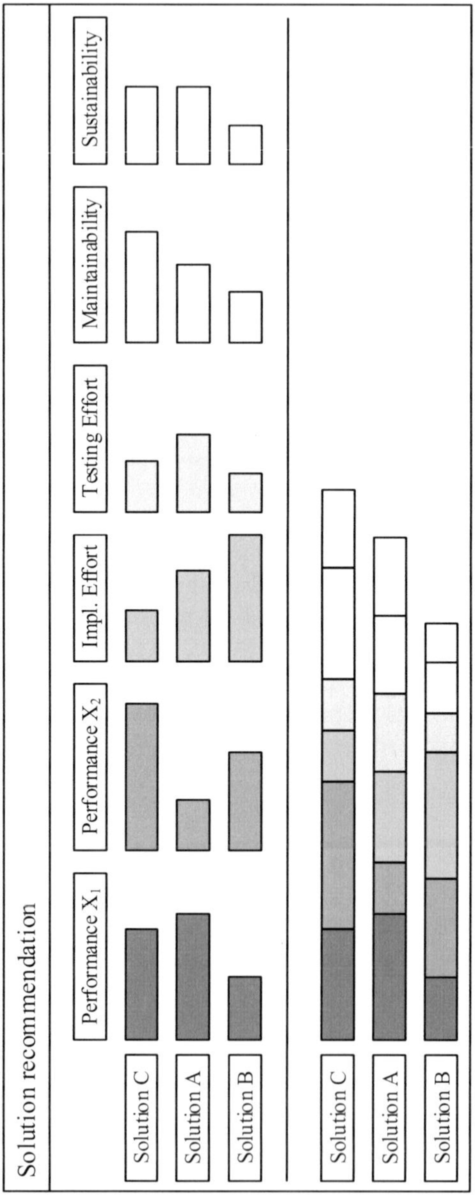


**Figure 5.11.:** Value chart example for recommending solutions

Solution proposals on the other hand have to be prioritized in each individual case because characteristics of solution proposals with respect to decision criteria may be case specific. Furthermore, the number of proposed solutions is also case specific. While the prioritization effort of the criteria may amortize over time, solution prioritization is a recurring effort that significantly depends on the number of solutions as well as the number of criteria. A possibility to reduce this effort is described in Section 5.8.4.

### 5.8.3. Decision Documentation

How the AHP approaches decision problems is comparable with how the GQM method approaches systematically experiment design problems. Both approaches are goal-oriented which is defined first. The goal is then refined into questions in the case of a GQM plan and refined into criteria in the case of the decision criteria hierarchy of AHP. The criteria define the necessary data for each alternative. In the GQM plan, the questions are refined into metrics that define what is to be measured and thus what data is to be collected. The data of each alternative for each criterion can be measured with performance evaluation experiments (e.g., timing behavior, resource utilization, and throughput) or needs to be specified by an individual practicing a certain role (e.g., a developer estimates the implementation effort for each alternative).

A benefit of the goal-oriented and systematic approach to decision problems is the potential to document the rational why the decision was made, e.g., why the particular solution alternative is selected. The decision criteria hierarchy of AHP already documents what is important for the decision maker in terms of the criteria and the priorities. The alternatives in the hierarchy document the possible actions, i.e., the possible solutions. The priorities of the solutions document which alternative is most favored. The pairwise comparisons of the alternatives can also be extended with the specification of the rational why one alternative is favored over another. This would document the decision in a traceable way.

### 5.8.4. Prioritization Alternative

When a thorough decision is not necessary and more "quick-and-dirty" decision is demanded, the decision maker can use the 100-dollar test (Leffingwell et al., 1999) to prioritize the criteria in the criteria hierarchy and the solution alternatives for each criterion. The decision maker has one hundred imaginary units (e.g., points, hours, money) to distribute between the criteria and between the alternatives for each criterion. The amount of imaginary units can also be larger than one hundred (e.g., 1,000, 10,000, or 100,000) to give more freedom to the decision maker (Regnell et al., 2001).

# 6. Java Persistence API Change Hypotheses

This chapter introduces eight change hypotheses for the Java Persistence API (JPA) as starting point to develop the corpus of elicited expert knowledge to satisfy requirement R2. The change hypotheses target three software performance and scalability problems that can be caused by using JPA without the consideration of the consequences for software performance and scalability. Because JPA is a specification and delegates relevant details to the implementation, the change hypotheses use implementation-specific extensions and features of the reference implementation EclipseLink (The Eclipse Foundation, 2015). EclipseLink is the recommended persistence provider for the SAP HANA Cloud persistence service (SAP SE, 2015) and the default persistence provider in the Oracle Glassfish application server (Oracle, 2015). The proposed change hypotheses may be non-exhaustive. Potential solution concepts that we have not investigated are fetch groups and the modification of the queries within the specification of the JPQL Query API and Criteria API.

The main sources for the development of the change hypotheses are the JPA specification (Java Persistence 2.1 Expert Group, 2013), the EclipseLink concept guide (The Eclipse Foundation, 2013b), the Java Persistence API (JPA) extension reference for EclipseLink (The Eclipse Foundation, 2014), the EclipseLink API reference (The Eclipse Foundation, 2013a), as well as examples (e.g., Sutherland et al., 2013; J. Krogh et al., 2012; OBrien et al., 2012; Oracle, 2013b), and practitioner reports and discussions (e.g., Winand, 2012a; Sutherland, 2010; Brekken et al., 2008; Limburg et al., 2013).

The source code model in the remainder of the chapter refers to an instance of the JaMoPP Java metamodel (Heidenreich et al., 2010). The persistence configuration model refers to an Ecore-based metamodel instance of the persistence.xml configuration file (see Appendix A.1). The persistence configuration metamodel is elicited from the XML schema definition of the persistence configuration schema (Oracle, 2013a). The change types in the change plan are metamodel-dependent change types. The change plan excerpts only show JaMoPP Java metamodel-dependent change types, persistence configuration metamodel-dependent change types and relevant model elements omitting other elements of the source code model, persistence configuration model, and change plan for simplicity. We omit in particular the reference elements of the change plan model in many cases and use instead the reference relationship between a change instance and the target of a reference element for simplicity.

The chapter is structured as follows: Section 6.1 introduces the query hints change hypothesis (6.1.1), the mapping configuration change hypothesis (6.1.2), the shared cache change hypothesis (6.1.3), and the pagination change hypothesis (6.1.4) for the N+1 Selects problem. Section 6.2 introduces the logging level change hypothesis for the excessive logging problem. Section 6.3 introduces the query hints change hypothesis (6.3.1), the mapping configuration change hypothesis (6.3.2), and the shared cache change hypothesis (6.3.3) for the excessive data allocation problem. Section 6.4 discusses assumptions and limitations and Section 6.5 concludes the chapter with a summary.

## 6.1. N+1 Selects Problem Change Hypotheses

This section introduces four change hypotheses for the N+1 Selects problem in the context of the Java Persistence API implementation EclipseLink that uses the query hints, the mapping configurations, the persistence unit cache, and the pagination solution concepts to propose eight potential solutions.

### 6.1.1. Query Hints

The Java Persistence API (JPA) specification foresees the configuration of queries by providing query hints. The available query hints are implementation specific and depend on the concrete persistence provider. The persistence provider ignores query hints that are provided but not supported. We identified a non-exhaustive set of four query hints that can be applied to solve the N+1 Selects problem based on practitioner reports and the EclipseLink documentation (The Eclipse Foundation, 2014; The Eclipse Foundation, 2013b). Batch fetching configures the query to fetch relationships in batches instead of one query per element. Batching is known as an efficient interaction pattern with a server (Ballesteros et al., 2009). Join fetching configures the query to obtain the relationships as part of the result of the original query. An entity graph defines which attributes and relationships are to be returned. EclipsLink differentiates between a load graph and fetch graph. The difference relies in how relationships and attributes are handled that are not specified in the entity graph. All persistent properties that are not specified in the entity graph are fetched according to their configured fetch strategy when the entity graph is provided as load graph, and fetched lazy when the entity graph is provided as fetch graph.

The query hint to configure batch fetching and join fetching requires the navigation to the relationship expression from the root entity as value. This is a concatenation of the root entity name with the persistent property names of the relationships. The query hints to configure the load graph and fetch graph require the name of a named entity graph as value. Entity graphs use the persistent properties of the entities and subgraphs to define persistent properties of associated entities. To build the entity graphs, it is necessary to know the accessed entities and persistent properties.

Query hints are applied to a query through the setHint interface method of the Query interface and as additional parameter for the find method of the entity manager. In general, we do not have to differentiate between queries that are build using the Query API or the Criteria API. The query is executed in both cases with the getResultList method. A differentiation between Query and TypedQuery is also not necessary since TypedQuery extends Query. In the case of a named query that is statically defined with the named query annotation, a collection of query hints can also be specified as value for the hint annotation attribute. The query hints are defined with the query hint annotation. Named queries provide a means to organize the queries in a readable and maintainable way and are considered as performant. When a named query is used, the change hypothesis end points create a change plan that describes the addition of query hint annotations to the hint annotation attribute of the named query annotation. Entity graphs are defined with the named entity graph annotation.

Figure 6.1 shows the structure of the change hypothesis described with the change hypothesis description language in the form of a UML object diagram. The query hints change hypothesis consists of a test with a static analysis, a test with a static and dynamic analysis, and four end points with a static analysis.

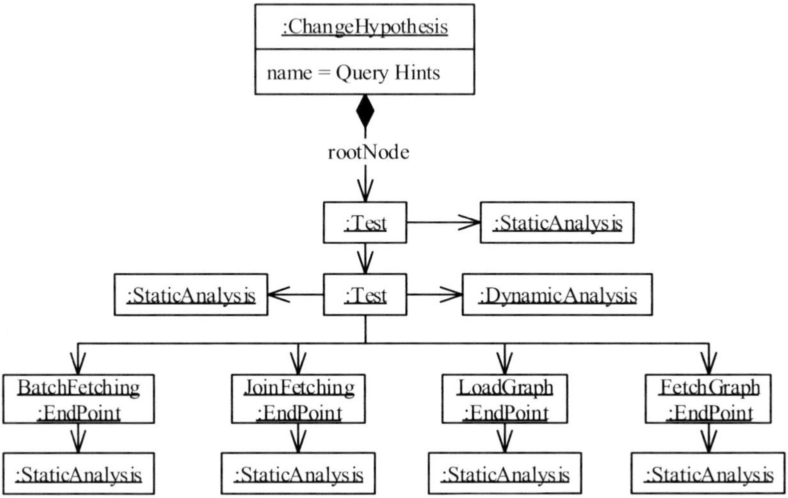


**Figure 6.1.:** N+1 Selects query hints change hypothesis overview

#### 6.1.1.1. Static Analysis

The static analysis of the first test analyses the performance profile instance that is given as input to Vergil. The performance profile must contain a performance aspect with the Query.getResultList interface method in the source code model instance as impacted element. The same performance aspect must also have a parameter in the parameter specification with the dimension for the number of SQL queries. The analysis concludes that the described problem is a Java Persistence API (JPA) problem where too many

SQL queries are send to the database when the described pattern matches. The static analysis of the second test is used to create the test profile and the static analyses of the end points are used to create the change plans.

#### 6.1.1.2. Dynamic Analysis

The dynamic analysis of the second test obtains the required complementary information to build the navigation to the relationship expressions and the entity graphs by analyzing the behavior of the software application. The goal is to match the N+1 Selects pattern on the SQL queries, to identify the used entity manager method for creating the query, to obtain a list of all accessed entities and persistent properties to build the entity graphs, and to build the navigation to the relationships.

To accomplish this, the dynamic analysis requests additional data by creating the appropriate test profile. The test profile requests the SQL query string of each SQL query that is send to the database, the timestamp of each SQL query, the entry and exit timestamps of all Servlet methods, of all getter and setter methods of each entity, and of the method that contains the impacted element. Furthermore the entry and exit timestamps of the entity manager's createQuery, createNamedQuery, and getCriteriaBuilder is requested. For the createNamedQuery method, the input parameter providing the name of the named query is also requested. The name of the named query is used to find the named query annotation in the source code model where the value of the annotation attribute name matches the name provided to the createNamedQuery method. The timestamps are requested in milliseconds. The dynamic analysis also requests the query hints that are already applied to the query.

The source code model allows to identify the relevant classes and methods that are to be monitored. Entity classes are identified by the entity annotation in the source code model. The test profile contains a performance aspect for each getter and setter method of an entity class. The accessed persistent properties are identified by the persistent property that is accessed inside an entity's getter or setter method. Servlet classes are identified based on the extension of the HttpServlet class. The test profile contains a performance aspect for each doGet and doPost method of a Servlet. The class method that

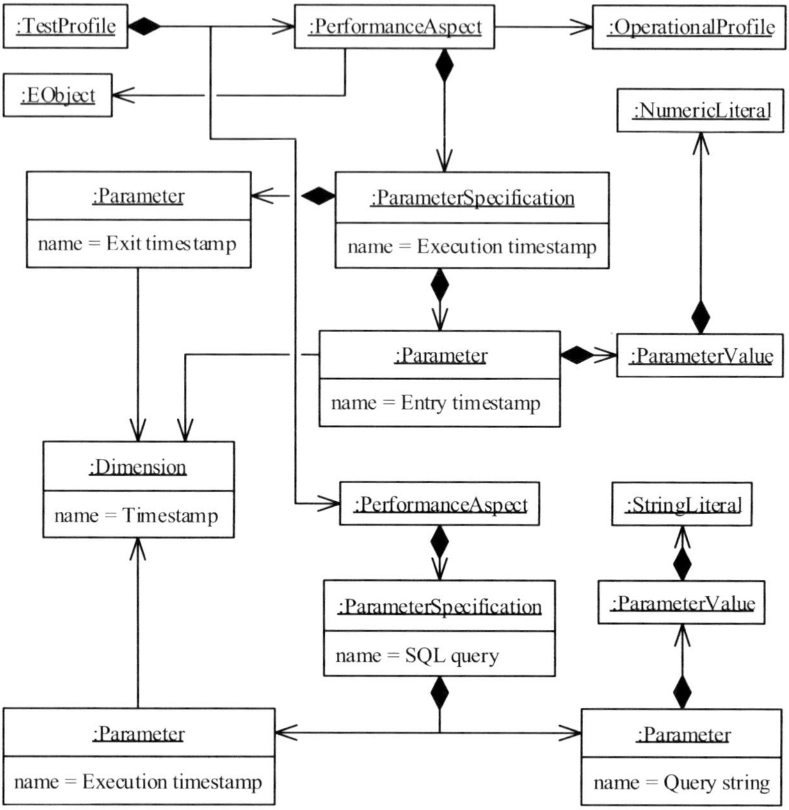


**Figure 6.2.:** Excerpt of the generated test profile

contains the method call referenced as impacted element in the performance profile is also determined through the source code model instance.

Figure 6.2 shows an excerpt of the test profile describing the SQL query aspect and the execution timestamp aspect in the form of a UML object diagram. The EObject element is used representatively in the example for a concrete class method element that is determined by the source code model analysis. In a concrete use case, an execution timestamp aspect is generated for each method of interest. The operational profile element is replaced with the operation profile that is referenced by the number of SQL query aspect in the performance profile. The workload is reduced to a degree that only one user is interacting with application at a time, e.g., the user attribute of the closed workload element is set to 1 user for the analysis regardless of what number of users is specified.

The test profile also serves as template for the performance profile providing the results to Vergil. A parameter element is replaced by an observation element with the same value for the name attribute and the observed value in the value literal. The parameter specification element and the required elements to describe the observation are multiplied as necessary. One parameter specification element describes one observation contained in the monitoring data to associate the entry and exit timestamp. In the case of the SQL query parameter specification, the parameter specification is multiplied to describe the observations since the association of the execution timestamp parameter and the query string parameter is required.

After receiving the results, the test uses the data first to find the SQL queries that are involved in the N+1 Selects problem. Therefore, the test uses the entry and exit timestamp of the Servlet methods and of the method containing the Query.getResultList method call element to determine in which Servlet method's context the getResultList method is executed. The entry and exit timestamp of this method and the execution timestamp of the SQL query is used to identify the relevant SQL Select queries. The test creates a histogram for this set of SQL queries to determine their frequency. The SQL Select query string for fetching an entity is the same when the parameter bindings are ignored. The test analysis the relative frequencies to find queries with a frequency of one and queries witch a frequency larger than one. The table and column names of the SQL query string are extracted and matched with JPA entities. A source code model analysis of the JPA entities analysis table and column annotations to identify which table and column name of the SQL query string corresponds to which entity and persistent property. When there are no column and table annotations present defaults are assumed. The resolved correspondences are then used by the referencing test to test each relationship for the existence of a SQL query with a relative frequency of larger than one that corresponds to the table that stores the relationship entity. This procedure is executed recursively and a set of navigation to the relationships is created. Elements of the set are pruned if another element exists that starts with the element that is to be pruned. When the resulting set of navigation to the relationship expressions is not empty, the N+1 Selects pattern is matched and the causing relationships are identified.

The test analyses the performance profile to determine for which getter and setter methods execution timestamps are specified. The persistent property of each executed getter method is determined by a source code model analysis. The analysis investigates whether the method contains an identifier reference with a persistent property of the class as target.

The analysis results are provided to the end points of the query hints change hypothesis to instantiate the solution proposals. The test of the query hints change hypothesis terminates when the N+1 Selects pattern is not matched since the solution proposals are considered to be not applicable.

#### 6.1.1.3. Batch Fetching

The batch fetching end point instantiates the batch fetching query hint solution proposal by taking the determined set of navigation to the relationship expressions and applying the batch fetching query hint for each navigation to the relationship expression with the navigation to the relationship expression as value to the query. In the case of a named query, the monitored value name of the query is used to find the named query annotation in the source code model instance. The query hint is applied to the query by adding a query hint annotation to the hints annotation attribute. The query hint is set as value for the name annotation attribute and the navigation to the relationship expression as value for the value annotation attribute. Adding the query hint to the named query was a design decision. The batch fetching end point applies the batch type query hint with the value IN as default to the query to configure the batch fetching type.

In all other cases, the query hint is applied to the query object on which the getResultList method is called. The batch fetching endpoint applies the setHint method call on the query object in front of the getResultList method call. The query hint and the navigation to the relationship expression are provided as parameters for the setHint method call. Figure 6.3 shows an excerpt of the generated change plan in the form of a UML object diagram. The excerpt only shows JaMoPP Java metamodel-dependent change types and relevant source code model elements omitting other elements of the source code model

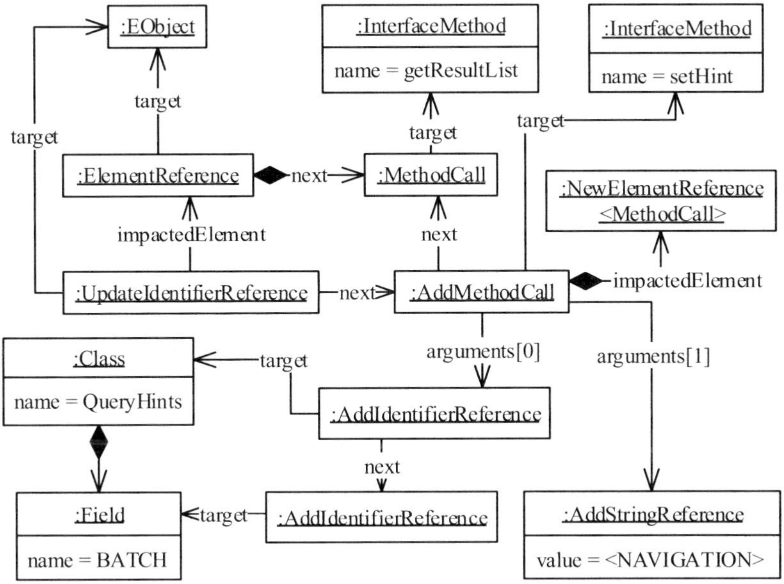


**Figure 6.3.:** Simplified excerpt of the change plan template for applying query hints to a query object

and change plan for simplicity. The labels of the relationships correspond to the attribute names. Values that depend on the particular instance are upper case and enclosed in pointed brackets. For simplicity, we omit in particular the reference elements of the change plan.

The change plan excerpt shows the insertion of the setHint method call in front of the getResultList method call. The necessary method call element and the argument for the method call are created. The insertion itself is given by the update identifier reference change that changes the value of the next reference of the element reference element which is a super type. In a concrete use case, the element reference can be a specialized type, e.g., a method call or an identifier reference for a variable. Accordingly, the EObject is then a method or a variable.

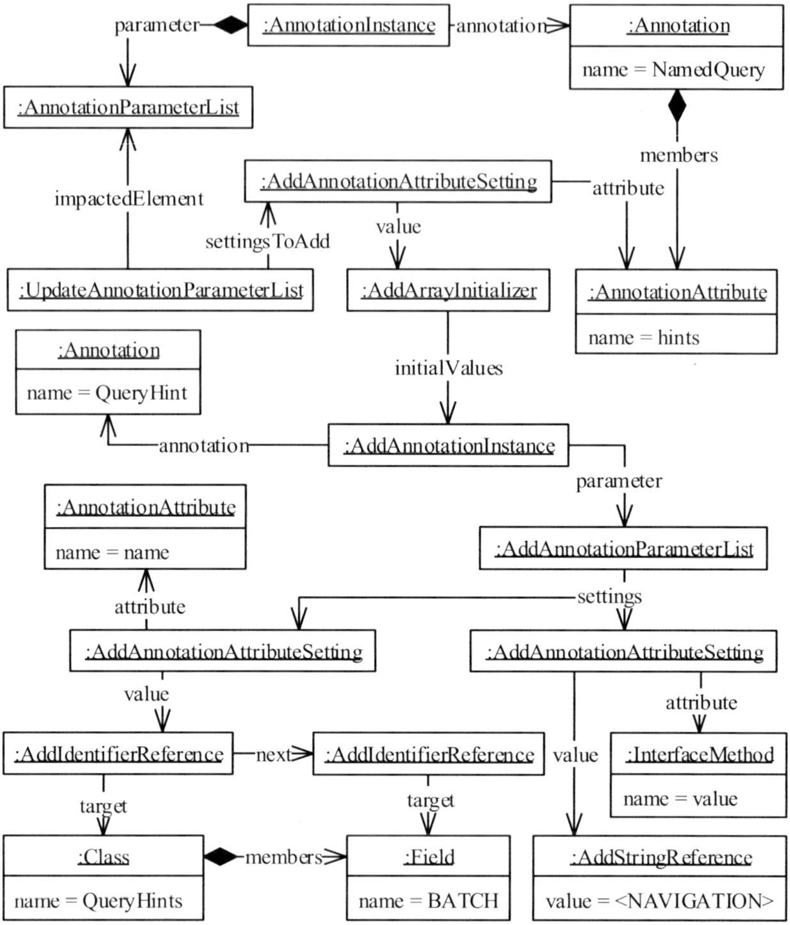


**Figure 6.4.:** Simplified excerpt of the change plan template for applying query hints to a named query annotation

Figure 6.4 shows the change plan excerpt in the form of a UML object diagram for adding the same query hint to a named query annotation for the case that no query hints are already specified. The excerpt only shows JaMoPP Java metamodel-dependent change types and relevant source code model elements omitting other elements of the source code model and change plan for simplicity. Values that depend on the particular model instance are upper case and enclosed in pointed brackets. A comparison of the change plan excerpts shows that more changes are necessary to apply the query hint to a named query annotation.

The annotation instance in the source code model instance that refers to the named query annotation is the annotation that defines the named query where the hints are to be added. The update annotation parameter list change is used to add a new annotation attribute setting to the settings attribute of the annotation parameter list of the annotation instance object. The add annotation attribute setting change refers to the hints annotation attribute object of the named query annotation in the source code model. The add array initializer change is set as value of the add annotation attribute setting change. The add annotation instance change is added to the initial values attribute and references the query hint annotation. The add annotation parameter list change is set as value of the parameter attribute of the add annotation instance change to define the annotation attribute settings. The add annotation attribute setting change referencing the name interface method of the query hint annotation has the batch fetch query hint as values. Therefore, two add identifier reference changes are used to reference the query hints class and the batch field. Another add annotation attribute setting change referencing the value interface method is used to define the navigation to the relationship expression as value.

#### 6.1.1.4. Join Fetching

The join fetching end point instantiates the join fetching solution proposal. The left fetch query hint supports nested fetch joins and allows null or empty values by using an outer join (The Eclipse Foundation, 2014). The instantiation procedure is analog to the procedure described for the batch fetching end point. The only difference is the query hint that is applied to the query. The application of the batch fetch type hint is replaced by the join fetch type hint. The examples for the change plan in Figure 6.3 and Figure 6.4 changes only minimally. The value of the field element becomes LEFT_FETCH instead of BATCH in both cases. The navigation to the relationship expression remains the same.

#### 6.1.1.5. Load Graph

The load graph end point instantiates the load graph solution proposal for the load graph query hint and a named entity graph. The application of the query hint to a query or named query is analogue to the batch fetching query hint. The field value in the change plan excerpts changes to JPA_LOAD_GRAPH and the name of the named entity graph replaces the navigation to the relationship expression.

The load graph end point uses the accessed persistent properties of the JPA entities to build the named entity graph. The named entity graph is specified with the named entity graph annotation. The named entity graph annotation is added to the class of the root entity. The name of the entity graph is specified as value for the name annotation attribute. A set of named attribute node annotations specifies all accessed persistent properties of the root entity. The set of named attribute node annotations for the root entity is specified as value for the attribute nodes attribute of the named entity graph annotation. The name of the persistent property is set as value for the named attribute node annotation. When the accessed persistent property of an entity is a relationship and one or more fields of the associated entity are also accessed, an additional subgraph is defined and the name of the subgraph is provided as value for the subgraph annotation attribute of the named attribute node annotation. A subgraph can contain named attribute nodes that reference another subgraph to build the entity graph. The subgraph itself is specified with the named subgraph annotation that has the same structure as the named entity graph. The set of one or more subgraphs is specified as value for the subgraphs annotation attribute of the named entity graph annotation.

#### 6.1.1.6. Fetch Graph

The fetch graph end point instantiates the fetch graph solution proposal. The instantiation is analogue to the load graph solution proposal but uses the fetch graph query hint to apply the named entity graph to a query or named query. The entity graph is build analogue to the procedure described for the load graph query hint. The resulting entity graph contains the accessed persistent properties. This is important in the case of the fetch graph since all persistent properties that are not specified in the entity graph are fetched lazily (Java Persistence 2.1 Expert Group, 2013).

### 6.1.2. Mapping Configuration

Batch fetching and join fetching for relationships can also be configured for persistent properties with the batch fetch and join fetch annotations. The difference to query hints is that the configuration how relationships are fetched is use case independent whereas query hints are use case dependent, i.e., query hints only affect the query on which the hints are applied. Consequently, the batch fetch and join fetch annotations may have a positive or negative impact on other use cases as well.

The concrete batch fetch type and join fetch type can also be configured like it is the case for the corresponding query hints. The batch fetch type to use is specified as value for the value annotation attribute of the batch fetch annotation as well as the join fetch type for the value annotation attribute of the join fetch annotation. The join fetch type outer is applied to allow null or empty values of a relationship (The Eclipse Foundation, 2014).

Figure 6.5 gives an overview on the mapping configuration change hypothesis. The change hypothesis consists out of a test with a static analysis, a test with a static and dynamic analysis, and the batch fetching end point and join fetching end point with a static analysis. The tests and referenced analysis are almost identical with the tests and referenced analysis of the query hints change hypothesis (see Section 6.1.1) with the difference that the dynamic analysis only has to collect the information to determine the navigation to the relationship expression. In consequence, the dynamic analysis has to be conducted only once and the collected data can be shared between the change hypotheses. This mitigates the data collection effort in the case of the N+1 Selects problem.

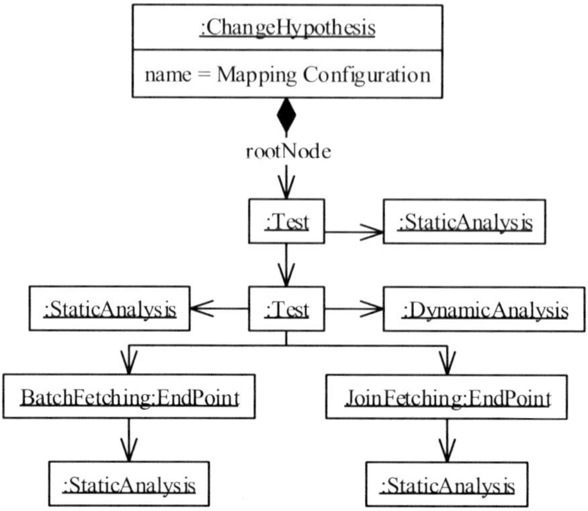


**Figure 6.5.:** Mapping configuration change hypothesis overview

#### 6.1.2.1. Batch Fetching

The batch fetching end point adds the batch fetch annotation to the persistent properties that reference other entities to instantiate the solution. The set of navigation to the relationship expressions are used to identify the persistent properties where the annotation is to be added. Beginning in the root entity, the change plan is built successively by visiting the persistent properties in the navigation to the relationship expressions. Based on the type reference of a relationship, the target entity is determined to follow the relation.

Figure 6.6 shows a simplified excerpt of the change plan that is created in the form of a UML object diagram for adding the batch fetch annotation with the batch fetch type IN to a persistent property. The persistent property is given by the field element of the source code model instance where the annotation is to be added. The name of the field is upper case and enclosed in pointed brackets to note that the name depends on the particular model instance. Particular elements of the change plan description language and the source code model have been omitted for simplicity. The update element annotations change instance is used to add the annotation to the annotations and modifiers attribute

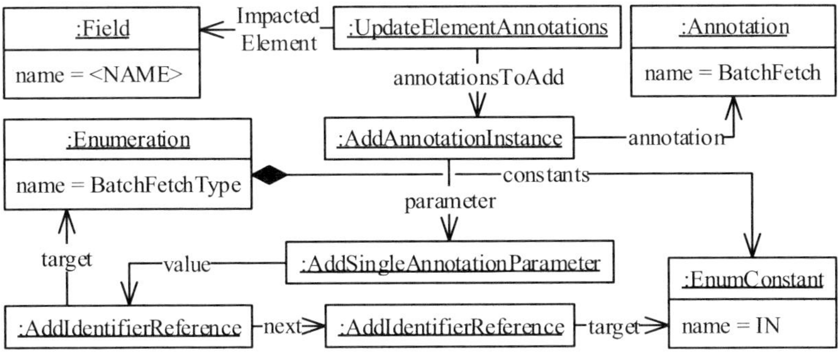


**Figure 6.6.:** Excerpt of the change plan describing the application of the batch fetch annotation to a persistent property

of the field object. The add annotation instance change has a reference to the batch fetch annotation. The add single annotation parameter change is added to the parameter attribute of the add annotation instance change to the define the parameter. The value of the add single annotation parameter change is the add identifier reference change with the batch fetch type enumeration of the source code model instance as target. Another add identifier reference change is set as value for the next attribute and has the enumeration constant element with the name IN as target.

#### 6.1.2.2. Join Fetching

The join fetching end point adds the join fetch annotation with the outer join parameter to the relevant persistent properties. Determining the relevant persistent properties is analog to the batch fetching end point. The difference relies in the concrete annotation that is added and the parameter and the value for the annotation attribute.

The change plan that is generated is also similar to the simplified change plan excerpt shown in Figure 6.6. What changes are the annotation, enumeration and enum constant elements that are referenced by the changes. This means, applied to the change plan excerpt, that the name attribute value of the annotation changes to JoinFetch, the value of name attribute of the enumeration changes to JoinFetchType, and the value of the name attribute of the enum constant changes to OUTER.

### 6.1.3. Shared Cache

EclipseLink provides a persistence context cache (L1) and a persistence unit cache (L2). The persistence unit cache contains recently read or written objects and the persistence context cache maintains objects while they participate in a transaction (The Eclipse Foundation, 2013b). Caching frequently accessed entities in the persistence unit cache can minimize database access. Selective caching of entities in the persistence unit cache is enabled either by adding the shared cache property for the entity to the persistence unit configuration or the cache annotation to the entity.

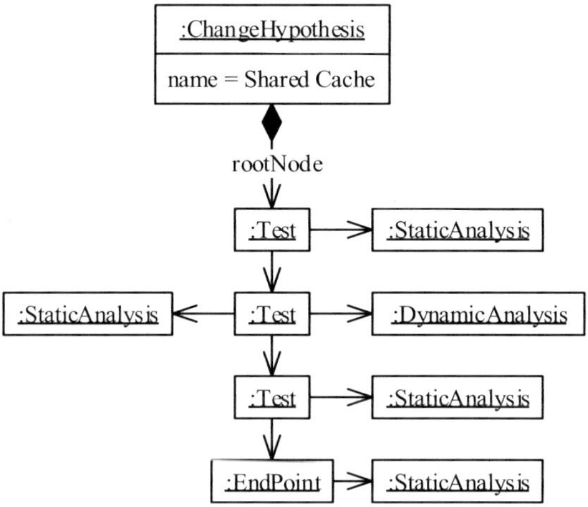


**Figure 6.7.:** Shared cache change hypothesis overview

The shared cache change hypothesis consists out of a test with a static analysis, a test with a dynamic and static analysis, a test with another static analysis, and an end point with a static analysis as shown in Figure 6.7. The static analysis and dynamic analyses of the first and second test are analogue to the tests of the query hints change hypothesis (see Section 6.1.1) but only the getter and setter methods are relevant for this change hypothesis. The static analysis of the third test analyses the persistence configuration model instance to check if the persistence unit cache is enabled. The persistence unit cache is enabled by default in EclipseLink. Depending on the concrete software application and persistence usage profile, the deactivation of the persistence unit cache can be necessary. The static analysis evaluates whether selective caching of an entity that is to be cached is explicitly enabled or disabled by analyzing the persistence unit configuration and the class annotations.

The end point instantiates the solution by enabling selective caching for the relevant entities with the help of the static analysis. This means that only specified entities are cached. The end point uses the executed getter and setter methods to determine the set of entities to be cache. For each entity contained in the set it is checked whether the cache annotation is present for each entity's class or the shared cache property is present in the persistence configuration model instance. If neither the annotation nor the property is present, the changes for adding the property to the persistence unit configuration are created. The relevant persistence unit is identified through the entities. The name of the property consists of the prefix eclipselink.cache.shared and the name of the entity concatenated with a dot. The value of the property has to be set to true.

Figure 6.8 shows the excerpt of the change plan that is created in the form of a UML object diagram. Values that depend on the particular model instance are upper case and enclosed in pointed brackets. For each entity that is to be cached, the add property change type is created together with the new element reference that inherits from the property element type. The unchanged element reference has the persistence unit element as target to signal that the property is added to the properties attribute of the persistence unit element in the persistence configuration model instance.

### 6.1.4. Pagination

The N+1 Selects problem can be an indication of a design flaw when all objects are displayed in the Web-based user interface. For example, if a single query reads all customer orders from the database and *n* queries read the order lines for the orders from the database, this potentially means that the whole database is read. When the database grows and the number of rows in the

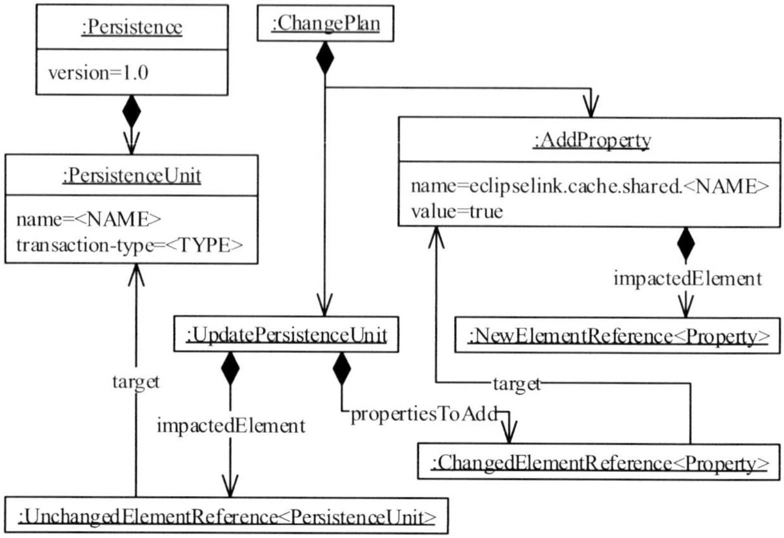


**Figure 6.8.:** Excerpt of the generated change plan to enable selective caching

order table and order line table increases, the application does not scale with the data. A solution to this scalability issue is the introduction of pagination. The goal of pagination is to limit the result list display on a Web page and to provide controls to navigate to the next or previous result page.

The JPA specification provides the pagination feature by applying the setFirstResult method and the setMaxResults method of the Query interface to the Query object. The pagination feature implemented in EclipseLink is usable on queries that do not use fetch joins (The Eclipse Foundation, 2013a). Recommended for pagination is also to apply batch fetching of relationships with the batch fetch type IN to only read the objects that are not in the cache (The Eclipse Foundation, 2013a).

The outcome of the pagination change hypothesis is twofold: the proposed changes configure the query with the hint to batch fetch the relationships which actually solves the N+1 problem. Specifying the first result and the maximum number of results for the query limits the length of the result list and

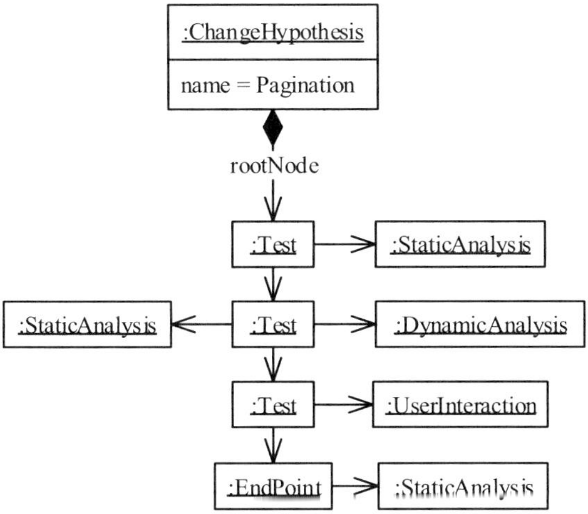


**Figure 6.9.:** Pagination change hypothesis overview

enables the software application to scale with a growing database. This can have a significant impact on the response time of the software application.

The introduction of pagination requires further changes. A method is to be added to the class that counts the number of objects of the root entity in the database and calculates the number of pages in dependence of the specified number of objects per page. This information has to be passed to the Web-based user interface to provide the number of pages to the controls for navigation, e.g., next page, previous page, or page selection by page number.

The pagination change hypothesis consists of a test with a static analysis, a test with a static and dynamic analysis, a test with a user interaction, and an end point with a static analysis as shown in Figure 6.9. The static and dynamic analyses of the first and second test are analogue to the analyses of the tests for the query hint change hypothesis to determine the navigation to the relationship expressions. The user interaction of the third test prompts the developer to find out whether all read objects from the query are passed to the Web-based user interface and visible to the user. If this is not the case, the read entity instances are most likely processed in some way, e.g., statistics are computed, where all entity instances are necessary and the introduction of the pagination concept is not applicable as it is thought in this change hypothesis. A potential solution for this scenario is to use the pagination feature inside a loop to iterate over the pages or to use the scrollable cursor feature that is recommended for batch processing and server processes.

When the read entity instances are passed to the Web-based user interface, the end point instantiates the pagination solution proposal with the help of the static analysis by applying the setFirstResult and setMaxResults method of the Query interface to the query. Additionally, the end point applies the batch fetching query hint to the query to solve the N+1 Selects issue (see Section 6.1.1). Two additional method parameters are added to the parameter list of the surrounding method that contains the getResultList method call that is referenced in the performance profile as impacted element. One method parameter for the page number and another parameter for the number of objects per page is added. The end point also adds the changes to the change plan to create a new method that counts the number of instances in the database for the root entity.

An excerpt of the change plan that is generated by Vergil describing the addition of the page number and object per page method parameters as well as the addition of the new class method to count the number of objects of the root entity in the database is shown in Figure 6.10 in the form of a UML object diagram. Names of classes and methods that depend on the particular model instance are upper case and enclosed in pointed brackets.

The class object of the source code model instance is the class containing the existing class method object as member. The update parametrizable change and the add ordinary parameter changes are used to add the page number and objects per page parameter to the parameter list of the class method. The update concrete classifier change is used to add the new class method to return the number of pages for a given number of objects per page to the member list of the class. The add int change is set as value for the type reference attribute of the add class method change to specify the return type. The add ordinary parameter change is added to the parameters attribute to define the method parameter. The add int changes specify the type of the parameters and set as value of the add ordinary parameter changes.

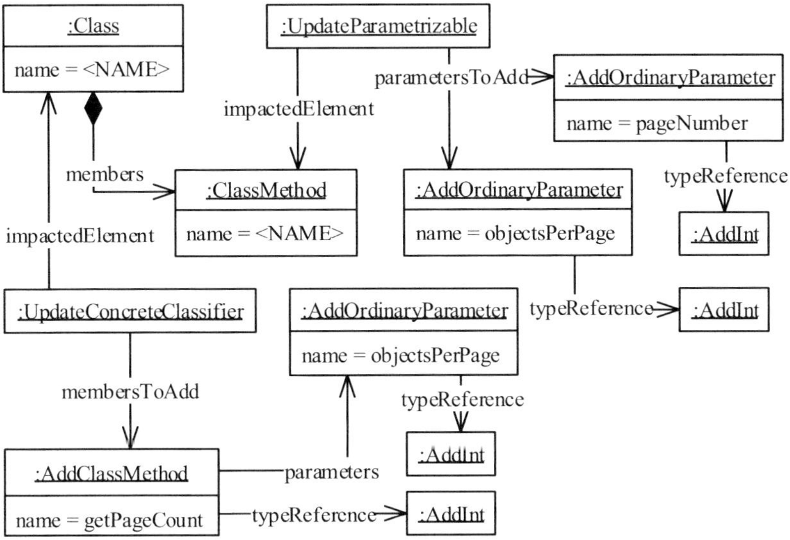


**Figure 6.10.:** Simplified excerpt of the generated change plan to introduce pagination

## 6.2. Excessive Logging Problem Change Hypothesis

The logging level change hypothesis asses the logging configuration of the persistence unit in the persistence configuration model instance. The goal of the change hypothesis is to assert that appropriate logging levels are configured.

The logging level change hypothesis consists of a test with a static analysis and an end point with a static analysis. The static analysis of the first test analyses the persistence unit configuration in the persistence configuration model instance and checks the presence of the property and configured value for the logging level property eclipselink.logging.level, the SQL logging level properties eclipselink.logging.level.sql, and the logging of parameters property eclipselink.logging.parameters.

The end point uses the referenced static analysis to instantiate the solution proposal when the logging levels are not configured appropriately. The logging level is set to INFO and the logging of SQL statements and parameters is disabled. An excerpt of the generated change plan for the logging level property is shown in Figure 6.11 in the form of a UML object diagram. The name and transaction type of the persistence unit depend on the particular model instance. The placeholders are upper case and enclosed in pointed brackets. The update property change in the change plan excerpt defines which property is to be changed and how. The name attribute of the property remains the same and does not have to be changed. The value attribute of the property has to be changed as defined in the value attribute of the update property change.

The logging level change hypothesis uses only the static analysis of the persistence configuration model instance. Additional analyses are not performed. This checks for an appropriate configuration of the logging levels whenever Vergil is applied to solve a particular problem. This design decision enables Vergil to proactively propose appropriate logging levels even when an excessive logging problem has not observed. This raises the awareness for potential problems.

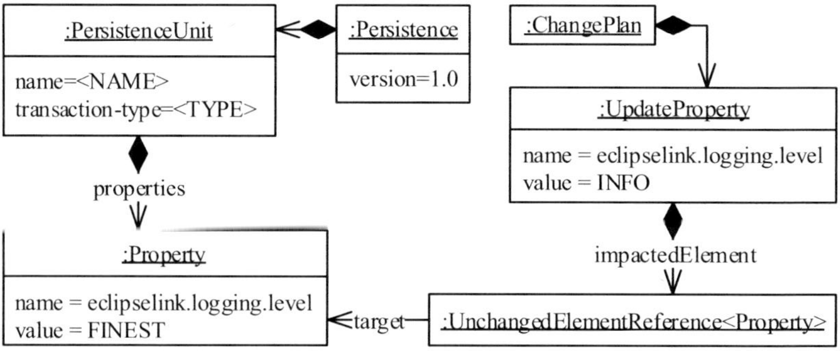


**Figure 6.11.:** Excerpt of the generated change plan to adjust the logging configuration

## 6.3. Excessive Dynamic Allocation Problem Change Hypotheses

This section introduces three change hypothesis for the excessive data allocation problem that use the fetch graph, lazy fetch type and the persistence unit cache as solution concepts to propose potential solutions.

### 6.3.1. Query Hint

The query hint change hypothesis for the excessive data allocation problem applies the fetch graph query hint to the query (see Section 6.1.1) to only read the accessed persistent properties from the database. Therefore, the change hypothesis uses analysis analogue to the relevant analyses of the N+1 Selects query hints change hypothesis (see Section 6.1.1) to create the fetch graph query hint. The change hypothesis is structured into a test with a static analysis following a test with a static and dynamic analysis and an end point with a static analysis.

- *Static Analysis*: The static analysis of the first test analyses the provided performance profile and checks the performance profile for the memory footprint dimension in a parameter specification referencing a class method element in the source code model. When the pattern matches, the applicability of the change hypothesis is concluded and the processing continues. The static analysis of the second test is used to create the test profile and the static analysis of the end point is used to create the change plan.
- *Dynamic Analysis*: The second test of the query hint change hypothesis uses the dynamic analysis to obtain the required information to build the entity graph by analyzing the behavior of the application. The goal is to obtain a list of all accessed entities and attributes to build the entity graph. The test profile is created analogue to the N+1 Selects query hints change hypothesis to obtain the relevant information to apply the fetch graph query hint. In contrast to the dynamic analysis of the N+1 Selects query hints change hypothesis the stack trace for the find method, the getResultList method, and the getSingleResult method when they are executed has to be requested because the performance

profile does not contain this information in the case of the excessive data allocation problem. Dedicated performance aspects are created for the stack traces of the find, getResultList and getSingleResult methods in the test profile. The returned performance profile then contains a parameter specification for each observation contained in the collected data to associate the entry and exit timestamp, and the stack trace. The timestamps of the getResultList, getSingleResult and find method are used to determine which method is used. The stack trace of this method is then used to locate the Query object on which the method call is applied. Therefore, the method is determined from which the call originates and a source code model analysis is performed to isolate the getResultList or getSingleResult method call, and the query object or the find method call. This way, the dynamic analysis determines where the query is created independent from where in the request processing the persistent properties are accessed or the query is created since this can happen in different methods and classes.

- *Fetch Graph End Point*: The end point instantiates the fetch graph solution proposal that is based on the fetch graph query hint and a named entity graph analogue to the fetch graph end point of the N+1 Selects query hints change hypothesis (see Section 6.1.1).

### 6.3.2. Mapping Configuration

The mapping configuration change hypothesis applies the lazy fetch type to persistent properties with associated entities that are not accessed. One-to-one and many-to-one relationships are fetched eagerly by default. The eager fetch type may have also been applied to relationships in the past to satisfy the needs of a previous application usage profile. Different to the lazy fetch type which is only a hint to the persistence provider, the eager fetch type forces the persistence provider to fetch the relationship eagerly (The Eclipse Foundation, 2013b). For example in Java EE, lazy loading is performed for one-to-one relationships when the lazy fetch type is specified as value for the fetch annotation attribute, whereas in Java SE the fetch attribute is ignored (The Eclipse Foundation, 2013b).

The mapping configuration change hypothesis consists of a test with a static analysis, a test with a static and dynamic analysis, and an end point with a static analysis.

- *Static Analysis*: The static analysis of the first test checks the performance profile for the presence of the memory footprint dimension. The static analysis of the second test is used to create the test profile and the static analysis of the third test is used to create the change plan.
- *Dynamic Analysis*: The dynamic analysis of the second test requests additional data about the software application's behavior to determine which persistent properties and entities are accessed analog to the query hint change hypothesis. The exception is that the stack trace is not requested because information is irrelevant. The persistent properties are located by the static analysis of source code model. The dynamic analysis matches the accessed entities and persistent properties with the observations to isolate the relevant persistent properties.
- *Fetch Type End Point*: The end point instantiates the solution proposal by applying lazy fetching to the value of the fetch type annotation attribute of the relationship annotation.

### 6.3.3. Shared Cache

The excessive data allocation problem is characterized by frequent creation and destruction of many objects. When a request is processed, the read objects from the database are cached in the persistence context cache and usually destroyed after the processing of the request completes. The goal of the shared cache change hypothesis is to cache frequently used objects in the persistence unit cache to minimize frequent object creation and destruction.

This change hypothesis builds upon the shared cache change hypothesis described in Section 6.1.3 for the N+1 Selects problem. The difference is that the first static analysis checks for the presence of the memory footprint dimension. The analysis of the persistence unit configuration in the persistence configuration model instance and the class annotations remain the same. The static analysis of the third test checks whether the shared cache is enabled or disabled and whether entities that are to be cached are defined or explicitly excluded from selective caching. Therefore, the monitoring data of the executed getter and setter methods is used to determine the set of entities that are to be cached. For each entity contained in the set, the static analysis checks whether the cache annotation is present for each entity's class or the shared cache property is present in the persistence unit configuration.

If neither the annotation nor the property is present, the end point instantiates the solution by enabling selective caching for the relevant entities. The changes for adding the property to the persistence unit configuration are created in the change plan. When an annotation or property is defined to exclude an entity from caching, the annotation or property is changed to enable caching for the entity.

## 6.4. Assumptions and Limitations

This section presents assumptions and limitations of the developed change hypotheses.

- *Metadata definition*: The change hypotheses assume that the object-relational mapping metadata is defined through annotations in the JPA entities and not through XML in the orm.xml file. When the metadata is defined in XML, the current designs of the analyses in the change hypotheses are unable to determine the mapping type. That a persistent property is a relationship with another entity can still be determined through the type reference of the persistent property in the source code model instance and the defined entities in the persistence configuration model instance. Support for the XML-based specification of object-relational metadata can be added to Vergil by the definition of an Ecore-based metamodel of the orm.xml file. Therefore, the XML schema definition of the orm.xml is used to create the Ecore-based metamodel analog to the definition of the persistence configuration metamodel that we have already created (see Section A.1). The orm.xml file is then parsed and a model instance is created (analogously for the EclipseLink specific eclipselink-orm.xml file).
- *Code revision*: Preliminary tests of the change hypotheses showed that the effectiveness of the proposed changes can depend on the revision of

the particular EclipseLink implementation. We executed the preliminary tests with EclipseLink version 2.5.0 contained in the Glassfish 4.0 application server and made a couple of interesting observations. The application of a named entity graph as fetch graph with the query hints annotation attribute to a named query causes an exception. Applying the same named entity graph as load graph on the other hand caused no exception. Applying the fetch graph query hint to the query object after the named query has been created caused also no exception. A possible solution for applying the fetch graph query hint to the query is to apply the setHint method to the query object when the named query was created with the createNamedQuery method. The result of the JPA case study presented in Section 7.3 show that the application of entity graphs as fetch graph or load graph have no significant impact on the number of queries that are used to read the objects from the database. Although, the JPA specification only specifies that the fetch graph and load graph determine when relationships are fetched but not how many queries are to be used. Whether and how the query hint is used by the persistence provider to optimize database access is unspecified. Practitioners on the other hand suggest the usage of fetch graphs or load graphs to avoid the N+1 Selects problem (Limburg et al., 2013). Another observation was that applying query hints to a named query with the query hints annotation and applying additional query hints to query object after the named query has been created caused an exception.

We made the observation that the application of the BATCH query hint to a JPQL query created with the createQuery method had no effect for nested relationships. This may be a problem of the specific revision of the used EclipseLink 2.5.0 implementation. A possible solution is to transform the JPQL query into a named query for the root entity and to apply the query hint with the query hints annotation to the named query.

We made the observation that adding the cache annotation to the class of an entity had no effect compared to adding the corresponding property to the persistence unit configuration. This may again be a problem of the particular EclipseLink revision. A possible solution is to take the revision into consideration when proposing changes.

- *Query joins*: We have not investigated the potential impact of batch fetching and join fetching query hints on queries that define joins. Further tests are necessary to identify potential conflicts and to extend the analysis contained in the change hypotheses appropriately.
- *Data model complexity*: We consider the identification of the accessed persistent properties based on the getter and setter methods to be able to deal with large and complex data models. However, we have currently no experience with applying the analyses to large and complex data models. We have also not investigated the impact of inheritance in data models on the solution proposals.

Despite the described concerns, the assumptions and limitations can be considered as temporary. Case study results can be used to iteratively extend the change hypotheses to weaken the assumptions and to overcome the limitations.

## 6.5. Summary

We defined eight change hypotheses for three software performance and scalability problems proposing twelve potential solutions. Fetch types, shared caching of entity instances, pagination and persistence configuration are the basic concepts behind the defined change hypotheses for JPA. This includes implementation specific features of the EclipseLink persistence provider that is the reference implementation of JPA and indicates that change hypotheses cannot be defined solely based on the JPA specification. However, the change hypotheses use concepts that originate from the JPA specification where possible such as the load graph, and the fetch graph query hints or concepts that have correspondences in implementations such as Hibernate like the join fetching and batch fetching mapping annotation or the persistence unit cache.

Excerpts of the generated test profiles and change plans show how Vergil describes the information with description languages introduced in Section 4. The change plans show how the metamodel-dependent change types for the JaMoPP Java metamodel describe what needs to be changed and how. The test profile excerpts show how data are requested for analysis without a close coupling between Vergil and monitoring tools. The test profile excerpts also show that adapters can be developed that translate the test profiles into instrumentation descriptions for tools such as the Adaptable Instrumentation and Monitoring (AIM) monitoring tool (Wert et al., 2015c) and the monitoring records back into the performance profile for Vergil. Therefore, the test profile also describes implicitly the expectation of Vergil how the requested data is described.

The defined change hypotheses indicate that solution concepts are reusable in the context of different performance and scalability problems. Fetch strategies, entity graphs, and shared object caching as solution concepts are applied in the context of the N+1 Selects problem and the excessive data allocation problem.

We apply the defined change hypothesis in the case study presented in Section 7.3 where they successfully propose solutions that solve the performance and scalability problems.

# 7. Validation

This chapter presents the validation of the hypotheses to satisfy the requirements and to attain the goal. The structure of the chapter is as follows: Section 7.1 introduces the design of the validation including the presentation of different validation types, an overview on the conducted studies and the coverage of the hypotheses. Section 7.2 presents the results of the online survey with respondents from industry and academia. Section 7.3 presents the results of the Java Persistence API (JPA) case study. Section 7.4 presents the results of using Palladio Component Model (PCM) as alternative means for performance evaluation of a solution proposal. Section 7.5 concludes the chapter with a summary of the results.

## 7.1. Validation Design

The goal of the conducted validation was to validate the defined hypotheses in Section 1.6 to overcome the challenges and to satisfy the requirements (see Section 1.3). In the following, we distinguish four different types of validations from literature and align their scope to the particular case of validating Vergil. Subsequently, we give a brief overview on the conducted studies before outlining how the studies cover the validation of the hypotheses.

### 7.1.1. Types

Böhme et al. (Böhme et al., 2008), Koziolek(H. Koziolek, 2008), and Becker (Becker, 2008) distinguish three different types of validating model-based software performance prediction approaches. The types have already been adapted by other researchers, e.g., for the area of design decision guidance, software architecture model improvement, and business process simulations (Durdik, 2014; A. Koziolek, 2013; Heinrich, 2014). Each type informs how thoroughly the research subject is studied in a particular case. In their original description, a validation of Type 1 validates the feasibility of the model-based prediction approach in terms of the accuracy of the prediction results through the authors. A validation of Type 2 validates the practicability of the approach through the application of the approach in particular cases by others. A validation of Type 3 validates the cost-benefit ratio through the application of the approach in real industrial software development projects. We describe the extension and alignment of the validation types as well as the relation with respect to Vergil in the following:

- *Type 0 (Appropriateness)*: The validation of theoretical concepts and description languages through theoretical assessments is considered as a validation of Type 0. In the case of description languages, this typically includes the instantiation of language constructs using examples of particular cases. In the case of theoretical concepts, the validity is often assessed through qualitative analysis or logical conclusions. We apply this type of validation to validate the appropriateness of the description languages and the workflow activities.
- *Type 1 (Feasibility)*: The application of theoretical concepts through the authors of Vergil in laboratory experiments or proof of concept case studies is considered as a validation of Type 1. This typically includes the injection of performance and scalability problems into a high-performance and scalable software application based on case reports from industry. A validation of Type 1 can also include a particular case example from industry as research subject in the form of a software application with known software performance and scalability issues. This type of validation includes the validation of Type 0 for the theoretical concepts and description languages of Vergil. We use this type of validation to validate Vergil's proof of concept. This study ensures that Vergil delivers the expected results under the assumption that Vergil's inputs were valid (H. Koziolek, 2008). Related examples are (Xu, 2008; A. Koziolek, 2013).
- *Type 2 (Practicability)*: The application of Vergil by the target audience instead of Vergil's developers to particular cases in order to evaluate

the practicability is considered as a validation of Type 2. This typically includes to provide a mature proof of concept implementation of Vergil that offers a reasonable usability often exceeding early prototypes. Case studies for Type 2 validations may involve students or practitioners (Böhme et al., 2008). Multiple participants are often necessary to reduce influence of individuals and to generalize the results (H. Koziolek, 2008). A Type 2 study asses not only the practicability by the target audience but also the practicability of creating change hypotheses to persist and provide solution knowledge by performance experts. A mature implementation of Vergil with appropriate usability that can be used to conduct a validation of Type 2 is not available at the time of conducting this validation. For this reason, we do not conduct a validation of Type 2. Related examples are (A. Koziolek, 2013).

- *Type 3 (Cost-Benefit)*: The application of Vergil in real industrial software development and evolution projects to compare the costs and benefits of Vergil with other existing approaches is considered as a validation of Type 3. Due to the novelty of Vergil, this means to compare Vergil with no-approach situations or with situations where performance experts assist the developer. This typically includes the quantification of cost savings in comparison with additional up-front costs and efforts to apply and establish Vergil. For example, additional up-front costs and effort include the creation of a reasonable repository of change hypotheses. A Type 3 study often requires to convince an organization to conduct the same project at least twice (Böhme et al., 2008). Due to the high costs, Type 3 studies are seldom conducted. Alternatively, researchers often prefer long running studies that include multiple industrial software development projects to amortize the initial up-front costs and efforts. This assumes, that software development projects are comparable and that some projects are conducted with the support of Vergil and others without. The benefit is then assessed by comparing costs and efforts between the projects with and without Vergil. For these reasons, we do not conduct a Type 3 validation in this thesis. However, survey respondents were asked to prioritize different support possibilities that a tool should include that supports the target audience in solving software performance and scalability problems. We interpret the distributed priorities of the respondents as indication where the respondents see the benefits when solving software performance and scalability problems and their agreement to the statement that the currently available support is insufficient. An example are the studies evaluating the cost-benefit of software performance evaluation methods (Martens et al., 2011).

### 7.1.2. Studies

This section gives a brief overview on the conducted online survey, Java Persistence API case study, and performance prediction case study to validate Vergil.

- *Online Survey*: We surveyed researchers and practitioners to validate the motivation and theoretical concepts of Vergil. We use self-administered questionnaires as research instrument where the respondents had to answer questions about their experience with solving software performance and scalability problems. This included questions about the settings of problem and solution cardinality, currently available support, the relevance of the support provided by Vergil and others. The results have been used to revise the theoretical concept of Vergil prior to the Java Persistence API case study.
- *Java Persistence Case Study*: We conduct a proof of concept validation of Type 1 of Vergil in laboratory experiments. We use case reports from industry related to the Java Persistence API (JPA) to reproduce particular case examples as research subject using fault injection techniques. For this purpose, we use the Media Store application as foundation. The conceptional idea behind this research sample application can be compared with established software applications in industries, e.g., Apple iTunes or Google Play. The application has already been used by other researchers of different areas as research subject, e.g., model-based software performance prediction (H. Koziolek, 2008; Becker, 2008). While the Media Store application is small and less complex compared to industry-size applications, the Media Store includes many of the industrially used concepts of distributed applications like Enterprise Java Beans (EJBs), component-based software architecture and Java Persistence API (JPA). In the first part of the case study, we apply Vergil to the N+1 Selects problem. In the seconds part, we apply Vergil to the

excessive logging problem, and in the third part, we apply Vergil to the excessive data allocation problem.

- *Performance Prediction Case Study*: We conduct a proof of concept validation of Type 1 in a laboratory experiment to evaluate the performance of solution proposals with model-based software performance prediction instead of measurement-based experiments. We use the Palladio Component Model (PCM) of the Media Store application for this purpose. Prior the performance evaluation of the research subject, we calibrated the PCM of the Media Store with actual performance measurements of the implementation. We use the solution proposal to introduce a caching component into the Media Store architecture as research subject. We analyze the prediction accuracy with the actual implementation of the solution.

### 7.1.3. Coverage

This section describes how the validation studies cover the hypotheses specifying our expectations on how to satisfy the requirements (see Section 1.3). Table 7.1 repeats the hypotheses and gives an overview on the type of validation that has been conducted.

The online survey validates the motivation behind Vergil and the potential benefit of the provided support as seen by practitioners. This also includes the collection of data to justify the workflow activities based on the responses of the respondents for questions about their experiences on solving software performance and scalability problems in industry. The survey results are used for a validation of Type 0 for the hypothesis H4.

In the context of the Java Persistence API case study, all hypotheses undergo a validation of Type 1. The validation of Type 1 consists of two parts. The first part includes the creation of the Java Persistence API change hypotheses. The creation of the change hypotheses for reported problem cases from industry includes the validation of Type 1 for H2, H3. The second part includes the application of Vergil to the particular case examples. In the course of applying Vergil, we execute the validation of Type 1 for the workflow activities H4 (see Section 5) by performing them step-by-step. The validation of Type 1 for the hypotheses H1, H2, H3, and H5 is inherently included in the application of

Vergil on a particular case example. In the context of the Java Persistence API case study, we also inherently validate the expressiveness of the description languages (see Chapter 4) by describing the necessary information.

The performance prediction case study assesses the use of simulations to evaluate the performance improvement instead of measurements. Simulations often use timing or resource demand estimates from the method developers to conduct the predictions due to the fact, that the surrounding studies target early design phases of software development projects where no implementation of the software application is available. However, to prioritize solution proposals for which some have been evaluated with measurements and others with simulation, an appropriate accuracy is necessary. For example, in literature, a deviation of the point estimator that is below 30% is often considered as satisfying (H. Koziolek, 2008). This implies that performance differences of solution proposals with heterogeneous performance evaluations have to be larger than 30% in order to be considerable to be different. This also applies to the performance improvement. While the case study does not cover a particular hypothesis of Table 7.1, it covers the hypothesis that simulation is an alternative means to evaluate solution properties prior to prioritization as considered by Vergil.

## 7.2. Online Survey

The online survey validates the motivation of Vergil and the need for the supported workflow activities based on the experience and opinion of the respondents.

Figure 7.1 gives an overview on the activities that we have executed to conduct the online survey in the form of a UML activity diagram. We started with the creation of a Goal Question Metric (GQM) plan to design and conduct the survey systematically and goal-oriented. We defined the goals and refined the goals into questions that are to be answered and we refined the questions into metrics that are to be measured with the survey questions. We conducted expert reviews of the GQM plan and revised the GQM plan until the reviewers have not raised any major concern. We designed the survey based on the GQM plan and conducted also expert reviews of the survey design. We revised the survey design until no major concerns have been raised by the reviewers.

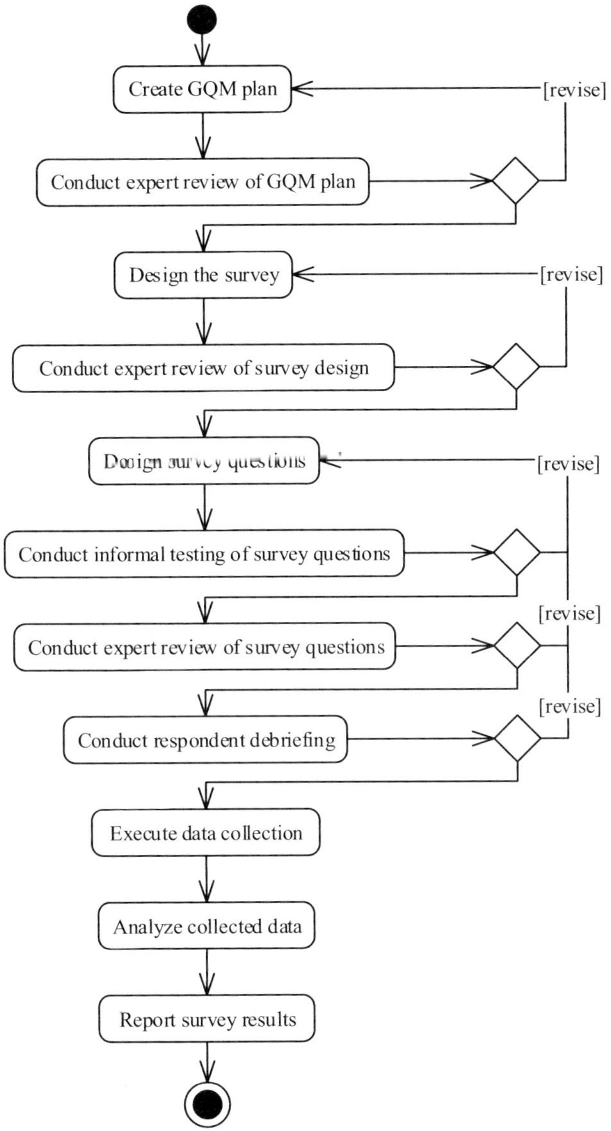


**Figure 7.1.:** Survey activities overview

We developed the survey questions based on the metrics of the GQM plan and conducted informal tests of the survey questions whenever a change to a survey question occurred and we tested the questions against question design principles. We conducted expert reviews of the survey questions until the experts had not any major concerns. We let test respondents complete the survey and conducted respondent debriefings. We asked the test respondents several questions to investigate how they have understood the survey questions. After the testing phase, we collected the data in the field. We analyzed the collected data and report the results in the remainder of this section.

The remainder of this section is structured as follows: Section 7.2.1 presents the goals of the GQM plan. Section 7.2.2 refines the goals of the GQM plan into questions that we answer with the survey results and refines the questions into metrics that we measure with the survey questions. Section 7.2.3 justifies the research instrument that we have used to collect the data. Section 7.2.4 discusses the survey design and describes the design principle that we followed to ensure proper survey design. Section 7.2.5 discusses the survey question design and the design principles that we followed to ensure that the survey questions measure the intended data. Section 7.2.6 describes the testing approach for the survey questions. Section 7.2.7 presents the survey results and answers the questions of the GQM plan. Section 7.2.8 concludes the section with a discussion of potential threats to validity.

### 7.2.1. Goals

This section presents the two goals of the online survey and the transformation of the goals into the structure template of the GQM plan to define the goals in the GQM plan. The goals are:

- *Validate the hypothesis that software performance and scalability problems can be classified in a general classification (G1)*: In (Jain, 1991), Jain notes that "Most performance problems are unique" (Jain, 1991) and that "The metrics, workload, and evaluation techniques used for one problem generally cannot be used for the next problem" (Jain, 1991). If this is the case for the great majority of software performance and scalability problems, it entails the risk that identifying solution patterns by testing change hypotheses is inadequate. Change hypotheses encapsulate software performance and scalability solution knowledge derived by eliciting performance expert knowledge. The fundamental concept of a change hypothesis is that solution patterns are reusable. The tests and embodied reasoning of a change hypothesis could render a change hypothesis as inapplicable for solving the problem if the solution concepts cannot be reused.

Specialized literature and experience reports from industry, on the other hand side, suggests that many software performance and scalability problems are often caused by simple oversights, misconceptions, and lack of knowledge about software programming concepts, technology usage, service consumption, and software configuration (C. Smith et al., 2002; Dudney et al., 2003; Tate et al., 2003; Karwin, 2010; Winand, 2012b; Haines, 2014). This supports the hypothesis of Vergil that software performance and scalability problems are recurrent with structural similar problem patterns. The proposed solutions in literature also suggest that there are common solution patterns. Common solution patterns mitigate the risk that identifying solution patterns by testing change hypotheses is inadequate.

From a research perspective, there is no unambiguous information available. Consequently, a clear assessment about the current situation is necessary to validate the hypothesis that solution patterns are reusable for software performance and scalability problem instances.

- *Validate the hypothesis that there is a need for the supported workflow activities (G2)*: Vergil guides developers to performance and scalability solutions with workflow activities that are composed to a systematic workflow (see Chapter 5). In general, the purpose of the workflow and the supported workflow activities is to identify potential solutions and to select the most appropriate solution among alternatives. The systematic approach of Williams and Smith (Williams et al., 2002a) includes the identification of potential solutions, performance evaluation of solutions, quantification of implementation effort and a cost-benefit analysis to select the most appropriate solution. This affirms the set of supported workflow activities entailing the risk that it does not satisfy the actual needs of developers.

  Consequently, a clear assessment about the current need is necessary to validate the hypothesis that there is a need for the workflow activities supported by Vergil and the description languages to exchange information for this purpose.

We use the Goal Question Metric (GQM) method (Runeson et al., 2012; Solingen et al., 1999; Basili et al., 1994) as goal-oriented measurement technique. We use the GQM method to define the metrics that are to be measured and to mitigate the risk that we collect unnecessary data or that we miss data as recommended in case study research (Runeson et al., 2012). We first reformulate G1 and G2 according to the GQM template (Basili et al., 1994). We define the questions (see Section 7.2.2) based on the reformulated goals. We derive the metrics that are to be measured with the questions in the survey based on the defined questions. This ensures that relevant metrics are collected (Runeson et al., 2012). According to the GQM template, G1 and G2 can be reformulated as:

- *G1*: Quantitatively evaluate [purpose] the validity [issue] of the motivational hypothesis of Vergil [object] from the viewpoint of performance experts and developers [viewpoint] in comparison to their daily business [comparison object].
- *G2*: Quantitatively evaluate [purpose] the need [issue] of the workflow activities and data representation of Vergil [object] from the viewpoint of performance experts and developers [viewpoint] in comparison to their daily business [comparison object].

### 7.2.2. Questions and Metrics

We refine G1 and G2 (see Section 7.2.1) into eleven questions to support data interpretation by deriving a measurement goal. We can conclude whether G1 and G2 are reached by answering the questions (Solingen et al., 1999). We formulate the expected answers for each question as hypotheses. This makes our knowledge about the current situation in industry and our expected answers explicit (Solingen et al., 1999). We use the formulated hypotheses during data interpretation for comparison with the actual measurement results. This supports us in the analysis of the causes if the actual measurement results deviate from our expectations (Solingen et al., 1999). Table 7.2 shows the refinement of G1 into the six questions Q1–Q6 and G2 into the five questions Q7–Q11.

We let two individual experts review the aforementioned eleven questions and hypotheses to ensure that the questions and hypotheses capture and correctly formulate our knowledge about the current situation in industry as recommended in case study research (Solingen et al., 1999).

Table 7.3 shows the refinement of the questions into metrics that we measure with the survey. The metrics provide all the quantitative information that we need to answer the questions (Solingen et al., 1999).

### 7.2.3. Research Instrument

In (de Leeuw, 2007), different data collection methods are presented and discussed together with recommendations when each data collection method is most appropriate. De Leeuw lists the potential respondents, expected response rate, financial costs and timeliness as criteria that are to be considered for the selection of an appropriate data collection method. Note, the features to describe the data collection methods in the remainder of this section are taken from (de Leeuw, 2007). In the following, we describe the three requirements that we have for the data collection method:

- *The completion of the survey should be independent from time (within a specified time frame) and location for respondents (RI-R1)*: Developers and performance experts are potential respondents for the survey. Developers and performance experts are often very busy with the projects they are involved. When we get the attention and interest of the developers and performance experts to participate in the survey, we have to encourage them to complete the survey. We can strengthen the encouragement by giving developers and performance experts the control about when (time) and where (location) they complete the survey.
- *The data to answer the questions should be collected within two weeks (RI-R2)*: Our project schedule allows us two weeks to collect the data to answer the questions. The data collection method has to collect the necessary data without affecting data quality.
- *The data to answer the questions should be collected using a small amount of resources without affecting data quality (RI-R3)*: Our budget is constrained and we have only a limited amount of manpower. The

data collection method has to scale with the number of respondents without requiring additional resources.

In general, the data to answer the questions can be collected with standardized interviews and self-administered questionnaires (de Leeuw, 2007). Interview surveys can be in person or over the telephone and includes the presence of an interviewer asking the questions to the participant and logs the participant's responses. A modern variant of self-administered questionnaires are online surveys, e.g., in form of a special survey Web site (de Leeuw, 2007).

In (de Leeuw, 2007), de Leeuw recommends online surveys when the required time to collect the data is important. Online surveys also have the lowest costs for completed questionnaires and have the ability to scale with an increasing number of potential respondents (de Leeuw, 2007). Consequently, a large amount of completed questionnaires can be collected in a time and cost efficient way (de Leeuw, 2007). This satisfies RI-R2 and RI-R3. Online surveys are also able to reach an international population of potential participants. De Leeuw points out that online surveys can be highly successful to survey special groups. The online survey gives the respondent the control about when *time* and where *location* the questions are answered and at what pace (de Leeuw, 2007). This satisfies RI-R1 and also gives the respondent the opportunity to look up information that are necessary to answer the questions.

### 7.2.4. Design of Survey

The goal of proper survey design is to minimize coverage error, sampling error, nonresponse error and measurement error that can affect survey results (de Leeuw et al., 2007; Lohr, 2007). According to (Lohr, 2007), all four sources of error are to be considered at design time to ensure the success of the survey. We follow the recommendations and guidelines from (de Leeuw et al., 2007; Lohr, 2007) to design the survey.

There are no lists of the population of developers and performance experts that can be used to obtain a random probability sample of selected participants to reduce coverage error. The coverage problem of online surveys is a known problem (de Leeuw et al., 2007; Lohr, 2007). Convenience samples are often used as solution to the problem (de Leeuw et al., 2007). In a convenience sample, respondents are volunteering (de Leeuw et al., 2007). For example, respondents are volunteering when a Web site offers a link to arbitrary visitors to participate in the survey. Convenience samples do not reduce coverage error (de Leeuw et al., 2007). The coverage error of convenience samples can also not be determined (Lohr, 2007). A solution that mitigates coverage error is to contact potential respondents through telephone or email and to ask them to participate in the online survey (Lohr, 2007). We have collected a list with the names and email addresses of 40 potential respondents from the academic software performance research community and industrial companies specialized on software performance. We use this list to contact the potential respondents through an email and to ask them to fill out the online survey. We use prenotifications for supervisors to ensure trustworthiness of the email invitations. We send a reminder to the potential respondents after one week that have not already responded, during the data collection period of two weeks. We used selected groups of the business networking platform LinkeIn as additional data source. We wrote a post in each group explaining our intention and encouraged members to participate in the survey. We wrote an additional post as reminder after the first week of the data collection period had passed.

The unknown population of developers and performance experts also avoids that we can determine the sampling error. The nonprobability sample is inappropriate and unreliable for the application of statistical inference in order to generalize the survey results to the general population of developers and performance experts and to estimate confidence intervals and to perform significance tests (de Leeuw et al., 2007; Lohr, 2007). In (Lohr, 2007), Lohr points out, that strong and often untestable assumptions are necessary about the similarity of the respondents included in the nonprobability sample and the people not included in the sample to use statistical inference. We apply descriptive statistics, e.g., mean values, standard deviation, or histograms, to analyze the collected data and to answer the questions for the population of our survey respondents (Runeson et al., 2012). Runeson et al. recommend to use nonparametric statistics for data that is collected with questionnaires (Runeson et al., 2012).

To reduce nonresponse error, we use prenotification, personalized invitation, reminders and we talked to supervisors to build trust and reduce refusal. We pay attention to question and questionnaire design to reduce item nonresponse (see Section 7.2.5).

We follow the recommendations in (de Leeuw et al., 2007) to reduce measurement error through thorough evaluation and pretests of the questionnaire and questions. We make sure that questions are clear and the terms have the same semantic for all respondents. We make also sure that the response alternatives for closed questions are well defined and exhaustive (see Section 7.2.5) (de Leeuw et al., 2007).

### 7.2.5. Design of Survey Questions

The goal of question design is to have questions that are as clear as possible to avoid misunderstanding and to have questions that measure the intended data. Note, the aspects of good question design that are described in this section are taken from (F. Fowler et al., 2007). Another concern of question design is that the responses to the questions are reliable and valid (F. Fowler et al., 2007). The data that is to be measured with the survey questions is defined in the metrics M1–M21 (see Section 7.2.2). The metrics are refined into survey questions to obtain the information from the respondents. The validity and reliability of the collected data depends on the refinement of the objectives of the metrics into the survey questions (F. Fowler et al., 2007). We follow the recommendation and guidelines in (F. Fowler et al., 2007) to refine the metrics into survey questions.

We mitigate the risk of misunderstandings by defining questions that are consistently understood by all respondents (F. Fowler et al., 2007). We evaluate that questions are consistently understood with expert reviews and pretests (see Section 7.2.6). We also specify a time frame when we give respondents the task to recall the information from their memory. This is especially important when the expected response depends on the time unit, e.g., from day to day, week to week (F. Fowler et al., 2007). We mitigate the risk of nonresponse by using simple words, providing definitions for words and phrases and provide *"Don't know"* and *"Other (Please specify)"* response options (F. Fowler et al., 2007). We also include descriptions in questions to reduce misunderstandings (F. Fowler et al., 2007).

We mitigate the risk that respondents cannot retrieve the answers to the questions by asking questions about information that the respondents have and are able to recall the information from their memory (F. Fowler et al., 2007). We avoid questions where respondents have to provide information about other people. The accuracy of the information depends on the elapsed time and impact (F. Fowler et al., 2007). We use larger periods, e.g., three years, when we are interested in information that had a major impact and we use shorter periods, e.g., in the last month, when we are interested in information that had only a minor impact (F. Fowler et al., 2007). We also avoid complex and multiple questions (F. Fowler et al., 2007).

We mitigate the risk of inappropriate responses by clearly specifying the response task (F. Fowler et al., 2007). We describe how the question is thought to be answered and align the response task to the questions that is asked (F. Fowler et al., 2007). We use mutually exclusive and exhaustive response alternatives for closed-ended questions that are obvious to the respondent (F. Fowler et al., 2007). We clearly specify the information of our interest for open-ended questions (F. Fowler et al., 2007). We use the direct question form to formulate questions and the imperative to specify the response task (F. Fowler et al., 2007). We use four response categories for the direct rating task which is easier for the respondent while we may have to accept a small decline in data quality (F. Fowler et al., 2007). We ask the respondents whether they agree or disagree with the statement that the existing support for finding a solution for a detected software performance and scalability problem is insufficient instead of formulating the response task as statement in order to mitigate the effect that respondents are more likely to agree when the question is in the form of a statement (F. Fowler et al., 2007). We avoid that respondents select response alternatives in a nice-to-have manner where multiple choices are allowed by tasking the respondent to distribute hundred points among the response alternatives.

We mitigate the risk that respondents are unwilling to answer the questions by assuring that the answers of the respondents are confidential and are only published in the aggregate (F. Fowler et al., 2007). This ensures that the answers cannot be associated with the individual respondent who provided the answer (F. Fowler et al., 2007).

### 7.2.6. Test of Survey Questions

Testing survey questions has the goal to evaluate that all survey questions are conform with the questionnaire design principles (see Section 7.2.5) (Campanelli, 2007). In (Campanelli, 2007), Campanelli recommends a three step approach for testing survey questions thoroughly when resources are constrained. We employ the recommended approach for testing our survey questions in the form of informal testing, expert reviews and respondent debriefing. In the informal testing step, we evaluate the survey questions against the questionnaire design principles. We perform informal testing continuously whenever changes are applied to the questionnaire design to identify issues early. In the second step, we conduct expert reviews. We requested an expert to evaluate the survey questions against the questionnaire design principles which is already considered as useful (Campanelli, 2007). A senior researcher served as expert (Campanelli, 2007). When major issues have been identified, we fixed the issues in the questionnaire design. We conducted the expert reviews iteratively with each revision of the questionnaire until the expert is unable to find any major issues. We performed three iterations until we executed step three. In step three, a group of testers completed the survey. After a tester completed the survey, we asked questions about the original survey questions in order to determine the understanding of the tester (Campanelli, 2007). We used a group of four testers. The group included a PhD student, two Master students and a Bachelor student. All testers in the group have experience with software performance and scalability.

### 7.2.7. Survey Results

The goal of this section is to provide a narrative description and analysis of the survey in a linear-analytic structure (Runeson et al., 2012). We also perform a negative case analysis to improve validity through the formulation of explanation alternatives where applicable (Runeson et al., 2012). We use explanation building to identify patterns and to find potential explanations for the identified patterns where it is beneficial for the analysis and for answering the questions Q1–Q11 (see Section 7.2.2) (Runeson et al., 2012).

The structure of this section is as follows: the section first describes the context of the survey and the population of respondents in terms of metadata that we have collected with additional survey questions. Thereafter, the section answers the questions Q1–Q11 and concludes with a summary of the survey results.

#### 7.2.7.1. Context

We implemented the questionnaire and collected the data with the survey platform SoGoSurvey (*SoGoSurvey* 2015). SoGoSurvey is an established platform in industry and academia for conducting online surveys. Customers of SoGoSurvey are among others ACM, FedEx, IBM, and Boston University (*SoGoSurvey* 2015). We collected the data in December 2014 within a time span of two weeks. We prenotificated supervisors to establish trustworthiness for the email invitations that we sent to the potential respondents. We sent personalized email invitations to 40 potential respondents that we have selected from our academic research community and companies with which we are in contact. We sent email remainders after one week has passed to potential respondents who had not participated.

In parallel, we created a clone of the survey and invited members of the Java Developers group and Performance Specialists group on the business networking platform LinkedIn. We used the Java Developers group and the Performance Specialists group as population register for potential respondents. We used an unpersonalized blog post in each group to establish trustworthiness and to invite potential respondents. We consider that the probability is low that the blog post in each group is read by people that are not in our target population. The rationale is that the groups are very focused on discussing problems and providing help to these particular topics. This is different to inviting arbitrary visitors of a Web site to participate in the survey. The blog post can be compared to sending unpersonalized emails to a list of collected email addresses. Whether the respondent reads the email is in control of the respondent. This is the same for reading the blog post.

In total, we had 44 responses. We had 26 responses from the invited 40 potential respondents. We were able to make contact with all 40 potential respondents. We had 14 nonresponses due to refusal (de Leeuw et al., 2007; Rässler et al., 2007). We had 18 responses from the potential respondents of the invited group members on LinkedIn.

We collected data specifically to understand the population of respondents. We positioned questions in the questionnaire that collected data about the practiced roles of respondents, the environments in which the respondents work, the number of employees of the organizations of the respondents, the engagement in solving software performance and scalability problems and whether the respondents ever solved a software performance and scalability problem in an industrially used software application.

**Practiced roles** Roles are not individuals and individuals can practice different roles. The respondents were able to specify that they practice multiple roles by selecting multiple response alternatives (closed-ended survey question). We provided nine response alternatives and additionally the option *Other* to specify a potential role of the respondent that does not match with the provided list of response alternatives and to avoid item nonresponse. Two respondents selected the option *Other*. One of the two respondents specified "Team Lead" as role. The other of the two respondents specified "Performance Test Analyst" as role. Figure 7.2 shows the percentage of respondents that practice a certain role. The roles that are practiced by most of the respondents are *Performance Engineer* and *Software Engineer/Developer* (henceforth referred to as Developer). Eleven respondents specified that they practice the role of the *Developer* but not the role of the *Performance Engineer*. Sixteen respondents specified that they practice the role of the *Performance Engineer* but not the role of the *Developer*. Seven respondents specified that they practice the role of the *Performance Engineer* and the role of the *Developer*. This leads to 77.3% of the respondents that practice either the role of the *Performance Engineer*, the role of the *Developer* or both. Consequently, the great majority of respondents represents the viewpoint of interest on the subject as defined in the goals G1 and G2 of the GQM plan (see Section 7.2.1).

**Work environments** We were interested in which environment the respondents work when they are working on software performance and scalability problems. We provided *University*, *Industry*, and *Consulting* as response alternatives. Additionally, we provided the possibility to select the option *Other* to specify an environment that is not in the list. The respondents were able to select multiple response options. Two respondents selected the response alternative *Other*. One of the two respondents specified "Research Institute" as environment. The other of the two respondents specified "Staffing" as environment. Figure 7.3 shows the percentage of respondents that work in a certain environment. The majority of respondents with 59.1% specified that they are working in *Industry*. 38.6% of the respondents specified that they do *Consulting*. 34.1% of the respondents specified that they work for

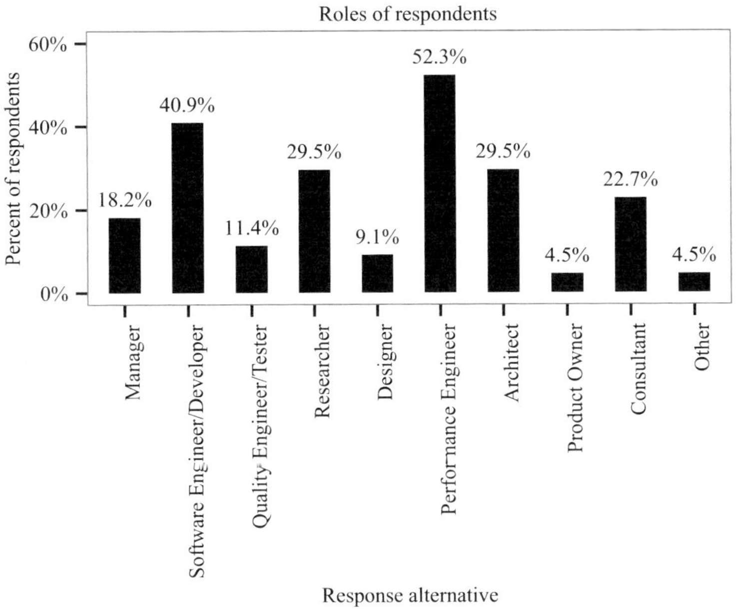


**Figure 7.2.:** Roles of respondents

the *University*. Eight respondents specified that they are working in *Industry* and do *Consulting*. Three respondents specified that they work at the *University* and do *Consulting*. Six respondents specified that they work for the *University* and in *Industry*. Thirteen respondents specified that they only work in *Industry*. Seven respondents specified only *Consulting* and another seven respondents only specified *University*. Consequently, 84.1% of the respondents have industrial experience. The strong industrial background of the respondents also supports the goals G1 and G2 of the GQM plan.

**Size of organizations** We collected data about the size of the organization in which the respondents work. We provided four response alternatives and the obligatory *Don't know* option. In this case without the possibility to specify a size that is not contained in the list. We registered one item nonresponse for this survey question. Consequently, only the responses of

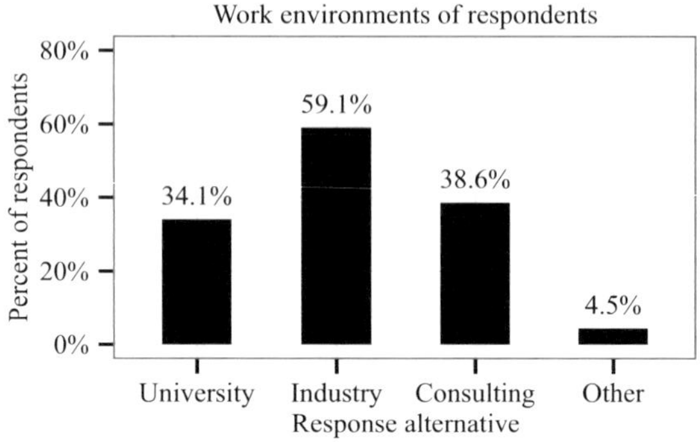


**Figure 7.3.:** Work environment of respondents

the remaining forty three respondents are analyzed. Figure 7.4 shows the percentage of respondents that work in an organization with a certain size. The majority with 37.2% of the respondents works in large organizations with more than five thousand employees. 25.6% of the respondents work for organizations that have more than one hundred employees to five hundred employees. 23.3% of the respondents work in smaller organizations with less than hundred employees. Only 11.6% of the respondents work in organization with more than five hundred to five thousand employees. One respondent selected the *Don't know* option. Roundabout a half works in organizations that are smaller than five hundred employees while roughly the other half works in lager organizations.

**Engagements** We were also interested in the time that the respondents already engage themselves in the context of solving software performance and scalability problems. We collected data about how many years the respondents already engage themselves in this context. We provided five response alternatives and the obligatory *Don't know* option. The respondents had to select one. No respondent selected the *Don't know* option. Figure 7.5 shows the percentage of respondents that engage themselves for a certain number of years in the context of solving software performance and scalability problems. 29.5% of the respondents specified that they engage themselves for more than three years to five years. 27.3% of the respondents specified that they engage

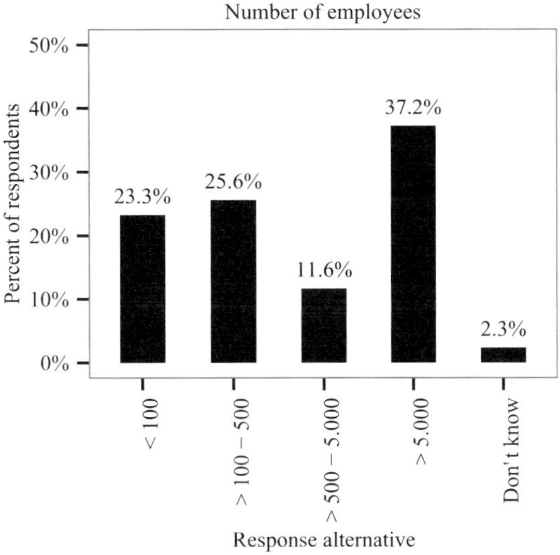


**Figure 7.4.:** Number of employees

themselves for more than five years to ten years. 22.7% of the respondents specified that they engage themselves for even more than ten years. 18.2% of the respondents specified that they engage themselves for more than one year to three years. One respondent has specified that she engages herself for less than one year. The majority with 79.5% of the respondents specified that they engage themselves in the context of solving software performance and scalability problems for more than three years. 50% of the respondents engage themselves for more than 5 years. We consider the majority of the respondents as experienced in solving software performance and scalability problems.

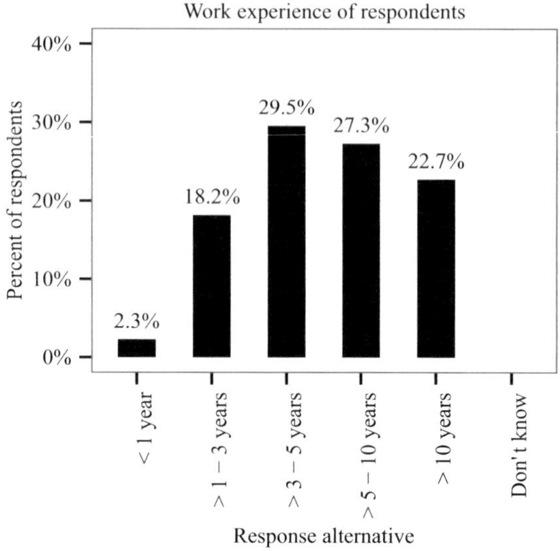


**Figure 7.5.:** Engagement of respondents in solving software performance and scalability problems

**Solution application** We collected data whether respondents have solved a software performance and scalability problem in an industrially used application. We provided *Yes* and *No* as response alternatives together with the obligatory *Don't know* option. One respondent selected the *Don't know* option. Figure 7.6 shows the percentage of respondents that have selected a particular response alternative. The great majority with 90.0% of the respondents specified that they have solved at least one software performance and scalability problem in an industrially used application. 6.8% of the respondents specified that they have not solved a software performance and scalability problem in an industrially used application.

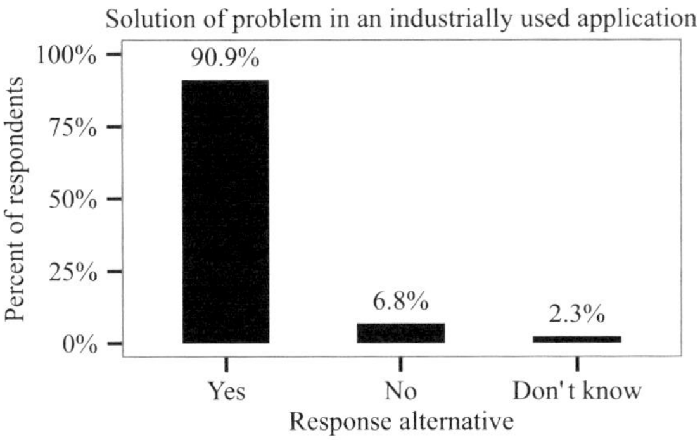


**Figure 7.6.:** Solution of a software performance and scalability problem in an industrially used application

### 7.2.7.2. Answering Questions

The following section presents the analysis results of the collected data and concludes the answers for the questions Q1–Q11 (see Section 7.2.2). For each question, the section repeats the question to answer, outlines the data collection, notes nonresponses and presents the analysis result.

**Q1** We collected M1 and M2 with one survey question for each metric to answer the question Q1: *"Are there software performance and scalability problems which are of recurring nature in industry?"*. The respondents had to specify in the survey question for M1 in how many percent of the cases they have seen the same problem already in the past, e.g., in the context of another application. We provided five response alternatives and the obligatory *Don't know* option. The respondents had to select one response alternative. Figure 7.7 shows the relative frequency of response alternatives that are selected by respondents. 52.3% of the respondents specified that they have seen the same problem already in the past in fifty to less than seventy five percent of the cases. 22.7% of the respondents specified that they have seen the same problem already in the past in twenty five to less than fifty percent of the cases. 13.6% of the respondents specified that they have seen the same problem already in the past in less than twenty five percent of the cases. 11.4%

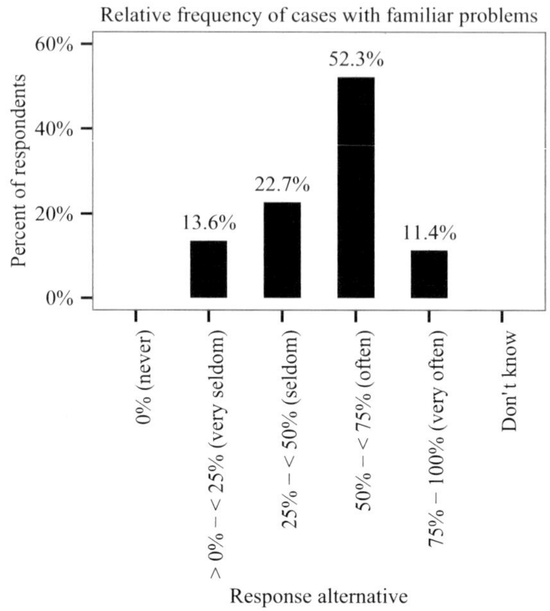


**Figure 7.7.:** Relative frequency of cases with familiar problems

of the respondents specified that they have seen the same problem already in the past in seventy five to one hundred percent of the cases. Consequently, 63.7% of the respondents specified that they had to solve a recurring software performance and scalability problem in at least 50% of the cases. This means that at least every second software performance and scalability problem that was to be solved was known by the majority of the respondents. Conversely, this means that less than 50% of the software performance and scalability problems have been new to the majority of the respondents.

The respondents had to specify in the survey question for M2 how many percent of the software performance and scalability problems that they have seen in the past three years have been new to them. The respondents had to specify the number in percent for this open-ended question. Figure 7.8 shows the percentage of respondents that specified a certain percentage as cumulative distribution function. 25% of the respondents specified that twenty

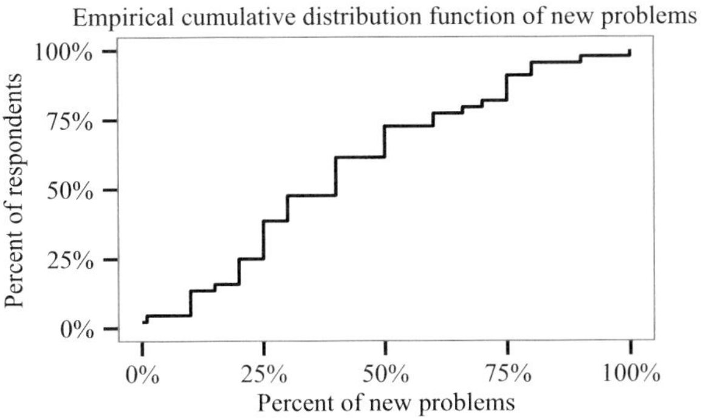


**Figure 7.8.:** Distribution of new problems

percent of the problems have been new to them at maximum. 50% of the respondents specified that forty percent of the problems have been new to them at maximum. 75% of the respondents specified that sixty percent of the problems have been new to them at maximum. Conversely, 75% of the respondents specified that they have seen at least forty percent of the problems already in the past. This means that almost a half or more of the occurring software performance and scalability problems can potentially be solved with Vergil.

We recognized that the collected data for the metrics M1 and M2 of individual respondents do not fit closely. We used the collected data for metric M2 where respondents specified the percentage of software performance and scalability problems that have been new to them in the last three years and transformed them to comply with metric M1. We computed the relative frequency of cases with problems that the respondents have already seen in the past from the collected data of metric M2. We took the inverse number of the respondents specified percentage and applied the response alternatives used to collect the data for metric M1 as bins. Figure 7.9 shows the relative frequency of cases where the respondents have already seen the same problem in the past three years derived from the collected data of metric M2 (on the right side) side by side with the collected data of metric M1 (on the left side). The percent of respondents that specified that they have seen the same problem already in the past in seventy five to one hundred percent of the cases is 27.2% higher

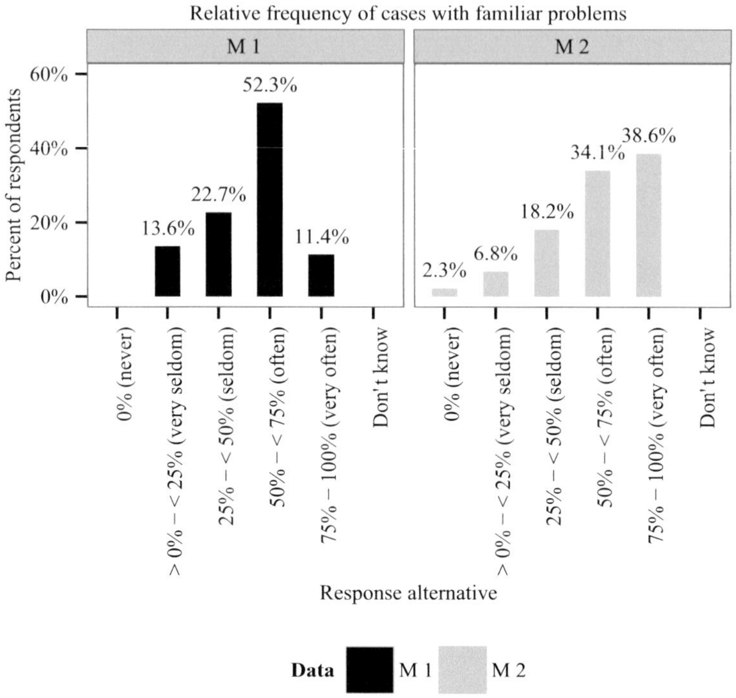


**Figure 7.9.:** Direct versus indirect relative frequency

in the data of metric M2. The percent of respondents that specified that they have seen the same problem already in the past three years in fifty to less than seventy five percent of the cases is 18.2% lower in the data of metric M2. Overall, the percent of respondents that specified that they have seen the same problem already in the past three years in more than fifty percent of the cases increased. An explanation building for the slightly different relative frequencies can be that we have specified a time frame of the past three years in the survey question that collected the data for metric M2. Individual respondents may have used different time frames to recall the information to answer the survey question that collected the data for metric M1. This would indicate that if the respondents used a time frame larger than the past three years, the number of cases where respondents have already seen the same problem in the past has increased in the past three years. A time frame larger than the past three years is compliant to the engagement of more than three years of the majority of respondents (see Figure 7.5).

In conclusion, the analysis of the collected data for metric M1 and M2 shows that we can answer the question Q1 in the affirmative. There are software performance and scalability problems of recurring nature in industry.

**Q2** We collected data for metric M3 and M4 with individual survey questions to answer the question Q2: *"Are there solutions to performance and scalability problems which are of recurring nature in industry?"*. In the survey question for metric M3, respondents had to specify in how many percent of the cases they apply solutions that they have already applied in the past, e.g., in the context of a different application or problem. We provided five response alternatives and the obligatory *Don't know* option to mitigate the risk of item nonresponse. No respondent selected the *Don't know* option. Figure 7.10 shows the relative frequency of the responses of the respondents (in the bar plot on the left side). The majority with 68.2% of respondents specified that they apply solutions that they have already applied in the past in at least 50% of the cases. 47.7% of the respondents specified that they apply solutions that they have already applied in the past in fifty to less than seventy five percent of the cases. 20.5% of the respondents specified that they apply solutions that they have already applied in the past in seventy five to one hundred percent of the cases. 20.5% of the respondents also specified that they apply solutions that they have already applied in the past in twenty five to less than fifty percent of the cases. Only 11.4% of the respondents specified that they apply solutions that they have already applied in the past in less than twenty five percent of the cases.

In the survey question for metric M4, respondents had to specify in how many percent of the cases they apply solutions that others have already applied in the past, e.g., a solution that they found in a book about software performance and scalability problems or a performance pattern. We provided the same five response options and the obligatory *Don't know* option as in the survey question that collected the data for metric M3. 4.5% of the respondents selected the *Don't know* option. Figure 7.10 shows the relative frequency of responses of the respondents (in the bar plot on the right side). 20.5% of

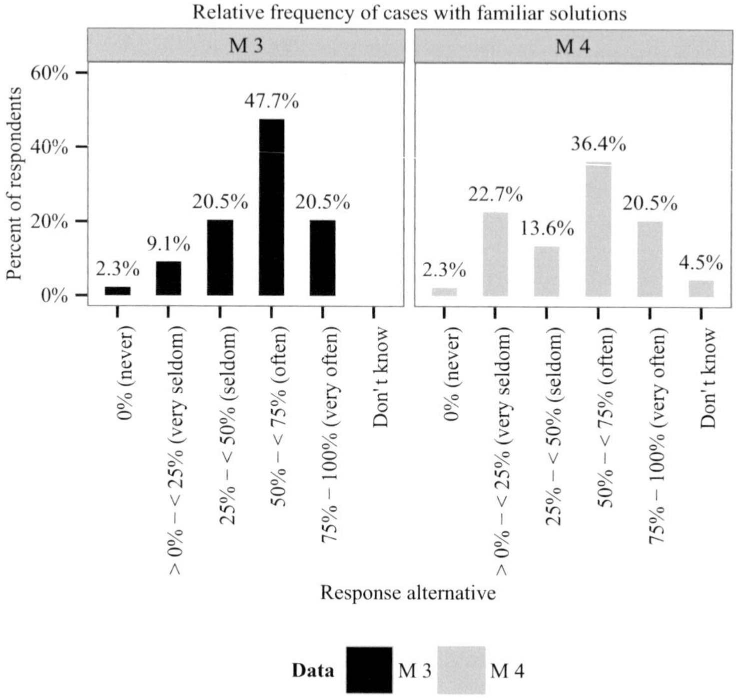


**Figure 7.10.:** Relative frequency of cases with familiar solutions

the respondents specified that they apply solutions that others have already applied in the past in seventy five to one hundred percent of the cases. 36.4% of the respondents specified that they apply solutions that others have already applied in the past in fifty to less than seventy five percent of the cases. The majority with 56.9% of the respondents specified that they apply solutions that others have already applied in the past in more than 50% of the cases.

Overall, the majority of respondents applies solutions that have been already applied in the past by themselves or by others in more than fifty percent of the cases. We conclude that we can also answer the question Q2 in the affirmative.

**Q3** We collected the data for metric M5 with a single survey question to answer the question Q3: *"Is there an established process for solving performance and scalability problems?"*. The respondents had to specify whether they follow an established process that is also used by others or they follow their own process. We provided five response alternatives and the obligatory *Don't know* option. We invited respondents to describe the process if they follow their own process. We also provided the response alternative that respondents have been able to specify that they have not solved any software performance and scalability problem in the past. 2.3% of the respondents selected the *Don't know* option. This corresponds to one respondent. 2.3% of the respondents also specified that they have not solved any software performance and scalability problem in the past. Figure 7.11 shows the relative frequency of the responses. The vast majority with 77.3% of the respondents specified that they decide from case to case what they do. 13.6% of the respondents specified that they use an established process. 4.5% of the respondents specified that they follow their own process. The two respondents who specified that they follow their own process provided the following descriptions (word citation):

> "Each performance problem needs to be tackled in an individual way. However the generic Measure - Analyse - Validate Hypothesis - Propose and Evalute [sic] Alternatives works quite well."

> "I use(d) queuing theory, statistics, measurement, and prediction [sic]"

The author of the latter description specified to practice the role of an architect with an engagement of more than five to ten years in solving performance and scalability problems working in industry and consulting for an organization with more than five hundred to five thousand employees. The author of the first description specified to practice the roles of a manager, performance expert and architect with an engagement of more than five to ten years in solving software performance and scalability problems working at the university, in industry and consulting for an organization with more than one hundred to five hundred employees.

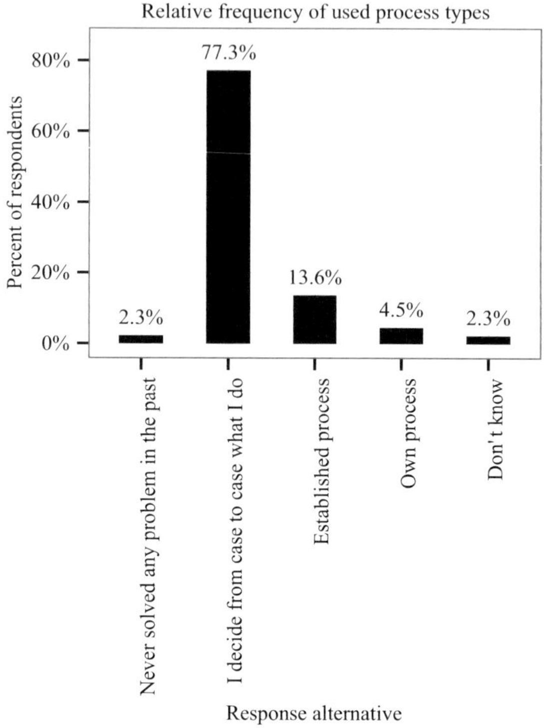


**Figure 7.11.:** Relative frequency of process types

An explanation building for the significant number of respondents that specified a from case to case decision in what they do is potentially that they recalled the information on a very low level of abstraction. When they consider the measurement of different metrics at different places in the software application already as a process difference can explain the 77.3% of respondents that selected this response alternative. Another explanation building is that the solution process is really case-specific. This would include that even on a high level of abstraction, as cited in the first citation above, a generic process is either not applied or not applicable. A third explanation building is that there are factors, e.g., project schedule, budget, development resources that determine the case-specific solution process. In this case, a generic process can be applicable but parts of the process can be ignored due to project-specific reasons.

Only 13.6% of the respondents specified that they use an established process when they solve a software performance and scalability problem. This corresponds to six respondents. Consequently, we answer question Q3 in the negative. We have not found a clear indication that there is an established process.

**Q4** We collected the data for the metric M6, M7, M8, M9, and M10 with a single survey question to answer the question Q4: *"Is it time consuming to solve an identified performance and scalability problem?"*. The respondents had to distribute one hundred points across five specified time spans according to how often the respondents are busy with solving a software performance and scalability problem for that time span. We have one item nonresponse and one invalid answer. One respondent distributed more than one hundred points. Consequently, we do not consider the collected data of these two respondents in the analysis. One point corresponds to one percent of the cases. Figure 7.12 shows the cumulative distribution for the distributed points for each time span that we have defined. 50% of the respondents specified that they are

- 10% of the cases at maximum busy for less than a few hours,
- 20% of the cases at maximum busy for a few hours to a day,
- 27.5% of the cases at maximum busy for more than a day to a week,
- 10% of the cases at maximum busy for more than a week to a month, and
- 0% of the cases at maximum busy for more than a month

for solving a software performance and scalability problem. 75% of the respondents specified that they are

- 30% of the cases at maximum busy for less than a few hours,
- 30% of the cases at maximum busy for a few hours to a day,
- 43.8% of the cases at maximum busy for more than a day to a week,
- 20% of the cases at maximum busy for more than a week to a month, and
- 10% of the cases at maximum busy for more than a month

for solving a problem. According to the collected data, the most software performance and scalability problems are solved within a couple of hours to a week. We consider a week as a long time span when a developer is busy with solving one software performance and scalability problem. An explanation building is that the effort for identifying a solution, conducting performance evaluation experiments, and proposing and evaluating alternative solutions is high. According to the data collected for metric M4, 56.9% of the respondents specified that they apply solutions that others have already applied in the past. Looking up potential solutions in books or talking to colleagues and transferring a potential solution into the problem-specific context can take time. Another explanation building is that developers are not working on the solution of a software performance and scalability problem without interruption. Developers have to attend meetings, discuss solution alternatives with the team and may have to wait until a solution is approved by the decision maker.

In conclusion, 50% of the respondents specified that they are 27.5% of the cases busy for more than a day to a week when they solve a software performance and scalability problem. Consequently, we answer the question Q4 in the affirmative.

**Q5** We collected the data for the metric M11, M12, M13, and M14 with a single survey question to answer the question Q5: *"What association scenario between problems and solutions occurs most often?"*. The respondents had to distribute one hundred points across four different association scenarios between problems and solutions that we have defined. The respondents had to distribute one hundred points according to how often they have been in the scenarios in the past. One point corresponds to one percent of the cases. We had two invalid responses. One respondent distributed more than one hundred points. Another respondent distributed less than one hundred points.

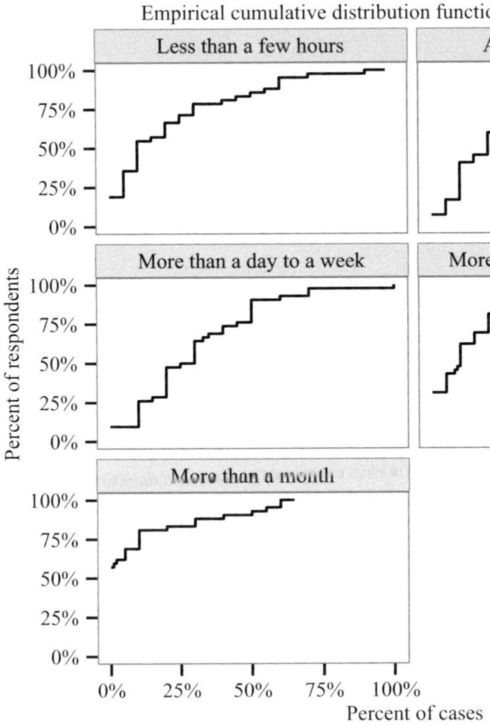


**Figure 7.12.:** Cumulative distribution functions of solution duration

The collected data of these two respondents is not considered in the analysis. Figure 7.13 shows the cumulative distribution function for the distributed points for each defined scenario. 50% of the respondents specified that they have been

- 10% of the cases at maximum in a one problem, one solution scenario,
- 27.5% of the cases at maximum in a one problem, more than one possible solution,
- 10% of the cases at maximum in a multiple problems, one possible solution per problem scenario, and

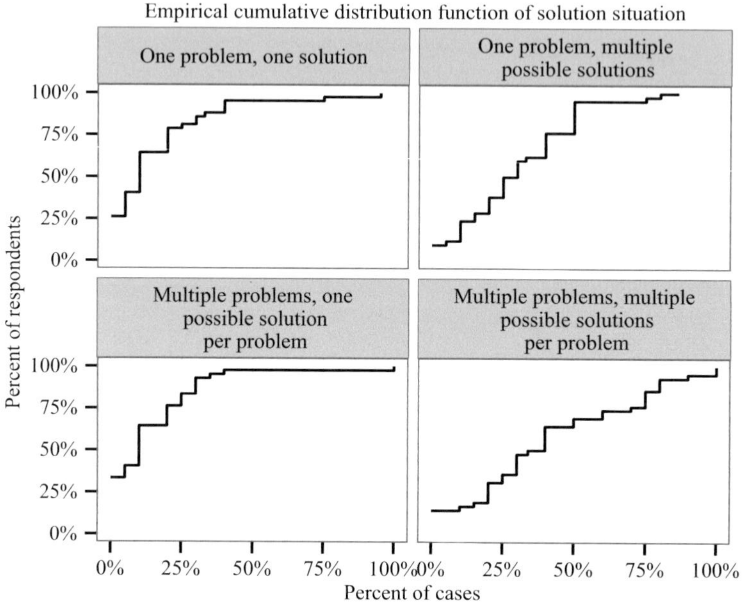


**Figure 7.13.:** Cumulative distribution functions of solution situation

- 37% of the cases at maximum in a multiple problems, multiple possible solutions per problem scenario

when they have worked on software performance and scalability problems in the past. 75% of the respondents specified that they have been

- 20% of the cases at maximum in a one problem, one solution scenario,
- 40% of the cases at maximum in a one problem, more than one possible solution,
- 20% of the cases at maximum in a multiple problems, one possible solution per problem scenario, and
- 67.5% of the cases at maximum in a multiple problems, multiple possible solutions per problem scenario

when they have worked on software performance and scalability problems in the past. The scenarios that most respondents have experienced in the past are one-to-many scenarios and many-to-many scenarios. 50% of the respondents specified that they have been in 27.5% of the cases at maximum in a one problem, more than one possible solutions scenario. 50% of the respondents also specified that they have been in 37% of the cases at maximum in a multiple problems, multiple possible solutions per problem scenario. 75% of the respondents specified that they have been in 40% of the cases at maximum in a one problem, more than one possible solution scenario. 75% of the respondents also specified that they have been in 67.5% of the cases at maximum in a multiple problems, multiple possible solutions per problem scenario when they have worked on software performance and scalability problems in the past. Consequently, we answer the question Q5 as follows: the scenario that the respondents experienced most often in the past are many-to-many scenarios where the most appropriate solution had to be selected among alternatives.

**Q6** We collected the data for the metric M15 with a single survey question to answer the question Q6: *"Is there sufficient support for finding a solution for performance and scalability problems?"*. The respondents had to specify whether they agree or disagree with the statement that the existing support for finding a solution for a detected software performance and scalability problem is insufficient. We provided four response alternatives and the obligatory *Don't know* option. We had two item nonresponses. Consequently, we analyzed the collected data from forty two respondents. Figure 7.14 shows the relative frequencies of the response alternatives. The majority with 76.2% of the respondents agrees that the existing support for finding a solution for a detected software performance and scalability problem is insufficient. 45.2% of the respondents strongly agrees with the statement. 31% of the respondents slightly agrees with the statement. 19% of the respondents slightly disagrees with the statement. No respondent strongly disagrees with the statement. We conclude from the collected data that no respondent is really satisfied with the existing support.

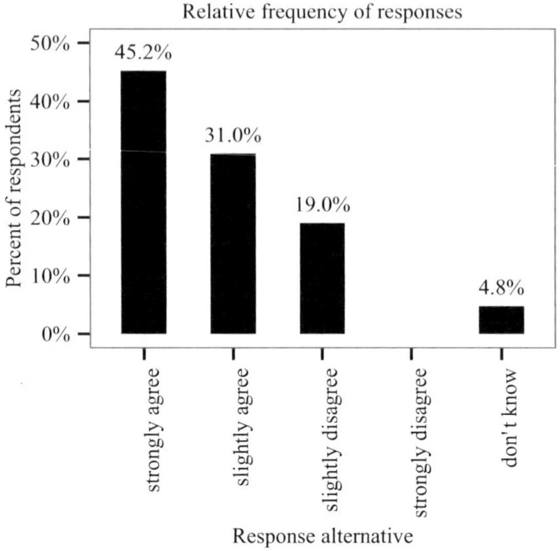


**Figure 7.14.:** Relative frequency of responses for statement agreement

We provided the option that the respondents can describe what kind of support they currently have to solve a detected software performance and scalability problem. Thirty three respondents described the support that they currently have (eleven item nonresponses). A respondent that practices the role manager, software engineer, designer, performance expert, architect, and consultant, who slightly disagrees with the statement provided the following description (word citation):

> "It's not like that there is a tool which will help you at any day to solve a performance problem if you identified one. The problem is not that the solution of the problem is the hurdle, but the identifying of it is time consuming and not that easy. Solving a problem (depending on where the problem is) involves tuning existing hardware, a rearchitecture of the application, optimization of a specific component or anything else like in the normal software development cycle"

In contrast, a respondent that practices the role manager, quality engineer/tester, and performance engineer, who slightly agrees with the statement provided the following description (word citation):

> "Forums, Expert Blogs, Books, Google, Experts in my Company/Network, tools like yslow"

Profiling and monitoring tools are mentioned often in the descriptions of the thirty three respondents. We conclude from the collected data that the respondents have support in terms of profiling and monitoring tools to validate hypotheses. We also conclude that the respondents are not supported in proposing hypotheses about what potentially solves the problem. In conclusion, 76.2% of the respondents agrees that the existing support for identifying a solution for a detected software performance and scalability problem is insufficient. Consequently, we answer the question Q6 in the negative.

**Q7** We collected the data for the metric M16 and M17 in a single survey question to answer the question Q7: *"Is it necessary to tailor generic solution patterns to the software application?"*. The survey question also collected the data for the metric M20, and M21. The respondents had to imagine a tool that supports them in solving software performance and scalability problems. We defined five different support features. The respondents had to distribute one hundred points (cf. 100 dollar test (Berander et al., 2005)) across the defined support features of the imaginary tool according to how important it is for the respondents that the tool provides this kind of support. This question design avoids that the respondents select the support features in a nice-to-have manner. The question design also shows the importance of one support feature versus the others. One point corresponds to one percent. We consider twenty percent as the baseline for a support feature. When the respondent assigns twenty percent to each support feature then all five support features are equal important. A support feature with more than twenty percent is more important. A support feature with less than twenty percent is less important. We had one respondent who distributed more than one hundred percent. We do not consider the collected data of this respondent in the analysis.

Figure 7.15 shows the cumulative distribution function for the distributed points for each defined support feature. 50% of the respondents specified that the completely automated proposal of generic solution patterns that they have to transfer into the actual application and problem context without the tool interacting with them has an importance of 5% at maximum. 75% of the respondents specified that the aforementioned support provided by the imaginary tool has an importance of 10% at most. An explanation building is that the proposal of generic solution patterns like to distribute functionality evenly among components does not add a significant benefit in the opinion of the respondents. The respondents still have to transfer the generic solution pattern into the problem and application-specific context, e.g., which functionality of which component has to be moved and where it is to be moved. Consequently, we consider the proposal of generic solution patterns even if completely automated as unimportant for the respondents.

In contrast, 50% of the respondents specified that the semi-automatic proposal of application and problem specific solutions while the imaginary tool is interacting with them has an importance of 20% at maximum. 75% of the respondents specified that aforementioned support provided by the imaginary tool has an importance of 27.5% at maximum. Tailored solution proposals are factor four more important than proposing generic solution patterns when we consider 50% of the respondents. When we consider 75% of the respondents it is almost factor three more important. This also is the third highest importance among the defined support possibilities when we consider the responses of 75% of the respondents. An explanation building is that the imaginary tool takes over the work of applying a generic solution pattern to an application and problem specific context. The respondents are then able to review the solution proposal, develop the final solution proposal based on the work that the tool has already done.

In conclusion, the semi-automatic proposal of tailored solutions even when the imaginary tool has to interact with the respondents is more important than the completely automated proposal of generic solution pattern. Consequently, we answer the question Q7 in the affirmative.

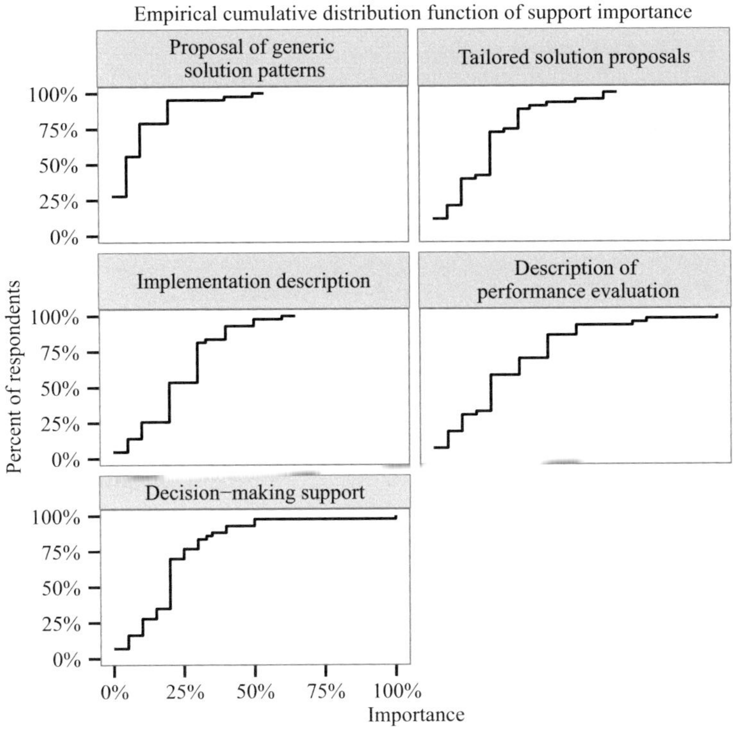


**Figure 7.15.:** Cumulative distribution functions of support importance

**Q8** We collected the data for the metric M18 with the same survey questions as the data for the metric M16, M17, M20, and M21 to answer the question Q8: *"Is it necessary to describe the performance evaluation experiments that are to be conducted?"*.

Figure 7.15 shows the cumulative distribution function for the distributed points for supporting performance evaluation experiments side by side with the other defined support features. 50% of the respondents specified that the description of the performance evaluation experiments that are to be conducted by the imaginary tool has an importance of 20% at maximum, e.g., what metrics are to be analyzed, where in the system and how the information is to be obtained. 75% of the respondents specified an importance of 40% at maximum for the aforementioned support possibility. This is the highest importance among the defined support possibilities when we consider the responses of 75% of the respondents.

An explanation building is that the imaginary tool provides an systematic approach to performance evaluation where the goals for each experiment are explicitly defined by the imaginary tool, goal-oriented performance evaluation experiments are conducted, relevant metrics are selected, and an appropriate evaluation technique is used. This mitigates the risk of unintentional mistakes in performance evaluation (Jain, 1991).

In conclusion, the support of the imaginary tool through the description of performance evaluation experiments that are to be conducted when performance and scalability problems are solved has been recognized with the highest relative importance by 75% of the respondents. We answer the question Q8 in the affirmative.

**Q9** We collected the data for the metric M19 with a single survey question to answer the question Q9: *"Is there a need to consider multiple criteria to rank solutions?"*. The respondents had to recall situations in which they had to decide on which solution of a software performance and scalability problem they implement. The respondents had to list some of the decision criteria that they consider in making the decision, e.g., performance improvement, implementation effort. We coded the responses according to the criteria that the respondents listed most often. We had one nonresponse and three responses that we cannot code. The three respondents provided responses that are too generic, i.e., *"All depends on the issue."*, or that are not compliant with the defined response task. We do not consider the four responses in the analysis. Consequently, one hundred percent of the respondents corresponds to forty respondents. Figure 7.16 shows the relative frequency of the coded decision criteria. 70% of the respondents specified that they consider the performance improvement when they decide which solution is to be implemented. 65% of the respondents specified the implementation effort as decision criterion. 30% of the respondents specified that maintainability is a concern when they select the solution. 22.5% of the respondents specified the complexity of the solution as decision criteria. 60% of the respondents also specified other criteria that are of concern when they decide on which solution to implement.

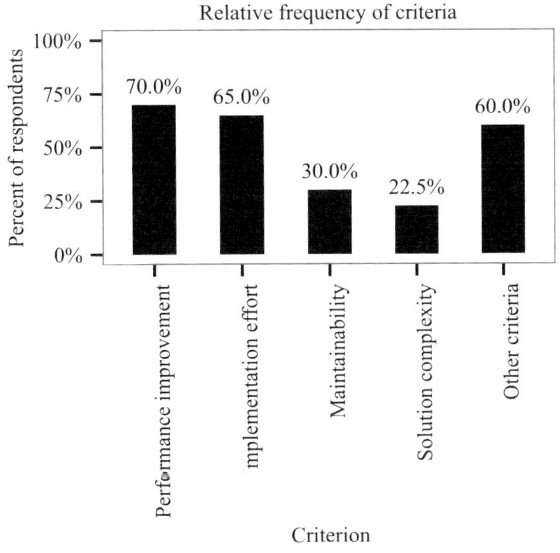


**Figure 7.16.:** Relative frequency of coded decision criteria

An explanation building for the high relative frequency of the decision criteria performance improvement and implementation effort is that the respondents repeated the examples that we gave in the survey question. A look into the responses of the respondents indicates that they have recalled the criteria and not simply repeated the examples. The following example supports our conclusion (word citation):

> "1. which one has the best performance improvement
> 2. (with same importance as 1) How fast/easy can the solution be realized
> 3. which one has the best maintenance on a long perspective"

The response also shows that decision criteria may have different priorities. A further indication for the recall of decision criteria by the respondents is that not all responses included both example criteria like the following example (word citation):

> "- time to realize
> - complexity at the end
> - maintenance effort afterwards"

Another explanation building is that performance improvement and implementation effort are obvious decision criteria when the respondents have to make the decision on which solution to implement. The high relative frequency is a logical consequence.

The following response of a respondent shows that the side effects and the propagation of changes is also a concern in making the decision (word citation):

> "performance improvement, effort for redesign and implementation, costs, affected (sub-)systems, risks of refactoring, impact on other quality characteristics such as reliability, security or privacy."

Overall, the responses show that there is a set of decision criteria which are of concern by most of the respondents. 60% of respondents also consider other decision criteria that we have not coded. This shows that the decision criteria are context-specific. We conclude that multiple decision criteria are to be considered when selecting a solution. The median of the number of specified decision criteria is three. We answer the question Q9 in the affirmative.

**Q10** We collected the data for the metric M20 with the same survey question as the data for the metric M16, M17, M18, and M21 to answer the question Q10: *"Is there a need to describe solutions at the implementation level?"*.

Figure 7.15 shows the cumulative distribution function of the distributed points for supporting the implementation of a solution side by side with the other support features. 50% of the respondents specified an importance of 20% at maximum for the support of describing the implementation of solution proposals by the imaginary tool, e.g., describing the implementation with change activities, listing of parts of the architecture, components, classes, and methods that are impacted by changes. 75% of the respondents specified an importance of 30% at maximum that the imaginary tool provides the aforementioned support possibility. This is the second highest importance among the defined support possibilities when we consider the responses of 75% of the respondents. An explanation building is that the implementation description entailing the impacted elements of the software application supports the respondents in reviewing and comparing solution proposals. The respondents can analyze the properties of a solution for factors that have been specified as common decision criteria by the respondents (see Q9), e.g., the complexity of a solution, the impact on maintainability, whether the solution is future-proof and fits to the available resources.

In conclusion, 75% of the respondents specified the second highest relative importance among the support possibilities for the description of the implementation of solution proposals by the imaginary tool. Consequently, we answer the question Q10 in the affirmative.

**Q11** We collected the data for the metric M21 with the same survey question as the data for the metric M16, M17, M18, and M20 to answer the question Q11: *"Is there a need to support the decision maker in making a decision about the solution to implement?"*. Figure 7.15 shows the cumulative distribution function of the distributed points for supporting the decision making process side by side with the other support features.

50% of the respondents specified an importance of 20% at maximum that the imaginary tool supports the respondents in making a decision about the solution to implement. 75% of the respondents specified an importance of 25% that the imaginary tool supports the aforementioned support feature. This is the fourth highest importance among the defined support feature when we consider the responses of 75% of the respondents.

An explanation building is that the selection of the most appropriate solution among solution alternatives when multiple decision criteria are involved is not trivial in many cases. The decision criteria can have different priorities. The imaginary tool supports the decision making process by taking over the work to propose the most appropriate solution. The imaginary tool considers the decision criteria, the properties of each solution alternative with respect to the defined decision criteria and priorities for the decision criteria.

Consequently, we answer the question Q11 in the affirmative.

#### 7.2.7.3. Summary

This section presented the survey results and answered the eleven questions Q1–Q11. The population of respondents is dominated by respondents that practice at least the roles of the developer and/or the role of the performance engineer. The majority of respondents has industrial experience and works for organizations with up to five hundred employees. Most of the respondents engage themselves for more than five years in the context of solving software performance and scalability problems and has solved at least on software performance and scalability problem in an industrially used application.

In the following, we summarize the results for the questions Q1–Q11. Table 7.4 lists the questions and the corresponding answer. According to our respondents, they are often in cases in which they solve a software performance and scalability problem that they have already seen in the past. They often apply solutions that they or others have already applied in the past to solve software performance and scalability problems. The majority of respondents decides from case to case what they do when they solve a software performance and scalability problem. We found no indication that there is an established process. They solve most of the problems within a time span of more than a day to week. Most of the cases are many-to-many situations where more than one problem is present and where more than one solution for each problem exists. The majority of respondents considers the existing support for finding a solution to software performance and scalability problems as insufficient. It is important for most of the respondents that a tool supports them in solving software performance and scalability problems by tailoring generic solution patterns to the application, describing the implementation of the solution at the implementation level, describing the performance evaluation experiments that are to be conducted, and supporting the decision making process to select the most appropriate solution. In the decision making process, multiple decision criteria are considered by most of the respondents.

We found three extra ordinary insights in the survey results. We have indication that decision criteria are context-specific and that decision criteria can have different priorities. We have also indication that the process of solving software performance and scalability problems is case-specific. We had an additional survey question where the respondents had to describe at least one of the problems abstractly that they have solved in an industrially used application. Problems are often caused by inappropriate database interaction, e.g., too many queries, querying too much data that is not needed. Many of the problems are already known in literature and still occur obviously in industry (Haines, 2014; Dudney et al., 2003; Still, 2013). One of the respondents noted that the abstraction within the software application through an object-relational mapper reduces the performance awareness of the developers.

### 7.2.8. Threats to Validity

In case study research, Runeson et al. (Runeson et al., 2012) consider construct validity, internal validity, external validity and reliability validity. The concern of construct validity is that the intended measurement and the actual measurement comply. The concern of internal validity is the causal relationship between the investigated factor and other factors. The concern of external validity is how far the study-specific findings are generalizable for other studies. The concern of reliability validity is how much the findings are researcher-specific (Runeson et al., 2012).

#### 7.2.8.1. Construct Validity

A potential threat to construct validity is that the survey questions and the questionnaire design have not been tested in the field under realistic conditions prior to the collection of the actual data. We used a GQM plan to systematically derive what the survey questions have to measure. We used a recommended testing approach (Campanelli, 2007) to mitigate the risk that the defined survey questions do not measure the intended data. This included change-triggered informal testing of the survey question, several expert reviews of the survey questions and the GQM plan, and a respondent debriefing where selected test respondents had to complete the survey prior to answering questions about how they have understood the survey questions. We have also made our knowledge explicit in form of hypotheses about the expected answers prior to collecting the data as recommended in (Solingen et al., 1999). The actual answers of the questions comply with our expectations and we have also no anomaly in the collected data indicating that the survey questions have not been consistently understood.

Another potential threat to validity is that we have not measured the time to solve a software performance and scalability problem in relation to the size of the project. This is why we cannot conclude from the collected data whether the specified amount of time is significant with respect to the project schedule.

#### 7.2.8.2. Internal Validity

A potential threat to internal validity is that the respondents of the research community and the companies we are in contact with knew the author of the survey. The respondents might thus be biased towards responses that support our goal. This is why we got a list of potential respondents within a company from supervisors. This lists included potential respondents with which we have not been in contact before to foster the objectivity of the respondents. The responses do not differ significantly when we compare the responses with the responses of unknown respondents from the groups of LinkedIn. There is no indication that the respondents have been biased.

#### 7.2.8.3. External Validity

A potential threat to external validity is that no random probability sample has been drawn. There is no population of developers and performance engineers from which we could have drawn a statistically representative random probability sample. The findings of the survey are only representative for the respondents of the survey. It is not possible to generalize the finding of the survey to the general population of developers and performance engineers. However, the intention of this survey is to better understand the current situation in industry and the potential need for support in solving software performance and scalability problems. The findings are relevant and are valuable for the design of Vergil. The context description of the survey (see Section 7.2.7) may help to identify a potential relevance of the survey for another case.

#### 7.2.8.4. Reliability Validity

The majority of survey questions that collect data to answer the questions are closed-ended questions. The respondents have to select a response from a list of defined response alternatives. There is no interpretation needed that may lead another researcher to different conclusions. Quantitative metrics are used to answer the questions. The highest relative frequency of response alternatives for the particular metric determined the question answer in most cases. The questionnaire included one open-ended survey question that collected relevant data to answer a question. The interpretation of the responses here is limited to counting the different decision criteria within the response. A closed-ended survey question used the *"Other (Please specify)"* option. No interpretation was needed to answer the question since the relative frequency of responses was relevant. Thus, we expect that other researchers come to the same conclusions when they conduct the same survey.

## 7.3. Case Study – Java Persistence API

This section presents the conducted case study of Type 1 to validate the hypothesis (see Table 7.1) with respect to the feasibility of Vergil. The remainder of this section is structured as follows: Section 7.3.1 introduces the goals of the case study. Section 7.3.2 introduces the Media Store application as research subject. Section 7.3.3 introduces the operational profiles that have been used for dynamic analyses. Section 7.3.4 explains the design of the case study. Section 7.3.5 gives an overview on the measurement environment where the Media Store application has been executed for performance testing and how relevant data about the Media Store application has been collected through application performance monitoring. Section 7.3.6 explains how the relevant model instances have been extracted from the implementation of the Media Store application. Section 7.3.7 introduces the decision criteria that are used for prioritization of solution proposals. Section 7.3.8 introduces the change constraints that we have defined for the implementation. Section 7.3.9 describes the results of applying Vergil to the N+1 Selects problem. Section 7.3.10 describes the results of applying Vergil to the excessive logging problem and Section 7.3.11 the results of applying Vergil to the excessive data allocation problem. After describing the results, Section 7.3.12 gives a brief overview on how the solution proposals are described. Section 7.3.13 discusses potential threats to validity. Section 7.3.14 summarizes the case study results and draws a conclusion on goal attainment. Section 7.3.15 provides an overall discussion of the case study, extraordinary insights and difficulties.

### 7.3.1. Goals

The goal of the case study is to validate the hypotheses H1–H5 and that Vergil provides the expected output when the inputs were valid. For this reason, we apply Vergil to three software performance and scalability problems in the context of the Java Persistence API. During the course of the case study, the description languages are used to describe the relevant information of real problems used to exchange information between different workflow activities as well as between Vergil and the experimenter using Vergil. We refined the aim of the case study into three goals:

- *G1*: Quantitatively evaluate [purpose] the solution of the N+1 selects problem in the context of the Java Persistence API [issue] with Vergil [object].
- *G2*: Quantitatively evaluate [purpose] the solution of the excessive logging problem in the context of the Java Persistence API [issue] with Vergil [object].
- *G3*: Quantitatively evaluate [purpose] the solution of the excessive data allocation problem in the context of the Java Persistence API [issue] with Vergil [object].

### 7.3.2. Media Store Application

The subject of the case study is the Media Store application that allows its users to upload and download audio files (H. Koziolek, 2008; Becker, 2008). We use an implementation of the Media Store application that was originally implemented by students during a practical course at the university. We extended the original implementation by introducing the album, audio blob and comment JPA entities. The modifications have been implemented by a bachelor student. This also includes the modification of the Web-based user interface to display all albums, the audios for each album, and a Web page to search for a particular album.

The remainder of this section describes the components and component assembly and the JPA entities.

#### 7.3.2.1. Component Assembly

The Media Store application is implemented with Java EE 6 technology. A component corresponds to a stateless Enterprise Java Bean (EJB). The components and the assembly of the components is shown in Figure 7.17 in the form of a UML component diagram. The IWebGuiBean interface is a facade that acts as interface between the Servlets of the Web application and the enterprise Java beans. The IUserManagementBean interface is responsible for creation and authentication of users. The functionality to read and write user objects to the database is provided by the IUserDBAdapterBean interface. The IMediaStoreBean interface acts as mediator between the IWebGuiBean interface and the IAudioDBAdapterBean, IEncoderBean, and IPackagingBean interface. The AudioDBAdapterBean EJB provides the functionality to read and write all JPA entity instances from and to the database except the user entity. The IEncoderBean interface is responsible for providing the functionality to re-encode an audio file in a lower bitrate than the uploaded bitrate. The IPackagingBean interface is used to compress multiple audio files into an archive when a collection of audio files is downloaded.

The Media Store application has one component for each defined interface that implements the particular interface. The EncoderBean EJB executes the particular encoder in a separate process and copies the audio file to the local file system, starts the encoding process, and reads the re-encoded audio file into memory. The PackagingBean EJB creates a zip file that contains the collection of audio files that the user requested to download. The UserDBAdapterBean EJB and the AudioDBAdapterBean EJB use the JPA as object-relational mapper to read and write objects from and to the database.

The Web-based user interface uses six Java Server Pages and Servlets to provide the functionality of the Media Store application to users. All Servlets use the IWebGUIBean interface to use the functionality of the EJBs. The Servlet Register allows visitors of the Web application to create a user account.

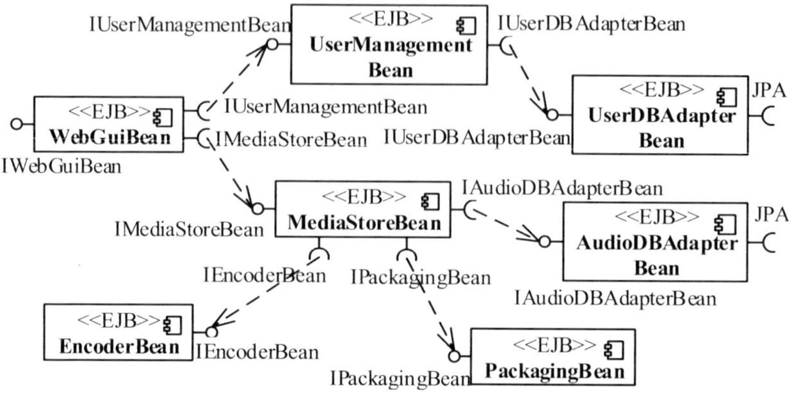


**Figure 7.17.:** Overview on the component assembly

The Servlet Login enables users to log in. The Download Servlet shows all albums and contained audios and provides the download capabilities of audios. The Servlet Upload enables users to upload an audio file into the database. The users can use the SearchAlbum Servlet to look for a particular album and to download audios from the search result. The Logout Servlet logs the user out and terminates the session.

#### 7.3.2.2. Java Persistence

The Media Store application uses five JPA entities to manage the relevant information about users and audio files. The entities are shown in Figure 7.18 in the form of a UML class diagram. Each persistent property of an entity has corresponding getter and setter methods. An exception is the identifier persistent property id where only a getter method is provided since the identifier is generated by the persistence provider.

The central entity is the Audio entity that contains all relevant meta-information about an audio file. The bytes of an audio file are stored in the AudioBlob entity. The Album entity describes a collection of audios as well as the potential different album artist and name. The User entity contains the relevant information about a user and a list of audios that each particular user contributed. The Comment entity stores the comments that user can make for audios.

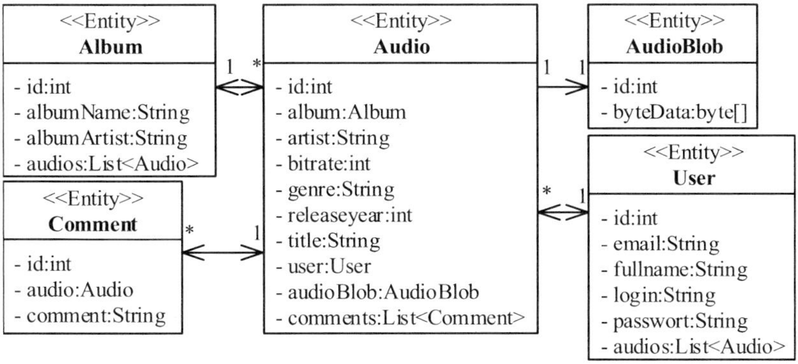


**Figure 7.18.:** Overview on the JPA entity classes

Table 7.5 shows the relationships between the entities and the configured fetch type. The name of the table in the database corresponds to the name of the entity that is stored in the table. An exception is the table for the user entity where the table name user is reserved by the database management system. Instead, the table containing the user entities has the name users. The Album entity has a one-to-many relationship to the Audio entity. The configured fetch type for the mapping is lazy fetching which is the default fetch type for one-to-many relationships. The Audio entity has a many-to-one relationship to the Album entity with the default fetch configuration of eager fetching. The mapping and fetch type applies to the many-to-one relationship between the Audio entity and the User entity. The fetch configuration of the one-to-many relationship between the Audio and Comment entity is also configured with the default fetch type. An exception is the fetch configuration of the one-to-one mapping of the relationship between the Audio entity and the AudioBlob entity. The default eager fetch type for a one-to-one mapping is overwritten with the lazy fetch type. The one-to-many mapping between the User and Audio entity as well as the many-to-one mapping between the Comment and Audio entity use the default fetch type of the mapping.

We implemented a database content generator for the Media Store application that generates Album, Audio, User, Comment, and AudioBlob entities randomly within specified parameters. We use a MP3 encoded audio file as sample to generate the audio file for the AudioBlob entity. The data generator also creates MP3 tags for each audio file using random strings for the attributes. The sample audio file has a file size of three kilobyte.

The database tables had the following number of rows: the database table storing the Album entities had 500 rows, the table storing the Audio entities had 3724 rows, the table storing the User entities had 500 rows, the table storing the Comment entities had 111885 rows, and the table storing the AudioBlob entities had 3724 rows. Each album has at minimum five and at maximum ten audios. Each audio has between ten and fifty comments (inclusively). Each user uploaded the audios for an individual album.

### 7.3.3. Operational Profiles

We use two operational profiles in the case study. When a simulated user downloads an audio, the audio is requested in the encoded bitrate as it is stored in the database. This avoids the re-encoding of the audio file in another bitrate and mitigates the risk that the encoding component becomes a bottleneck.

- *Multiple user operational profile*: One operation profile for the performance test with multiple users (200 users for the N+1 Selects problem, 100 users for the excessive logging problem, and 50 users for the excessive data allocation problem) and another operational profile for a single user test. Figure 7.19 shows the usage profile used for the performance test in form of a UML state machine diagram with transition probabilities. The entry behavior of each state denotes the called method in form of the Servlet class name concatenated with the class method name by a dot. A user first logs in to the Media Store application providing user name and password. All users are redirected to the album overview where all albums and all audios are displayed. A user downloads a audio file from the list of all albums and audios with a probability of ten percent. A user also uploads an audio file with a probability of ten percent. Most of the users search for a particular album with a probability of fifty five percent. There are also users that logout from the Media Store application after viewing all albums with a probability of twenty five percent. A user logs out after the download or upload of an audio file completes. A user who searched for a particular album downloads an audio file with a probability of ten percent or logs out with a probability

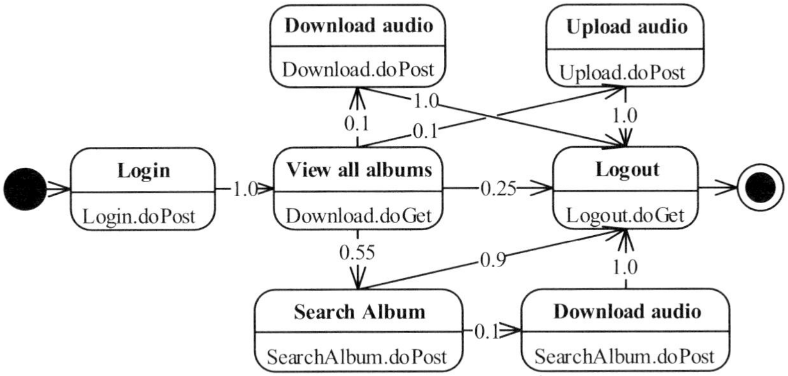


**Figure 7.19.:** Media Store usage profile with transition probabilities for performance test

of ninety percent. We use a closed workload and a think time of the user between three and five seconds. We simulate the users that follow the described usage profile with Apache JMeter™ (The Apache Software Foundation, 2015) and the extension Markov4JMeter (van Hoorn et al., 2008). We use this operational profile to monitor the response time of Servlet methods that are called as entry behavior of each state. The response time of five Servlet methods are used as criteria in decision making (see Section 7.3.7).

- *Single User Operational Profile*: Aside the probabilistic multiple users operational profile, we also use a deterministic single user operational profile to monitor specific data. Figure 7.20 shows this usage profile in the form of UML state machine with the called Servlet methods as entry behavior of each state. The transition probabilities are set to 1.0. The user in the single user test logs in to the Media Store application and views views all albums and audios. Thereafter, the user searches for a particular album and uploads an audio file afterwards. The user logs out when the upload completes. We use a closed workload with one user and a think time of zero seconds. We also simulate the user that uses the Media Store application as specified in the usage profile with JMeter and the extension Markov4JMeter. We apply the single user test to monitor the SQL queries that the JPA implementation issues

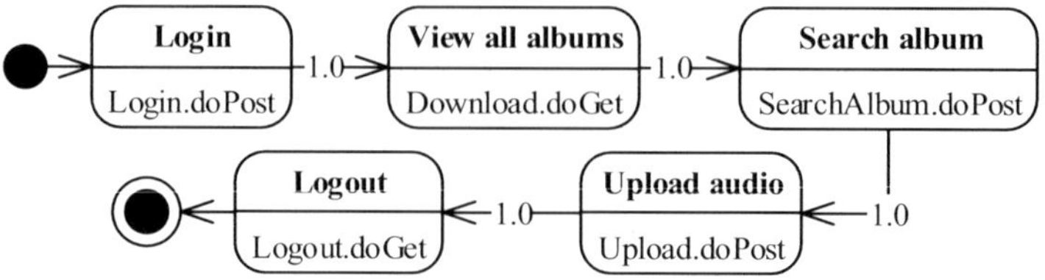


**Figure 7.20.:** Media Store usage profile with transition probabilities for single user test

to the database and to monitor the execution of all getter and setter methods of the JPA entities, i.e., Album, Audio, User, Comment, and AudioBlob. The memory footprint of methods is also measured with the single user test. The single user test mitigates the risk of potential side effects caused by parallel execution, e.g., SQL statements issued by several executing threads.

### 7.3.4. Case Study Design

The case study assumes a thoughtless usage, misconception, oversight or a lack of knowledge in using the Java Persistence API. Thoughtless means in this case that the Java Persistence API and the entities are used without consideration of the potential impact on relational data retrieval from the database which is a common case in industry (Haines, 2014; Grabner, 2013). For example, entities and contained relationships are accessed like objects where no application tailored configurations are applied to the Java Persistence API features, e.g, relationship fetch strategies and types.

We investigate the solution of three general and well known software performance and scalability problems that also occur in the context of the Java Persistence API as a consequence of thoughtless usage, lack of knowledge or simple oversight. The N+1 Selects problem has been recognized and reported by researchers and practitioners (Haines, 2014; Winand, 2012a; Brekken et al., 2008; Limburg et al., 2013; Grabner, 2010). The same applies for the excessive logging (Hunt et al., 2012; Grabner, 2012) and excessive data allocation problem (C. Smith et al., 2003; Hunt et al., 2012; T.-H. Chen et al., 2014).

We used the description of the root causes in the reports of practitioners to inject the problems into the Media Store application. Problem injection is a valid research method (Hsueh et al., 1997; Duan et al., 2008). The problems are injected as follows:

- *N+1 Selects Problem Injection*: The Media Store uses a named query to read all album entities from the database. The named query is statically defined with the named query annotation inside the named queries annotation in the album entity class. The named query is identified through the given name and used when all albums are viewed on the Web-based user interface. The specified JPQL query is as follows: *Select a from Album a*. The result list of the executed query is parsed into a return object of the surrounding method. All album attributes and all audio attributes except the comment entity relationship and audio blob entity relationship is accessed. From the user entity only the login attribute is accessed.

  The Java persistence provider uses $1+500+503=1004$ SQL queries to read the data from the database. In 1 query, all album entities are read from the database. 500 queries are used to read the user entities and 503 queries are used to read the audio entities.

  Table 7.6 shows the resulting impact of the 1004 SQL queries on the Download.doGet Servlet method that is called when all albums are viewed and gives an overview on the observed response times of the other Servlet methods. The values in the table show that other Servlet methods are not affected by the problem. The values are as follows: the 90%ile of the Login.doPost Servlet method is 0.003 seconds, the 90%ile of the Download.doGet method is 1.324 seconds, the 90%ile of the Download.doPost method is 0.056 seconds, the 90%ile of the SearchAlbum.doPost method is 0.037 seconds, the 90%ile of the Upload.doPost method is 0.015 seconds, and the 90%ile of the Logout.doGet method is 0.001 seconds. The response time value of the Download.doGet method is significantly impacted by the N+1 Selects problem. We measured the response time as described in Section 7.3.5 with the multiple user operational profile as described in Section 7.3.3.

- *Excessive Logging Problem Injection*: We build on top of the N+1 Selects problem for the excessive logging problem. We configured the persistence unit to log the SQL queries and the used parameters. We applied the settings to the persistence unit by adding the corresponding properties to the persistence unit in the persistence.xml file. We applied the log level SEVERE as value for the EclipseLink logging level property, FINEST as value for the EclipseLink SQL query logging level property, and true as value for the parameter logging property. This results in at least 1004 log entries for the logged queries and their parameter bindings for each execution of the Download.doGet method. This has a significant impact on the method's response time.

Table 7.6 shows the resulting response times with the excessive logging problem. We measured the response times with the multiple user operational profile and applied one hundred users (see Section 7.3.3). Considering that only half of the number of users are applied in the operational profile compared to the N+1 Selects problem, the excessive logging problem increases the 90%itle of the response time of the Download.doGet method from 1.324 seconds to 2.339 seconds. The response time of the other methods increased only slightly by about 1 to 18 milliseconds for the 90%ile. The dispersion of the measurements around the mean value increased also. This shows the increased variance from 0.034 to 0.203 compared to the response times of the N+1 Selects problem. The mean value of the Download.doGet method is 1.078 seconds with the N+1 Selects problem and 1.749 seconds with the excessive logging problem.

The measurement results of the excessive logging problem shows that logging of SQL queries in cases where many SQL queries are used to obtain the data from the database adds a significant response time overhead.

- *Excessive Data Allocation Problem Injection*: We avoided the N+1 Selects problem by configuring the named query with query hints to batch fetch relationships. We introduced the excessive data allocation problem by setting the fetch type of the one-to-one relationship in the audio entity for the audioblob entity from LAZY to EAGER. This is the default fetch type for a one-to-one relationship that is used when no fetch type is specified explicitly. In consequence, the associated audioblob entity containing the audio file is fetched from the database together with the audio entity itself. This means that when all albums are viewed by the user, 3724 audio entities and 3724 audioblob entities are read from the database. This has a significant impact on the response time of the Download.doGet method and the memory footprint of the method in which the named query is executed. The mean value of the memory footprint is 75.5 MB.

Table 7.6 shows the response times for the Servlet methods for the excessive data allocation problem. The excessive data allocation problem has a significant higher impact on the response time than the N+1 Selects or the excessive logging problem considering that only a fourth of the number of users compared to the N+1 Selects problem and a half of the number of users compared to the excessive logging problems are applied. We measured the response time with the multiple user operational profile and fifty users (see Section 7.3.3). The 90%tile of the response time of the Download.doGet method is 7.625 seconds. This is almost factor five higher than the response time with N+1 Selects problem and more than factor tree compared to the response time of the excessive logging problem. The Media Store application also had to handle only a fourth of the number of users compared to the N+1 Selects problem and only a half of the users compared to the excessive logging problem. The response times of the other Servlet methods do not show a significant impact. The dispersion of the measurements from the mean value is less than the dispersion in the excessive logging case. The variance is 0.448 and the mean value is 6.736 seconds.

### 7.3.5. Measurement Environment

The measurement environment consisted of three computers. The first computer was the load generator that was responsible for simulating users. The simulated users use the Media Store application according to the specified script. We used Apache JMeter (The Apache Software Foundation, 2015) as workload generator software and the Markov4JMeter plugin (van Hoorn, 2014a) for simulating probabilistic user behavior (see Section 7.3.3). The load generator was equipped with an Intel® Core™ i7 2640M @ 2.80GHz CPU with four cores, a memory size of 8GB RAM, and Windows 7 Enterprise SP 1 64bit as operating system. The second computer was the application server that was responsible for hosting the Media Store application (see Section 7.3.2). The application server was equipped with an Intel® Xeon® L5630 @ 2.13GHz CPU providing sixteen cores, a memory size of 16GB RAM, and Linux Enterprise Server 11 SP2 64bit as operating system. We used Glassfish 4.0 (Oracle, 2015) as Java application server. This includes EclipseLink 2.5.0 (The Eclipse Foundation, 2015) as implementation of the Java Persistence API. We used Java 1.7.0_51 as Java™ SE Runtime Environment to execute Glassfish. The third computer was the database server that was responsible for hosting the database of the Media Store application. The hardware and operation system of the database server was identical to the hardware and operating system of the application server. We used Apache Derby 10.10.1.1 (The Apache Software Foundation, 2014) as database management system and Java 1.7.0_51 as Java™ SE Runtime Environment to execute Apache Derby. All three computers were attached to the network with a 1 Gbit link.

We used the Adaptable Instrumentation and Monitoring (AIM) (Wert et al., 2015b; Wert et al., 2015c) tool to monitor the Media Store application and to collect the required data for the case study. AIM uses Java bytecode instrumentation to collect data about an application. What is to be measured and where in the system is described with the Instrumentation Description Model (IDM) description language (Wert et al., 2015d). AIM is capable of monitoring the entry and exit timestamp of methods, SQL statements that are send to the database, the memory utilization of the Java heap space, and others. AIM uses instrumentation probes that insert monitoring code reversibly into the bytecode of an application. Monitoring records are created whenever a method is executed that is instrumented. A monitoring record contains the instrumentation probe specific data together with meta-information, e.g., the thread identifier of the executing thread and a sequentially incremented unique method call identifier. We used AIM also to sample the CPU utilization of the application server with a sampling rate of $\frac{1}{100ms}$.

### 7.3.6. Model Extraction

We extracted the Java source code model with the Java Model Parser and Printer (JaMoPP) (Heidenreich et al., 2010) completely automated and resolved all references from the source code files and relevant dependencies, i.e., Java Persistence API, and relevant source code files of EclipseLink. We selectively parsed the source code to avoid a high execution time and memory consumption that preliminary tests have indicated when parsing the complete EclipseLink source code into a single model instance. The Java Model Parser and Printer (JaMoPP) parses the source code of an application based on compilation units, i.e., *.java file. This allows to deal with a large application code base through loading only the required compilation units into memory.

We parsed the content of the persistence.xml file into a persistence configuration model instance. We performed this step manually. An automated parser for the persistence.xml file that creates the corresponding persistence configuration model instance is an XML parser that iterates through the elements and attributes of in the XML file and creates an instance of the corresponding metamodel element.

### 7.3.7. Decision Criteria

We validate the performance solution description language for expressing the decision criteria hierarchy of the Analytic Hierarchy Process (AHP). We describe the characteristics of solutions with respect to the leafs in the decision criteria hierarchy in the remainder of the case study.

We only consider Servlet methods that are important for the attractiveness of the Media Store to its users and that have a high probability to be used according to the usage profile (see Section 7.3.3). The response time of the selected Servlet methods is important for the responsiveness of the application as it is directly perceived by users. We are interested in the 90% percentile of the response time measured in seconds as performance metric (Kopp, 2012b). While a solution that is able to provide the lowest response time may require disproportionally high implementation effort or may not be able to be sustainable as reported by our survey respondents (see Section 7.2.7, Q9), we also consider the implementation effort and the sustainability as decision criteria. We also consider the compliance with the defined constraints as decision criteria (see Section 7.3.8). Table 7.7 lists the decision criteria with the determined local and global priorities. The global priorities are determined for the leafs in the criteria hierarchy. The selection of decision criteria is driven by selecting as less criteria as possible by still reflecting the most important concerns in deciding about the solution to implement.

We used the AHP to determine the priorities for the decision criteria (see Section 5.8). In total, we performed $\frac{5*(5-1)}{2} + \frac{4*(4-1)}{2} = 16$ pairwise comparisons to determine the priorities for the criteria in the hierarchy. The Consistency Ratio (CR) is below five percent for all pairwise comparisons for each level in the hierarchy which is below the ten percent that are recommended at maximum for CR.

Achieving a low Consistency Index (CI) was not trivial. We used additional tool support that highlights where judgements are logically inconsistent and that proposes how consistency can be improved (Goepel, 2014). This kind of support also has to be integrated in the implementation of Vergil to support the decision maker in making logically consistent judgements. Attaining logically consistent judgements becomes also more difficult with the number of criteria in a group that are to be compared pairwise. The fewer criteria are in a group, the easier it is to achieve a low consistency index. This conclusion can also be drawn from the Random Index (RI) for different numbers of criteria where the RI increases with the number of criteria (Saaty, 2008). This also allows a higher CI in the judgements since $CR = \frac{CI}{RI}$.

The performance solution description language is capable of expressing the decision criteria hierarchy and the priorities. Each criterion that is listed in Table 7.7 is expressed with a criterion element. The name attribute of the criterion element is set to the name of the criteria in the hierarchy. The subcriteria relationship is expressed with the corresponding relationship of the description language. The criteria for the Servlet methods have an impacted element relationship with the corresponding class method element in the source code model. The priorities of the criteria are expressed with the associated parameter specification. The dimension of the priority parameter is a numeric dimension with valid values $v : 0 \leq v \leq 1$. Each parameter specifies the priority as numeric literal with the priority set as value. During the pairwise comparisons of the criteria in each group for each level in the hierarchy, the priority parameter specifies the local priority of the criteria. After all pairwise comparisons are completed and a desired CI is attained, the global priorities are determined and the local priority values of numeric literals are replaced with the global priority values.

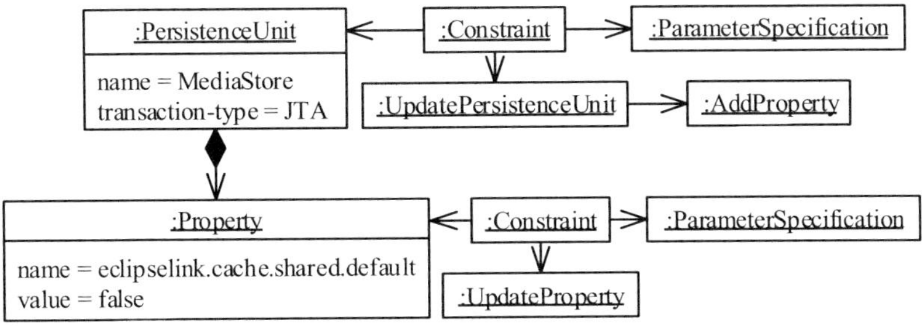


**Figure 7.21.:** Excerpt of the defined constraints

### 7.3.8. Constraints

We validate the expressiveness of the constraints description language by defining constraints for the Media Store application. The constraints are used in the remainder of the case study in the context of assessing the impact of the necessary changes to implement a solution.

We defined constraints for the interfaces that are implemented by EJBs to express architectural concerns, e.g., IAudioDBAdapterBean, IMediaStoreBean, and IWebGUIBean. In particular, we constrain the addition and deletion of interface methods and the addition and deletion of interface method parameters. Adding or deleting a method from an interface impacts classes that implement the interface. Consequently, changes have also to be applied to the implementing classes. This is the same for adding or deleting parameters from an interface method.

We also constrain changes of the persistence configuration. Configuring the persistence unit with properties keeps the application portable since the persistence.xml file can be easily exchanged to consider the particular needs of a certain environment. Consequently, we prefer to add properties to the persistence configuration and to update existing properties.

Figure 7.21 shows an excerpts with constraints for the persistence configuration. The update persistence unit change with the referenced add property change constrains the addition of properties to the persistence unit. The update property change constrains the update of the existing property for the shared cache.

We noticed that expressing the constraints manually by defining the elements can become a tedious task when many constraints are to be defined. The implementation of Vergil can be extended to support the decision maker with the specification of the constraints by enabling the selection of the elements in the Java source code. The particular element can then be looked up in the source code model instance. A tailored list of possible change types further supports the decision maker in selecting the change to constrain.

### 7.3.9. N+1 Selects Results

We successfully described all relevant information of the N+1 Selects problem with the performance profile description language as input for Vergil (see Section 4.2).

#### 7.3.9.1. Performance Profile

The performance profile includes the description of the response time of the Servlet methods that are executed during the performance test as specified in the applied operational profile (see Section 7.3.3). The performance profile also includes the description of the amount of SQL queries that are sent to the database in the context of viewing all albums when the named query is executed with the method Query.getResultList.

- *Response Time Aspect*: Figure 7.22 shows the excerpt of the performance profile describing the response time observation in form of the 90% percentile of the Servlet method Download.doGet for the performance test with two hundred users. The performance aspect references the doGet method of the class Download in the source code model instance as impacted element. The performance aspect also references the operational profile for the performance test. The referenced closed workload describes the different properties of the workload. The parameter specification specifies the observation for the response time dimension. The observed value of 1.324 seconds is the 90% percentile value of the monitored data. The response time observation for the other five executed Servlet methods (see Section 7.3.7) is described analogously.

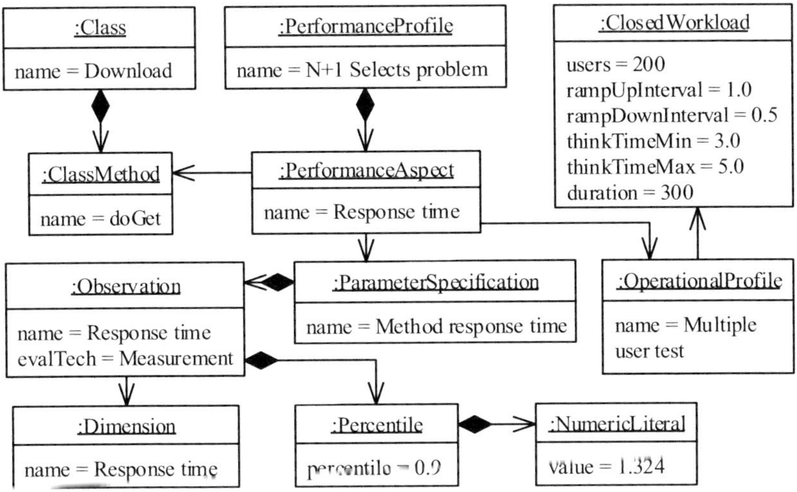


**Figure 7.22.:** Excerpt of the performance profile for the N+1 Selects problem describing the response time of the Servlet method Download.doGet

- *SQL Queries Aspect*: The number of SQL queries is described with the performance profile description language as maximum value observation. The JPA provider sends 1004 SQL queries to the database to read the required information (see Section 7.3.4). Figure 7.23 shows an excerpt of the performance profile describing the number of SQL queries aspect. The dimension is a numeric dimension with valid values $v : v \geq 0$. The method call element in the source code model instance with the Query.getResultList interface method as target is referenced as impacted element. The method call executes the named query and obtains the result list of all album entity instances. The operational profile describes the single user test and denotes when the SQL queries have been observed.

#### 7.3.9.2. Query Hints Change Hypothesis

The query hints change hypothesis tests the applicability of the change hypothesis and creates four different change plans: one change plan to apply the

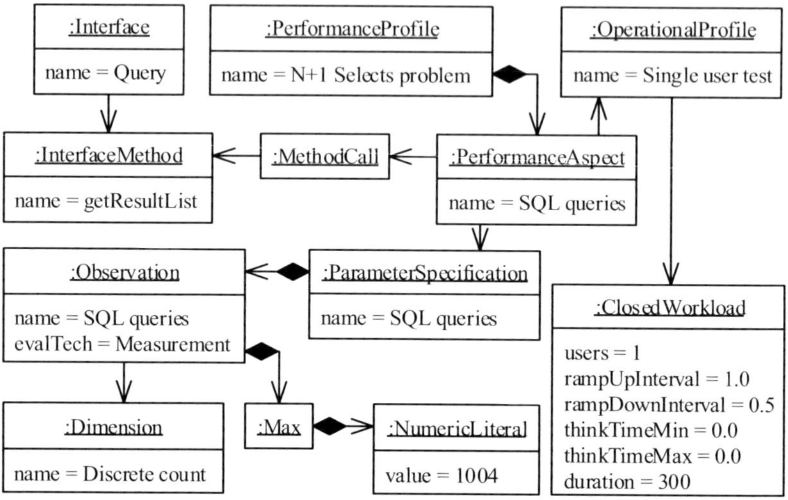


**Figure 7.23.:** Excerpt of the performance profile for the N+1 Selects problem describing the number of SQL queries when the Download.doGet is executed

batch fetch query hint to the query, one for the left fetch (join) query hint, one for the fetch graph query hint and another one to apply the load graph query hint.

- *Analysis Results*: The static analysis matches the number of SQL queries parameter and the method call of the Query.getResultList method (see Section 6.1.1). The dynamic analysis creates the test profile as described in Section 6.1.1. This includes a performance aspect that requests the SQL query string of each SQL query that is send to the database and the timestamp of each SQL query. This also includes 12 performance aspects that request the entry and exit timestamps of the doGet and doPost methods of the six Servlets of the Media Store application. 45 individual performance aspects are created for all getter and setter methods of the entities to request the entry and exit timestamps. An individual performance aspect requests the entry and exit timestamp of the private AudioDBAdapterBean.getAlbumAudioMap method that contains the Query.getResultList method call referenced as impacted element. Furthermore, 3 performance aspects are created to request the entry and exit timestamps of the entitiy manager's createQuery, createNamedQuery, and getCriteriaBuilder methods. An additional performance aspect is created to request the input parameter name of the createNamedQuery method together with a timestamp. The last performance aspect that is created requests the query hints that are already applied to the query. In total, the test profile contains 64 performance aspects to describe what is to be measured and where in the Media Store application. The single user operational profile of the number of SQL queries aspect in the performance profile is taken over as operational profile for the test profile. The number of users attribute for the closed workload element is already set to 1 user.

The performance profile that describes the monitoring result based on the test profile as template was dominated by observations for the getter and setter methods with 150,922 performance aspects. The observations have been collected within a measurement period of only 5 minutes. This indicates that a manual description of the monitoring results with the performance profile description language as input for Vergil when raw data is requested is inappropriate. Tool support is necessary to create the performance profile from the observations.

The SQL queries are analyzed for each of the 4 executions of the Download.doGet method. The computed histogram for the SQL queries contains a select query for the album table with a frequency of 1, a select query for the users table with a frequency of 500, and a select query for the audio table with a frequency of 503. The frequencies are equal for all 4 execution contexts of the Download.doGet method. Based on the frequencies of the queries and the mappings in the JPA entity classes, the navigation to the relationship "Album.audios.user" is determined by the analysis. The analysis of the observations for the getter and setter methods shows, that only the getter methods of album (all), audio (all except getComments and getAudioBlob), and user (only getLogin) are accessed in the context of the Download.doGet method. Neither a getter nor a setter method of the audio blob or comment entity is accessed in the context of the Download.doGet method. The observed parameter for the name of the named query is "Album.getAll". No observations have been made for query hints because no query hints are applied to the named query.

- *Solution Proposals*: The analysis results are used to apply the batch fetch query hint to the query. The performance profile contains observations for the createNamedQuery method. The monitored name of the named query is "Album.getAll". The analysis of the source code model instance locates the named query in the JPA entity album. The batch fetching end point creates the changes for the addition of query hint BATCH with the value "Album.audios.user" to the named query (see Section 6.1.1). Analog to the batch fetch query hint, the join fetch query hint is added analogously as query hint annotation to the named query annotation. The change plan contains the changes for the addition of the query hint LEFT_JOIN as hint and the navigation to the relationship expression "Album.audios.user" as value (see Section 6.1.1).

  The accessed persistent properties of the JPA entities are used to create the named entity graph that is applied as load graph or fetch graph to the named query. The named entity graph is defined for the root entity album and is also added to the class of the album entity. A subgraph is used for the accessed relationship audios to define the persistent properties of the Audio entity. Another subgraph is used for the user relationship of the audio entity to define the persistent properties of the user entity. The named entity for the root entity defines 4 persistent properties where the named attribute node annotation references the audio subgraph. The subgraph for the audio entity defines 8 persistent properties where the named attribute node annotation for the persistent property user references the user subgraph and the subgraph for the user entity defines only the persistent property login (see Section 6.1.1).

- *Implementation*: We implemented the proposed changes to evaluate the performance. During the implementation and preliminary testing we recognized, that applying the fetch graph query hint to the named query through the query hint annotation causes an exception when the getResultList method is executed. Applying the same entity graph as load graph causes no exception. We solved this issue by applying the fetch graph query hint to the query object where getResultList method is applied in order to evaluate the performance.

#### 7.3.9.3. Mapping Configuration Change Hypothesis

The mapping configuration change hypothesis tests the applicability of adding the batch fetching or join fetching annotation to the relationship mapping. The test result of the mapping configuration change hypothesis is the creation of two change plans. One change plan for adding the batch fetching annotation to the album.audios and audio.user persistent properties and another change plan describing the same changes for adding the join fetch annotation to both persistent properties.

- *Analysis Results*: Analog to the query hints change hypothesis results, the relevant pattern in the performance profile describing the N+1 Selects problem is matched. The monitoring data has to be obtained only once and are reused in the case of the mapping configuration change hypothesis. The implemented JPA entities album and audio neither have batch fetch nor join fetch annotations applied to audios persistent property of the album entity or user persistent property of the audio entity. Consequently, the annotation cannot be updated. The annotations have to be added to the mappings.
- *Solution Proposal*: The determined navigation expression "Album.audios.user" is used to locate the relationship mappings where the batch fetch annotation or join fetch annotation is to be added. In both cases, beginning in the root entity album, the changes are created for adding the annotation to the persistent property audios of the album entity which is the relationship from the album entity to the audio entity (see Section 7.3.2.2). This already deals with the "Album.audios" part of the navigation to the relationship expression. The type audio of the persistent property audios is used to deal with the "audios.user" part of the navigation to the relationship expression. The static analyses of the end points go to the JPA entity audio in the source code model instance to locate the persistent property user and to create the changes for adding the annotation to the persistent property (see Section 6.1.2.
- *Implementation*: We implemented the changes with IN as the batch fetch type for the batch fetch annotation and OUTER as the join fetch type for the join fetch annotation. The performance evaluation results are described in Section 7.3.9.6.

#### 7.3.9.4. Shared Cache Change Hypothesis

The shared cache change hypothesis tests the applicability of selective caching and creates the change plan to enable selective caching for the album, audio, and user JPA entity.

- *Analysis Results*: Like in the case of the query hint and mapping configuration change hypothesis, the static analysis matches the number of SQL queries parameter in the performance aspect describing the SQL queries problem. The created test profile requests the same data as in the case of the mapping configuration change hypothesis and contains the same number of 58 performance aspects where the majority of the aspects is necessary to request the entry and exit timestamps of the getter and setter methods contained in the JPA entity classes. We used the same observations as in the case of the query hint and mapping configuration change hypothesis. This is possible because only a subset of the data is requested compared to the query hint change hypothesis. The analysis results of the persistence unit cache show that neither the persistence unit cache is enabled nor the selective caching of JPA entities. The eclipselink.cache.shared.default property in the persistence configuration model instance is set to false.

- *Solution Proposal*: The determined JPA entities through the accessed persistent properties are album, audio, and user. For each of the three JPA entities, an update persistence unit change referencing a add property change is created. The value of the name attribute of the add property change is set to eclipselink.cache.shared.Album for the album entity (analog for the audio and user entity). The value attribute is set to true to enable selective caching of the entity in the persistence unit cache (see Section 6.1.3).

- *Implementation*: To evaluate the performance, we implemented the proposed changes in the persistence.xml file. A benefit of applying changes to the persistence configuration is that the application does not have to be re-compiled and deployed since no changes are applied to the source code. Only a restart of the application is necessary that the properties become effective. When an application contains a mechanism to change the properties at runtime, even a restart is not necessary, e.g., by periodically checking the persistence configuration.

#### 7.3.9.5. Pagination Change Hypothesis

The pagination change hypothesis tests the applicability of introducing pagination of the query result set. The resulting change plan contains the changes to apply pagination and the batch fetching query hint to the query.

- *Analysis Results*: In addition to the static and dynamic analysis to determine the navigation to the relationship expressions, the pagination change hypothesis also defines a test with a user interaction to prompt the user of Vergil. We answer the question whether all album entity instances that are read from the database are passed to the user interface with 'yes'. The getAlbumAudioMap method of the class AudioDBAdapter returns the read entity instance as map with the AlbumInfo object as key and the collection of AudioInfo objects for the particular album instance as value. The AlbumInfo and AudioInfo objects contain the data of the album, audio, and user entity instances that are read from the database. The monitored execution of the getter methods is the access of the JPA entity persistent properties to create the AlbumInfo and AudioInfo objects. The resulting map of key value pairs is returned from the AudioDBAdapter.getAlbumAudioMap method and passed through to the Download.doGet method where the map is forwarded to the Java Server Page to display all albums and their audios.
- *Solution Proposal*: The end point uses the determined navigation to the relationship expression "Album.audios.user" to create the changes for the addition of the batch fetch query hint to the named query "Album.getAll" (analog to the description in Section 7.3.9.2). The named query name has been observed as query name when the createNamedQuery method was called. The location of the named query annotation is determined through the observed query name and the name attribute of the named query annotation. The end point uses the referenced getResultList method call in the performance profile describing the N+1 Selects problem to determine the Query object element in the source code model to create the add method call changes for the setFirstResult and setMaxResults method calls. Both method calls are applied by updating the next relationship of the query object element in the source code model instance with an update identifier reference change with the add method call change for the setFirstResult method as next reference

that has the add method call change for the setMaxResults method as next reference that as the original method call element as next reference. The update parametrizable change referencing two add ordinary parameter changes is created to add the parameter objectsPerPage and the parameter pageNumber, both of type int, to the empty method parameter list of the getAlbumAudioMap method. The end point also creates the update concrete classifier change and others for adding the method getPageCount to the AudioDBAdapter class that contains the surrounding method getAlbumAudioMap of the method call element in the source code model instance. The class is determined with the static analysis through the container relationship of the relevant source code model elements (see Section 6.1.4).

- *Change Plan and Change Propagation*: The generated change plan only contains the initial set of changes compared to the other change plans that already describe all necessary changes. The changes of the extended parameter list of the getAlbumAudioMap method impact the IAudioDBAdapter interface. Since the IAudioDBAdapter interface is a required interface of the MediaStoreBean component, the changes propagate to the getAlbumAudioMap method of the IMediaStoreBean interface. The changes propagate then to the IWebGUIBean interface where changes propagate to the Download.doGet method. The changes also impact the Java Server Page 'download.jsp'. The current scope of Vergil ends at the Servlet scope. Consequently, the Java Server Page is out of the current scope of Vergil. The changes that have propagated to the interfaces also propagate to the implementing classes. The changes also propagate to the method calls of the impacted interface methods. We propagated the impact manually. For each method element in the source code model instance that is impacted from the changes applied to the parameters of the getAlbumAudioMap class method element, an update parametrizable change and two add ordinary parameter changes and add int changes are created to add the parameters also to the parameters of the impacted method element. An update concrete classifier change referencing an add class method or add interface method change with relevant add ordinary parameter changes and add int changes are created to add the method to the impacted classifier.
- *Implementation*: We partially implemented the changes to evaluate the performance. We applied the batch fetch query hint and the set-

FirstResult method and setMaxResults method to the query. We also implemented the getPageCount method to calculate the number of pages for a given number of objects per page. We omitted the implementation of the changes for the addition of the objectsPerPage and pageNumber parameters that propagate through the Media Store implementation and used prototyping instead. We used 25 objects per page and called the getPageCount method from the getAlbumAudioMap with 25 as value for the objectsPerPage parameter. From the returned result, a randomly selected page number multiplied by 25 is provided as parameter for the setFirstResult method. The parameter value for the setMaxResults method is given by 25. The design decision on how changes can only partly be implemented to evaluate their effect without sacrificing confidence is the task of the developer. Prototyping recommendations can also be provided by Vergil and is considered as future work.

#### 7.3.9.6. Performance Evaluation

The performance evaluation assesses the response time impact of the solution proposals with respect to the response time criteria of the decision criteria hierarchy that defines the response time of five Servlet methods (see Section 7.3.7).

**Performance Test** We used the multiple user operational profile with 200 simulated users that was specified in the performance profile for the response time performance aspect (see Section 7.3.9 and Section 7.3.3). Figure 7.24 gives an overview on the raw response time observations for the relevant Servlet methods in the form of boxplots. The diagrams are arranged in a grid with three columns and two rows where an individual diagram shows the observations for a particular Servlet method. The first row shows the response time observations for Download.doGet, Download.doPost, and Login.doPost method. The second row shows the observations for the Logout.doGet, SearchAlbum.doPost, and Upload.doPost method. The associated Servlet method is given by the label above each diagram. The scales are free throughout the diagrams. The 90% percentile values for each case are summarized in Table 7.8 together with the mean values that are enclosed in square brackets computed from the raw measurement data.

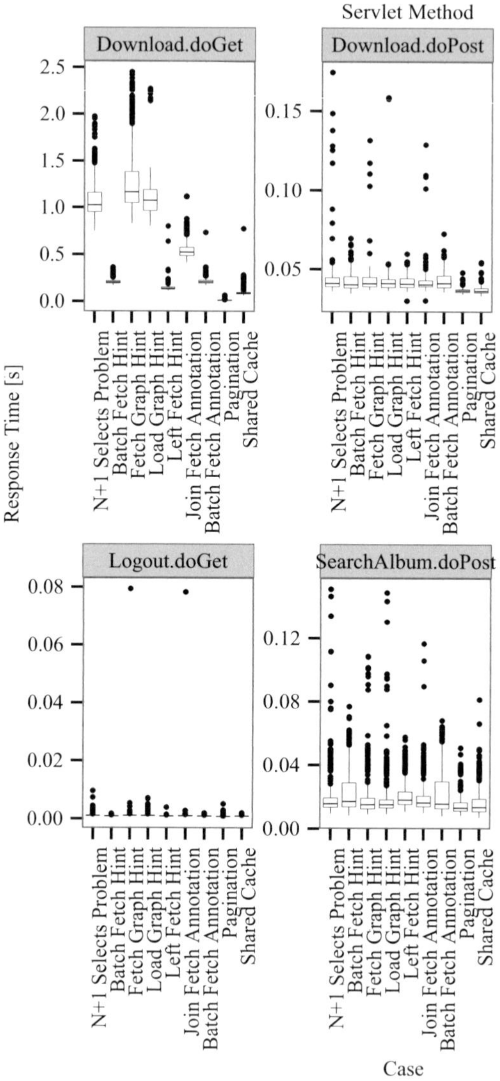


**Figure 7.24.:** Response time of the N+1 Selects solution proposals

**Significant Effects** Table 7.8 as well as Figure 7.24 show significant differences in the response time for the observations of the N+1 Selects Problem compared to the solution cases for the Download.doGet method. We validated the differences through the application of the Welch's t-test. We applied the central limit theorem and applied the Shapiro-Wilk test to each case to test for normal distribution with a significance level of 0.05. The Shapiro-Wilk test did not reject the null hypothesis that the population for each case is normal distributed. We checked the rest of the results with quantile-quantile plots. In pairwise comparisons between the N+1 Selects problem case with the solution proposals, we tested the null hypothesis that the mean values of the populations are equal with a significance level of 0.05. In all pairwise comparisons, the test rejected the null hypothesis. We analyzed the statistically significant differences in the mean values. The comparison of the mean values of the fetch graph query hint and the load graph query hint with mean value of the N+1 Selects problem shows a performance degradation. About 0.183 seconds in the case of the fetch graph query hint and about 0.016 seconds in the case of the load graph query hint. The mean values of the other solution proposals show a significant performance improvement. The performance improvement for the pagination solution is 1.065 seconds, for the shared cache 0.986 seconds, for the left fetch query hint 0.935 seconds, for the batch fetch query hint 0.869 seconds, for the batch fetch mapping annotation 0.867 seconds, and for the join fetch mapping annotation 0.536 seconds. We applied Welch's t-test with a significance level of 0.05 also to test the observations of the batch fetch query hint and the batch fetch mapping annotation for statistically significant difference. The result of the Welch's t-test showed that there is no statistically significant difference.

**Significant Side Effects** A negative side effect refers to the case where the application of a solution proposal leads to a performance degradation of a Servlet method that is not impacted by the N+1 Selects problem. A positive side effect refers to the case where the response time of the Download.doPost, Login.doPost, Logout.doGet, SearchAlbum.doPost or Upload.doPost response time increases in the case of an applied solution compared to the case with the N+1 Selects problem. The mean values show deviations of only a few milliseconds. In the case of the pagination solution proposal, the mean value of the response time for the Download.doPost method improves by about 12 milliseconds. However, such small differences in the response time can still be caused by the stochastic nature of performance measurements (Liu, 2009) and may not be an effect of the changes. When such small differences are important, additional repetitions of the measurements for the N+1 Selects problem and the pagination solution can be conducted and the mean values across the measurement series can be compared. When the statistically significant difference between the N+1 Selection problem measurements and the pagination solution measurements persist, and there are no statistically significant differences in between the measurement series of each case then an effect of the changes can be concluded. Nevertheless, the test results of the Welch's t-test show statistically significant differences. The practical relevance of such small differences is questionable due to the stochastic nature of performance measurements and has to be considered in decision making.

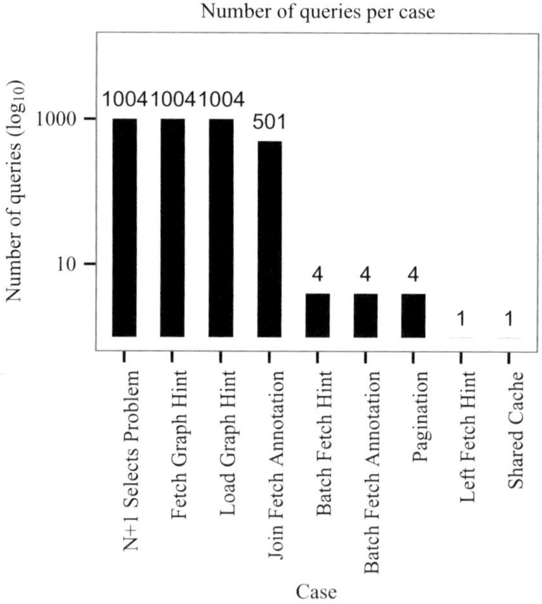


**Figure 7.25.:** Number of queries per case

**N+1 Selects Resolution** Figure 7.25 shows the impact on the number of SQL queries in each case in the context of the Download.doGet method. The fetch graph hint and the load graph hint have no impact on the number of SQL queries. The SQL queries in the case of the load graph hint are identical with the SQL queries in the N+1 Selects problem case. In the case of fetch graph hint, the queries are also identical with the queries of the N+1 Selects problem except the query that reads the instances of the user entity. This query only reads the persistent property login of the entity. The join fetch annotation reduces the number of queries to 501. A single join query reads the instances of the album entity and the audio entity, and 500 queries read the user entity instances. This indicates that the persistence provider may not take the join fetch annotation for the nested relationship between audio and user into consideration when the database query is composed.

The batch fetch hint and the batch fetch annotation have identical results. In total, four queries are used in each case to read the entity instances from the database. One query reads the instances of the album entity, another query reads the instances of the user entity, and two queries read the instances of the audio entity in batches.

In the case of pagination with 25 objects per page, four queries are also used to read the data. One query counts the number of instances in the database of the album entity. Another query reads up to 25 instances of the album entity that correspond to the specified page number. One query reads the instances of the audio entity by the album entity instances, and another query reads the instances of the user entity referenced by the audio entity instances.

Only a single query is sent to the database in the cases of the left fetch hint and the shared cache. The left fetch hint reads the instances of the entities album, audio, and user in a single query. In the shared cache case, the persistence provider only reads the instances of the album entity from the database.

#### 7.3.9.7. Solution Ranking

In the following, we assess the constraint compliance of the solution proposals, prioritize the solution proposals with respect to the decision criteria to complete the AHP, and rank the solutions according to their total priority. We conclude the section with the description of the solution validation results.

**Constraint Compliance** The constrains model (see Section 7.3.8) defines the constraints and preferences for changing particular elements of the Media Store application. The pagination solution conflicts with the constraints for the Media Store interfaces for adding new methods to an existing interface and for adding new method parameters to a method. In total, the pagination solution impacts three interfaces, i.e., IAudioDBAdapterBean, IMediaStoreBean, and IWebGUIBean. The shared cache solution supports the expressed willingness to change the persistence configuration by adding appropriate properties. The query hint solution proposals and the mapping configuration solution proposals do not conflict with any defined constraint.

**Solution Prioritization** We continue the AHP and prioritize the solution alternatives with respect to the eight leaf decision criteria of the decision criteria hierarchy (see Section 7.3.7). We prioritized the solution proposals with respect to each criterion in pairwise comparisons. In total, we performed $8 * \frac{8*(8-1)}{2} = 224$ comparisons to determine the local priorities for each solution proposal with respect to each criterion. The CR for the pairwise comparisons is below ten percent for each set of pairwise comparisons with 9.1% at maximum. We used a equal priority in all pairwise comparisons with respect to the response time decision criteria Login.doPost, Download.doPost, SearchAlbum.doPost, Upload.doPost based on the performance evaluation results that show no significant impact.

**Solution Recommendation** The pagination solution proposal is ranked at the top and dominates the ranking by more than factor two with respect to the global priority of the shared cache solution proposal. Interesting is the higher ranking of fetch graph query hint (ranked fifth) and the load graph query hint (ranked sixth) compared to the batch fetch annotation configuration (ranked seventh) and the join fetch mapping configuration (ranked eighth). The join fetch mapping configuration and the batch fetch mapping configuration have an equal or higher priority for all criteria except for sustainability. For sustainability, the fetch graph query hint and the load graph query hint achieve a priority that is almost factor four higher than the priority of the mapping configuration solution proposals. The sustainability criterion has the highest priority among the leaf criteria in the hierarchy. This is the explanation why the fetch graph query hint and the load graph query hint are not ranked last.

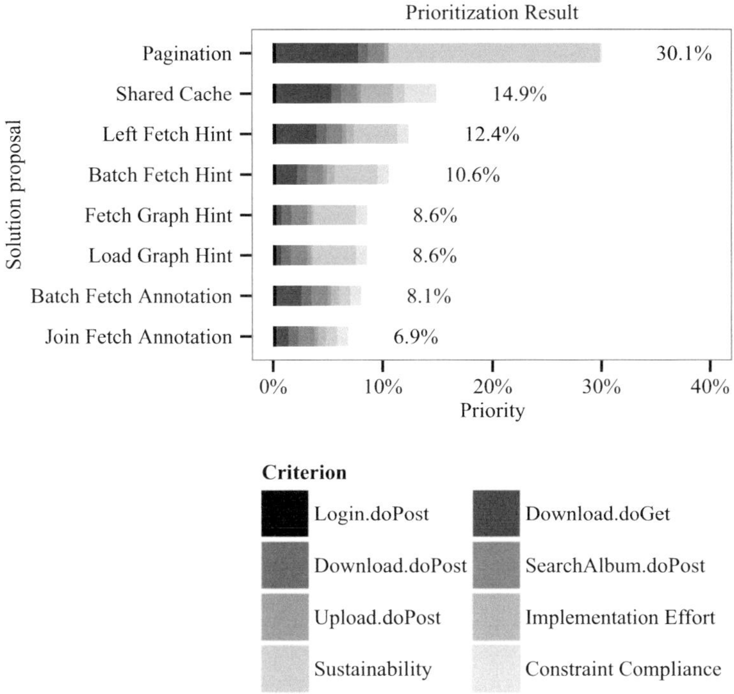


**Figure 7.26.:** Prioritization results visualization as stacked bars

**Ranking Visualization** Figure 7.26 and Figure 7.27 show the visualization of the prioritization results for the solution proposals as solution recommendation for the developer as described in Section 5.8 in the form of bar charts for each of the criterion and in the form of a stacked bar charts. In both charts, the global priorities are used as priority. In Figure 7.26, the developer can draw a conclusion on which solution proposal contributes most to the goal of solving the N+1 Selects problem. Figure 7.27, on the other hand, shows how much an individual solution proposal contributes to a particular criterion. For example, the pagination solution proposal contributes most to the overall goal. This

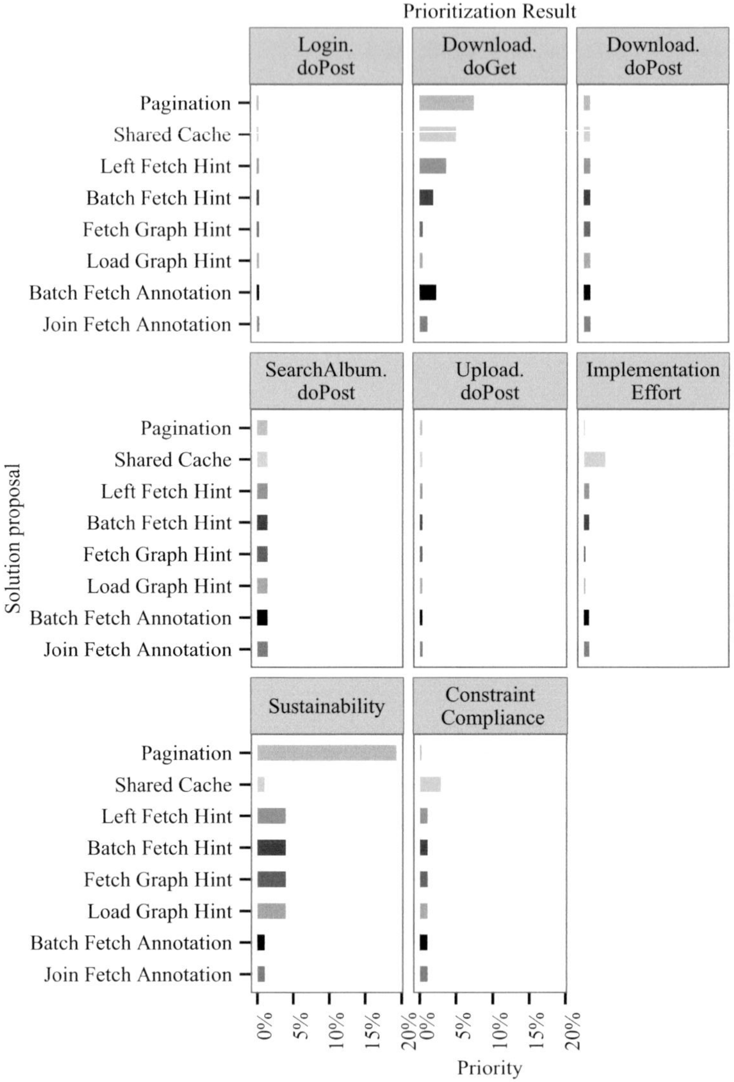


**Figure 7.27.:** Prioritization results visualization per criterion

solution proposal achieves also the highest response time improvement for the Download.doGet method and dominates the other solution proposals with respect to sustainability. The drawbacks of the pagination solution proposal are also visible. The implementation effort is the highest and it is the least constraint compliant solution which is given by the lowest priority in both cases.

**Solution Validation** We follow the recommendation and select the pagination solution proposal as the solution that is to be implemented. We evaluated the implemented pagination solution with a performance test. We applied the multiple user operation profile with 200 users and a duration of 1 hour. We modified the operational profile that the users also select another page. The 90% percentile of the doGet method of the download Servlet is 0.016 seconds.

### 7.3.10. Excessive Logging Results

The excessive logging problem affects the CPU utilization and the response time of the Media Store application's view all albums functionality. This section describes the excessive logging problem as input for Vergil, the static analysis results of the persistence configuration, the proposed changes, and the performance evaluation results. We test only one change hypothesis in the context of the excessive logging problem creating a single solution proposal. Consequently, we will only assess the constraint compliance of the solution proposal and omit the solution ranking.

- *Performance Profile*: The performance profile describing the problem as input for Vergil describes the response time of the Download.doGet method analog to Section 7.3.9. The 90% percentile response time value of the Download.doGet method specified by the numeric literal is replaced with the value of 2.339 seconds. Figure 7.28 shows the raw response time observations in the form of a boxplots. For the excessive logging problem, a slightly different closed workload was applied. The operational profile used a closed workload with 100 simulated users and duration of 600 seconds. The users attribute and the duration attribute of the closed workload element have the appropriate values.

The CPU utilization performance aspect has no impacted element. The observation describes the mean value of the CPU utilization of 0.451 that corresponds to 45.1%. The dimension is a numeric dimension with valid values $x : 0 \leq x \leq 1$ (see Section 4.1.2.1).

- *Analysis Results*: The analysis recognizes three relevant properties in the persistence configuration model instance. The value of the logging level property is set to the logging level SEVERE that provides less details than the INFO logging level. The value of the logging level property for SQL statements is set to the logging level FINEST and the value of the logging of parameters property is set to true. The configured logging level SEVERE does not violate the logging level recommendation for production. The logging level property for SQL statements and the logging of parameters property cause the logging of the SQL queries and the bound parameters. The number of log entries is supported by the presence of the N+1 Selects problem. However, the performance evaluation results show that the logging has a significant impact on the response time of the Download.doGet method.
- *Change Plan*: The change plan contains two update property changes. One update property change element for the logging level property for SQL statements and another one for the logging of parameters property. The update property changes propose to set the value of the logging level property for SQL statements to OFF and the value of the logging of parameters property to false. The update property changes reference the corresponding property elements in the persistence configuration model instance. The change plan is similar to the example in Section 6.2.
- *Constraint Compliance*: The update property changes in the change plan support the specified positive preference to change the persistence configuration. There are no conflicts with other defined constraints.

#### 7.3.10.1. Performance Evaluation

We implemented the proposed changes by updating the property values as suggested. We applied the multiple user operational profile with 100 users and a duration of 600 seconds as described by the performance profile. Table 7.9 summarizes the raw observations in the form of 90% percentile values

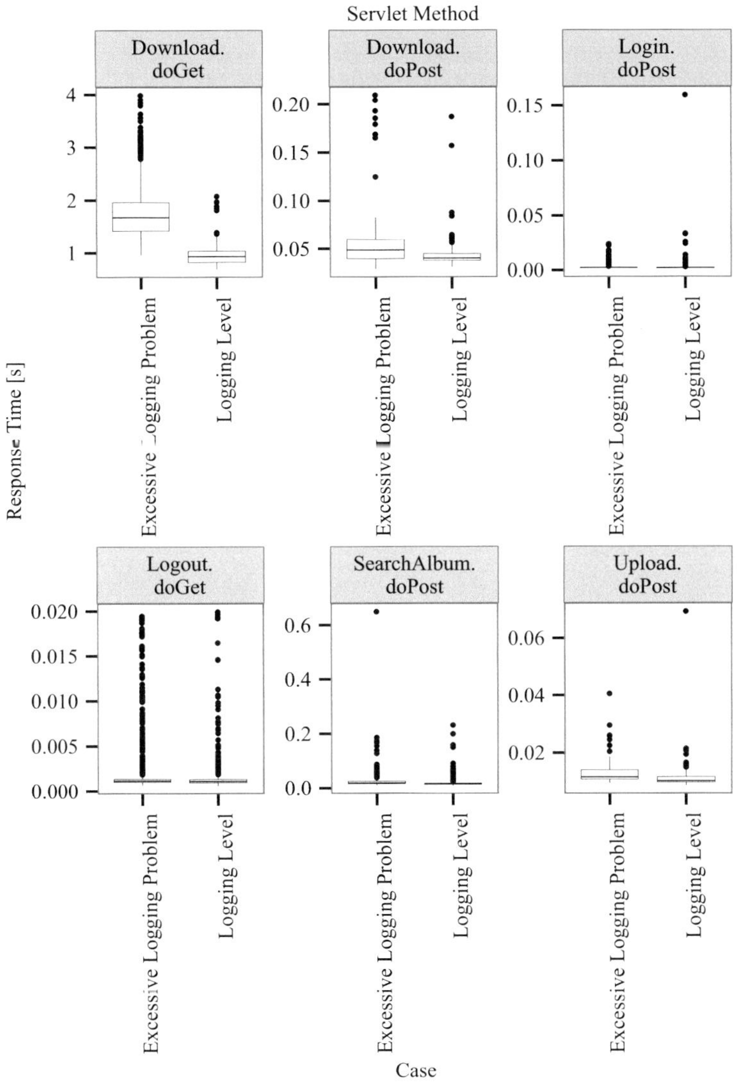


**Figure 7.28.:** Response time with the excessive logging problem

and mean values that are enclosed in square brackets. Figure 7.28 gives an overview on the raw response time observations in the form of boxplots for each case. The diagrams are arranged in two rows and three columns. The first row includes the diagrams for the Download.doGet, Download.doPost, and Login.doPost method. The second row includes the Logout.doGet, SearchAlbum.doPost, and Upload.doPost method. Figure 7.29 shows the raw CPU utilization measurements in the form of a boxplot. The analysis results of the observations and the identified significant differences are described in the following.

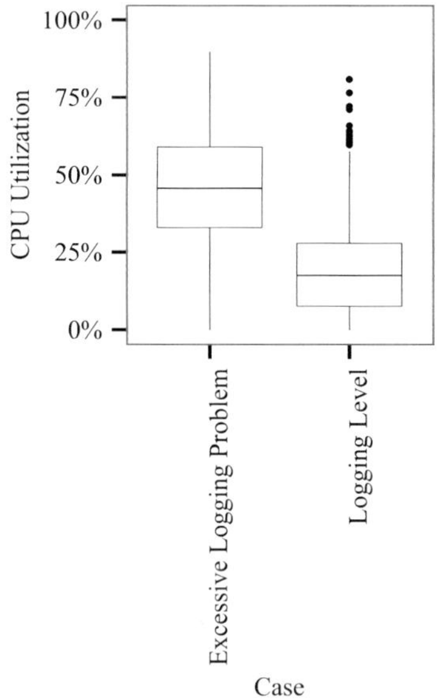


**Figure 7.29.:** CPU utilization with the excessive logging problem

**Significant Effects** The results show that the mean value of the CPU utilization is reduced by about 59.0% from 45.1% to 18.5%. The 90% percentile value improves by about 59.5% from 2.339 seconds to 0.948 seconds. The test result of Welch's t-test for a significance level of 0.05 supports the observation and shows a statistically significant difference between the mean value of each case for the Download.doGet method. The same applies to the CPU utilization. The test result of Welch's t-test also shows a statistically significant difference between the mean value of each case. For the response time observations of the Download.doGet method and the CPU utilization in both cases, we applied the central limit theorem and the Shapiro-Wilk test to test for normal distribution with a significance level of 0.05 before applying Welch's t-test.

**Significant Side Effects** We have not been able to identify significant side effects where the logging level configuration changes cause a performance degradation. The mean response time values of the other Servlet methods show only a small variation of up to 12 milliseconds. This is similar to the variations observed in the results of the N+1 Selects problem. We consider that the deviations are caused by measurement noise and the stochastic nature of measurements in the case of the Download.doPost, Login.doPost, Logout.doGet, SearchAlbum.doPost, and Upload.doPost.

## 7.3.11. Excessive Data Allocation Results

The excessive data allocation problem significantly impacts the response time of the doGet method of the download Servlet and causes a mean response time of 7.625 seconds (see Table 7.6). The memory footprint of the AudioDBAdapter.getAlbumAudioMap method with 75.5 MB on average is also significant. This section describes the problem description with the performance profile description language, the tests of the change hypotheses, the performance evaluation results of the proposed changes and the completion of the AHP to rank the solution proposals. The results show that the proposed changes improve the mean response time by up to 98.3% and reduce the mean memory footprint by up to 88.9%.

### 7.3.11.1. Performance Profile

The performance profile contains a description of the response time and the memory footprint. The 90% percentile value of response time for the

Download.doGet method is described analog to the description given in Section 7.3.9. The value of the numeric literal that specifies the parameter value for the 90% percentile is set to 7.625. Figure 7.30 gives an overview on the raw response time observations in the form of a boxplot. The memory footprint aspect specifies the mean value of the difference between the memory usage when the control flow enters the AudioDBAdapter.getAlbumAudioMap and when the control flow leaves the method at the end. The referenced dimension is a numeric dimension with valid real values $x : 0 \leq x$, and a relation semantic of lower is better. The memory footprint aspect references the AudioDBAdapter.getAlbumAudioMap class method element in the source code model instance as impacted element. The number of users and the duration of the closed workload are different. In the case of the excessive data allocation problem, 50 simulated users are used and a duration of 900 seconds. The values of the users attribute and the duration attribute of the closed workload element are set accordingly. The response time aspect references the multiple user operational profile. The memory footprint aspect references the single user operational profile.

#### 7.3.11.2. Query Hint Change Hypothesis

The query hint change hypothesis for the excessive data allocation problem tests the applicability of the change hypothesis and creates a change plan to a apply a fetch graph query hint to the query to specify which persistent properties are to be loaded eagerly and which persistent properties are to be loaded when first accessed.

- *Analysis Results*: The static analysis matches the pattern of the memory footprint aspect in the performance profile given as input with AudioDBAdapter.getAlbumAudioMap as impacted class method and the memory footprint dimension as parameter dimension. The dynamic analysis creates the test profile to request the required data. This test profile requests entry and exit timestamps of the doGet and doPost methods of the Servlets download, login, logout, register, search album, and upload as well as of the AudioDBAdapter.getAlbumAudioMap method. Therefore, 13 performance aspects are created. The entry and exit timestamps of the createQuery, createNamedQuery, getCriteriaBuilder, and the find method of the entity manager as well as the getResultList and getSingleResult method of the Query interface are requested too. Therefore, 6 performance aspects are created. An individual performance aspect requests the value of the method parameter name in the case of the createNamedQuery method together with a timestamp. Another individual aspect requests the applied query hints. In the case of the find, getResultList, and getSingleResult method the stack trace when the method is executed is requested. The test profile contains 45 performance aspects requesting the entry and exit timestamps for the methods contained in the JPA entity classes. The test profile specifies to apply the single user operational profile to obtain the requested data with the value of the user attribute set to one.

The collected information show that the AudioDBAdapter.getAlbum AudioMap method call is located in the context of the Download.doGet method. The accessed persistent properties in this context are all persistent properties of the album entity, all except the comments and the persistent property audio blob of the audio entity, and the persistent property login of the user entity. The query object is located through the method call of the getResultList method that is located in the AudioDBAdapter.getAlbumAudioMap method.

- *Solution Proposal*: The 13 accessed persistent properties are used to create the named entity graph for the album entity including two individual subgraphs: one subgraph for the persistent properties of the audio entity and another subgraph for the persistent properties of the user entity. The named entity graph is added to the class of the JPA entity album. The named entity graph is applied to the query object as fetch graph through the setHint method.
- *Change Plan*: The essential changes created in the change plan describe the creation of the named entity graph and the application of the setHint method to the query object. For example, an update concrete classifier change referencing an add annotation instance change is created to add the named entity graph annotation to the class album.

#### 7.3.11.3. Mapping Configuration Change Hypothesis

The mapping configuration change hypothesis for the excessive data allocation problem tests the applicability of the change hypothesis and creates a change plan to apply lazy fetching to relationship mappings that are not accessed and configured for eager fetching.

- *Analysis Results*: The static analysis matches the memory footprint aspect containing the parameter that has the memory footprint dimension as parameter dimension analog to the description given in Section 7.3.11.2. The created test profile requests the entry and exit timestamps of the doGet and doPost methods of the 6 Servlets, the getAlbumAudioMap method of the AudioDBAdapter class, and the getter and setter methods contained in the JPA entities. Therefore, 58 performance aspects are created to describe the required data. The test profile specifies the single user operational profile with a single user for the closed workload. We used the same observations to create the performance profile that is given back to Vergil as in Section 7.3.11.2. The domination of the performance profile by performance aspects describing the entry and exit timestamps of the getter and setter methods of JPA entities persists. The analysis results are comparable. The AudioDBAdapterBean.getAbumAudioMap method call is located in the context of the Download.doGet method. The entry and exit timestamps of the Download.doGet method are used to isolate the accessed persistent properties. As described in the previous section, in the context of the Download.doGet method, 13 persistent properties are accessed in total distributed across the album, audio and user entities.
- *Solution Proposal*: The 13 accessed persistent properties are investigated in the source code model instance with the static analysis to locate the relationships where lazy fetching is to be applied. The persistent property audio blob in the audio entity is isolated as one-to-one relationship mapping that is eagerly fetched and not accessed in the context of the doGet method of the download Servlet.
- *Change Plan*: The fetch attribute of the one-to-one mapping annotation is set to the eager fetch type explicitly. The change plan contains an update identifier reference change referencing the enum constant LAZY of the fetch type enumeration as target.

#### 7.3.11.4. Shared Cache

The shared cache change hypothesis in the context of the excessive data allocation problem test the applicability of the change hypothesis and creates a change plan for the persistence configuration for the selective caching of the album, audio, and user entity.

- *Analysis Results*: Like in the case of the query hint and mapping configuration change hypothesis, the static analysis matches the memory footprint dimension referenced by a parameter in the performance aspect describing the memory footprint problem. The created test profile requests the same data as in the case of the mapping configuration change hypothesis and contains the same number of 58 performance aspects where the majority of the aspects is necessary to request the entry and exit timestamps of the methods contained in the JPA entity classes. We used the same observations as in the case of the query hint and mapping configuration change hypothesis. This is possible because only a subset of the data is requested compared to the query hint change hypothesis. The static analysis of the persistence configuration model instance shows that the persistence unit cache is disabled explicitly by the eclipselink.cache.shared.default property set to false. The persistence configuration model instance contains no properties for the album, audio, and user entity that explicitly enable or disable selective caching. The same applies to the classes of the JPA entities that do not contain cache annotation.
- *Solution Proposal* Vergil: uses the 13 accessed persistent properties to determine the album, audio, and user entity that are to be cached in the persistence unit cache. The EclipseLink shared cache properties for the album, audio, and user entities with the property value set to true are added to the persistence configuration to enable selective caching.
- *Change Plan*: The change plan contains an update persistence unit change referencing three add property changes with the corresponding property name for each of the three entities and the value set to true.

#### 7.3.11.5. Performance Evaluation

We assess the response time impact of the solution proposals with respect to the defined response time criteria in the decision criteria hierarchy. The response time criteria are given by the leaf criteria of the five Servlet methods (see Section 7.3.7). We also collect the data to answer the questions of the GQM plan (see Section 7.3.1).

**Performance Test** We applied the multiple user operational profile with 50 simulated users that was specified in the performance profile for the response time performance aspect to evaluate the performance of the solution proposals. Figure 7.30 gives an overview on the raw response time observations for the excessive data allocation problem, the fetch graph query hint solution proposal, the lazy fetching mapping configuration solution proposal, and the shared cache solution proposal. The raw observations are summarized in the form of boxplots for each individual case. The diagrams for each Servlet method are arranged in a grid with two rows and three columns. The first row includes the Download.doGet, Download.doPost, and Login.doPost method. The second row includes the Logout.doGet, SearchAlbum.doPost, and Upload.doPost method. The scales are free throughout the diagrams. The observations are summarized in Table 7.10 in the form of the 90% percentile values together with the mean values that are enclosed in square brackets.

**Significant Effects** The observations show obvious significant differences between the excessive data allocation problem and the three solution proposals for the Download.doGet Servlet method. The comparison of the mean values for the Download.doGet method show a reduction of the response time by up to 98.3%. The mean values for the same method for the fetch graph query hint case and the lazy fetch type differ by about 43 milliseconds. Figure 7.31 gives an indication for the difference in the form of a boxplot for the memory footprint. The mean value for the memory footprint of the fetch graph query hint is 27.20 MB and for the lazy fetch type 10.66 MB. The larger memory footprint can be the reason for the response time difference. This is supported by the observations of the shared cache case where an even lower memory footprint results in lower response times.

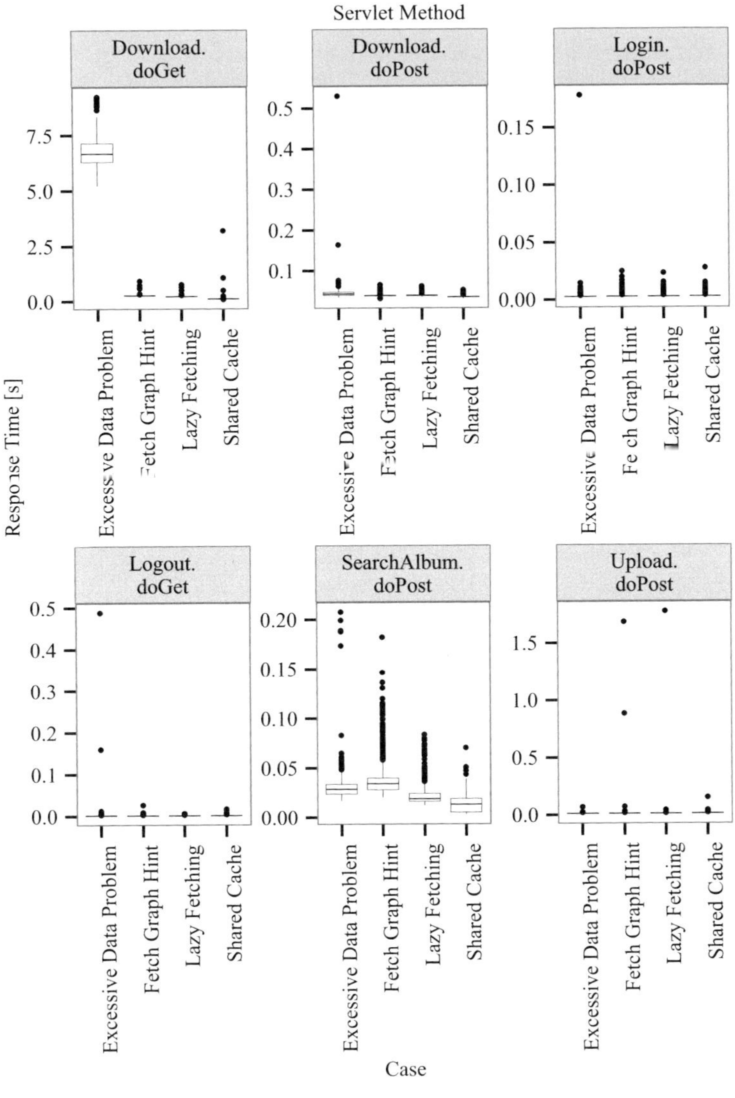


**Figure 7.30.:** Response time with the excessive data allocation problem

**Significant Side Effects** The performance evaluation results show no significant changes for the Login.doPost or the Logout.doGet method when we applied the solution proposals. The Upload.doPost method has higher mean values of up to 20 milliseconds when we applied the solution proposals. The higher mean values show that the response time of the Upload.doPost method experiences a performance degradation after the application of the solution proposals. However, the difference of 20 milliseconds can be caused by measurement noise and the stochastic nature of performance measurements. In the role of the decision maker, we do not consider the difference as a significant performance degradation because from the perspective of a user of the Media Store application, the difference between a mean response time of 0.013 and 0.033 may not be noticeable. This shows the importance of assessing and prioritizing the solution proposals by the decision maker with respect to the decision criteria. Otherwise, thresholds are necessary to automatically decide if a performance degradation is really considered as degradation in the context of a particular application when the significance test shows a statistically significant difference. Such thresholds are often application specific. The mean values for the Download.doPost method and SearchAlbum.doPost method on the other hand are lower after the application of the changes with the mean value for the SearchAlbum.doPost method in the case of the fetch graph query hint as an exception. Liu recommends to be cautious in interpreting performance improvement of degradations due to code changes of less than 10% due to the stochastic nature of performance measurements (Liu, 2009). While the differences exceed the 10% recommendation, they are still in the single digit milliseconds range. Due to this fact, we attribute the changes to measurement noise and the stochastic nature of performance measurements. In situations where such small differences already count, we recommend repetitions of the performance evaluation experiment to analyse whether the differences persist across several repetitions.

**Excessive data allocation Resolution** All solution proposals reduce the memory footprint of the AudioDBAdapterBean.getAlbumAudioMap by at least about 64% from 75.50 MB on average to 27.20 MB on average in the case of the fetch graph query hint solution proposal. The largest reduction is achieved by the shared cache solution proposal that reduces the memory footprint to 8.35 MB on average. The lazy fetch type solution proposal reduces the mean value of the memory footprint to 10.66 MB.

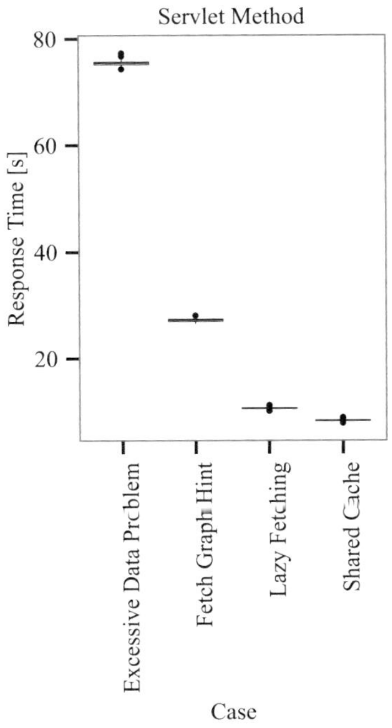


**Figure 7.31.:** Memory footprint

#### 7.3.11.6. Solution Ranking

In the following, we assess the constraint compliance of the solution proposals, and prioritize the solution proposals with respect to the decision criteria to complete the AHP. We use the results to rank the solution proposals according to their total priority. We conclude the section with the description of the solution validation results.

**Constraint Compliance** The lazy fetch type mapping configuration solution proposal conflicts not with any of the defined constraints. The fetch graph query hint solution proposal does also not conflict with any defined constraint in the constraints model. The changes of the shared cache solution proposal are supported by the positive constraints for adding or updating properties of the persistence configuration. This supports the necessary changes of the shared cache solution proposal.

**Solution Prioritization** We prioritized the solution proposals with respect to each decision criteria to complete the AHP. In total, we performed $8 * \frac{3*(3-1)}{2} = 24$ pairwise comparisons. The CR is below ten percent for all groups of pairwise comparisons with 7.4% at maximum. This time, in contrast to the solution prioritization in Section 7.3.9.7, we considered the small performance deviations in the response time observations determined as side effects. This means that the performance degradation is prioritized in pairwise comparisons between solution proposals with respect to the reference in the case of the excessive data allocation problem. For example, in the pairwise comparison between the fetch graph query hint and the shared cache solution proposal with respect to the Upload.doPost criteria, the prioritization is in favor of the fetch graph query hint, even though both have larger 90% percentile response time values compared to the case of the excessive data allocation problem. Consequently, solution proposals with the least performance degradation should obtain the largest priority compared to the others. This is also the case when a solution proposal improves performance whereas other may reduce performance. We prioritized the solution proposals with respect to the implementation effort and sustainability criterion.

**Solution Recommendation** The shared cache solution proposal is ranked first and contributes most to the goal of solving the excessive data allocation problem. The fetch graph query hint is ranked second, and the lazy fetch type mapping configuration is ranked third. The shared cache solution proposal obtains a total priority of 42.9% that is about 1.4 times the priority of fetch graph query hint. The three solution proposals have an equal contribution to the Login.doPost criteria. The shared cache solution proposal contributes most to the Download.doGet, Download.doPost, SearchAlbum.doPost, implementation effort, and constraint compliance criteria. The fetch graph solution proposal contributes most to the sustainability criterion. This reflects the use-case-specific nature of the fetch graph solution proposal in contrast to the shared cache and lazy fetch type mapping configuration solution proposal that affect all use cases.

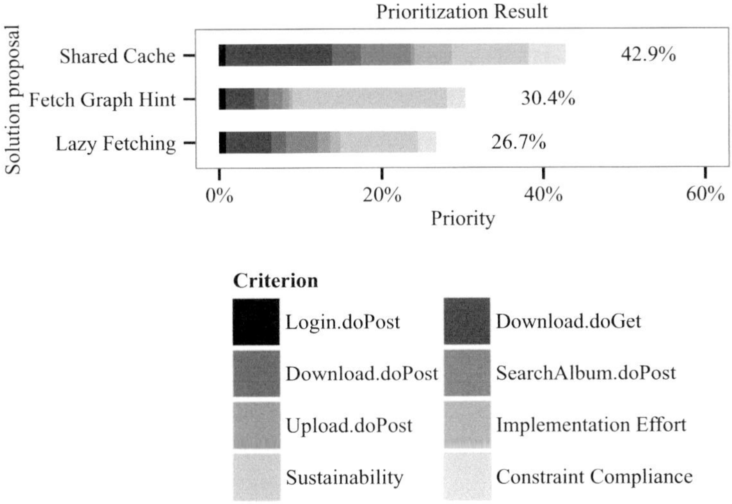


**Figure 7.32.:** Prioritization results visualization as stacked bars

**Ranking Visualization** Figure 7.32 and Figure 7.33 visualizes the prioritization results for the developer in the form of a stacked bar chart and bar charts for each criterion. We used the global priorities of the solution proposals to create the diagrams. The developer can draw a overall conclusion from Figure 7.32 to determine which solution proposal contributes most to the goal and Figure 7.33 allows the developer to have a more detailed look on how much each solution proposal contributes to a specific decision criteria. The developer then selects the solution proposal to be implemented. We follow the recommendation of Vergil and select the shared cache solution proposal.

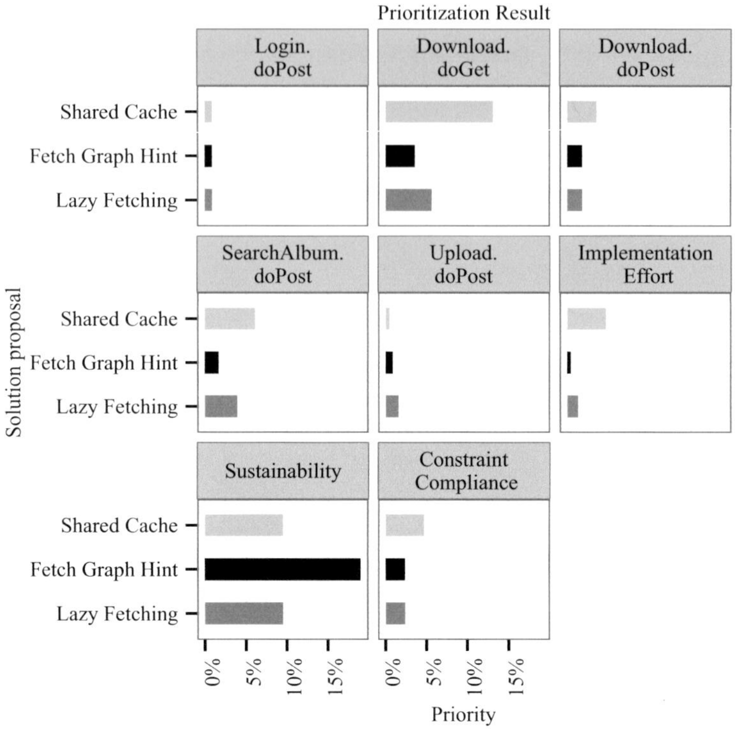


**Figure 7.33.:** Prioritization results visualization per criterion

## 7.3.12. Solution Description

An excerpt of the solution description model for the pagination solution proposal is shown in Figure 7.34. The excerpt describes the Download.doGet response time criteria and the associated global priority. The priority dimension is a numeric dimension with valid values $x : 0 \leq x \leq 1$, and a relation semantic of higher is better. The global priority of the criterion is specified by the associated parameter specification that specifies a value of 0.222 as global priority (see Section 7.3.7). The excerpt also describes the sustainability crite-

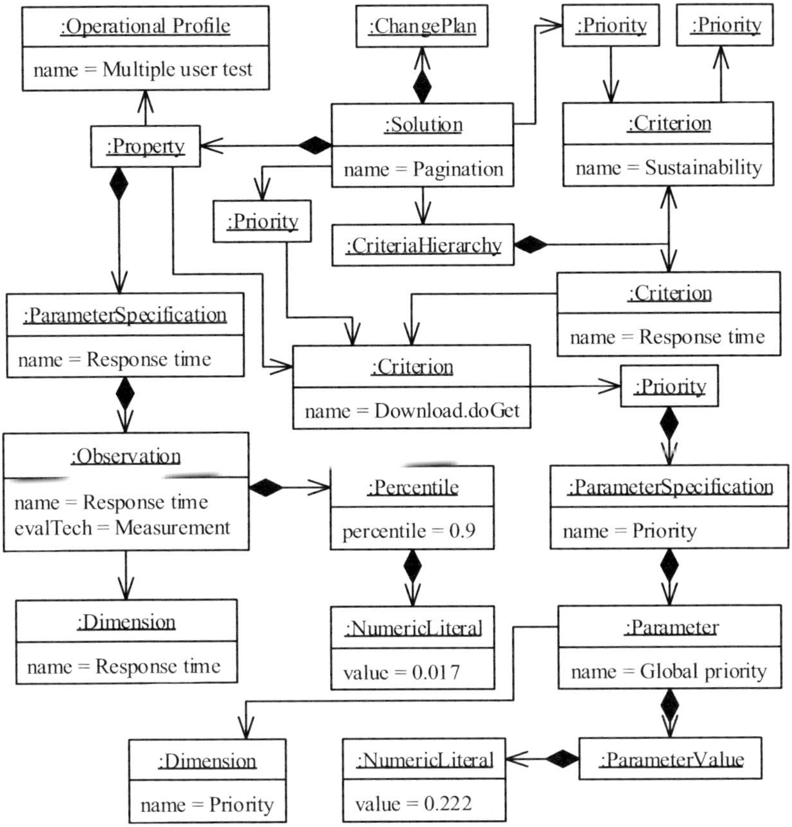


**Figure 7.34.:** Excerpt of the solution description of the pagination solution proposal

rion of the criteria hierarchy. The solution element references the change plan for the pagination solution, and the property specifying the 90% percentile of the response time observations of the Download.doGet method.

### 7.3.13. Threats to Validity

The validity of the case study results are assessed with construct validity, internal validity, external validity, and reliability validity (Runeson et al., 2012). The concern of each threat to validity has already been described in Section 7.2.8.

#### 7.3.13.1. Construct Validity

A potential threat to construct validity is that we measure unintended measures instead of the intended measures. To mitigate this threat, we broke the overall validation goal to validate that Vergil provides the expected output when the inputs were valid down into a GQM plan with refined goals, questions, and metrics. In answering the refined questions and assessing goal attainment, we have been able to draw a conclusion for validating goal attainment. We have also used multiple sources of evidence in the form different problems that can occur when an application uses the Java Persistence API.

#### 7.3.13.2. Internal Validity

A potential threat to internal validity is that we as the developers of Vergil conducted the study and may introduce an experimenter bias due to our knowledge about Vergil. We mitigate this potential threat by using quantitative metrics and providing comprehensive results and justifications for prioritization. This enables to understand the results comprehensibly.

#### 7.3.13.3. External Validity

A potential threat to external validity is the representativeness of the sample application. We are aware that enterprise business applications of much larger size exist and are used in industry. This includes a more complex business logic, and more complex JPA entities. However, we argue that the Media Store application can be considered as representative for the purpose of a proof of concept validation conducted in this study. Small sample applications have already been used by other researchers in case studies, e.g., (H. Koziolek,

2008; van Hoorn, 2014b). Applying Vergil to industry-size application may require more sophisticated change hypotheses especially with respect to the conducted tests. The activities that are performed to guide the developer from testing the change hypotheses to solution prioritization remain the same. The defined change hypotheses for the case study may need to be refined for industrial applications, but they depend only on the JPA implementation and not on a particular application. Another threat to external validity is the representativeness of the injected problems. The injected problems are reported cases from industry and also well known in academic research. For this reason, we argue that the problems can be considered as representative as we followed practitioner reports. The selected operational profile and workload may also be perceived as a potential threat to external validity. However, both are given as input to Vergil where they are then used as reference. Despite the potential threats to external validity, we consider the results that Vergil provides the expected output when the inputs were valid to be generalizable.

### 7.3.14. Summary

This section summarizes the case study results and draws a conclusion on goal attainment.

- *N+1 Selects Problem*: The fetch graph query hint and the load graph query hint did neither reduce the number of SQL queries that are sent to the database from the persistence provider nor did they improve the 90% percentile response time value of the Download.doGet method. In contrast, the batch fetch query hint and the left fetch query hint achieve a significant performance improvement of the Download.doGet method. They also significantly reduce the number of SQL queries that are necessary to read the entities' objects from the database. A significant performance degradation of the other Servlet methods does not take place.

  The batch fetch mapping annotation and the join fetch mapping annotation reduce the 90% percentile value of the response time for the Download.doGet method significantly. Comparing both against each other, the batch fetch mapping annotation achieves better results. This is due to the still significant number of SQL queries that are used to the objects of the User entity from the database. The join fetch mapping annotation has no effect for the nested relationship. When the number of objects for the Audio entity increases, the number of queries increases too. For the reason of the incomplete resolution of the problem, we take a pessimistic position and consider the problem as not solved in the case of the join fetch mapping annotation. We have not identified a significant performance degradation.

The activation of selective caching in the persistence unit cache achieved the second-best performance improvement without causing a performance degradation. The number of SQL queries is reduced to one.

The introduction of pagination results in the most significant performance improvement in the context of the N+1 Selects problem. The number of SQL queries is also reduced not only due to the limitation of the result list but also due to the additionally introduced fetching of the relationships in batches. The pagination solution also causes no performance degradation.

In light of the results, we conclude goal attainment for solving the N+1 Selects problem in the context of the JPA with Vergil.

- *Excessive Logging Problem*: The logging level change hypothesis reduces the 90% percentile value of the response time as well as the CPU utilization of the application server. Side effects in the form of a performance degradation of other Servlet methods do not occur. In light of the results, we conclude goal attainment for solving the excessive logging problem in the context of the JPA with Vergil.

- *Excessive Data Allocation Problem*: This time, the application of the fetch graph query hint achieves a significant performance improvement. The response time as well as the memory footprint is reduced without causing significant performance degradations of other application parts. This behavior is also expected by the use case specific impact of the changes that affect only the query where the fetch graph query hint is applied to.

  The lazy fetch type mapping configuration results in the second-best performance improvement for both, the response time as well as the memory footprint. Despite the potential risk of impacting other use cases through the use case independent changes, we have not identified a major performance degradation of any Servlet method.

Activating selective caching provides the best performance results. The 90% percentile response time value as well as the mean memory footprint is the lowest. The 90% percentile value of the response time for uploading audio files increased in the single digit millisecond range. This can be due to cache updates. However, the response time deviation is not significant. In light of the results, we conclude goal attainment for solving the excessive data allocation problem in the context of the JPA with Vergil.

## 7.3.15. Discussion

The case study shows that if Vergil is applied correctly, Vergil provides the expected results in the considered case. This includes the formulation of appropriate change hypotheses. In the complete implementation and prototyping of solution proposals, the prioritization of solution proposals, the size of the performance profile describing requested data, and the employment of significance testing.

### 7.3.15.1. Performance Evaluation

We have selected a measurement duration in dependence with the applied number of users. We used 300 seconds and 200 users in the case of the N+1 Selects problem, 600 seconds and 100 users in the case of the excessive logging problem, and 900 seconds and 50 users in the case of the excessive data allocation problem. The measurement duration does not include the time for starting the simulated users at the beginning as well was stopping the simulated users at the end. The data collection period started after all simulated users had been started and stopped before the first simulated user was stopped. This was enough for this case study to obtain a large number of measurements to draw a conclusion about performance improvement or degradation with an acceptable confidence. In general, the required measurement duration and the data collection period have to be balanced with the particular characteristics of the software application, usage profile, workload, and the required confidence.

This includes the repetition of experiments to assess whether deviations in the response time are to be attributed to the stochastic nature of performance measurements or to the applied changes.

#### 7.3.15.2. Solution Prototyping

We implemented most solution proposals completely to evaluate the performance prior to solution prioritization. This was done in a couple of minutes for each solution proposal. This does not include additional effort for redeployment of the application and a reset of the database prior to each experiment as well as restarting the application server. In the case of the pagination solution proposal, a complete implementation of the changes has not been necessary. In contrast, a prototype implementation without changing the interfaces and the Web-based user interface was enough to evaluate the performance improvement in order to prioritize the solution proposal. However, the most appropriate solution evaluation method depends on the particular solution and is a balance between effort and confidence.

#### 7.3.15.3. Solution Prioritization

The prioritization of the criteria in the decision criteria hierarchy is a onetime effort (for an application) when the priorities and criteria are stable. The prioritization effort amortizes with the number of applications over time. The application of Vergil ranges ideally from the development to the evolution of a software application. This typically includes scenarios where an application has to cope with changing usage profiles or workloads. The prioritization of the solution alternatives has to be done every time. Due to the nature of AHP, the number of pairwise comparisons depends on the number of solution alternatives and criteria. This shows the number of 24 comparisons in the case of the excessive data allocation problem versus the 224 in the case of the N+1 Selects problem. The solution ranking activity of Vergil is designed to support the developer in selecting a solution to implement. When only one solution proposal exists, as in the case of the excessive logging problem, prioritization is without benefit and can even not be performed with AHP due to the missing counterpart for the pairwise comparison.

#### 7.3.15.4. Performance Profile

The number of performance aspects in the performance profile describing the requested observations for the dynamic analysis was very large when all monitored data is given back. This problem can be easily solved by the implementation of Vergil. For example, despite the application of sampling a possibility is to only return one set of samples without duplicates. Another possibility is to request aggregated or pre-analyzed data in the analysis of a change hypothesis instead of raw data.

#### 7.3.15.5. Significance Test

The difference between the mean values can be assessed with statistical hypothesis tests like the two-sample t-test. Unfortunately, performance measurements often do not satisfy the normality distribution and equal variance assumptions of the t-test. We can overcome the equal variances assumption with Welch's t-test and the central limit theorem to overcome the normal distribution assumption. Following the central limit theorem, the new sample set is derived from the original one by building groups of samples and taking the average of each group. We followed this procedure to assess the statistically significance of the differences in our observations. We experienced that the groups often have to include several ten thousands of samples of the performance measurement to pass the Shapiro-Wilk normality test for a significance level of 0.05. This leads to a very small standard deviation to such a degree that Welch's t-test rejected the null hypothesis in most cases. We consider deviations in the single digit millisecond range to be practically negligible due to the stochastic nature of performance measurements (Liu, 2009). We draw the conclusion that statistical hypothesis tests to assess differences in mean values to conclude a performance improvement or degradation where the differences are not obvious is of limited benefit. This leads to the conclusion that the decision maker plays a key role in assessing performance improvements or degradations in such cases.

## 7.4. Case Study – Caching Component Evaluation

Vergil foresees the recommendation of model-based performance prediction by simulation to evaluate the performance impact of solution proposals prior to solution prioritization instead of measurement. For this reason, we conducted this case study validate the feasibility of simulation as alternative means. We also draw conclusions about what has to be considered when creating change hypotheses that recommend to use this performance evaluation means. Note, this case study has already been published in (Heger et al., 2014b). Parts of the description of the case study are taken from there. The remainder of the section is structured as follows: Section 7.4.1 describes the goal of the case study, introduces the question that is to be answered with the results based on the defined metrics. Section 7.4.2 outlines the design of the case study before Section 7.4.3 introduces the used PCM model. Section 7.4.4 describes the calibration of the PCM model instance. Section 7.4.5 presents the results of the case study followed by a discussion of the results in Section 7.4.6. Section 7.4.7 concludes the section with a discussion of potential threats to validity.

### 7.4.1. Goal, Question, and Metrics

The goal of the case study is to assess the feasibility of using model-based performance prediction by simulation to evaluate the performance of solution proposals with the Palladio Component Model (PCM). This includes to draw a conclusion whether it is feasible to prioritize solution proposals based on characteristics that have been obtained with different performance evaluation means.

The question that is to be answered in particular is whether the prediction accuracy is high enough to use the predicted values instead of actual measurements to avoid an implementation of the solution proposal prior to the final solution selection. This means that the prediction error has to be small enough to replace a measurement-based performance evaluation experiment with a model-based performance prediction evaluation experiment. While a prediction error of less than 30% is already considered as acceptable (H.

Koziolek, 2008), the decision maker has to keep the prediction accuracy in mind when assessing solution proposals.

The metrics that are to be measured to answer the question is the prediction error for the point estimator of the mean value and the 90% percentile value for the response time of the download method of the WebGUIBean component.

### 7.4.2. Case Study Design

We continue with the Media Store application as sample application (see Section 7.3.2). In contrast to the Java Persistence API case study, the encoding of audio files in a bit rate that is less compared to the uploaded one is of particular interest. The research subject is the encoding component that is a software bottleneck due to the high CPU demand of the re-encoding procedure. The Media Store application is not identical to the implementation used in the Java Persistence API case study. The implementation used in this case study misses some of the extensions like the album entity and the view of audios per album. Instead, a list of audio files is displayed on the user interface. The database contains also significantly less entries compared to the Java Persistence API case study. We used three different file sizes (i.e., 3.92 MB, 4.62 MB, and 8.02 MB) to create the 81 audio files contained in the database. The file sizes are equally distributed among the audio files in the database. The original bit rate of the uploaded audio files is 190 kBit/s.

For the purpose of this case study, we consider a usage scenario of the Media Store application where multiple users download an audio file $\alpha \in AudioFiles$ randomly with a bit rate $\beta \in B = \{32, 64, 128, 160\}$ that is less compared to the uploaded bit rate of 190 kBit/s to force the re-encoding of $\alpha$ with bit rate $\beta$. Mathematically, the encoding function is defined as follows:

$$encode(\alpha, \beta) = \alpha' \tag{7.1}$$

where $\alpha'$ is the re-encoded audio file $\alpha$ in the desired bit rate $\beta$. We simulate three power users with zero think time who execute the usage profile in a closed workload scenario using HP LoadRunner (LoadRunner 2014). The simulated usage profile is as follows: users login, select the desired audio file $\alpha$ and bit rate $\beta$ randomly following a uniform distribution, download the re-encoded audio file $a'$, and logout. In contrast to the JPA case study, we do not use a probabilistic usage profile in terms of transition probabilities between individual Servlets (Heger et al., 2014b).

A prerequisite for caching is that the encode method (as formalized in Equation 7.1) returns for the same input tuple $(\alpha, \beta)$ the same result $\alpha'$. In the case of a data access profile following a uniform distribution like in this example, the cache hit probability $P$ only depends on the size of the cache and the total number of elements. For example, to achieve a hit probability $P = 0.8$, the cache size can be determined as follows:

$$\lceil |AudioFiles| * |B| * P \rceil = \lceil 81 * 4 * 0.8 \rceil = 260 \tag{7.2}$$

where the result is rounded to the next integer. However, the size of the cache can be limited by the amount of memory that is available for caching objects (Heger et al., 2014b).

### 7.4.3. Palladio Component Model

The PCM model instance for the Media Store application contains a basic component for each EJB of the implementation. Figure 7.35 shows a combined static and deployment view of the Media Store architecture's most relevant components as an excerpt from the PCM model instance. Also shown is the modeling of the performance-relevant behavior in form of the SEFF for the IMediaStoreBean.download and RDSEFF for the IEncoderBean.encode method. The architecture shows only the application server tier that is the open-source variant of Oracle's Glassfish application server. The SEFF models the performance-relevant behavior of the MediaStoreBean's download method and consists of the external call action to fetch an audio file from the database and the external call action to encode the audio file in a specified audio bit rate. The RDSEFF models the re-encoding as internal action that specifies the non-parametric resource demand as stochastic expression (Heger et al., 2014b).

### 7.4.4. Model Calibration

We calibrated the PCM model instance semi-automatically by determining the stochastic expression used in the RDSEFF as non-parametric resource

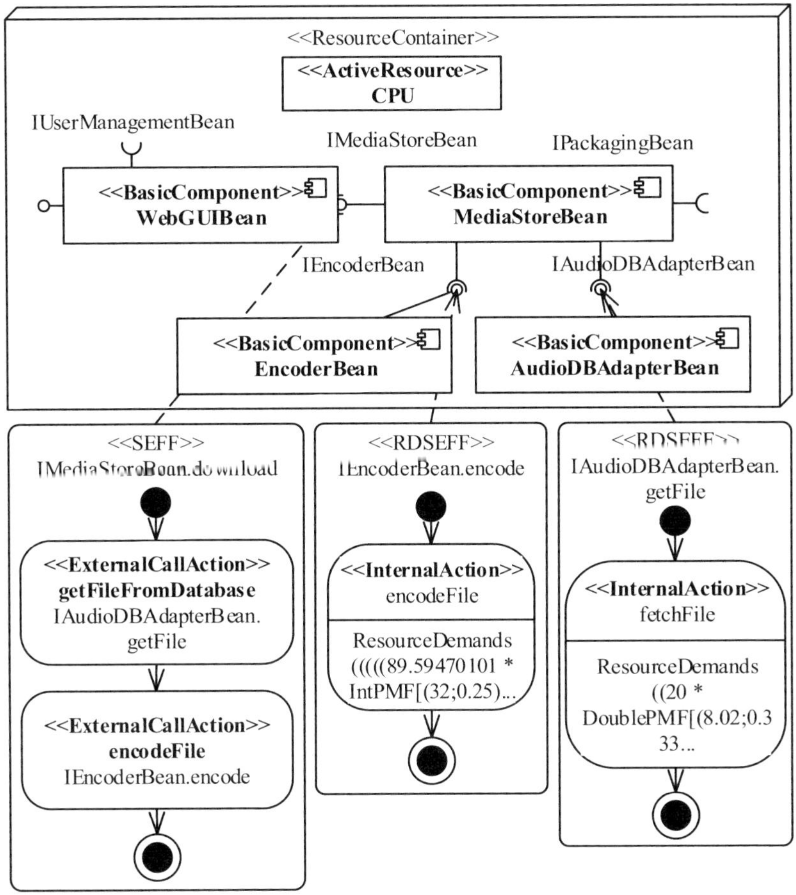


**Figure 7.35.:** Media Store PCM model instance excerpt based on (Heger et al., 2014b)

demand. Therefore, the Media Store application was deployed to the same measurement environment as described in Section 7.3.5. While RDSEFFs allow the specification of platform-independent resource demands, we used platform-dependent timing values as resource demands in the stochastic expression. The timing values used as resource demands are in milliseconds. For this reason, we set the processing rate of the CPU resource to 1000 to have the prediction results already converted from milliseconds to seconds. The modeling of middleware performance is not necessary. The timing values implicitly include middleware performance (H. Koziolek, 2008).

We extracted the timing values through measurements with single user tests for the AudioDBAdapterBean.getFile method individually for each of the three file sizes by instrumenting the method with AIM. We extracted the timing values for the EncoderBean.encode method also through single user tests by instrumenting the method and measuring the response time for all possible combinations of file size and bit rate. We applied a linear regression on the results with file size and bit rate as parameters. We then used the determined coefficients to build the stochastic expression as linear regression with the determined probability functions for file size and bit rate in the case of the EncoderBean.encode method and only file size in the AudioDBAdapter-Bean.getFile method (Heger et al., 2014b).

We calibrated the PCM model instance with the determined timing values and simulated the usage profile with three users and a workload with think time 0 to obtain the series of reference measurements as shown in Figure 7.37 for the Prediction Problem case. In the cumulative distribution function, we observed a predicted median response time of 14.39 seconds for the case where encoding becomes a software bottleneck (Heger et al., 2014b).

We instrument the WebGUIBean's download method with AIM and monitor the response time of the method. In the monitoring results, shown as cumulative distribution function in Figure 7.37 for the case Measurement Problem, we observe a median response time of 14.29 seconds (Heger et al., 2014b).

### 7.4.5. Results

We manually transform the SEFF of the IMediaStoreBean.download method as shown in Figure 7.36. Examples for how the transformation can be automated is shown in literature, e.g., (Trubiani et al., 2011; Arcelli et al., 2013b; A. Koziolek et al., 2011). We introduced a branch action and two Probabilistic Branch Transitions (PBTs) to simulate the cache. We assign the hit probability $P = 0.8$ to the cache hit PBT and the miss probability $1 - P = 0.2$ to the cache miss PBT. We assume that the cache access time to be negligible, based on our practical experience (fetching an $\alpha'$ from the cache takes on average $0.02\mu s$

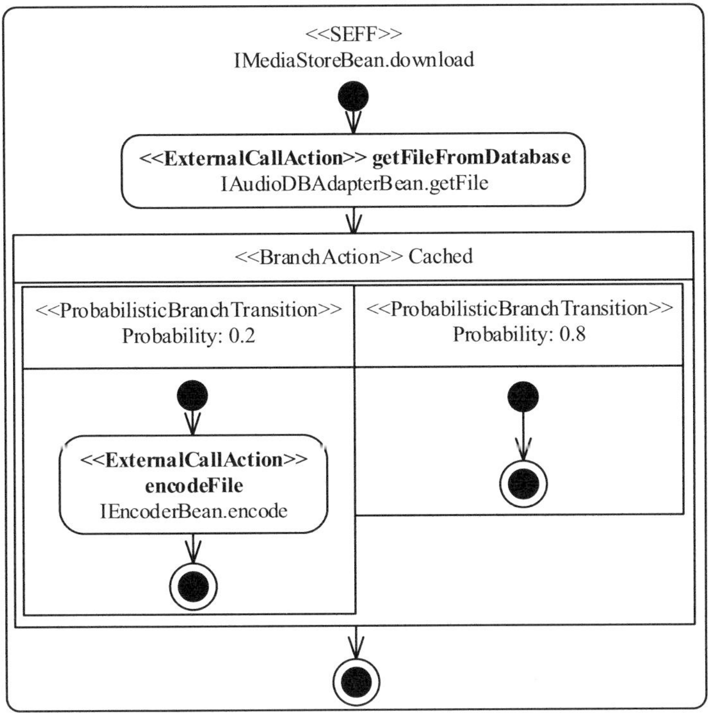


**Figure 7.36.:** Modified SEFF with simulated cache (Heger et al., 2014b)

with the implemented caching solution). The simulation results are shown in Figure 7.37 as cumulative distribution function for the Prediction Cache case. The simulation predicts a median response time of 2.95 seconds. Based on the evaluation results, a performance improvement of 487% is estimated for the changes (Heger et al., 2014b).

To validate the simulation results, we implemented the cache as an EJB using Google's Guava libraries (Google 2014). In the implementation of the MediaStoreBean.download method, we introduced a conditional branch to check the cache first for the tuple $(\alpha, \beta)$. When the requested audio file is not present in the cache, $\alpha$ is fetched from the database and re-encoded with bit rate $\beta$. The resulting $\alpha'$ is then added to the cache. We set the cache size to 260 objects and repeated the performance test. The initial warm-up of the cache is done during the ramp-up phase of the load test. In the monitoring results (as shown in Figure 7.37 for the Measurement Cache case), we observed a median response time of 2.71 seconds. The measured response times show a performance improvement of 527% (Heger et al., 2014b).

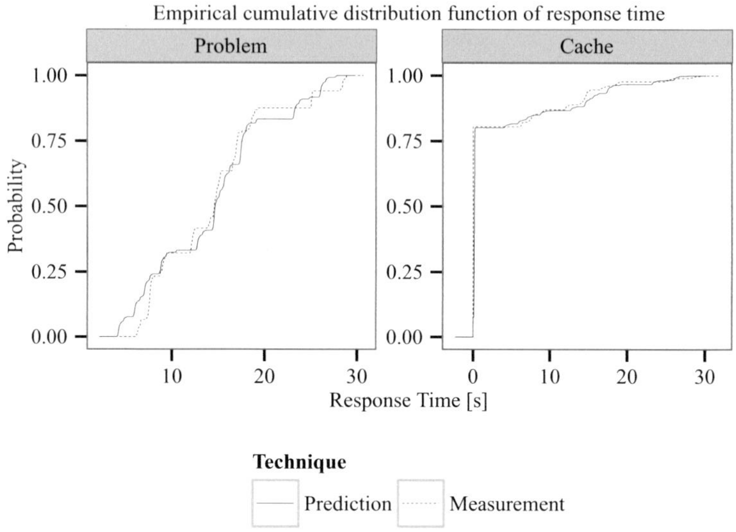


**Figure 7.37.:** Measured and predicted response times (Heger et al., 2014b)

## 7.4.6. Discussion

The prediction error between the measured mean value and the predicted mean value without the cache is about 0.7%. The prediction error for the 90% percentile values is 5.1%. The recommendation to be cautious about the interpretation of deviations of less than 10% was given by (Liu, 2009) for the comparison of performance measurements to compare the effects of code or configuration changes. In the context of Vergil, measurement results have to be compared to prediction results when solution proposals are prioritized with respect to decision criteria. Consequently, when we apply the 10% rule to interpret the deviation between the measured and predicted mean values leads to the conclusion that the deviation is below 10% and we consider the deviation is not significant enough. This implies that the prediction results can be compared with measurement results of potential solution alternatives. However, this requires that the prediction error needs to be assessed prior to the performance evaluation of solution proposals with the application of the particular operational profile. The determined prediction error has then to be considered by the decision maker when prioritizing solution proposals.

A remaining question is how to deal with the unknown prediction error when changes are applied to the model. The prediction error in this case is -8.7% for the mean value and -3.2% for the 90% percentile value. To quantify the prediction error for the solution proposal, the changes have to be applied to the implementation and a performance evaluation experiment has to be conducted. Thus, we consider the prediction error of the changed model instance as unknown.

The results indicate that assessing the performance improvement of solution proposals with model-based performance prediction and the comparison with measurement-based performance evaluation results of other solution proposals is possible to prioritize solution proposals. The a priori unknown prediction error for the changed model instance requires the decision maker to be cautious when comparing characteristics of solution proposals that originate from different performance evaluation means.

When a performance model does not exist, the effort for creating and calibrating the model might be higher compared to implementing the solution proposal and measure the performance impact. For example, the implementation of the caching solution took significantly less effort compared to creating and calibrating the model. If a performance model was already created to assess early design decisions, a calibration of the model might still be necessary. Another concern is to maintain the model. This requires that the model evolves with the implementation. If this is not the case, the model has to be updated prior to the performance evaluation. This may include structural changes as well as behavioral changes. In light of these observations, we argue that evaluating the performance with prediction, may be a benefit when a model is already maintained and integral part of the software development process.

### 7.4.7. Threats to Validity

In this section, we discuss potential threats to validity of the case study results. Section 7.2.8 gives a short overview on the concern of each threat.

#### 7.4.7.1. Construct Validity

A potential threat to construct validity is the model calibration due to potential measurement overhead. The inclusion of the overhead of the instrumentation can cause a bias in the obtained timing values that are used to create the resource demand functions. To mitigate the risk of introducing such a bias in the timing values, we measured the relevant methods in isolation with a single instrumentation probe that is used to instrument the application. We elaborate the employed method and asses the overhead in (Wert et al., 2015c) where the method resulted in the most accurate prediction results compared to other measurement methods and tools.

#### 7.4.7.2. Internal Validity

A potential threat to internal validity is the performance evaluation experiments and the applied changes to the model instance. We mitigated the risk of observing changes in the dependent variables (i.e., the response time) that are not caused by the changes of the independent variable (i.e., the applied model changes) by executing the same performance evaluation experiments. Consequently, only one independent variable has been modified between the experiments. Another potential threat to internal validity is a potential experimenter bias due to the fact that the experimenter knows the developers of PCM. However, the experimenter is not involved in the development and the conclusions have been solely drawn from the achieved prediction accuracy of the mean value and 90% percentile value.

#### 7.4.7.3. External Validity

A potential threat to external validity is the size and complexity of the sample application. We are aware that much larger software applications in size and complexity exist in industry. Nevertheless, applications of similar size and complexity have also been used in other case studies as well, e.g., (H. Koziolek, 2008; Becker, 2008). However, the application of PCM to larger software applications in industry has already been shown in literature, e.g., (A. Koziolek, 2013; Gooijer et al., 2012). The case study results indicate that a sufficient prediction accuracy is achievable. In general, the prediction accuracy may decrease when performance experts have to make model abstractions in order to create a model with reasonable effort (H. Koziolek, 2008). This is often a balance between prediction accuracy and modeling effort.

## 7.5. Summary

This chapter presented the results of the conducted online survey, the JPA case study, and the evaluation of simulation. The online survey results show the validity of the motivational hypotheses and the need for more support in solving software performance and scalability problems. Software performance and scalability problems can be classified into a general classification (i.e., software performance antipatterns) and solution concepts can be reused for particular problem instances. The respondents agreed that the current support in solving software performance and scalability problems is insufficient.

The results of the JPA case study show the feasibility of Vergil and the validity of the hypotheses to satisfy the requirements for an approach to build a recommendation system that supports developers who are novices in software performance engineering and responsible for solving software performance and scalability problems without the assistance of a software performance expert. Elicited performance expert knowledge can be formalized into rules that consist of tests with different analyses and end points instantiating a particular solution concept when the conditions are satisfied. The case study results also show that the workflow of Vergil provides a valid output given valid input and that the most appropriate solution proposal is recommended to the developer.

The case study on evaluating the usage of simulation as alternative for measurement showed promising results but also necessary extensions to Vergil in terms of model extraction to know the level of detail of the models required to develop change hypotheses that recommend simulation instead of measurement as evaluation means. The unknown prediction accuracy of the changed model instance is an issue for the confidence of the prediction result. In the particular case example, the calibration of the model instance with measurements took more effort than implementing the solution in the source code.

**Table 7.1.:** Validation design overview

| Hypothesis | | Validation Survey | Type 0 | Type 1 |
|---|---|---|---|---|
| H1 | Model-Driven Software Development (MDSD) techniques provide the facilities to consider various implementation artifacts to identify possible solutions. | — | ✓ | ✓ |
| H2 | Domain-specific description languages provide the required data representations. | — | ✓ | ✓ |
| H3 | Solutions for software performance and scalability problems are identifiable with rules and static analysis, dynamic analysis and user interaction. | — | ✓ | ✓ |
| H4 | The activities in a workflow to guide novice developers are to identify possible solutions, to identify the impacted elements, to estimate the implementation effort, to evaluate the properties of solutions, and to prioritize solution alternatives. | ✓ | ✓ | ✓ |
| H5 | Model-Driven Software Development techniques and rules enable the derivation of an implementation description. | — | ✓ | ✓ |

**Table 7.2.:** Questions and hypotheses

| Question | | Hypothesis |
|---|---|---|
| Q1 | Are there software performance and scalability problems which are of recurring nature in industry? | There is a set of frequent occurring software performance and scalability problem patterns. |
| Q2 | Are there solutions to performance and scalability problems which are of recurring nature in industry? | There is a set of frequent applicable solution patterns for the set of recurring problem patterns. |
| Q3 | Is there an established process for solving performance and scalability problems? | There is no established process in industry for solving software performance and scalability problems. |
| Q4 | Is it time consuming to solve an identified performance and scalability problem? | The amount of time that is spent for solving software performance and scalability problems is case-specific and depends on the experience, creativity and knowledge about common solutions and performance evaluation methods of the developer. |
| Q5 | What association scenario between problems and solutions occurs most often? | Developers often experience a one problem and more than one solution alternative (one-to-many) situations as well as a more than one problem and more than one solution alternative (many-to-many) situation. |
| Q6 | Is there sufficient support for finding a solution for performance and scalability problems? | There is no support in form of a tool that guides developers from a software performance and scalability problem to a solution. |

| | | |
|---|---|---|
| Q7 | Is it necessary to tailor generic solution patterns to the software application? | The tailoring of generic solution patterns is necessary to clarify the intend of the solution for less experienced and less trained developers. |
| Q8 | Is it necessary to describe the performance evaluation experiments that are to be conducted? | The description of performance evaluation experiments is necessary to support less experienced and less trained developers. |
| Q9 | Is there a need to consider multiple criteria to rank solutions? | It is necessary to consider qualitative and quantitative criteria to rank solutions. |
| Q10 | Is there a need to describe solutions at the implementation level? | It is necessary to describe solutions at the implementation level to tailor a solution pattern to the concrete software application. |
| Q11 | Is there a need to support the decision maker in making a decision about the solution to implement? | It is necessary to support the decision maker in selecting the solution that is to be implemented. |

**Table 7.3.:** Metrics

| Metric | | Q |
|---|---|---|
| M1 | Percentage of respondents that report that they have often or very often seen the same software performance and scalability problem already in the past. | Q1 |
| M2 | Percentage of software performance and scalability problems that have been new to the respondents. | Q1 |
| M3 | Percentage of respondents that report that they often or very often apply solutions to solve software performance and scalability problems that they have already applied in the past. | Q2 |
| M4 | Percentage of respondents that report that they often or very often apply solutions to solve software performance and scalability problems that others have already applied in the past. | Q2 |
| M5 | Percentage of respondents that report that they follow an established process to solve software performance and scalability problems. | Q3 |
| M6 | Median of the reported relative frequency that respondents spent less than a few hours on solving a performance and scalability problem. | Q4 |
| M7 | Median of the reported relative frequency that respondents spent a few hours to a day on solving a performance and scalability problem. | Q4 |
| M8 | Median of the reported relative frequency that respondents spent more than a day to a week on solving a performance and scalability problem. | Q4 |
| M9 | Median of the reported relative frequency that respondents spent more than a week to a month on solving a performance and scalability problem. | Q4 |
| M10 | Median of the reported relative frequency that respondents spent more than a month on solving a performance and scalability problem. | Q4 |

| | | |
|---|---|---|
| M11 | Median of the reported relative frequency that respondents are in a one problem, one solution scenario. | Q5 |
| M12 | Median of the reported relative frequency that respondents are in a one problem, more than one possible solution scenario. | Q5 |
| M13 | Median of the reported relative frequency that respondents are in a more than one problem, one possible solution for each problem scenario. | Q5 |
| M14 | Median of the reported relative frequency that respondents are in a more than one problem, more than one possible solution for each problem scenario. | Q5 |
| M15 | Percentage of respondents that slightly agree or strongly agree that the available support for solving performance and scalability problems is insufficient. | Q6 |
| M16 | 75% quantile of the reported importance for generic solution proposals. | Q7 |
| M17 | 75% quantile of the reported importance for tailored solution proposals. | Q7 |
| M18 | 75% quantile of the reported importance for describing the performance evaluation experiments that are to be conducted. | Q8 |
| M19 | Median of the reported number of criteria that the respondents consider in making a decision on which solution to implement. | Q9 |
| M20 | 75% quantile of the reported importance for describing the implementation of solutions at the implementation level. | Q10 |
| M21 | 75% quantile of the reported importance for supporting decision making about the solution to implement. | Q11 |

**Table 7.4.:** Summary question answers

| Question | | Answer |
|---|---|---|
| Q1 | Are there software performance and scalability problems which are of recurring nature in industry? | Yes |
| Q2 | Are there solutions to performance and scalability problems which are of recurring nature in industry? | Yes |
| Q3 | Is there an established process for solving performance and scalability problems? | No |
| Q4 | Is it time consuming to solve an identified performance and scalability problem? | Yes |
| Q5 | What association scenario between problems and solutions occurs most often? | many-to-many |
| Q6 | Is there sufficient support for finding a solution for performance and scalability problems? | No |
| Q7 | Is it necessary to tailor generic solution patterns to the software application? | Yes |
| Q8 | Is it necessary to describe the performance evaluation experiments that are to be conducted? | Yes |
| Q9 | Is there a need to consider multiple criteria to rank solutions? | Yes |
| Q10 | Is there a need to describe solutions at the implementation level? | Yes |
| Q11 | Is there a need to support the decision maker in making a decision about the solution to implement? | Yes |

**Table 7.5.:** Mapping configuration of Java persistence entities

| Mapping | Association | Fetch Type |
|---|---|---|
| Album → Audio | one-to-many | lazy |
| Audio → Album | many-to-one | eager |
| Audio → User | many-to-one | eager |
| Audio → Comment | one-to-many | lazy |
| Audio → AudioBlob | one-to-one | lazy |
| User → Audio | one-to-many | lazy |
| Comment → Audio | many-to-one | eager |

**Table 7.6.:** Observed response times for each problem

| Servlet Method | 90%ile [s] | | |
|---|---|---|---|
| | N+1 Selects | Excessive logging | Excessive data allocation |
| Login.doPost | 0.003 | 0.004 | 0.003 |
| Download.doGet | 1.324 | 2.339 | 7.625 |
| Download.doPost | 0.056 | 0.074 | 0.051 |
| SearchAlbum.doPost | 0.037 | 0.040 | 0.042 |
| Upload.doPost | 0.015 | 0.016 | 0.015 |
| Logout.doGet | 0.001 | 0.002 | 0.003 |

**Table 7.7.:** Decision criteria hierarchy with priorities

| Criteria | Local Priority | Global Priority |
|---|---|---|
| Response time (90%ile) | 0.463 | — |
| ⊢ Login.doPost | 0.055 | 0.026 |
| ⊢ Download.doGet | 0.480 | 0.222 |
| ⊢ Download.doPost | 0.152 | 0.071 |
| ⊢ SearchAlbum.doPost | 0.251 | 0.116 |
| ⊢ Upload.doPost | 0.061 | 0.028 |
| Implementation effort | 0.063 | 0.063 |
| Sustainability | 0.380 | 0.380 |
| Constraint compliance | 0.094 | 0.094 |

**Table 7.8.:** 90%ile values of the response time in seconds with the mean values enclosed in square brackets

| Case | Download.doGet | Download.doPost | Login.doPost | Logout.doGet | SearchAlbum.doPost | Upload.doPost |
|---|---|---|---|---|---|---|
| N+1 Selects Problem | 1.324 [1.078] | 0.056 [0.049] | 0.003 [0.002] | 0.001 [0.001] | 0.037 [0.020] | 0.015 [0.013] |
| Batch Fetch Hint | 0.241 [0.209] | 0.055 [0.043] | 0.005 [0.003] | 0.001 [0.001] | 0.041 [0.023] | 0.020 [0.012] |
| Fetch Graph Hint | 1.747 [1.261] | 0.050 [0.045] | 0.003 [0.003] | 0.001 [0.001] | 0.039 [0.020] | 0.014 [0.011] |
| Load Graph Hint | 1.273 [1.094] | 0.048 [0.044] | 0.003 [0.003] | 0.001 [0.001] | 0.031 [0.019] | 0.014 [0.013] |
| Left Fetch Hint | 0.171 [0.143] | 0.050 [0.042] | 0.004 [0.003] | 0.001 [0.001] | 0.037 [0.021] | 0.017 [0.012] |
| Join Fetch Annotation | 0.653 [0.542] | 0.051 [0.044] | 0.003 [0.002] | 0.001 [0.001] | 0.038 [0.020] | 0.020 [0.017] |
| Batch Fetch Annotation | 0.241 [0.211] | 0.057 [0.044] | 0.005 [0.003] | 0.001 [0.001] | 0.042 [0.022] | 0.023 [0.014] |
| Pagination | 0.017 [0.013] | 0.040 [0.037] | 0.002 [0.002] | 0.001 [0.001] | 0.025 [0.016] | 0.013 [0.010] |
| Shared cache | 0.109 [0.092] | 0.043 [0.038] | 0.004 [0.003] | 0.001 [0.001] | 0.035 [0.017] | 0.015 [0.012] |

**Table 7.9.:** 90%ile values of the response time in seconds with the mean values enclosed in square brackets

| Case | Download.doGet | Download.doPost | Login.doPost | Logout.doGet | SearchAlbum.doPost | Upload.doPost |
|---|---|---|---|---|---|---|
| Excessive Logging Problem | 2.339 [1.749] | 0.074 [0.057] | 0.004 [0.004] | 0.002 [0.002] | 0.040 [0.025] | 0.016 [0.013] |
| Logging Level | 1.152 [0.948] | 0.053 [0.045] | 0.003 [0.003] | 0.002 [0.001] | 0.038 [0.019] | 0.014 [0.011] |

**Table 7.10.:** 90%ile values of the response time in seconds with the mean values enclosed in square brackets

| Case | Download.doGet | Download.doPost | Login.doPost | Logout.doGet | SearchAlbum.doPost | Upload.doPost |
|---|---|---|---|---|---|---|
| Excessive Data Problem | 7.625 [6.736] | 0.051 [0.049] | 0.003 [0.003] | 0.003 [0.002] | 0.042 [0.031] | 0.015 [0.013] |
| Fetch Graph Hint | 0.292 [0.263] | 0.045 [0.040] | 0.003 [0.003] | 0.002 [0.002] | 0.055 [0.038] | 0.018 [0.033] |
| Lazy Fetching | 0.246 [0.220] | 0.043 [0.040] | 0.003 [0.003] | 0.002 [0.001] | 0.039 [0.023] | 0.015 [0.027] |
| Shared Cache | 0.124 [0.113] | 0.038 [0.036] | 0.003 [0.003] | 0.002 [0.002] | 0.034 [0.014] | 0.021 [0.015] |

# 8. Related Work

This section presents related work to Vergil from different domains and outlines the differences. Thereby, the focus relies on recommendation systems in software engineering and model-based and measurement-based performance solution approaches that share similar high-level objectives, software performance problem and solution definitions, software performance problem detection, self-adaptive resource allocation, and change description and propagation. Because Vergil guides the developer, this section describes related work with the aim to answer the following questions (where appropriate and where the required information is provided by the authors):

- Who is the intended user?
- What is the supported task?
- What is the cognitive support?
- What are the proposed information?

The remainder of the section shows that to the best of our knowledge, there are no closely related approaches available, except software performance experts. Hence, distinctive points of Vergil compared to existing related approaches are already given in many cases by the intended answers to the questions above. Software performance antipatterns describe possible solutions but the developer has to transfer the solution concept into the particular context without additional support. Performance problem detection approaches support the developer in detecting software performance and scalability problems early but do not support the developer in the solution process. Source code-based recommendation systems support the developer with code completion, method reuse, and prevent wrong API usages to complete a development task but focus on the functional aspects rather than the quality aspects with respect to the behavior of how the functionality is provided. Model-based performance solution approaches focus on the software architecture design while most measurement-based performance solution approaches focus on the configuration of the application. Self-adaptive resource allocation approaches combine model-based and measurement-based techniques to autonomously enable the application to adapt to a changing operational profile. While Vergil does not exclude software architecture changes, application configuration changes, and resource allocation changes that are also covered by other approaches, there is a gap to support developers at the software implementation level. This includes especially the usage of APIs, frameworks and libraries with respect to performance and scalability quality attributes of an application.

The section is structured as follows: Section 8.1 presents related work with respect to the definition of software performance antipatterns. Section 8.2 presents approaches that solely focus on the detection of software performance problems. Section 8.3 presents recommendation systems in software engineering. Section 8.4 presents model-based approaches to detect and solve software performance problems. Section 8.5 presents approaches that use measurements to solve software performance problems. Section 8.6 presents approaches for self-adaptive allocation of resources. Section 8.7 presents related work that is related to describing and propagating changes.

## 8.1. Performance Problem and Solution Definition

Software performance antipatterns document common software performance problems and their solutions. A performance antipattern description includes a name for the performance antipattern (e.g., the one lane bridge, excessive dynamic allocation, or circuitous treasure hunt), a description of the symptoms and root causes, and solutions (C. U. Smith et al., 2000). Hereby, software performance antipatterns can be technology independent or technology dependent as well as defined on different levels of abstraction.

Smith and Williams define 14 technology-independent software performance antipatterns in (C. U. Smith et al., 2000; C. U. Smith et al., 2002; C. Smith et al., 2002; C. Smith et al., 2003). Dudney et al. defined in total 52 J2EE technology-specific antipatterns that can cause performance problems as well as maintainability issues and in total 45 potential solutions (Dudney et al., 2003). The proposed solutions affect different levels of an application. On average, Dudney et al. propose 1 solution for each antipattern with 4 solution proposals at maximum. According to the description, 23 performance antipattern have an impact on performance. The solution descriptions range from source code fragments to concepts that are described in natural language and diagrams. Dugan et al. define in (Dugan Jr. et al., 2002) the sisyphus database retrieval antipattern. Dugan et al. propose 4 possible solutions where 1 solution requires the application of 1 complementary solution and 1 solution requires also the application of 2 complementary solutions. Hallal et al. define 38 Java multithreading-specific antipatterns (Hallal et al., 2004). Smaalders reports on performance antipatterns experienced during the work at the Solaris operating system (Smaalders, 2006). Węgrzynowicz defines in (Wgrzynowicz, 2013) 5 performance antipatterns for the one-to-many relation between entities of the object-relational mapping framework Hibernate. Tate et al. define in (Tate et al., 2003) EJB specific performance antipattern. Karwin and Winand describe performance problems and solutions related to SQL (Karwin, 2010; Winand, 2012b). Haines reports in (Haines, 2014) on common Java performance problems and possible solutions experienced in practice.

While performance antipatterns provide solution concepts for software performance and scalability problems, developers still have to transfer the concepts into the context of the particular application where the problem is to be solved manually. This task can be especially complex for novice developers or developers that are unfamiliar with the application. A performance expert can use the defined antipatterns as support to develop change hypotheses for Vergil. Vergil can then use the change hypotheses to support novice developers and developers that are unfamiliar with the application.

## 8.2. Performance Problem Detection

In literature, performance problem detection approaches have been presented that solely focus on performance problem detection. Approaches of this category often use monitoring data from dynamic analysis of the application under test collected either during tests or productive use. Approaches that consider both, performance problem detection and the proposal of solutions are mostly based on design models not the source code of an application. This section presents the approaches that do not consider the proposal of solutions. Section 8.4 presents approaches that consider solution proposals.

NiPAD detects and classifies software performance antipatterns with machine learning techniques based on system performance metrics from dynamic analysis (Peiris et al., 2014b).

PAD detects Java EE software performance antipatterns in component-based software systems by means of dynamic analysis and predefined rules (Parsons, 2007; Parsons et al., 2008).

StackMine uses postmortem analysis of call stack traces to identify performance bugs by mining a large number of call stack traces and clustering identified patterns (Han et al., 2012).

LagHunter detects software performance bugs in Java GUI applications by measuring the latency of user actions and combining data from different application deployments to produce a report that supports the developer in identifying and fixing the root cause (Jovic et al., 2011).

DynamicSpotter automatically detects software performance antipatterns through measurement-based experiments and adaptive instrumentation of the application. Therefore, DynamicSpotter executes experiments to test whether a particular performance antipattern is present in the software application. The results of the systematic search are detected software performance antipatterns and their root causes (Wert et al., 2013; Wert et al., 2014).

PAMD detects the Blob software performance antipattern in fUML design models by analyzing the executed activities when the design model is simulated (Arcelli et al., 2015).

Shang et al. detect performance regressions in a new revision of the application based on the prediction error of regression models created for the last revision. The approach uses available performance counters and selects the relevant counters to build regression models for the relevant counters (Shang et al., 2015).

Jiang et al. identify possible performance problems by analyzing execution logs of the application created during load tests. The approach uses a performance baseline obtained from previous load tests and compares the current execution logs against them based on the response time distribution. The approach creates a performance analysis report as result for the developer (Jiang et al., 2009).

In our own work, we utilized performance unit tests to detect software performance regressions during software development and to isolate the root cause. Our approach compares the performance evaluation results of the latest revision with the results of the previous revision. The performance regression as well as the isolated root cause, e.g., a method call that has a significantly higher response time (Heger et al., 2013).

PAD supports the developer in identifying performance anomalies in distributed systems and finding the root causes by analyzing, correlating, visualizing, and comparing performance counter logs. The PAD-assisted investigation process includes automated and manual tasks (Peiris et al., 2014a).

Paradyn uses performance measurements collected during the execution of a parallel application to detect software performance bottlenecks in terms of parts of the application that consume the most resources. Padadyn uses adaptive instrumentation techniques to control what performance data is collected and when. Paradyn tests defined hypotheses about potential performance problems and their root cause (Miller et al., 1995).

FOREPOST supports the test engineer in finding methods that are software performance bottlenecks by creating rules from execution traces of the application and by applying the rules to select the input data for the application. The execution traces are collected through runtime monitoring of the application (Grechanik et al., 2012).

Yan et al. identify potential performance problems, i.e., excessive memory usage, by tracking object references. The approach also provides a ranking of the identified problems and metrics to access how difficult or (impossible) a code transformation is (Yan et al., 2012).

Ehlers et al. detect performance anomalies and isolate the root cause of a performance problem through self-adaptive monitoring techniques based on the Kieker monitoring framework. Response time forecasts based on time series and hypothesis tests are used to detect when the response time deviates from the expectation (given by the response time forecast) (Ehlers et al., 2011).

Waller et al. include the MooBench micro-benchmark into continuous integration to detect performance regressions for the monitoring overhead of the Kieker application performance monitoring framework. The benchmark results are visualized for each build and presented to the developers that have to draw a conclusion whether a performance regression occurred (Waller et al., 2015).

Mirgorodskiy and Miller diagnose performance problems in distributed applications when the applications are operated in production. Self-adaptive runtime monitoring is used to collect execution traces. The successful and failed execution traces are then analyzed to identify the causes of problems. The problems are ranked for the performance analyst by importance (Mirgorodskiy et al., 2008).

Vergil neither includes software performance and scalability problem detection nor a tight coupling with a particular problem detection approach. Software performance and scalability problem detection is not in the scope of Vergil. That's why Vergil expects a performance profile as input that can be created by any performance problem detection tool or manually by the developer. However, based on the research context behind Vergil, to provide developers with a holistic performance problem and solution recommendation approach, our intent is to couple Vergil with DynamicSpotter (Wert et al., 2013; Wert et al., 2014), if necessary.

## 8.3. Recommendation Systems in Software Engineering

To support a developer in completing a task, various recommendation systems are proposed to support software engineering. Many of the recommendation systems support the developer in understanding the usage of a particular API, in understanding the source code of an application, or in reusing existing methods. Other recommendation systems support the developer with code completion. Many of the recommendation systems are described to support the developer during maintenance and evolution of a software application. None of the source-code-based recommendation system's aim is to support the developer in solving software performance and scalability problems. The recommendation systems focus on supporting the developer in implementing and changing what the software application does but not on how the software application does what it is expected to do. This is also the main difference to Vergil. The recommendation systems often propose code fragments without supporting the developer in integrating the code fragment into the source code. An important aspect that is unconsidered by most recommendation systems is that changes on a particular element can cause changes on another element. The remainder of this section briefly describes an excerpt of 25 recommendation systems for software engineering.

The Smell-Driven Performance Tuning (SDPT) technique semi-automatically helps developers of visual dataflow programming languages to solve performance problems. SDPT applies changes to the dataflow code semi-automatically in order to solve performance problems. SDPT proposes solution alternatives to remove the problem. SDPT considers different types of interactions depending on the possible degree of automation, e.g., by asking questions to the developer. Human input and judgment are required in cases where the changes cannot be applied automatically. SDPT guides the developer through the manual solution process. In other cases, the developer has to provide additional information in order to execute the transformation reliably. SDPT extends the Smell-Driven Performance Analysis (SDPA) that detects the problems and reports the problems by inserting icons into the dataflow program. SDPA also provides explanations about the problems. SDPT extends SDPA by providing transformation alternatives for restructuring affected portions of the code. A pane in the user interface provides information about the transformations (Chambers et al., 2015).

RASCAL proactively recommends a set of methods to be called that the developer may want to use next by analyzing similar classes. Input is the Java class on which the developer is working. RASCAL uses information about component usage of developers and applies data mining techniques on the code repository (McCarey et al., 2005).

FrUiT guides novice Developers in using a framework. FrUiT uses rules extracted from existing framework instantiations to recommend which methods to call or what objects to instantiate. FrUiT is reactive and provides recommendations upon request (Bruch et al., 2006).

Strathcona supports the developer in using an API and provides source code examples describing the use of the API upon request. The developer selects the

Java source code fragment as input and Strathcona uses heuristics to determine examples from other applications using the same API. Each provided example includes an overview on the structural similarity, a rational for the example in the form of a textual description, and source code with details (Holmes et al., 2006).

Hipikat supports the developer who joins an existing development team by recommending project artifacts (e.g., source code, problem reports, or articles) that are relevant to the current maintenance task of the developer. Hipikat provides the recommendations upon request by the developer who has to provide a query as input. Hipikat retrieves the relevant artifacts from the history of the project based on the source code, change history, issue reports, the documentation, and others (Čubranić et al., 2005).

CodeBroker supports the developer in reusing unknown methods by recommending relevant methods to the developer. CodeBroker uses the JavaDoc documentation comments and method signatures of the currently developed source code where the cursor of the developer is currently located to identify relevant methods. The list of method recommendation is tailored to the developer and task by removing methods that are irrelevant for the current task and by removing methods that the developer already knows. CodeBroker recommends the methods proactively. CodeBroker provides the recommendation as a ranked list according to the relevance of a method. The recommendation includes the name of the method, its signature as well as the full JavaDoc documentation upon request (Ye et al., 2005).

Mendel supports the developer with recommendations about structural properties (e.g., naming conventions, types) of the source code entity that the developer currently develops in the course of software evolution. Mendel analyses similar source code entities that are related to the current source code entity to obtain the recommendations. Mendel uses the differences to identify the properties exhibited by relevant entities that are missing in the currently developed one (Lozano et al., 2011).

Jigsaw supports the developer in reusing small portions of code. In difference to other recommendation systems that provide similar support, Jigsaw also supports the developer in integrating the code into the developer's current code. The developer has to specify the target (e.g., a class, or a method) and the method to reuse. Jigsaw then integrates the method while the developer has to focus on differences like inheritance, control flow, or exception handling.

Jigsaw prompts the developer to resolve conflicts during integration, e.g., when a statement corresponds to more than one other statement (Cottrell et al., 2008).

API Explorer supports novice and expert developers reactively in discovering required API methods and objects to instantiate in order to complete the development task. API Explorer uses structural relationships between API elements to make the recommendations. The input is an incomplete statement and the output is a set of proposals, e.g., how to instantiate a particular object. API Explorer automatically creates the required code (Duala-Ekoko et al., 2011).

Prospector supports the developer in using an API by recommending code fragments. Prospector uses synthesizing from method signatures and a corpus of other code using the API to make the recommendations. The developer requests recommendations by specifying the input and output type and Prospector proposes methods or sequences of methods that take the input type as input and return the output type as output. Prospector ranks the proposals and inserts the selected code fragment into the source code of the developer (Mandelin et al., 2005).

Precise supports the developer reactively in using an API by recommending the parameters for a method call to use while other approaches often focus on recommending the method to call. Precise automatically provides recommendations in the form of a list of ranked parameter alternatives based on the similarity of contexts and the frequency of usage. Precise extracts the recommendations from the source code of existing applications. Input to Precise is the current context, e.g., a method call statement in the source code (Zhang et al., 2012).

Mens at el. present an approach to support the developer in developing and maintaining Smalltalk applications. Programming patterns (e.g., design patterns) are expressed as logical rules and used to check whether a certain portion of the code satisfies the pattern, to find portions of the code that match the pattern, to detect violations of the pattern, and to generate code fragments (Mens et al., 2002).

uContracts informs the developer when specified usage contracts of methods are violated either due to changes to the source code entity or due to changes to the contract. The tool checks all usage contracts of a method whenever a change to the source code occurs. Usage contracts encode structural regularities defining the expectations and assumptions on how the method is to be reused (Lozano et al., 2015).

Castro et al. present an approach that assists the developer in the diagnosis and correction of inconsistencies between specified structural design rules and the source code of an application, e.g., coding conventions, idioms, or design patterns. The approach reports all source code elements for which the structural design rules are not satisfied. Developers have to create the structural design rules that apply for an application. The approach applies changes directly to the abstract syntax tree of an application to solve the violations (Castro et al., 2011).

MEnToR supports novice and expert developers in inferring concepts and features of a source code entity. Association rules mining is used to discover regularities from the source code of an application, e.g., naming conventions. The regularities are then used by MEnToR to check whether a source code element complies with the regularities and to recommend implementation changes in terms of missing characteristics. Input to MEnToR are the method that is currently browsed by the developer. Output to the developer are a list with the unsatisfied regularities that represents potential errors, a list with suggestions in the form of partially satisfied regularities, and another list with regularities that are completely satisfied (Lozano et al., 2010).

DebugAdvisor supports developers in debugging an issue by recommending information such as people, source code files, and methods that are relevant to the current issue. Input to DebugAdvisor is a mixture of structured and unstructured data. DebugAdvisor mines software repositories (e.g., version control systems, issue tracker) to make recommendations by analyzing the relationships between the entities (Ashok et al., 2009).

SemDiff supports the developer in maintaining the source code of an application that uses a non-trivially evolved framework. SemDiff recommends changes to adjust the usage of the framework to comply with the evolved version. SemDiff takes selected method calls as input where the methods are no longer provided by the framework. SemDiff recommends methods to be called instead as replacement together with a confidence value. To make recommendations, SemDiff determines high level changes by analyzing the source code repository of the framework and determining how the framework has been adapted to its own changes, e.g., determining which method is called by a method that previously called the deleted method. The recommendations are presented in a list and ranked according to the confidence value (Dagenais et al., 2008).

MAM supports the developer in migrating an application from one programming language to another one (e.g., from Java to C#). MAM takes the source code of a set of applications as input. The source code of an application has to be provided for both languages. MAM analyses the source code of the applications for both languages to determine how an API of one language maps to an API of another language. The output of MAM are API mapping relations for API classes and methods (Zhong et al., 2010).

ROSE guides the developer in applying changes to an application by proposing further change locations in order to prevent incomplete changes. ROSE predicts further change locations based on initial changes. ROSE mines the data of the source code repository to create association rules. ROSE uses the association rules to predict further changes based on the change history. ROSE presents related changes to the developer in a view when the developer applies changes to an entity. ROSE checks for further changes when the developer commits the changes to the source code repository. The recommendations are ranked by confidence (Zimmermann et al., 2005).

Dora supports the Developer in exploring the source code of an application to complete software maintenance and evolution tasks by recommending relevant methods. Dora takes a natural language query and the call graph of the application as input and outputs the relevant methods. Dora scores the methods according to their relevance. Dora presents relevant parts of the call graph together with the relevant methods to the developer (E. Hill et al., 2007).

Suade supports the developer (novice developers and developers who are unfamiliar with the application) in understanding the source code of an application by recommending potentially relevant elements upon request. Suade takes a set of source code elements as inputs that are of interest for the developer and outputs a set of other source code elements that may be of interest (Robillard, 2008).

Altair supports the developer in API navigation by recommending related API methods. Altair takes a query as input and outputs a ranked set of related API methods. To make recommendations, Altair uses static analysis of the source code to extract structural information (Long et al., 2009).

Bruch et al. present a code completion system that supports the developer with relevant and context-sensitive recommendations on what method to call. The system derives its knowledge through mining an existing codebase. Input to the system is the variable and the output of the system is a list of method calls ranked by confidence (Bruch et al., 2009).

Mylar supports developers in completing a task by persisting the elements and relations that are relevant to the task. Mylar observes the interaction of the developer with source code elements as input to model the task and to learn the task context. Mylar uses the information to filter the source code elements so that the developer can focus on the relevant elements. Mylar also recommends structural related elements that may be of interest for the developer (Kersten et al., 2006; Kersten et al., 2005).

MAPO supports the developer in understanding API usages by recommending API usage patterns in the form of method call sequences. MAPO takes a query describing a method, class, or package for an API as input. MAPO searches open source code repositories for source code files relevant to the query and applies different processing and mining steps to make the recommendations. MAPO does currently not support the insertion of the code fragments into the source code of the developer (Xie et al., 2006).

SABER supports the developer in detecting incorrect usages of the J2EE framework that have a serious impact on performance by looking for patterns in the source code. The patterns are encoded into rules. SABER takes Java classes as input and analysis whether the classes comply with the rules. SABER can be executed in batch mode or interactively as part of an integrated development environment. The output of SABER are an explanation of the rational of the detected pattern, potential reasons for the pattern to be a false positive, and information that may explain why the pattern occurred (Reimer et al., 2004).

FixWizard supports the developer in changing the source code of an application by recommending parts of the application where the changes also have to be applied and by recommending changes for the task the developer is working on based on similar changes in the past. FixWizard uses similarities in structure and object usage to make recommendations. FixWizard recommends relevant editing operations and parameters (Nguyen et al., 2010).

## 8.4. Model-based Performance Solution

Most approaches that provide recommendations to solve performance and scalability problems have the software architect or designer as target audience not the developer. Hence, the model-based approaches expect design models as input that are often transformed into performance models to collect performance data. The output is often one or more complete design model alternatives. While the approaches support the software architect in finding a software architecture that satisfies certain quality attributes, the implementation of the software application is often neglected also due to the reason that it does often not yet exist. The level of abstraction and the simplifications and assumptions that are often present in the modeling languages make it difficult if not impossible to correct, for example, the improper usage of an API to solve performance and scalability problems. This is a distinctive point between Vergil and the approaches presented in the remainder of the section.

### 8.4.1. Antipattern-based Approaches

Closely related to Vergil is the work of the group of Cortellessa (Di Marco et al., 2014; Cortellessa et al., 2007; Cortellessa et al., 2014; Cortellessa et al., 2012; Cortellessa et al., 2010a; Cortellessa et al., 2010c; Cortellessa et al., 2009; Arcelli et al., 2013c; Arcelli et al., 2013b; Arcelli et al., 2013a; Arcelli et al., 2015) and joint work of this group with other groups (Trubiani et al., 2014; Trubiani et al., 2011; Cortellessa et al., 2015; Mirandola et al., 2012). The input to their approach are design models in the form of UML model instances (Cortellessa et al., 2010c) or PCM model instances (Trubiani et al., 2014; Trubiani et al., 2011). They use rules derived from software performance antipatterns and formalized in first-order logic to detect software performance antipatterns in design models based on performance indices determined through performance models. Solutions are provided as refactoring recommendations of the design model. In their recent work (Arcelli et al.,

2013b; Arcelli et al., 2013a), they use model transformation techniques to automate the software architecture model refactoring. Their process starts with the software architecture model that is transformed into a performance model. Thereafter, a model solution step is used to generate the required performance indices. The performance indices are used together with performance antipatterns in the results interpretation and feedback generation step to identify antipatterns in the model and to propose solutions. When multiple antipatterns are identified, a ranking is used to isolate the antipatterns that are the real causes (Trubiani et al., 2014; Trubiani et al., 2011). In their recent work (Di Marco et al., 2014), they extended their existing approach to obtain the performance indices from actual measurements when the software application is executed. While the intended task to support is similar to the intention of Vergil, there are some obvious distinctive considerations. The supported audience of Vergil are developers not software architects or designers. Hence, the main input of Vergil are implementation artifacts not design models without the limitation that design models may be used as complementary information. The solution description of Vergil refers to implementation artifacts in the form of what elements are impacted and how they must be changed. Another obvious distinctive point is that Vergil does not include software performance antipattern detection. The consideration of design models as corpus limits the solvable antipatterns due to the assumptions, simplifications, and abstraction of the modelling language (Trubiani et al., 2014; Trubiani et al., 2011). This is especially the case where implementation details are important.

Williams and Smith present in (Williams et al., 2002b) their performance assessment of software architecture method that they use in their role as performance consultants. The method takes the software architecture as input to identify potential software quality risks and to identify possible strategies to mitigate or remove the risks. The method consists of ten steps beginning with an introduction to the method itself for all stakeholders (e.g., managers, developers) and ends with an economic analysis. The assessment can take several weeks when performance measurements and modeling is necessary to quantify the impact of potential problems. The most significant difference to Vergil is that their method foresees that the performance expert takes part in the actual solution process whereas the goal of Vergil is to exclude the performance expert from the actual solution process.

Lin and Kavi present in (Lin et al., 2014) an approach that follows similar concepts like the approach of Cortellessa et al.. They use multiple models as abstraction and profiling to collect performance indices. However, many details are not evidently part of the description. Hence, important details are missing to make the differences between their approach and Vergil clear. For example, it is unclear how solutions are concretely proposed and what level of detail is employed, e.g., natural language description or tailored to the context with concrete changes.

### 8.4.2. Rule-based Approaches

Rule-based approaches are related to antipattern-based approaches. They use rules to apply predefined solutions to the model in order to solve the problem (Etemaadi et al., 2015).

Xu presents a prototype called Performance Booster (PB). The input to PB is a set of UML design models that are annotated with performance annotations. PB transforms the design models into performance models, i.e., Layered Queueing Network (LQN), to automatically identify bottlenecks and long path problems. Rules are used to detect problems and identify architecture level changes at the level of the performance model in order to solve the problems. The considered changes include configuration changes such as the number of CPUs as well as design changes of the performance model. The rules for detecting the problems also trigger the rules to recommend changes. PB uses the performance model to search for possible solutions. Subsequently, altered performance models are created. Performance and cost are used as criteria to rank the possible alternatives in order to select the candidates for the next iteration. The recommended changes for the performance model have to be translated back manually into changes of the design model by the designer. Xu outlines various extension possibilities ranging from additional rules to using measurements for deployment and design tuning as well as using other design models as starting point. Nevertheless, the most significant differences to Vergil are the supported role of the designer and the non-consideration of the implementation level of a software application. The work presented in (Xu, 2010) builds upon the work in (Franks et al., 2006) where the identification of layered bottlenecks (i.e., software bottlenecks) and the recommendation of changes in LQN performance models is treated (Xu, 2008; Xu, 2010).

Baber et al. use the RARE and ARCADE tool to guide the iterative derivation of software architectures in terms of allocating functionality and data to domain reference architecture classes. The focus of RARE is to suggest allocations based on heuristics derived from expert experience. Suggestions are given in the form of a sequence of actions, e.g., to move a certain service from one domain reference architecture class to another. ARCADE focuses on dynamic analysis such as simulations and provides the evaluation results to RARE. Hereby, ARCADE supports untrained and less experienced stakeholders in conducting the evaluation (Barber et al., 2002).

Bachman et al. present ArchE as software architecture design assistant. ArchE supports the software architect with advice how quality attributes of the design can be satisfied. The software architect has to interpret the given advice for the domain of the software application. Input to ArchE is the functionality that the software application has to provide and quality requirements. ArchE uses the input and requests additional information from the software architect like execution times to propose an initial design together with possible transformations of the design when not all quality requirements are satisfied. The software architect selects a transformation and provides necessary information. Iteratively, the design is improved until all quality requirements are satisfied (Bachmann et al., 2007).

Kavimandan and Gokhale use a heuristic-based model transformation to support developers of distributed, real-time, and embedded component-based systems in deployment and configuration decisions to satisfy quality of service requirements (Kavimandan et al., 2009).

Drago presents QVT-Rational, a feedback provisioning system to support the designer. QVT-Rational uses a multi-modeling approach to allow a domain expert to specify the domain-specific system metamodels, quality models, model transformations, and a quality prediction tool chain in order to propose alternative designs when the designer asks QVT-Rational for feedback. The domain expert includes what quality properties may be of interest and how the quality properties can be evaluated. The goal is to provide complete design alternatives that satisfy certain quality requirements (Drago, 2012; Drago et al., 2011).

Potena, Mirandola, and Cortellessa present an approach to adapt service-oriented architectures. The adaptation plans propose changes on how to change the structure and behavior through service replacement and modification of interactions between services. An optimization model proposes the most appropriate adaptation plan that satisfies constraints for performance, reliability, and availability. The adaption plans can be defined by the designer or the maintainer of the system or created by the system at runtime (Potena, 2013; Cortellessa et al., 2010b; Mirandola et al., 2010).

Mirandola and Trubiani propose an approach to combine quality of services analysis results from design time and runtime quality of service models in order to support the designer and software engineer in applying changes to the design model. The proposed approach considers the Analytic Hierarchy Process to prioritize the quality attributes (Mirandola et al., 2012).

Kim et al. present an approach to compose an initial software architecture design based on a set of non-functional requirements and architectural tactics. Architectural tactics are rules describing generic solutions to satisfy quality attributes. In the case of performance, architectural tactics include, for example, the usage of priority scheduling, the introduction of concurrency, or the introduction of caching. Multiple tactics are composed and instantiated to create the initial architectural design (Kim et al., 2009).

The presented approaches provide support for the software architect or designer which is a different target audience as the developer in the case of Vergil. Even when the authors use the role of the developer as the intended user like in (Kavimandan et al., 2009), the changes remain on the architecture level and a different domain of software systems. While the goal of solving software performance problems appears to be similar, the supported task of finding a software performance architecture that meets quality requirements is different. Because a commonality between Vergil and the approaches is the employment of rules, performance experts can use the already formalized knowledge on architectural changes to create change hypotheses to change the architecture when a software performance and scalability problem cannot be solved at the implementation level, e.g., changes to the deployment configuration, or replacement of existing components. The rules of Vergil in the form of changes hypotheses are not predefined solutions compared to the model-based approaches. A change hypothesis includes tests and analysis and embodies a solution concept that has to be instantiated by Vergil in each particular context of a problem to obtain the concrete solution proposal.

### 8.4.3. Metaheuristic-based Approaches

In contrast to antipattern-based and rule-based approaches, meta-heuristic-based approaches see the solution of performance problems as optimization problem and try to iteratively improve the software architecture design for the defined quality attributes (Etemaadi et al., 2015).

Canfora et al. propose an approach to compose Web services using genetic algorithms in order to meet quality of service constraints, e.g., cost and response time (Canfora et al., 2008; Canfora et al., 2005).

ArcheOpterix supports the software architect in component deployment problems of embedded systems. ArcheOpterix takes software architecture models as input and applies evolutionary algorithms to find solutions that consider all constraints and objectives. The output of ArcheOpterix is a set of software architecture models (Aleti et al., 2009).

PerOpteryx supports the software architect in finding the best software architecture that satisfies quality requirements and cost constraints, e.g., maximizing availability and performance, and minimizing costs. PerOpteryx automatically proposes a set of Pareto-optimal design alternatives as solutions using analytical optimization techniques and evolutionary algorithms. PerOpteryx takes a functional-requirements-fulfilling PCM model instance as input. The output of PerOpteryx in form of the Pareto-optimal design alternatives are also PCM model instances. The software architect has to specify what are viable changes to the software architecture, i.e., the allocation of components, the server configuration (e.g., processing rate of the CPU), and component selection. The automated optimization process includes the formulation of the search problem, the optimization with analytical techniques, the optimization with evolutionary algorithms, and the presentation of the results. PerOpteryx uses LQNs as performance models to evaluate availability and performance (A. Koziolek et al., 2013; A. Koziolek, 2013; A. Koziolek et al., 2011).

The AQOSA framework supports the software architect by automatically generating alternative software architecture designs for embedded systems using evolutionary algorithms. AQOSA supports multiple quality attributes and takes a set of components and their interactions as functional part of the system as input together with usage scenarios, the architecture properties to be optimized, and a set of hardware and software component specifications. The output are Pareto-optimal solutions (Etemaadi et al., 2015; Etemaadi et al., 2012).

Grunske presents an approach that employs evolutionary algorithms and multiple objective optimization techniques to identify software architecture design alternatives that satisfy multiple quality requirements. Input to the approach is an initial architectural design that satisfies the functional requirements. The approach then proposes a set of Pareto-optimal design alternatives (Grunske, 2006).

The intended user of the meta-heuristic-based approaches and the supported task is identical compared to the antipattern-based and rule-based approaches. The approaches differ in how they improve an initial architectural design model not in what they do. Hence, the distinctive points compared to Vergil are similar. A significant difference is that Vergil is a rule-based approach and due to this they differ also in how recommendations are determined.

### 8.4.4. Design Space Exploration Approaches

Design space exploration approaches guide the architect in exploring possibly huge design spaces considering any possible combination of parameters.

Planner2 supports the software designer in priority assignment and allocation of tasks in distributed real-time systems to meet soft and hard deadlines. Planner2 searches the design space and uses LQNs to collect measures in order to evaluate priority assignments and allocations whether deadline requirements are satisfied (Zheng et al., 2003).

The DeepCompass framework supports the architect in designing software and hardware architectures of embedded systems that has to satisfy multiple quality attributes. The DeepCompass framework includes guidance in designing alternatives, evaluates the performance of each alternative as well as identifying bottlenecks, and provides a trade-off comparison of the alternatives. The process consists of a modeling phase in which the architect creates software and hardware components, a system design phase in which the architect creates the software and hardware architecture of each alternative, a performance analysis phase in which simulations are used to evaluate performance and behavior, and a analysis phase to compare design alternatives with respect to the quality criteria. Inputs are the results from source code analysis, simulations, profiling, and measurements. Also considered as input are usage profiles, simulation techniques, and priorities for the quality attributes. The architect uses a Pareto analysis to identify the most appropriate alternative (Bondarev et al., 2007).

Ipek et al. use artificial neural networks as predictive models to support the architect in exploring the design space in order to perform cost-benefit analysis among design alternatives, or to find design subspaces that satisfy certain quality constraints. The architect can investigate parameter correlations and perform sensitivity analyses, evaluate new features of the architecture, assess the performance impact of changes, and diagnose performance bottlenecks (Ipek et al., 2008).

Ardagna et al. present a two-step approach to support the application designer in finding a deployment configuration for Cloud-based applications that satisfies performance requirements and minimizes costs. The approach takes a PCM model instance as input together with an extension of the PCM. In the first step, an initial deployment configuration is determined that is iteratively improved in the second step. A LQN performance model is employed to evaluate the quality of service of design alternatives (Ardagna et al., 2014).

The design space exploration approaches differ in the intended user and the supported task and are limited to architectural changes.

## 8.5. Measurement-based Performance Solution

Measurement-based approaches are closer to Vergil than model-based approaches in terms that they use measurements of the application for reasoning and expect the availability of an implementation.

Chen at el. present an automated framework to detect object-relational mapping performance antipatterns through static code analysis. The framework provides suggestions to the developer to prioritize the solution of the detected instances of the antipatterns by assessing the decrease in response time. Realistic operational profiles are used to assess the impact of the performance antipatterns and to prioritize the solutions. The solution of instances of the excessive data performance antipattern is prioritized through changing the fetch type from eager fetching to lazy fetching where appropriate. The changes are applied manually. The impact of the changes is evaluated by measuring the response time before and after solving the excessive data antipattern instances. The solution of instances of the one-by-one processing antipattern is prioritized by monitoring the repetitive SQL statements and execution of the monitored SQL statements in batches. The results are used to determine the effect size (i.e., trivial, small, medium, large) that supports the developer in the decision on what instances of the antipatterns to solve (T.-H. Chen et al., 2014). While the focus of this approach is on detecting antipatterns through static code analysis, they consider the evaluation of changes and prototype implementations to measure the impact in order to prioritize the solution. However, the proposal of solutions to the developer is not part of the approach.

Lengauer and Mössenböck propose a method to support the task of configuring the Java memory management by automatically finding the most appropriate garbage collector configuration for an application. The optimization algorithm takes a parameter model and performance evaluation results as input, i.e., the median of the garbage collection time. The parameter model describes the parameters that can be changed and the valid values of each parameter. The objective function takes the parameter values as input executes the performance evaluation experiments and returns the median of the garbage collection time to the optimization algorithm (Lengauer et al., 2014). The approach is technology-specific and limited to the configuration of the Java memory management. Nevertheless, if it is difficult or impossible to create rules to support the developer in the configuration of the Java memory management which we have investigated in (Löwen, 2014), we consider the approach as complementary to Vergil. The approach could be used to determine the configuration that is proposed to the developer.

Bodík et al. propose a methodology to support operators in the identification of recurring availability and performance problems and to propose recovery actions that have been applied in the past. The methodology uses performance metrics collected throughout the data center on different levels (e.g., hardware, operating system, or application) to determine a data center's state through a subset of the collected performance metrics. The state of the data center is used as pattern and persisted. Recovery actions are proposed to the operator when a problem recurs, e.g., redirecting the traffic. The methodology matches the state of the data center to persisted patterns (Bodík et al., 2010). While the scope of the approach differs significantly from the scope of Vergil, the general idea to reuse knowledge in terms of applying similar solutions to recurring problems is shared.

Malek et al. present a design framework to support the architect in finding a new distributed deployment architecture that satisfies quality of service attributes and a given set of deployment constraints. Monitoring data of the running system is collected, alternative deployment architectures are identified and a redeployment of the system is performed. A model is used to represent the deployment architecture including hosts, components, physical links and logical links. An analyzer component determines a set of actions to enable the system to satisfy the objectives. The framework expects input from the architect at design time for parameters that may not be monitored. The architect can also specify deployment constraints like to what hosts a component can be deployed (Malek et al., 2004). The approach is limited to deployment configuration changes. A commonality with Vergil is that a set of actions is used to describe how the deployment is to be changed.

The Automated Configuration Tool (ACT) supports developers and administrators in the configuration of software systems. ACT supports a semi-automated process to conduct experiments in order to measure the effects of configurations. ACT expects the configuration parameters to vary and values for each parameter to test together with adapters to execute the experiments automatically as input. ACT outputs configurations that satisfy the expectations, as well as characteristics of the behavior and a predictive model for the behavior of the system. ACT uses the predictive model to identify an optimal configuration. The prediction results are evaluated together with similar configurations in order to identify the configuration that provides high and consistent performance (Sage, 2003). Similar to other approaches, ACT is limited to the configuration of a software system.

Horikawa proposes a method to identify and solve scalability bottlenecks in ACID-compliant relational database management systems. The proposed method uses event trace-based measurements to identify the scalability bottlenecks and improves the scalability by replacing the lock that is the bottleneck with more fine-grained locks (Horikawa, 2011). While relational databases are still an essential part of contemporary enterprise applications, databases are out of the current scope of Vergil.

## 8.6. Self-Adaptive Resource Allocation

Virtualization and cloud computing provide theoretically unlimited resources and allow an application to elastically cope with changes in the operational profile by allocating additional resources or releasing unnecessary resources for efficient resource utilization. Multiple approaches are proposed in literature to enable applications self-adaptive resource allocation at runtime, e.g., (Huber et al., 2011; van Hoorn, 2014b; Bennani et al., 2005; Ferretti et al., 2010; Jung et al., 2008; Li et al., 2009; Van et al., 2010; Padala et al., 2009; Steinder et al., 2007). The remainder of this section describes two approaches as an example in more detail.

The group of Kounev (Kounev et al., 2011b; Huber et al., 2011; Huber et al., 2012; Kounev et al., 2011a) proposes self-adaptive resource allocation in virtualized environments to adapt the allocated resources during application in order to cope with changes in the operational profile and ensure efficient resource utilization. Huber et al. employs the PCM for online performance prediction to predict the impact of changes in the operational profile of the application and reconfiguration actions (Huber et al., 2011). The S/T/A metamodel describes the reconfiguration scenarios (Huber et al., 2012). This includes high-level strategies and low-level tactics and actions. The aim of strategies is to attain a certain objective while tactics specify the actions to take.

Van Hoorn presents in (van Hoorn, 2014b) the SLAstic approach. The SLAstic approach manages the capacity of distributed component-based software systems at runtime by using reconfiguration operations. The five considered reconfiguration changes of the SLAstic approach are the replication and de-replication of software components, the migration of software components, and the allocation and de-allocation of execution containers. The SLAstic framework maintains architecture models of the application including quality properties derived from monitoring data. The monitoring data are continuously collected with the Kieker monitoring framework. The operations are applied to satisfy quality of service requirements while minimizing the usage of resources. PCM model instances are used to also provide a proactive approach. The description of the reconfiguration plans is the same as used by the group of Kounev.

The adaption actions of self-adaptive resource allocation approaches include, for example, the addition of a CPU to a virtual machine, the addition of a virtual machine, the replication of software components, or the migration of a component to another virtual machine (Huber et al., 2012). It is obvious that source code changes are out of scope of such approaches. Nevertheless, the knowledge encapsulated in the approaches is complementary and can be used by the performance expert to create change hypotheses for Vergil to propose architectural changes.

## 8.7. Change Description and Propagation

In literature, different change type classifications are introduced. Lehnert et al. reviewed studies that introduce change type classifications and proposed a taxonomy to overcome the identified issues (Lehnert et al., 2012). The proposed taxonomy consists of atomic change types and composite change types where composite change types are a set of atomic change types. The taxonomy includes the atomic changes add, delete, and property update. Furthermore, the composite change types move, merge, split, replace, and swap. The considered scope of changes includes requirements, architecture, source code, documentation, configuration files, and other documents (Lehnert et al., 2012).

Ren et al. use a course grained set of atomic changes to describe the difference between two revisions of the same Java application in the context of the change impact analysis tool Chianti. They also include dependencies between atomic changes, i.e., change $\alpha$ is a prerequisite of change $\beta$. The set of considered atomic changes includes 16 change types for adding and deleting a class, method, field, empty instance initializer, empty static initializer, and changing a method body, virtual method lookup, definitions of instance and static field initializer, instance initializer, and static instance initializer (Ren et al., 2004).

Karlsruhe Architectural Maintainability Prediction (KAMP) uses work activities to describe a software maintenance task as work plans based on a software architecture model, i.e., a PCM model instance, to enable the software architect to estimate the effort for implementing the changes. The considered work activities include add, change, and remove of the PCM elements, e.g., component, interface, or operation (Rostami et al., 2015; Stammel et al., 2011; Stammel et al., 2009).

Burger proposes to describe changes for metamodels and model instances by a change metamodel that distinguishes between metamodel-independent changes and metamodel-dependent changes. The metamodel-independent changes are specialized for each particular metamodel to derive the metamodel-dependent changes. The metamodel-independent change metamodel describes changes that can be applied to the Ecore metamodel. The change metamodel distinguishes between atomic changes and complex changes. The atomic changes are specialized into existence change, and feature change. Furthermore, feature change is specialized into attribute change and reference change. An existence change can be of type create or delete while a feature change can be of type add, remove, change, or unset (Burger, 2014).

The development of the change plan description language started with the concepts of (Lehnert et al., 2012) and (Stammel et al., 2009; Stammel et al., 2011) as foundation. In difference to this concepts, the change plan description language has to include the dependencies between changes that is inspired by (Ren et al., 2004). While the change plan description language was not sufficient enough to describe the intended changes based on the change types, the change plan description language includes the concept of metamodel-dependent changes from (Burger, 2014) to describe the different aspects of a particular change. Especially because the changes focus on the source code model that the JaMoPP Java metamodel in this thesis.

To complete a change plan that has been created by a change hypothesis, a change impact analysis is necessary by propagating the changes. The change impact analysis discipline is well addressed as the review of 150 approaches by Lehnert shows (Lehnert, 2011). According to this study, the large majority of the studied approaches assess the impact of source code changes at the source code level. Other approaches assess the impact of changes on architectural models, requirements models, documentation, or configuration files. There are also approaches that include several kinds of implementation artifacts in the assessment, e.g., source code and architecture (Lehnert, 2011). The developed approaches use different techniques to assess the change impact, e.g., call graph analysis, program slicing, or explicit rules (Lehnert et al., 2013). Explicit rules are specific impact propagation rules that are derived through expert knowledge elicitation. The rules determine how a certain type of change affects other elements that are in a relation with the changed element. For example, when the intended change is to delete a certain method from a particular interface, the implementation of that particular method in all classes implementing the interface are also to be deleted (Lehnert, 2011). In (Lehnert et al., 2013), Lehnert et al. highlight two insights: many approaches support only one type of artifact, and many approaches do not take the individual change type into consideration. Both observations are important for our goal attainment. Vergil builds on various models that represent different aspects of the software application (see Section 3.3) and supports the developer with a change plan as implementation description of a solution where different types of changes are distinguished (see Section 4.3).

Briand et al. use rules to synchronize and ensure consistency of the architecture and source code of a software application (Briand et al., 2003). Lehnert et al. go beyond architecture and source code and use rules to propagate the impact within and between heterogeneous software artifacts (Lehnert et al., 2013). Their approach uses an Ecore-based model representation of software artifacts, e.g., source code, architecture, tests or configuration file, to apply the propagation rules. Lehnert et al. provide a set of impact propagation rules in the context of the EMFTrace tool (*EMFTrace* 2014; Lehnert et al., 2013). A rule-based dependency analysis is used to establish the dependency relations between the models including different UML models, Java source code and JUnit tests. A dependency relation specifies the type of relation between a source model and a target model, e.g., equivalences of elements, and enables the traceability between the source model and the target model. The rule-based impact propagation uses the changed element, the type of change and any other element that has a relation to the changed element in order to determine if and how the other elements are impacted. Infinite loops during impact propagation are prevented through storing the changed element, type of change, and impacted element (Lehnert et al., 2013).

The support of heterogeneous software artifacts renders the concept of this approach for assessing the consequences of changes well suited for the needs of Vergil. A communality is that Vergil considers also Ecore-based models.

A change hypothesis creates a change plan with the intended changes that are to be implemented to solve the software performance and scalability problem. The change plan includes the change types and impacted elements of the source code model instance. All elements that are in relation with the impacted element are provided by the relations within the same model instance containing the impacted element and the dependency relations to elements of other model instances. The rules use this information to determine if and how related elements are impacted. The result for each impact propagation is determined by a propagation rule. The rule adds one or more changes for the impacted element to the change plan. This includes the creation of the ancestor relation in the change plan. This aspect is different to the original rule design in (Lehnert et al., 2013) where the result of a propagation rule is the creation of a new entry in a report. The propagation rules of Vergil can also include user interaction where the developer has to provide additional information, e.g., when parameters are added to a method signature and the changes propagate to the caller of the method then the developer has to specify whether the parameter values can be provided.

# 9. Conclusion

This chapter concludes the thesis with a summary of the main contributions and validation results in Section 9.1, a discussion of the scientific merit of the contributions in Section 9.2 and the presentation of the resulting benefits in Section 9.3. Section 9.4 presents the assumptions this thesis builds upon and discusses the limitations of the approach before Section 9.5 points out possible directions of future work.

## 9.1. Summary

Motivated by the frustration of users and developers caused by performance and scalability problems and the impact on a business's revenue, this thesis proposed Vergil to explicitly consider implementation artifacts to solve software performance and scalability problems in enterprise applications to overcome the shortcomings of existing solutions. The formulated goal of the thesis was the "Development of an approach that satisfies the requirements and enables developers who are novices in software performance engineering to solve software performance and scalability problems without the assistance of a software performance expert" to cope with the decreasing number of software performance experts that are capable of managing performance during development due to retirement and non-replacement with comparably skilled people (C. U. Smith, 2015). To attain that goal and to provide sufficient support to developers who are novices in software performance engineering, the main scientific contributions of this thesis are:

- *Explicit consideration of the implementation level to recommend solutions for software performance and scalability problems*: To support the developer at the implementation of a software application where most of the software performance and scalability problems have their cause (Compuware 2015), Vergil utilizes Model-Driven Software Development (MDSD) techniques to consider different implementation artifacts as main corpus of data sources to recommend possible solutions. Implementation artifacts (e.g., source code files and configuration files) are parsed into model-based representations that are utilized by static analyses of elicited rules from performance expert knowledge. Complementary information is provided by dynamic analysis of the software application's implementation, e.g., performance tests. Thereby, Vergil uses the model-based representation of implementation artifacts as data source to create a test profile that describes the dynamic analysis in terms of what information is to be collected, where in the software application's implementation the data is to be measured and when, with respect to the operational profile. Complementary information can also be provided by design models and performance models due to the employment of MDSD techniques. The selection of simulation as evaluation means when measurements are infeasible supports the "convergence of measurement and modeling methods" (Woodside et al., 2007) for software performance evaluation. Vergil provides the solution proposals as a change plan describing the necessary implementation changes to implement the solution proposal. We validated the feasibility of this contribution with a case study that had the Java Persistence API as research subject. We injected three common software performance and scalability problems into a performant and scalable application based on accessible reports from developers. The results show that Vergil identifies possible solutions to solve the injected problems.

- *Description languages for data representation and human computer interaction*: We designed Vergil as a reactive approach and proposed description languages for data representation and human computer interaction to enable Vergil to interact with the developer. Building upon the parameter dimension and specification description language, the performance profile description language describes the performance problem as input as well as collected information from dynamic analysis. The test profile, a specialization of the performance profile, supports the conduction of the dynamic analysis providing guidance by describing what information to collect and where in the software application's implementation the data should be monitored. The performance solution description language builds also upon the parameter dimension and specification language and describes the relevant decision criteria and the properties of a solution with respect to the decision criteria. The change plan description language uses metamodel-dependent change types to describe how the implementation of the software application should be changed to implement the solution. The change hypothesis description language provides the framework for the software performance expert to create rules that Vergil applies to the given input to recommend solutions. The constraints description language constrains changes to the implementation by specifying change types that cannot be applied. In the course of the JPA case study, we validated the expressiveness of the description languages and showed that the necessary information is describable.

- *Workflow to guide developers through the solution process without the assistance of a software performance expert*: We proposed a workflow that mimics the structured approach of software performance experts to guide the developer through the solution process without the assistance of a software performance expert. The workflow includes the identification of possible solutions by testing the change hypothesis, the identification of impacted elements of the software application's implementation by propagating the initial changes in the change plan through the implementation, the estimation of the implementation effort based on the completed change plan, the evaluation of the solution properties with respect to the decision criteria, and the ranking of the solution proposals by priority to support the developer in selecting the most appropriate solution proposal. The workflow involves the role of the tester who is responsible for conducting dynamic analysis and the role of the decision maker who is responsible for creating the decision criteria and for prioritizing the decision criteria as well as the solution proposals with respect to the criteria. The case study results showed that Vergil provides valid output given valid input.
- *Instantiation of the approach for three common Java Persistence API (JPA) problems*: We instantiated Vergil for the Java Persistence API by creating change hypotheses for the N+1 Selects problem, the excessive data allocation problem and the excessive logging problem. We developed the rules based on the API documentation, published best practices and antipattern documentations. The contained changes range from configuration changes of the persistence unit to architectural

changes of the employed software application. We injected the problems as research subject into a performant and scalable application and applied Vergil to solve the problems. We injected the problems based on available reports from developers. The case study results showed that we have been successful with solving the problems with Vergil.

## 9.2. Scientific Merit

The research presented in this thesis was motivated by the significant impact of software performance and scalability problems on the satisfaction of end-users (Compuware 2015; Lazar et al., 2006; Bouch et al., 2000; Ramsay et al., 1998; Skadberg et al., 2004; Ceaparu et al., 2004), the revenue of a business (Kohavi et al., 2007), the difficulty for developers to properly learn the usage of APIs (Jin et al., 2012; Robillard, 2009), the reports from managers that most software performance scalability problems are caused by the implementation (Compuware 2015) (supported by the results of our conducted online survey), the decreasing number of software performance experts (C. U. Smith, 2015) and the shortcomings of existing solutions that neither have the developer as target audience nor consider the implementation of a software application.

The contributions of this thesis showed that the shortcomings of existing solutions can be overcome to enable developers who are novices in software performance and scalability to solve software performance and scalability problems without the assistance of a software performance expert. Thereby, MDSD techniques have shown to be a practical means for an explicit consideration of implementation artifacts. The contributions also show that software performance expert knowledge (i.e., test, analyses, and reasoning) can be elicited and formalized into rules to build a recommendation system for developers. This is not limited to but applies in particular to solve software performance and scalability problems that are the result of inappropriate usage of APIs. The results of this thesis also indicate that it is possible to support the convergence of measurement and modeling methods (Woodside et al., 2007) to solve software performance and scalability problems.

## 9.3. Benefits

The contributions of this thesis beneficially supports software engineering in the following main aspects:

- *Reduced workload of software performance experts*: While the number of software performance experts that are capable of managing software performance during development is perceived as decreasing (C. U. Smith, 2015), Vergil reduces the workload of software performance experts by making use of the trend of documenting frequent software performance and scalability problems as antipatterns. Software performance experts can focus on unknown software performance and scalability problems and elicit the new knowledge derived through the solution of the problem into rules for Vergil that are then made available to a large community of developers to solve similar problems.
- *Improved learning abilities for developers*: The created rules used by Vergil to make recommendations and the change plans describing the implementation implicitly support developers to learn and understand common performance and scalability concepts as well as an appropriate usage of APIs, frameworks and libraries for performance and scalability. The more developers internalize the implicitly learned performance and scalability solutions, the more aware they become to develop performant and scalable applications. Over time, the role of Vergil may change from advising solutions to validate solutions where a developer uses Vergil to confirm own solution proposals. Even in this role, Vergil may be able to point out alternative solutions that the developer may have not considered.
- *Improved quality and attractiveness of software applications*: While the vast majority of software performance and scalability problems are experienced by end-users (Compuware 2015) and the solution of software performance and scalability problems is considered to be most challenging (Jovic et al., 2011) reducing the complexity of this task with tools like an implementation of Vergil that requires less performance expertise for solving software performance and scalability problems supports the solution of problems before they are noticed by end-users. This in turn increases the perceived quality of end-users (Bouch et al.,

2000) and the attractiveness of a software application (Skadberg et al., 2004).

## 9.4. Assumptions and Limitations

In the following, we present the assumptions this thesis builds upon and discuss the identified limitations of Vergil:

- *Availability of a representative measurement environment*: Vergil assumes that a representative measurement environment is available for conducting dynamic analysis and performance tests. This includes realistic test data in size and structure as well as usage profiles and workloads from test or operation under which the software performance and scalability problems occurred. Furthermore, this also includes that instrumentation and monitoring capabilities are available to instrument the software application and monitor the relevant data.
- *Validity of user input*: We assume that the input given to Vergil by the user is valid. This includes the performance and scalability problem description, complementary information from user interaction and conducted experiments and the prioritization of decision criteria and solution proposals. Especially in the case of performance tests, we have the assumption that the individual playing the role of the tester is capable of conducting statistically rigorous performance evaluation experiments (Georges et al., 2007).
- *Availability of metamodels*: Vergil makes use of MDSD techniques by parsing implementation artifacts into a model instance. To create that model instance, a metamodel is necessary to create the instance. While many metamodels have already been developed in literature like the JaMoPP Java metamodel provided by (Heidenreich et al., 2010), we assume that metamodels are developed for implementation artifacts based on the Ecore meta-metamodel like in the case of the persistence configuration metamodel.
- *Trace links between model instances*: We assume that trace links and correspondence relations between model elements of different model

instances are available. For example, trace links can be automatically determined on existing models using rules (Lehnert et al., 2013).

- *Limitations of automation*: It is possible to automate the conduction of experiments for dynamic analysis and performance tests to a large degree. Prioritizing solutions automatically is difficult. The difference between two solution alternatives with respect to a particular criterion may be important in one case but irrelevant in another case. Prioritizing solution proposals is highly context specific and requires knowledge about an application's domain. Technically, an automated prioritization is possible given the availability of the required properties. However, we rely on the manual prioritization by the decision maker. Another limitation is to apply changes automatically. While changes in our conducted case study can be applied automatically, more complex changes involving significant refactoring activities may not be applicable automatically.
- *Limitation of combinations of solutions*: Currently, Vergil is not capable of proposing combinations of solutions within an iteration in terms of a composition of the solution proposals of different change hypotheses. Vergil can provide combinations of solutions when it is included in a single change hypothesis as in the case of the pagination change hypothesis.

## 9.5. Future Work

In this section, we point out possible directions of future work:

- *Automating the collection of complementary information from dynamic analyses*: Vergil considers the role of the tester that is responsible for conducting the required experiments to collect complementary information from dynamic analysis. This task can be automated to a large degree as already utilized in the detection of software performance and scalability problems (Wert et al., 2013; Wert et al., 2014) and the derivation of performance models (D. J. Westermann, 2014). In our collaborative work with Wert et al., we have already developed the means to automatically instrument the implementation of software applications and to adapt the instrumentation without restarting the application (Wert et al., 2015c). The collaboration also includes the development of an instrumentation description language (Wert et al., 2015d). Building upon the developed automation in the context of this thesis and the available automation from our collaborative work, only a limited implementation effort remains to implement the required adapters in order to conduct dynamic analysis automatically.

- *Coupling with proactive software performance and scalability detection approaches that consider the implementation of the software application*: Vergil is designed as a reactive approach that provides recommendations upon request of the developer. Coupling Vergil with DynamicSpotter (Wert et al., 2015a), the implementation of the proactive automatic performance problem diagnostics approach (Wert, 2015), and integrating both into a continuous performance evaluation scenario as part of the continuous build infrastructure, enables to create reports for developers that provide information about detected performance and scalability problems in the application as well as possible solutions. Building upon the automation, detecting and solving software performance and scalability problems are considered throughout development, maintenance, and evolution of a software application.
- *Collaboration with performance experts from industry to identify needs and to develop additional rules*: In the course of this thesis, we have had exchanges with industry software performance experts. In personal conversations, they provided valuable insight into their daily business and reported what performance and scalability problems should be addressed with an approach like Vergil. Many of the problems were related to the usage of APIs and the configuration of components. Intensifying this exchange can guide the further development of Vergil and the development of rules. Furthermore, given an implementation of Vergil with acceptable usability, performance experts can evaluate the capabilities of Vergil and indicate required improvements.
- *Coupling with design decision documentation*: Solving a software performance and scalability problem with a particular solution proposal is a software design decision. The rationale for this design decision is already given by the decision criteria, the prioritization of the decision criteria and the prioritization of the solution proposals with respect

to the decision criteria. This rationale is not documented to support a design decision in the future. Research in the field of software evolution identified the benefits from reusing documented design decisions to improve future design decisions (Durdik et al., 2013; Könemann et al., 2010). The consideration of this research direction may allow to further support the solution of similar problems and to trace the rationale of why a particular problem has been solved with the implemented solution in the past.

- *Consideration of other quality attributes*: This thesis focuses on software performance and scalability problems in enterprise applications. The general approach of Vergil to use rules to identify possible solutions to a problem and to assess the properties of solution proposals with respect to decision criteria in order to select the most appropriate solution proposal in a context may also apply for other quality attributes, e.g., availability, reliability, or security. A prerequisite for this research direction is that the problem and solution knowledge can be elicited into rules and that solutions are available on the implementation level.
- *Integration of model extraction facilities*: To make simulation a feasible alternative for evaluating performance quality attributes of a solution proposal, model instances (i.e., PCM model instances) are required with a known level of detail. Knowing the level of detail is necessary for the development of the change hypotheses that may recommend simulation for performance evaluation. Requesting models as input entails the risk of the unknown degree of abstraction of the model instance and may lead to incorrect conclusions. The level of abstraction for the JaMoPP Java metamodel instance is known. Tools are already available to create a PCM model instance from an implementation including SoMoX (Becker et al., 2010) and Kieker (van Hoorn et al., 2012; van Hoorn, 2014b).
- *Explicit consideration of prototyping*: To validate the pagination solution proposal, we used prototyping in our JPA case study instead of implementing the solution proposal completely. The results show that Vergil should explicitly consider prototyping to evaluate solution proposals. For this reason, change hypotheses should include prototyping knowledge of the solution concept and create change plans that describe the prototype implementation.

# Bibliography

## Publications

Heger, C. (2013). „Systematic Guidance in Solving Performance and Scalability Problems.“ In: *Proceedings of the 18th International Doctoral Symposium on Components and Architecture*. WCOP '13. Vancouver, British Columbia, Canada. ACM, pp. 7–12.

Heger, C., J. Happe, and R. Farahbod (2013). „Automated Root Cause Isolation of Performance Regressions During Software Development.“ In: *Proceedings of the 4th ACM/SPEC International Conference on Performance Engineering*. ICPE '13. Prague, Czech Republic: ACM, pp. 27–38 (cit. on p. 279).

Heger, C. and R. Heinrich (2014a). „Deriving Work Plans for Solving Performance and Scalability Problems.“ In: *Computer Performance Engineering*. Ed. by A. Horváth and K. Wolter. Vol. 8721. Lecture Notes in Computer Science. Springer International Publishing, pp. 104–118 (cit. on pp. 70, 72, 83, 97, 104).

Heger, C., A. Wert, and R. Farahbod (2014b). „Vergil: Guiding Developers Through Performance and Scalability Inferno.“ In: *The Ninth International Conference on Software Engineering Advances (ICSEA)*. Ed. by H. Mannaert, L. Lavazza, R. Oberhauser, M. Kajko-Mattsson, and M. Gebhart. IARIA, pp. 598–608 (cit. on pp. 66, 70, 77, 79, 83, 252, 254–258).

Weiss, C., D. Westermann, C. Heger, and M. Moser (2013). „Systematic Performance Evaluation Based on Tailored Benchmark Applications.“ In: *Proceedings of the 4th ACM/SPEC International Conference on Performance Engineering*. ICPE '13. Prague, Czech Republic: ACM, pp. 411–420.

Wert, A., M. Oehler, C. Heger, and R. Farahbod (2014). „Automatic Detection of Performance Anti-patterns in Inter-component Communications.“ In: *Proceedings of the 10th International ACM Sigsoft Conference on Quality of Software Architectures*. QoSA ’14. Marcq-en-Bareul, France: ACM, pp. 3–12 (cit. on pp. 40, 94, 278, 280, 309).

Wert, A., H. Schulz, and C. Heger (2015c). „AIM: Adaptable Instrumentation and Monitoring for Automated Software Performance Analysis.“ In: *Proceedings of the 10th International Workshop on Automation of Software Test*. AST 2015. appears 2015. Florence, Italy: ACM (cit. on pp. 110, 149, 208, 260, 310).

Wert, A., H. Schulz, C. Heger, and R. Farahbod (2015d). „Generic Instrumentation and Monitoring Description for Software Performance Evaluation.“ In: *Proceedings of the 6th ACM/SPEC International Conference on Performance Engineering*. ICPE ’15. Austin, Texas, USA: ACM, pp. 203–206 (cit. on pp. 208, 310).

## Supervised Theses

Dadashi, A. (2013). „Data Generation for Performance Evaluation of Data-Centric Systems.“ MA thesis. Karlsruhe Institute of Technology.

Dogan, Y. (2013). „Detection of Relevant Variation Points in Software Workload Monitoring Data for Performance Antipattern Detection with Regression Analysis Techniques.“ Master’s Thesis. Karlsruhe Institute of Technology.

Erdogan, I. (2012). „Simulationsbasierte Erkennung von Performance Anti-Pattern in Palladio-Modellen.“ Master’s Thesis. Karlsruhe Institute of Technology.

Kohlhaas, S. (2014). „Systematic Investigation of Performance Anti-Patterns in In-Memory Database Queries.“ Bachelor’s Thesis. Karlsruhe Institute of Technology.

Komgang Djomgang, E. G. (2012). „Evaluation of Different Performance Feedback Types for Developers.“ MA thesis. Karlsruhe Institute of Technology.

Löwen, O. (2014). „Analyse der Speicherverwaltungskonfiguration in Java zur Lösung von Performance-Problemen.“ MA thesis. Karlsruhe Institute of Technology (cit. on p. 295).

Merkert, P. (2014). „An Empirical Study for the Evaluation of a Performance Problem Detection Approach.“ Bachelor's Thesis. Karlsruhe Institute of Technology (cit. on p. 6).

Muszynski, H. (2014). „Kosten-Nutzen-Analyse von kombinierten Lösungen für Performance Probleme.“ Bachelor's Thesis. Duale Hochschule Baden-Württemberg Karlsruhe.

Schulz, H. (2014). „Adaptive Instrumentation of Java-Applications for Experiment-Based Performance Analysis.“ Bachelor's Thesis. Karlsruhe Institute of Technology.

Tran, L.-H. S. (2013). „Measurement-Based Diagnosis of Performance Problems in Cloud Applications.“ Master's Thesis. Karlsruhe Institute of Technology.

## References

Albrecht, A. J. (1979). „Measuring application development productivity.“ In: *Proceedings of the Joint SHARE/GUIDE/IBM Application Development Symposium*. Vol. 10, pp. 83–92 (cit. on p. 105).

Aleti, A., S. Bjornander, L. Grunske, and I. Meedeniya (2009). „ArcheOpterix: An extendable tool for architecture optimization of AADL models.“ In: *Model-Based Methodologies for Pervasive and Embedded Software, 2009. MOMPES '09. ICSE Workshop on*, pp. 61–71 (cit. on pp. 7, 292).

Arcelli, D., L. Berardinelli, and C. Trubiani (2015). „Performance Antipattern Detection Through fUML Model Library.“ In: *Proceedings of the 2015 Workshop on Challenges in Performance Methods for Software Development*. WOSP '15. Austin, Texas, USA: ACM, pp. 23–28 (cit. on pp. 278, 287).

Arcelli, D. and V. Cortellessa (2013a). „Software model refactoring based on performance analysis: better working on software or performance side?“ In: *Proceedings 10th International Workshop on Formal Engineering Approaches to Software Components and Architectures*. Ed. by B. Buhnova, L. Happe, and J. Kofroň. Vol. 108. Electronic Proceedings in Theoretical Computer Science. Open Publishing Association, pp. 33–47 (cit. on pp. 79, 287, 288).

Arcelli, D., V. Cortellessa, and D. Di Ruscio (2013b). „Applying Model Differences to Automate Performance-Driven Refactoring of Software Models.“ In: *Computer Performance Engineering*. Springer, pp. 312–324 (cit. on pp. 256, 287).

Arcelli, D., V. Cortellessa, and C. Trubiani (2013c). „Experimenting the Influence of Numerical Thresholds on Mode-based Detection and Refactoring of Performance Antipatterns.“ In: *Electronic Communications of the EASST* (cit. on p. 287).

Ardagna, D., G. Gibilisco, M. Ciavotta, and A. Lavrentev (2014). „A Multi-model Optimization Framework for the Model Driven Design of Cloud Applications.“ In: *Search-Based Software Engineering*. Ed. by C. Le Goues and S. Yoo. Vol. 8636. Lecture Notes in Computer Science. Springer International Publishing, pp. 61–76 (cit. on pp. 7, 294).

Arnold, R. S. and S. A. Bohner (1996). *Software Change Impact Analysis*. IEEE Computer Society Press (cit. on p. 97).

Ashok, B., J. Joy, H. Liang, S. K. Rajamani, G. Srinivasa, and V. Vangala (2009). „DebugAdvisor: A Recommender System for Debugging.“ In: *Proceedings of the the 7th Joint Meeting of the European Software Engineering Conference and the ACM SIGSOFT Symposium on The Foundations of Software Engineering*. ESEC/FSE ’09. Amsterdam, The Netherlands: ACM, pp. 373–382 (cit. on pp. 8, 284).

Bachmann, F., L. Bass, P. Bianco, and M. H. Klein (2007). *Using ArchE in the Classroom: One Experience*. Tech. rep. CMU/SEI-2007-TN-001. Software Engineering Institute, Carnegie Mellon University (cit. on pp. 7, 94, 290).

Ballesteros, F. J., F. Kon, M. Patiño, R. Jiménez, S. Arévalo, and R. H. Campbell (2009). „Batching: A Design Pattern for Efficient and Flexible Client/Server Interaction.“ In: *Transactions on Pattern Languages of Programming I*. Ed. by J. Noble and R. Johnson. Vol. 5770. Lecture Notes in Computer Science. Springer Berlin Heidelberg, pp. 48–66 (cit. on p. 123).

Balsamo, S., A. Di Marco, P. Inverardi, and M. Simeoni (2004). „Model-based performance prediction in software development: a survey.“ In: *Software Engineering, IEEE Transactions on* 30.5, pp. 295–310 (cit. on p. 19).

Barber, K., T. Graser, and J. Holt (2002). „Enabling iterative software architecture derivation using early non-functional property evaluation.“ In: *Automated Software Engineering, 2002. Proceedings. ASE 2002. 17th IEEE International Conference on*, pp. 172–182 (cit. on pp. 7, 290).

Basili, V. R., G. Caldiera, and H. D. Rombach (1994). „The Goal Question Metric Approach." In: *Encyclopedia of Software Engineering*. Ed. by J. J. Marciniak. Wiley and Sons, pp. 528–532 (cit. on p. 160).

Becker, S. (2008). „Coupled model transformations for QoS enabled component-based software design." PhD thesis. Universität Oldenburg (cit. on pp. 151, 154, 198, 261).

Becker, S., M. Hauck, M. Trifu, K. Krogmann, and J. Kofroň (2010). „Reverse Engineering Component Models for Quality Predictions." In: *14th European Conference on Software Maintenance and Reengineering (CSMR)*, pp. 194–197 (cit. on p. 311).

Becker, S., H. Koziolek, and R. Reussner (2007). „Model-Based Performance Prediction with the Palladio Component Model." In: *Proceedings of the 6th International Workshop on Software and Performance*. WOSP '07. Buenes Aires, Argentina: ACM, pp. 54–65 (cit. on pp. 22, 23).

– (2009). „The Palladio component model for model driven performance prediction." In: *Journal of Systems and Software* 82.1. Special Issue: Software Performance - Modeling and Analysis, pp. 3–22 (cit. on pp. 19, 21, 22).

Bennani, M. N. and D. Menascé (2005). „Resource Allocation for Autonomic Data Centers using Analytic Performance Models." In: *Proceedings of the Second International Conference on Autonomic Computing (ICAC 2005)*, pp. 229–240 (cit. on p. 297).

Berander, P. and A. Andrews (2005). „Requirements Prioritization." In: *Engineering and Managing Software Requirements*. Ed. by A. Aurum and C. Wohlin. Springer Berlin Heidelberg, pp. 69–94 (cit. on pp. 31, 32, 187).

Bodík, P., M. Goldszmidt, A. Fox, D. B. Woodard, and H. Andersen (2010). „Fingerprinting the Datacenter: Automated Classification of Performance Crises." In: *Proceedings of the 5th European Conference on Computer Systems*. EuroSys '10. Paris, France: ACM, pp. 111–124 (cit. on pp. 8, 296).

Boehm, B., B. Clark, E. Horowitz, C. Westland, R. Madachy, and R. Selby (1995). „Cost models for future software life cycle processes: COCOMO 2.0." In: *Annals of Software Engineering* 1.1, pp. 57–94 (cit. on p. 105).

Boehm, B. (1984). „Software Engineering Economics." In: *Software Engineering, IEEE Transactions on* SE-10.1, pp. 4–21 (cit. on pp. 105, 107).

Böhme, R. and R. Reussner (2008). „Validation of Predictions with Measurements." In: *Dependability Metrics*. Ed. by I. Eusgeld, F. Freiling, and R. Reussner. Vol. 4909. Lecture Notes in Computer Science. Springer Berlin Heidelberg, pp. 14–18 (cit. on pp. 151, 153).

Bondarev, E., M. R. V. Chaudron, and E. A. de Kock (2007). „Exploring Performance Trade-offs of a JPEG Decoder Using the Deepcompass Framework.“ In: *Proceedings of the 6th International Workshop on Software and Performance*. WOSP ’07. Buenes Aires, Argentina: ACM, pp. 153–163 (cit. on pp. 7, 294).

Bondi, A. B. (2000). „Characteristics of Scalability and Their Impact on Performance.“ In: *Proceedings of the 2nd International Workshop on Software and Performance*. WOSP ’00. Ottawa, Ontario, Canada: ACM, pp. 195–203 (cit. on p. 2).

Bouch, A., A. Kuchinsky, and N. Bhatti (2000). „Quality is in the Eye of the Beholder: Meeting Users’ Requirements for Internet Quality of Service.“ In: *Proceedings of the SIGCHI Conference on Human Factors in Computing Systems*. CHI ’00. The Hague, The Netherlands: ACM, pp. 297–304 (cit. on pp. 2, 306, 307).

Briand, L. C., Y. Labiche, and L. O’Sullivan (2003). „Impact analysis and change management of UML models.“ In: *Software Maintenance, 2003. ICSM 2003. Proceedings. International Conference on*, pp. 256–265 (cit. on p. 300).

Bruch, M., M. Monperrus, and M. Mezini (2009). „Learning from Examples to Improve Code Completion Systems.“ In: *Proceedings of the the 7th Joint Meeting of the European Software Engineering Conference and the ACM SIGSOFT Symposium on The Foundations of Software Engineering*. ESEC/FSE ’09. Amsterdam, The Netherlands: ACM, pp. 213–222 (cit. on pp. 8, 286).

Bruch, M., T. Schäfer, and M. Mezini (2006). „FrUiT: IDE Support for Framework Understanding.“ In: *Proceedings of the 2006 OOPSLA Workshop on Eclipse Technology eXchange*. eclipse ’06. Portland, Oregon, USA: ACM, pp. 55–59 (cit. on pp. 8, 281).

Burger, E. J. (2014). „Flexible Views for View-based Model-driven Development.“ PhD thesis. Karlsruhe Institute of Technology (cit. on pp. 71, 299).

Campanelli, P. (2007). „Testing survey questions.“ In: *International handbook of survey methodology*. Ed. by E. D. de Leeuw, J. J. Hox, and D. A. Dillman. Lawrence Erlbaum Associates, pp. 176–200 (cit. on pp. 165, 166, 195).

Canfora, G., M. Di Penta, R. Esposito, and M. L. Villani (2005). „An Approach for QoS-aware Service Composition Based on Genetic Algorithms.“ In: *Proceedings of the 7th Annual Conference on Genetic and Evolutionary*

*Computation*. GECCO '05. Washington DC, USA: ACM, pp. 1069–1075 (cit. on pp. 7, 292).

Canfora, G., M. D. Penta, R. Esposito, and M. L. Villani (2008). „A framework for QoS-aware binding and re-binding of composite web services.“ In: *Journal of Systems and Software* 81.10. Selected papers from the 30th Annual International Computer Software and Applications Conference (COMPSAC), Chicago, September 7-21, 2006, pp. 1754–1769 (cit. on p. 292).

Carenini, G. and J. Loyd (2004). „ValueCharts: Analyzing Linear Models Expressing Preferences and Evaluations.“ In: *Proceedings of the Working Conference on Advanced Visual Interfaces*. AVI '04. Gallipoli, Italy: ACM, pp. 150–157 (cit. on p. 117).

Castro, S., C. De Roover, A. Kellens, A. Lozano, K. Mens, and T. D'Hondt (2011). „Diagnosing and correcting design inconsistencies in source code with logical abduction.“ In: *Science of Computer Programming* 76.12. Special Issue on Software Evolution, Adaptability and Variability, pp. 1113–1129 (cit. on pp. 8, 284).

Ceaparu, I., J. Lazar, K. Bessiere, J. Robinson, and B. Shneiderman (2004). „Determining Causes and Severity of End-User Frustration.“ In: *International Journal of Human-Computer Interaction* (3), pp. 333–356 (cit. on pp. 2, 306).

Chambers, C. and C. Scaffidi (2015). „Impact and utility of smell-driven performance tuning for end-user programmers.“ In: *Journal of Visual Languages & Computing* 28, pp. 176–194 (cit. on pp. 3, 94, 281).

Chen, T.-H., W. Shang, Z. M. Jiang, A. E. Hassan, M. Nasser, and P. Flora (2014). „Detecting Performance Anti-patterns for Applications Developed Using Object-relational Mapping.“ In: *Proceedings of the 36th International Conference on Software Engineering*. ICSE 2014. Hyderabad, India: ACM, pp. 1001–1012 (cit. on pp. 88, 110, 204, 295).

Chen, X., C. P. Ho, R. Osman, P. G. Harrison, and W. J. Knottenbelt (2014). „Understanding, Modelling, and Improving the Performance of Web Applications in Multicore Virtualised Environments.“ In: *Proceedings of the 5th ACM/SPEC International Conference on Performance Engineering*. ICPE '14. Dublin, Ireland: ACM, pp. 197–207 (cit. on p. 110).

Cheng, X. (2008). „Performance, Benchmarking and Sizing in Developing Highly Scalable Enterprise Software.“ In: *Performance Evaluation: Metrics, Models and Benchmarks*. Ed. by S. Kounev, I. Gorton, and K. Sachs.

Vol. 5119. Lecture Notes in Computer Science. Springer Berlin Heidelberg, pp. 174–190 (cit. on pp. 33, 34, 45, 55, 83, 86, 87, 89, 90, 104, 107, 109).

Clark, J. A. and D. K. Pradhan (1995). „Fault injection: a method for validating computer-system dependability.“ In: *Computer* 28.6, pp. 47–56 (cit. on p. 13).

Cortellessa, V., A. Di Marco, and C. Trubiani (2010a). „Performance Antipatterns as Logical Predicates.“ In: *Engineering of Complex Computer Systems (ICECCS), 2010 15th IEEE International Conference on*, pp. 146–156 (cit. on p. 287).

Cortellessa, V., A. di Marco, R. Eramo, A. Pierantonio, and C. Trubiani (2009). „Approaching the Model-Driven Generation of Feedback to Remove Software Performance Flaws.“ In: *Software Engineering and Advanced Applications, 2009. SEAA '09. 35th Euromicro Conference on*, pp. 162–169 (cit. on p. 287).

Cortellessa, V., R. Mirandola, and P. Potena (2010b). „Selecting Optimal Maintenance Plans Based on Cost/Reliability Tradeoffs for Software Subject to Structural and Behavioral Changes.“ In: *Software Maintenance and Reengineering (CSMR), 2010 14th European Conference on*, pp. 21–30 (cit. on p. 291).

Cortellessa, V., A. Di Marco, R. Eramo, A. Pierantonio, and C. Trubiani (2010c). „Digging into UML Models to Remove Performance Antipatterns.“ In: *Proceedings of the 2010 ICSE Workshop on Quantitative Stochastic Models in the Verification and Design of Software Systems*. QUOVADIS '10. Cape Town, South Africa: ACM, pp. 9–16 (cit. on pp. 3, 287).

Cortellessa, V., A. Di Marco, and C. Trubiani (2012). „Software Performance Antipatterns: Modeling and Analysis.“ In: *Formal Methods for Model-Driven Engineering*. Ed. by M. Bernardo, V. Cortellessa, and A. Pierantonio. Vol. 7320. Lecture Notes in Computer Science. Springer Berlin Heidelberg, pp. 290–335 (cit. on p. 287).

– (2014). „An approach for modeling and detecting software performance antipatterns based on first-order logics.“ In: *Software & Systems Modeling* 13.1, pp. 391–432 (cit. on p. 287).

Cortellessa, V. and L. Frittella (2007). „A Framework for Automated Generation of Architectural Feedback from Software Performance Analysis.“ In: *Formal Methods and Stochastic Models for Performance Evaluation*. Ed. by K. Wolter. Vol. 4748. Lecture Notes in Computer Science. Springer Berlin Heidelberg, pp. 171–185 (cit. on p. 287).

Cortellessa, V., R. Mirandola, and P. Potena (2015). „Managing the evolution of a software architecture at minimal cost under performance and reliability constraints.“ In: *Science of Computer Programming* 98.4, pp. 439–463 (cit. on p. 287).

Cottrell, R., R. J. Walker, and J. Denzinger (2008). „Semi-automating Small-scale Source Code Reuse via Structural Correspondence.“ In: *Proceedings of the 16th ACM SIGSOFT International Symposium on Foundations of Software Engineering*. SIGSOFT '08/FSE-16. Atlanta, Georgia: ACM, pp. 214–225 (cit. on pp. 8, 283).

Čubranić, D., G. C. Murphy, J. Singer, and K. S. Booth (2005). „Hipikat: a project memory for software development.“ In: *Software Engineering, IEEE Transactions on* 31.6, pp. 446–465 (cit. on pp. 8, 282).

Dagenais, B. and M. P. Robillard (2008). „Recommending Adaptive Changes for Framework Evolution.“ In: *Proceedings of the 30th International Conference on Software Engineering*. ICSE '08. Leipzig, Germany: ACM, pp. 481–490 (cit. on pp. 8, 285).

Dalkey, N. C., B. B. Brown, and S. Cochran (1969). *The Delphi method: An experimental study of group opinion*. Vol. 3. Rand Corporation Santa Monica, CA (cit. on p. 107).

de Leeuw, E. D. (2007). „Choosing the Method of Data Collection.“ In: *International handbook of survey methodology*. Ed. by E. D. de Leeuw, J. J. Hox, and D. A. Dillman. Lawrence Erlbaum Associates, pp. 113–135 (cit. on pp. 35, 36, 161, 162).

de Leeuw, E. D., J. J. Hox, and D. A. Dillman (2007). „The Cornerstones of Survey Research.“ In: *International handbook of survey methodology*. Ed. by E. D. de Leeuw, J. J. Hox, and D. A. Dillman. Lawrence Erlbaum Associates, pp. 176–200 (cit. on pp. 36, 162–164, 167).

Di Marco, A. and C. Trubiani (2014). „A model-driven approach to broaden the detection of software performance antipatterns at runtime.“ In: *Proceedings 11th International Workshop on Formal Engineering approaches to Software Components and Architectures, FESCA 2014, Grenoble, France, 12th April 2014*. Pp. 77–92 (cit. on pp. 287, 288).

Drago, M. L. (2012). „Quality Driven Model Transformations for Feedback Provisioning.“ PhD thesis. Politecnico di Milano (cit. on pp. 7, 290).

Drago, M. L., C. Ghezzi, and R. Mirandola (2011). „Towards Quality Driven Exploration of Model Transformation Spaces.“ In: *Model Driven Engineering Languages and Systems*. Ed. by J. Whittle, T. Clark, and T. Kühne.

Vol. 6981. Lecture Notes in Computer Science. Springer Berlin Heidelberg, pp. 2–16 (cit. on p. 290).

Duala-Ekoko, E. and M. Robillard (2011). „Using Structure-Based Recommendations to Facilitate Discoverability in APIs.“ In: *ECOOP 2011 - Object-Oriented Programming*. Ed. by M. Mezini. Vol. 6813. Lecture Notes in Computer Science. Springer Berlin Heidelberg, pp. 79–104 (cit. on pp. 8, 283).

Duan, S. and S. Babu (2008). „Guided Problem Diagnosis through Active Learning.“ In: *Autonomic Computing, 2008. ICAC '08. International Conference on*, pp. 45–54 (cit. on p. 205).

Dudney, B., S. Asbury, J. Krozak, and K. Wittkopf (2003). *J2EE antipatterns*. Wiley (cit. on pp. 71, 159, 195, 276).

Dugan Jr., R. F., E. P. Glinert, and A. Shokoufandeh (2002). „The Sisyphus database retrieval software performance antipattern.“ In: *WOSP*. ACM, pp. 10–16 (cit. on p. 277).

Durdik, Z. (2014). „Architectural Design Decision Documentation with Reuse of Design Patterns.“ PhD thesis. Karlsruhe Institute of Technology (cit. on p. 152).

Durdik, Z. and R. Reussner (2013). „On the Appropriate Rationale for Using Design Patterns and Pattern Documentation.“ In: *Proceedings of the 9th International ACM Sigsoft Conference on Quality of Software Architectures*. QoSA '13. Vancouver, British Columbia, Canada: ACM, pp. 107–116 (cit. on p. 311).

Ehlers, J., A. van Hoorn, J. Waller, and W. Hasselbring (2011). „Self-adaptive Software System Monitoring for Performance Anomaly Localization.“ In: *Proceedings of the 8th ACM International Conference on Autonomic Computing*. ICAC '11. Karlsruhe, Germany: ACM, pp. 197–200 (cit. on p. 279).

Eichelberger, H. and K. Schmid (2014). „Flexible resource monitoring of Java programs.“ In: *Journal of Systems and Software* 93, pp. 163–186 (cit. on p. 110).

Etemaadi, R. and M. R. Chaudron (2015). „New degrees of freedom in metaheuristic optimization of component-based systems architecture: Architecture topology and load balancing.“ In: *Science of Computer Programming* 97.3, pp. 366–380 (cit. on pp. 7, 289, 292, 293).

Etemaadi, R., M. Emmerich, and M. Chaudron (2012). „Problem-Specific Search Operators for Metaheuristic Software Architecture Design.“ In: *Search Based Software Engineering*. Ed. by G. Fraser and J. Teixeira de

Souza. Vol. 7515. Lecture Notes in Computer Science. Springer Berlin Heidelberg, pp. 267–272 (cit. on p. 293).

Ferretti, S., V. Ghini, F. Panzieri, M. Pellegrini, and E. Turrini (2010). „QoS–Aware Clouds." In: *Proceedings of the 2010 IEEE 3rd International Conference on Cloud Computing (CLOUD)*, pp. 321–328 (cit. on p. 297).

Fowler, F. and C. Cosenza (2007). „Writing effective questions." In: *International handbook of survey methodology*. Ed. by E. D. de Leeuw, J. J. Hox, and D. A. Dillman. Lawrence Erlbaum Associates, pp. 136–159 (cit. on pp. 36, 164, 165).

Fowler, M. (2002). *Patterns of Enterprise Application Architecture*. Boston, MA, USA: Addison-Wesley Longman Publishing Co., Inc. (cit. on pp. 32, 33).

Franks, G., D. Petriu, M. Woodside, J. Xu, and P. Tregunno (2006). „Layered Bottlenecks and Their Mitigation." In: *Quantitative Evaluation of Systems, 2006. QEST 2006. Third International Conference on*, pp. 103–114 (cit. on p. 289).

Frey, S., A. van Hoorn, R. Jung, W. Hasselbring, and B. Kiel (2011). *MAMBA: A Measurement Architecture for Model-Based Analysis*. Tech. rep. Christian-Albrechts-Universität zu Kiel (cit. on p. 56).

Frølund, S. and J. Koisten (1998). *QML: A Language for Quality of Service Specification*. Tech. rep. Technical Report HPL-98-10. Hewlett-Packard Laboratories (cit. on pp. 55, 56).

Georges, A., D. Buytaert, and L. Eeckhout (2007). „Statistically Rigorous Java Performance Evaluation." In: *Proceedings of the 22Nd Annual ACM SIGPLAN Conference on Object-oriented Programming Systems and Applications*. OOPSLA '07. Montreal, Quebec, Canada: ACM, pp. 57–76 (cit. on pp. 112, 308).

Gooijer, T. de, A. Jansen, H. Koziolek, and A. Koziolek (2012). „An Industrial Case Study of Performance and Cost Design Space Exploration." In: *Proceedings of the 3rd ACM/SPEC International Conference on Performance Engineering*. ICPE '12. Boston, Massachusetts, USA: ACM, pp. 205–216 (cit. on pp. 109, 261).

Gosling, J., B. Joy, G. Steele, and G. Bracha (2005). *The Java™ Language Specification, Third Edition*. 3rd ed. The Java™ Series. Addison-Wesley Professional (cit. on p. 29).

Grassi, V., R. Mirandola, and A. Sabetta (2005). „From Design to Analysis Models: A Kernel Language for Performance and Reliability Analysis of Component-based Systems." In: *Proceedings of the 5th International Workshop on Software and Performance*. WOSP '05. Palma, Illes Balears, Spain: ACM, pp. 25–36 (cit. on pp. 19, 34).

Grechanik, M., C. Fu, and Q. Xie (2012). „Automatically Finding Performance Problems with Feedback-directed Learning Software Testing." In: *Proceedings of the 34th International Conference on Software Engineering*. ICSE '12. Zurich, Switzerland: IEEE Press, pp. 156–166 (cit. on p. 279).

Grunske, L. (2006). „Identifying "Good" Architectural Design Alternatives with Multi-objective Optimization Strategies." In: *Proceedings of the 28th International Conference on Software Engineering*. ICSE '06. Shanghai, China: ACM, pp. 849–852 (cit. on pp. 7, 293).

Hallal, H., E. Alikacem, W. Tunney, S. Boroday, and A. Petrenko (2004). „Antipattern-based detection of deficiencies in Java multithreaded software." In: *Quality Software, 2004. QSIC 2004. Proceedings. Fourth International Conference on*, pp. 258–267 (cit. on p. 277).

Han, S., Y. Dang, S. Ge, D. Zhang, and T. Xie (2012). „Performance Debugging in the Large via Mining Millions of Stack Traces." In: *Proceedings of the 34th International Conference on Software Engineering*. ICSE '12. Zurich, Switzerland: IEEE Press, pp. 145–155 (cit. on p. 278).

Hatvani, L., A. Jansen, C. Seceleanu, and P. Pettersson (2010). „An Integrated Tool for Trade-off Analysis of Quality-of-service Attributes." In: *Proceedings of the 2Nd International Workshop on the Quality of Service-Oriented Software Systems*. QUASOSS '10. Oslo, Norway: ACM, 2:1–2:6 (cit. on p. 113).

Heidenreich, F., J. Johannes, M. Seifert, and C. Wende (2009). *JaMoPP: The Java Model Parser and Printer*. Tech. rep. Institut für Software- und Multimediatechnik, Technische Universität Dresden (cit. on pp. 29, 30, 34).

– (2010). „Closing the Gap between Modelling and Java." In: *Software Language Engineering*. Ed. by M. van den Brand, D. Gasević, and J. Gray. Vol. 5969. Lecture Notes in Computer Science. Springer Berlin Heidelberg, pp. 374–383 (cit. on pp. 29, 30, 121, 208, 308).

Heinrich, R. (2014). *Aligning Business Processes and Information Systems*. Springer Vieweg, p. 233 (cit. on p. 152).

Herbst, N. R., S. Kounev, and R. Reussner (2013). „Elasticity in Cloud Computing: What It Is, and What It Is Not." In: *Proceedings of the 10th International Conference on Autonomic Computing (ICAC 13)*. San Jose, CA: USENIX, pp. 23–27 (cit. on p. 1).

Hill, E., L. Pollock, and K. Vijay-Shanker (2007). „Exploring the Neighborhood with Dora to Expedite Software Maintenance.“ In: *Proceedings of the Twenty-second IEEE/ACM International Conference on Automated Software Engineering*. ASE '07. Atlanta, Georgia, USA: ACM, pp. 14–23 (cit. on pp. 8, 285).

Hill, M. D. (1990). „What is Scalability?“ In: *ACM SIGARCH Computer Architecture News* 18.4, pp. 18–21 (cit. on p. 2).

Holmes, R., R. Walker, and G. Murphy (2006). „Approximate Structural Context Matching: An Approach to Recommend Relevant Examples.“ In: *Software Engineering, IEEE Transactions on* 32.12, pp. 952–970 (cit. on pp. 6, 8, 282).

Horikawa, T. (2011). „An Approach for Scalability-bottleneck Solution: Identification and Elimination of Scalability Bottlenecks in a DBMS.“ In: *Proceedings of the 2Nd ACM/SPEC International Conference on Performance Engineering*. ICPE '11. Karlsruhe, Germany: ACM, pp. 31–42 (cit. on pp. 110, 297).

Hsueh, M.-C., T. Tsai, and R. Iyer (1997). „Fault injection techniques and tools.“ In: *Computer* 30.4, pp. 75–82 (cit. on pp. 13, 205).

Huber, N., F. Brosig, and S. Kounev (2011). „Model-based Self-Adaptive Resource Allocation in Virtualized Environments.“ In: *6th International Symposium on Software Engineering for Adaptive and Self-Managing Systems (SEAMS 2011)*. Waikiki, Honolulu, HI, USA: ACM, pp. 90–99 (cit. on pp. 109, 297).

Huber, N., A. van Hoorn, A. Koziolek, F. Brosig, and S. Kounev (2012). „S/T/A: Meta-Modeling Run-Time Adaptation in Component-Based System Architectures.“ In: *Proceedings of the 9th IEEE International Conference on e-Business Engineering (ICEBE 2012)*. Hangzhou, China: IEEE Computer Society, pp. 70–77 (cit. on pp. 33, 297, 298).

Hughes, R. T. (1996). „Expert judgement as an estimating method.“ In: *Information and Software Technology* 38.2, pp. 67–75 (cit. on pp. 105, 106).

Hunt, C. and J. Binu (2012). *Java™ Performance*. Addison-Wesley (cit. on pp. 27, 204).

Ipek, E., S. A. McKee, K. Singh, R. Caruana, B. R. d. Supinski, and M. Schulz (2008). „Efficient Architectural Design Space Exploration via Predictive Modeling.“ In: *ACM Trans. Archit. Code Optim.* 4.4, 1:1–1:34 (cit. on pp. 7, 294).

ISO/IEC/IEEE (2010). „Systems and software engineering – Vocabulary.“ In: *International Standard ISO/IEC/IEEE 24765:2010(E)*, pp. 1–418 (cit. on pp. 1, 5–7, 18, 21, 57).

Jain, R. (1991). *The Art of Computer Systems Performance Analysis*. John Wiley & Sons (cit. on pp. 4, 5, 7, 18, 19, 47, 54, 55, 57, 61, 67, 111, 112, 158, 190).

Java Persistence 2.1 Expert Group (2013). *JSR 338: Java$^{TM}$ Persistence API, Version 2.1* (cit. on pp. 24–26, 121, 133).

Jiang, Z. M., A. E. Hassan, G. Hamann, and P. Flora (2009). „Automated performance analysis of load tests.“ In: *Software Maintenance, 2009. ICSM 2009. IEEE International Conference on*, pp. 125–134 (cit. on p. 279).

Jin, G., L. Song, X. Shi, J. Scherpelz, and S. Lu (2012). „Understanding and Detecting Real-world Performance Bugs.“ In: *Proceedings of the 33rd ACM SIGPLAN Conference on Programming Language Design and Implementation*. PLDI '12. Beijing, China: ACM, pp. 77–88 (cit. on pp. 3, 306).

Jørgensen, M. (2004). „A review of studies on expert estimation of software development effort.“ In: *Journal of Systems and Software* 70.1-2, pp. 37–60 (cit. on p. 106).

– (2007). „Forecasting of software development work effort: Evidence on expert judgement and formal models.“ In: *International Journal of Forecasting* 23.3, pp. 449–462 (cit. on p. 106).

Jørgensen, M. and S. Grimstad (2008). „Avoiding Irrelevant and Misleading Information When Estimating Development Effort.“ In: *Software, IEEE* 25.3, pp. 78–83 (cit. on p. 106).

Jovic, M., A. Adamoli, and M. Hauswirth (2011). „Catch Me if You Can: Performance Bug Detection in the Wild.“ In: *Proceedings of the 2011 ACM International Conference on Object Oriented Programming Systems Languages and Applications*. OOPSLA '11. Portland, Oregon, USA: ACM, pp. 155–170 (cit. on pp. 3, 278, 307).

Jung, G., K. R. Joshi, M. A. Hiltunen, R. D. Schlichting, and C. Pu (2008). „Generating Adaptation Policies for Multi-tier Applications in Consolidated Server Environments.“ In: *Proceedings of the International Conference on Autonomic Computing (ICAC '08)*, pp. 23–32 (cit. on p. 297).

Karlsson, J., S. Olsson, and K. Ryan (1997). „Improved practical support for large-scale requirements prioritising.“ In: *Requirements Engineering* 2.1, pp. 51–60 (cit. on pp. 32, 113).

Karlsson, J., C. Wohlin, and B. Regnell (1998). „An evaluation of methods for prioritizing software requirements.“ In: *Information and Software Technology* 39.14–15, pp. 939–947 (cit. on p. 32).

Karwin, B. (2010). *SQL Antipatterns: Avoiding the Pitfalls of Database Programming*. Pragmatic Programmers. Pragmatic Bookshelf (cit. on pp. 159, 277).

Kavimandan, A. and A. Gokhale (2009). „Applying Model Transformations to Optimizing Real-Time QoS Configurations in DRE Systems.“ In: *Architectures for Adaptive Software Systems*. Ed. by R. Mirandola, I. Gorton, and C. Hofmeister. Vol. 5581. Lecture Notes in Computer Science. Springer Berlin Heidelberg, pp. 18–35 (cit. on pp. 7, 290, 291).

Kehrer, T., U. Kelter, and G. Taentzer (2011). „A rule-based approach to the semantic lifting of model differences in the context of model versioning.“ In: *Automated Software Engineering (ASE), 2011 26th IEEE/ACM International Conference on*, pp. 163–172 (cit. on p. 73).

Kersten, M. and G. C. Murphy (2005). „Mylar: A Degree-of-interest Model for IDEs.“ In: *Proceedings of the 4th International Conference on Aspect-oriented Software Development*. AOSD '05. Chicago, Illinois: ACM, pp. 159–168 (cit. on p. 286).

– (2006). „Using Task Context to Improve Programmer Productivity.“ In: *Proceedings of the 14th ACM SIGSOFT International Symposium on Foundations of Software Engineering*. SIGSOFT '06/FSE-14. Portland, Oregon, USA: ACM, pp. 1–11 (cit. on p. 286).

Kim, S., D.-K. Kim, L. Lu, and S. Park (2009). „Quality-driven architecture development using architectural tactics.“ In: *Journal of Systems and Software* 82.8. SI: Architectural Decisions and Rationale, pp. 1211–1231 (cit. on p. 291).

Kohavi, R. and R. Longbotham (2007). „Online Experiments: Lessons Learned.“ In: *Computer* 40.9, pp. 103–105 (cit. on pp. 2, 306).

Könemann, P. and O. Zimmermann (2010). „Linking Design Decisions to Design Models in Model-Based Software Development.“ In: *Software Architecture*. Ed. by M. A. Babar and I. Gorton. Vol. 6285. Lecture Notes in Computer Science. Springer Berlin Heidelberg, pp. 246–262 (cit. on p. 311).

Kounev, S., K. Bender, F. Brosig, N. Huber, and R. Okamoto (2011a). „Automated Simulation-Based Capacity Planning for Enterprise Data Fabrics.“ In: *4th International ICST Conference on Simulation Tools and Techniques*. Barcelona, Spain: ICST, pp. 27–36 (cit. on pp. 110, 297).

Kounev, S., F. Brosig, and N. Huber (2011b). „Self-aware QoS Management in Virtualized Infrastructures.“ In: *Proceedings of the 8th ACM International Conference on Autonomic Computing*. ICAC '11. Karlsruhe, Germany: ACM, pp. 175–176 (cit. on p. 297).

Koziolek, A. (2013). „Automated Improvement of Software Architecture Models for Performance and Other Quality Attributes.“ PhD thesis. Karlsruhe Institute of Technology (cit. on pp. 7, 109, 117, 152, 153, 261, 292).

Koziolek, A., D. Ardagna, and R. Mirandola (2013). „Hybrid multi-attribute QoS optimization in component based software systems.“ In: *Journal of Systems and Software* 86.10, pp. 2542–2558 (cit. on p. 292).

Koziolek, A., H. Koziolek, and R. Reussner (2011). „PerOpteryx: automated application of tactics in multi-objective software architecture optimization.“ In: *Proceedings of the joint ACM SIGSOFT conference (QoSA+ISARCS'11)*. Boulder, Colorado, USA: ACM, pp. 33–42 (cit. on pp. 109, 256, 292).

Koziolek, H. (2008). „Parameter dependencies for reusable performance specifications of software components.“ PhD thesis. Universität Oldenburg (cit. on pp. 151–154, 156, 198, 246, 252, 256, 261).

– (2010). „Performance evaluation of component-based software systems: A survey.“ In: *Performance Evaluation* 67.8. Special Issue on Software and Performance, pp. 634–658 (cit. on p. 19).

Kruchten, P. (2003). *The Rational Unified Process: An Introduction*. 3rd ed. Boston, MA, USA: Addison-Wesley Longman Publishing Co., Inc., p. 336 (cit. on p. 47).

Lazar, J., A. Jones, M. Hackley, and B. Shneiderman (2006). „Severity and impact of computer user frustration: A comparison of student and workplace users.“ In: *Interacting with Computers* 18.2, pp. 187–207 (cit. on pp. 2, 306).

Leffingwell, D. and D. Widrig (1999). *Managing Software Requirements: A Unified Approach*. Boston, MA, USA: Addison-Wesley Longman Publishing Co., Inc. (cit. on p. 119).

Lehnert, S. (2011). *A review of software change impact analysis*. Tech. rep. Ilmenau University of Technology (cit. on pp. 97, 299, 300).

Lehnert, S., Q. Farooq, and M. Riebisch (2012). „A Taxonomy of Change Types and Its Application in Software Evolution.“ In: *Engineering of Computer Based Systems (ECBS), 2012 IEEE 19th International Conference and Workshops on*, pp. 98–107 (cit. on pp. 71, 298, 299).

Lehnert, S., Q. Farooq, and M. Riebisch (2013). „Rule-Based Impact Analysis for Heterogeneous Software Artifacts.“ In: *Proceedings of the 17th Euro-*

*pean Conference on Software Maintenance and Reengineering (CSMR).* IEEE, pp. 209–218 (cit. on pp. 45, 71, 97, 100, 300, 301, 309).

Lehtola, L. and M. Kauppinen (2004). „Empirical Evaluation of Two Requirements Prioritization Methods in Product Development Projects." In: *Software Process Improvement.* Ed. by T. Dings. Vol. 3281. Lecture Notes in Computer Science. Springer Berlin Heidelberg, pp. 161–170 (cit. on p. 32).

Lengauer, P. and H. Mössenböck (2014). „The Taming of the Shrew: Increasing Performance by Automatic Parameter Tuning for Java Garbage Collectors." In: *Proceedings of the 5th ACM/SPEC International Conference on Performance Engineering.* ICPE '14. Dublin, Ireland: ACM, pp. 111–122 (cit. on pp. 8, 110, 295).

Li, J., J. Chinneck, M. Woodside, M. Litoiu, and G. Iszlai (2009). „Performance model driven QoS guarantees and optimization in clouds." In: *Proceedings of the ICSE Workshop on Software Engineering Challenges of Cloud Computing (CLOUD '09)*, pp. 15–22 (cit. on p. 297).

Libič, P., L. Bulej, V. Horky, and P. Tůma (2014). „On the Limits of Modeling Generational Garbage Collector Performance." In: *Proceedings of the 5th ACM/SPEC International Conference on Performance Engineering.* ICPE '14. Dublin, Ireland: ACM, pp. 15–26 (cit. on p. 110).

Lilja, D. J. (2005). *Measuring computer performance: a practitioner's guide.* Cambridge University Press (cit. on p. 21).

Lin, C.-E. and K. Kavi (2014). „Performance Engineering Using Performance Antipatterns in Distributed Systems." In: *Proceedings of The Ninth International Conference on Software Engineering Advances*, pp. 627–636 (cit. on p. 288).

Linstone, H. A., M. Turoff, et al. (1975). *The Delphi method: Techniques and applications.* Vol. 29. Addison-Wesley Reading, MA (cit. on p. 107).

Liu, H. H. (2009). *Software Performance and Scalability: A Quantitative Approach.* John Wiley & Sons, Inc. (cit. on pp. 21, 224, 240, 251, 258).

Lohr, S. L. (2007). „Coverage and sampling." In: *International handbook of survey methodology.* Ed. by E. D. de Leeuw, J. J. Hox, and D. A. Dillman. Lawrence Erlbaum Associates, pp. 97–112 (cit. on pp. 36, 162, 163).

Long, F., X. Wang, and Y. Cai (2009). „API Hyperlinking via Structural Overlap." In: *Proceedings of the the 7th Joint Meeting of the European Software Engineering Conference and the ACM SIGSOFT Symposium on The Foundations of Software Engineering.* ESEC/FSE '09. Amsterdam, The Netherlands: ACM, pp. 203–212 (cit. on p. 286).

Lozano, A., A. Kellens, and K. Mens (2011). „Mendel: Source code recommendation based on a genetic metaphor.“ In: *Automated Software Engineering (ASE), 2011 26th IEEE/ACM International Conference on*, pp. 384–387 (cit. on pp. 6, 8, 282).

Lozano, A., A. Kellens, K. Mens, and G. Arevalo (2010). „MEntoR: Mining Entities to Rules.“ In: *9th BElgian-NEtherlands EVOLution Workshop (BENEVOL), Lille* (cit. on pp. 8, 284).

Lozano, A., K. Mens, and A. Kellens (2015). „Usage contracts: Offering immediate feedback on violations of structural source-code regularities.“ In: *Science of Computer Programming*. in press (cit. on pp. 8, 284).

Maiden, N. A. and C. Ncube (1998). „Acquiring COTS Software Selection Requirements.“ In: *IEEE Softw.* 15.2, pp. 46–56 (cit. on p. 32).

Malek, S., M. Mikic-Rakic, and N. Medvidovic (2004). „An Extensible Framework for Autonomic Analysis and Improvement of Distributed Deployment Architectures.“ In: *Proceedings of the 1st ACM SIGSOFT Workshop on Self-managed Systems*. WOSS ’04. Newport Beach, California: ACM, pp. 95–99 (cit. on pp. 8, 296).

Mandelin, D., L. Xu, R. Bodık, and D. Kimelman (2005). „Jungloid Mining: Helping to Navigate the API Jungle.“ In: *Proceedings of the 2005 ACM SIGPLAN Conference on Programming Language Design and Implementation*. PLDI ’05. Chicago, IL, USA: ACM, pp. 48–61 (cit. on pp. 8, 283).

Martens, A., H. Koziolek, L. Prechelt, and R. Reussner (2011). „From monolithic to component-based performance evaluation of software architectures.“ English. In: *Empirical Software Engineering* 16.5, pp. 587–622 (cit. on p. 154).

Martinec, T., L. Marek, A. Steinhauser, P. Tůma, Q. Noorshams, A. Rentschler, and R. Reussner (2014). „Constructing Performance Model of JMS Middleware Platform.“ In: *Proceedings of the 5th ACM/SPEC International Conference on Performance Engineering*. ICPE ’14. Dublin, Ireland: ACM, pp. 123–134 (cit. on p. 110).

McCarey, F., M. Ó. Cinnéide, and N. Kushmerick (2005). „Rascal: A Recommender Agent for Agile Reuse.“ In: *Artificial Intelligence Review* 24.3-4, pp. 253–276 (cit. on pp. 6, 8, 281).

Menasce, D. A. and V. Almeida (2002). *Capacity Planning for Web Services: Metrics, Models, and Methods*. Prentice Hall (cit. on p. 20).

Mens, K. and A. Lozano (2014). „Source Code-Based Recommendation Systems.“ English. In: *Recommendation Systems in Software Engineering*.

Ed. by M. P. Robillard, W. Maalej, R. J. Walker, and T. Zimmermann. Springer Berlin Heidelberg, pp. 93–130 (cit. on pp. 5, 14, 38, 40–43).

Mens, K., I. Michiels, and R. Wuyts (2002). „Supporting software development through declaratively codified programming patterns.“ In: *Expert Systems with Applications* 23.4, pp. 405–413 (cit. on p. 283).

Miller, B., M. Callaghan, J. Cargille, J. Hollingsworth, R. Irvin, K. Karavanic, K. Kunchithapadam, and T. Newhall (1995). „The Paradyn parallel performance measurement tool.“ In: *Computer* 28.11, pp. 37–46 (cit. on pp. 91, 279).

Mirandola, R. and C. Trubiani (2012). „A Deep Investigation for QoS-based Feedback at Design Time and Runtime.“ In: *Engineering of Complex Computer Systems (ICECCS), 2012 17th International Conference on*, pp. 147–156 (cit. on pp. 287, 291).

Mirandola, R. and P. Potena (2010). „Self-Adaptation of Service Based Systems Based on Cost/Quality Attributes Tradeoffs.“ In: *Symbolic and Numeric Algorithms for Scientific Computing (SYNASC), 2010 12th International Symposium on*, pp. 493–501 (cit. on p. 291).

Mirgorodskiy, A. V. and B. P. Miller (2008). „Diagnosing Distributed Systems with Self-propelled Instrumentation.“ In: *Middleware 2008*. Ed. by V. Issarny and R. Schantz. Vol. 5346. Lecture Notes in Computer Science. Springer Berlin Heidelberg, pp. 82–103 (cit. on p. 280).

Moløkken, K. and M. Jørgensen (2003). „A review of software surveys on software effort estimation.“ In: *Proceedings of the International Symposium on Empirical Software Engineering*, pp. 223–230 (cit. on p. 105).

Al-Naeem, T., I. Gorton, M. A. Babar, F. Rabhi, and B. Benatallah (2005). „A Quality-driven Systematic Approach for Architecting Distributed Software Applications.“ In: *Proceedings of the 27th International Conference on Software Engineering*. ICSE ’05. St. Louis, MO, USA: ACM, pp. 244–253 (cit. on p. 113).

Ngo-The, A. and G. Ruhe (2005). „Decision Support in Requirements Engineering.“ In: *Engineering and Managing Software Requirements*. Ed. by A. Aurum and C. Wohlin. Springer Berlin Heidelberg, pp. 267–286 (cit. on p. 31).

Nguyen, T. T., H. A. Nguyen, N. H. Pham, J. Al-Kofahi, and T. N. Nguyen (2010). „Recurring Bug Fixes in Object-oriented Programs.“ In: *Proceedings of the 32Nd ACM/IEEE International Conference on Software Engineering - Volume 1*. ICSE ’10. Cape Town, South Africa: ACM, pp. 315–324 (cit. on p. 287).

Noorshams, Q., A. Martens, and R. Reussner (2010). „Using Quality of Service Bounds for Effective Multi-objective Software Architecture Optimization.“ In: *Proceedings of the 2nd International Workshop on the Quality of Service-Oriented Software Systems (QUASOSS '10), Oslo, Norway, October 4, 2010*. ACM, New York, NY, USA, 1:1–1:6 (cit. on pp. 56–58, 62, 64).

Padala, P., K.-Y. Hou, K. G. Shin, X. Zhu, M. Uysal, Z. Wang, S. Singhal, and A. Merchant (2009). „Automated Control of Multiple Virtualized Resources.“ In: *Proceedings of the 4th ACM European Conference on Computer Systems*. EuroSys '09. Nuremberg, Germany: ACM, pp. 13–26 (cit. on p. 297).

Parsons, T. (2007). „Automatic Detection of Performance Design and Deployment Antipatterns in Component Based Enterprise Systems.“ PhD thesis. University College Dublin (cit. on p. 278).

Parsons, T. and J. Murphy (2008). „Detecting Performance Antipatterns in Component Based Enterprise Systems.“ In: *Journal of Object Technology* (3), pp. 55–90 (cit. on p. 278).

Peiris, M., J. Hill, J. Thelin, S. Bykov, G. Kliot, and C. Konig (2014a). „PAD: Performance Anomaly Detection in Multi-server Distributed Systems.“ In: *Cloud Computing (CLOUD), 2014 IEEE 7th International Conference on*, pp. 769–776 (cit. on pp. 110, 279).

Peiris, M. and J. H. Hill (2014b). „Towards Detecting Software Performance Anti-patterns Using Classification Techniques.“ In: *SIGSOFT Softw. Eng. Notes* 39.1, pp. 1–4 (cit. on p. 278).

Potena, P. (2013). „Optimization of adaptation plans for a service-oriented architecture with cost, reliability, availability and performance tradeoff.“ In: *Journal of Systems and Software* 86.3, pp. 624–648 (cit. on pp. 7, 291).

Ramsay, J., A. Barbesi, and J. Preece (1998). „A psychological investigation of long retrieval times on the World Wide Web.“ In: *Interacting with Computers* 10.1. HCI and Information Retrieval, pp. 77–86 (cit. on pp. 2, 306).

Rao, R. and S. K. Card (1994). „The Table Lens: Merging Graphical and Symbolic Representations in an Interactive Focus + Context Visualization for Tabular Information.“ In: *Proceedings of the SIGCHI Conference on Human Factors in Computing Systems*. CHI '94. Boston, Massachusetts, USA: ACM, pp. 318–322 (cit. on p. 117).

Rässler, S., D. B. Rubin, and N. Schenker (2007). „Incomplete Data: Diagnosis, Imputation, and Estimation.“ In: *International handbook of sur-*

*vey methodology*. Ed. by E. D. de Leeuw, J. J. Hox, and D. A. Dillman. Lawrence Erlbaum Associates, pp. 370–386 (cit. on p. 167).

Regnell, B., M. Höst, J. N. och Dag, P. Beremark, and T. Hjelm (2001). „An industrial case study on distributed prioritisation in market-driven requirements engineering for packaged software.“ In: *Requirements Engineering* 6.1, pp. 51–62 (cit. on p. 120).

Reimer, D., E. Schonberg, K. Srinivas, H. Srinivasan, B. Alpern, R. D. Johnson, A. Kershenbaum, and L. Koved (2004). „SABER: Smart Analysis Based Error Reduction.“ In: *Proceedings of the 2004 ACM SIGSOFT International Symposium on Software Testing and Analysis*. ISSTA '04. Boston, Massachusetts, USA: ACM, pp. 243–251 (cit. on p. 286).

Ren, X., F. Shah, F. Tip, B. G. Ryder, and O. Chesley (2004). „Chianti: A Tool for Change Impact Analysis of Java Programs.“ In: *Proceedings of the 19th Annual ACM SIGPLAN Conference on Object-oriented Programming, Systems, Languages, and Applications*. OOPSLA '04. Vancouver, BC, Canada: ACM, pp. 432–448 (cit. on pp. 298, 299).

Reussner, R., S. Becker, E. Burger, J. Happe, M. Hauck, A. Koziolek, H. Koziolek, K. Krogmann, and M. Kupperberg (2011). *The Palladio Component Model*. Tech. rep. Faculty of Informatics, Karlsruhe Institute of Technology (cit. on pp. 21, 34).

Robillard, M. P. (2008). „Topology Analysis of Software Dependencies.“ In: *ACM Trans. Softw. Eng. Methodol.* 17.4, 18:1–18:36 (cit. on p. 285).

– (2009). „What Makes APIs Hard to Learn? Answers from Developers.“ In: *IEEE Software* 26.6, pp. 27–34 (cit. on pp. 3, 306).

Rokach, L. and O. Maimon (2008). *Data Mining with Decision Trees: Theory and Applications*. Vol. 69. Series in machine perception and artificial intelligence. World Scientific Publishing Company, Incorporated (cit. on p. 79).

Rostami, K., J. Stammel, R. Heinrich, and R. Reussner (2015). „Architecture-based Assessment and Planning of Change Requests.“ In: *Proceedings of the 11th International ACM SIGSOFT Conference on the Quality of Software Architectures (QoSA'15)*. QoSA'15. Montreal, QC, Canada: ACM (cit. on pp. 71, 105, 106, 299).

Runeson, P., M. Höst, A. Rainer, and B. Regnell (2012). *Case Study Research in Software Engineering: Guidelines and Examples*. John Wiley and Sons (cit. on pp. 112, 160, 163, 166, 195, 246).

Saaty, T. L. (2005). „The analytic hierarchy and analytic network processes for the measurement of intangible criteria and for decision-making.“ In: *Multi-*

*ple criteria decision analysis: state of the art surveys*. Ed. by J. Figueira, S. Greco, and M. Ehrgott. International Series in Operations Research & Management Science. Springer, pp. 345–405 (cit. on pp. 31, 75, 76, 115, 116).

Saaty, T. L. (2008). *Decision Making for Leaders - The Analytic Hierarchy Process for Decisions in a Complex World*. RWS Publications (cit. on pp. 116, 210).

Sage, A. (2003). „Observation-Driven Configuration of Complex Software Systems." PhD thesis. University of St Andrews (cit. on p. 296).

Shang, W., A. E. Hassan, M. Nasser, and P. Flora (2015). „Automated Detection of Performance Regressions Using Regression Models on Clustered Performance Counters." In: *Proceedings of the 6th ACM/SPEC International Conference on Performance Engineering*. ICPE '15. Austin, Texas, USA: ACM, pp. 15–26 (cit. on p. 278).

Skadberg, Y. X. and J. R. Kimmel (2004). „Visitors' flow experience while browsing a Web site: its measurement, contributing factors and consequences." In: *Computers in Human Behavior* 20.3, pp. 403–422 (cit. on pp. 2, 306, 308).

Smaalders, B. (2006). „Performance Anti-Patterns." In: *Queue* 4.1, pp. 44–50 (cit. on p. 277).

Smith, C. U. (2007). „Introduction to Software Performance Engineering: Origins and Outstanding Problems." In: *Formal Methods for Performance Evaluation*. Ed. by M. Bernardo and J. Hillston. Vol. 4486. Lecture Notes in Computer Science. Springer Berlin Heidelberg, pp. 395–428 (cit. on p. 46).

– (2015). „Software Performance Engineering Then and Now: A Position Paper." In: *Proceedings of the 2015 Workshop on Challenges in Performance Methods for Software Development*. WOSP '15. Austin, Texas, USA: ACM, pp. 1–3 (cit. on pp. 3, 8, 17, 46, 303, 306, 307).

Smith, C. U. and L. G. Williams (2000). „Software performance antipatterns." In: *Workshop on Software and Performance*. ACM, pp. 127–136 (cit. on p. 276).

– (2002). „New software performance antipatterns: More ways to shoot yourself in the foot." In: *Int. CMG Conference*, pp. 667–674 (cit. on p. 276).

Smith, C. and L. Williams (2002). „Software Performance AntiPatterns; Common Performance Problems and their Solutions." In: *CMG-CONFERENCE-*. Vol. 2, pp. 797–806 (cit. on pp. 159, 276).

– (2003). „More new software performance antipatterns: Even more ways to shoot yourself in the foot.“ In: *CMG-CONFERENCE-*, pp. 717–725 (cit. on pp. 27, 71, 204, 276).

Solingen, R. van and E. Berghout (1999). *The Goal/Question/Metric Method: a practical guide for quality improvement of software development.* McGraw-Hill Publishing Company (cit. on pp. 160, 161, 195).

Stahl, T., M. Völter, J. Bettin, A. Haase, and S. Helsen (2006). *Model-Driven Software Development: Technology, Engineering, Management.* John Wiley & Sons, Ltd (cit. on pp. 27, 28).

Stammel, J. and R. Reussner (2009). „Kamp: Karlsruhe architectural maintainability prediction.“ In: *Proceedings of the 1. Workshop des GI-Arbeitskreises Langlebige Softwaresysteme (L2S2): Design for Future-Langlebige Softwaresysteme*, pp. 87–98 (cit. on p. 299).

Stammel, J. and M. Trifu (2011). „Tool-supported estimation of software evolution effort in service-oriented systems.“ In: *Joint Proceedings of the First International Workshop on Model-Driven Software Migration (MDSM 2011) and the Fifth International Workshop on Software Quality and Maintainability (SQM 2011).* Vol. 708, pp. 56–63 (cit. on p. 299).

Steinder, M., I. Whalley, D. Carrera, I. Gaweda, and D. Chess (2007). „Server virtualization in autonomic management of heterogeneous workloads.“ In: *Proceedings of the 10th IFIP/IEEE International Symposium on Integrated Network Management (IM 2007)*, pp. 139–148 (cit. on p. 297).

Svahnberg, M. and C. Wohlin (2002). „Consensus Building when Comparing Software Architectures.“ In: *Product Focused Software Process Improvement.* Ed. by M. Oivo and S. Komi-Sirviö. Vol. 2559. Lecture Notes in Computer Science. Springer Berlin Heidelberg, pp. 436–452 (cit. on p. 113).

Tate, B., M. Clark, B. Lee, and P. Linskey (2003). *Bitter EJB.* Manning (cit. on pp. 159, 277).

Trubiani, C. and A. Koziolek (2011). „Detection and solution of software performance antipatterns in palladio architectural models.“ In: *Proceedings of the 2nd ACM/SPEC International Conference on Performance engineering.* Vol. 36. 5. ACM, pp. 19–30 (cit. on pp. 3, 4, 7, 107, 109, 256, 287, 288).

Trubiani, C., A. Koziolek, V. Cortellessa, and R. Reussner (2014). „Guilt-based handling of software performance antipatterns in palladio architectural models.“ In: *Journal of Systems and Software* 95, pp. 141–165 (cit. on pp. 287, 288).

van Hoorn, A. (2014b). „Model-Driven Online Capacity Management for Component-Based Software Systems.“ PhD thesis. Christian-Albrechts-Universität zu Kiel (cit. on pp. 247, 297, 311).

van Hoorn, A., M. Rohr, and W. Hasselbring (2008). „Generating Probabilistic and Intensity-Varying Workload for Web-Based Software Systems.“ In: *Proceedings of the SPEC International Workshop on Performance Evaluation: Metrics, Models and Benchmarks*. SIPEW '08. Darmstadt, Germany: Springer-Verlag, pp. 124–143 (cit. on p. 203).

van Hoorn, A., J. Waller, and W. Hasselbring (2012). „Kieker: A Framework for Application Performance Monitoring and Dynamic Software Analysis.“ In: *Proceedings of the 3rd ACM/SPEC International Conference on Performance Engineering*. ICPE '12. Boston, Massachusetts, USA: ACM, pp. 247–248 (cit. on pp. 110, 311).

Van, H. N., F. D. Tran, and J.-M. Menaud (2010). „Performance and Power Management for Cloud Infrastructures.“ In: *Proceedings of the 2010 IEEE 3rd International Conference on Cloud Computing (CLOUD)*, pp. 329–336 (cit. on p. 297).

Vuduc, R., J. W. Demmel, and J. A. Bilmes (2004). „Statistical Models for Empirical Search-Based Performance Tuning.“ In: *Int. J. High Perform. Comput. Appl.* 18.1, pp. 65–94 (cit. on p. 110).

Waller, J., N. C. Ehmke, and W. Hasselbring (2015). „Including Performance Benchmarks into Continuous Integration to Enable DevOps.“ In: *SIGSOFT Softw. Eng. Notes* 40.2, pp. 1–4 (cit. on p. 280).

Wgrzynowicz, P. (2013). „Performance antipatterns of one to many association in hibernate.“ In: *Computer Science and Information Systems (FedCSIS), 2013 Federated Conference on*, pp. 1475–1481 (cit. on p. 277).

Wert, A. (2015). „Performance Problem Diagnostics by Systematic Experimentation.“ appears 2015. PhD thesis. Karlsruhe Institute of Technology (cit. on p. 310).

Wert, A., J. Happe, and L. Happe (2013). „Supporting Swift Reaction: Automatically Uncovering Performance Problems by Systematic Experiments.“ In: *Proceedings of the 2013 International Conference on Software Engineering*. ICSE '13. San Francisco, CA, USA: IEEE Press, pp. 552–561 (cit. on pp. 40, 94, 110, 278, 280, 309).

Westermann, D. J. (2014). „Deriving Goal-oriented Performance Models by Systematic Experimentation.“ PhD thesis. Karlsruhe Institute of Technology (cit. on pp. 19, 56, 110, 309).

Westermann, D., J. Happe, and R. Farahbod (2013). „An Experiment Specification Language for Goal-driven, Automated Performance Evaluations.“ In: *Proceedings of the 28th Annual ACM Symposium on Applied Computing*. SAC '13. Coimbra, Portugal: ACM, pp. 1043–1048 (cit. on p. 56).

Weyuker, E. and F. Vokolos (2000). „Experience with performance testing of software systems: issues, an approach, and case study.“ In: *Software Engineering, IEEE Transactions on* 26.12, pp. 1147–1156 (cit. on p. 112).

Williams, L. G. and C. U. Smith (2002b). „PASA$^{SM}$: An Architectural Approach to Fixing Software Performance Problems.“ In: *International Computer Measurement Group Conference*, pp. 307–320 (cit. on p. 288).

Winand, M. (2012b). *SQL Performance Explained: Everything developers need to know about SQL performance*. Winand, Makus (cit. on pp. 159, 277).

Woodside, M., G. Franks, and D. C. Petriu (2007). „The Future of Software Performance Engineering.“ In: *Future of Software Engineering, 2007. FOSE '07*, pp. 171–187 (cit. on pp. 3, 5, 7–9, 18, 109, 304, 306).

Xie, T. and J. Pei (2006). „MAPO: Mining API Usages from Open Source Repositories.“ In: *Proceedings of the 2006 International Workshop on Mining Software Repositories*. MSR '06. Shanghai, China: ACM, pp. 54–57 (cit. on pp. 8, 286).

Xu, J. (2008). „Rule-based Automatic Software Performance Diagnosis and Design Improvement.“ PhD thesis. Carleton University (cit. on pp. 88, 104, 107, 110, 152, 289).

– (2010). „Rule-based automatic software performance diagnosis and improvement.“ In: *Performance Evaluation* 67.8. Special Issue on Software and Performance, pp. 585–611 (cit. on pp. 3, 7, 289).

Yan, D., G. Xu, and A. Rountev (2012). „Uncovering Performance Problems in Java Applications with Reference Propagation Profiling.“ In: *Proceedings of the 34th International Conference on Software Engineering*. ICSE '12. Zurich, Switzerland: IEEE Press, pp. 134–144 (cit. on p. 279).

Yau, S., J. Collofello, and T. MacGregor (1978). „Ripple effect analysis of software maintenance.“ In: *Computer Software and Applications Conference, 1978. COMPSAC '78. The IEEE Computer Society's Second International*, pp. 60–65 (cit. on pp. 4, 71, 97).

Ye, Y. and G. Fischer (2005). „Reuse-Conducive Development Environments.“ In: *Automated Software Engineering* 12.2, pp. 199–235 (cit. on pp. 8, 282).

Zhang, C., J. Yang, Y. Zhang, J. Fan, X. Zhang, J. Zhao, and P. Ou (2012). „Automatic parameter recommendation for practical API usage.“ In: *34th*

*International Conference on Software Engineering (ICSE)*, pp. 826–836 (cit. on pp. 6, 8, 283).

Zheng, T. and M. Woodside (2003). „Heuristic Optimization of Scheduling and Allocation for Distributed Systems with Soft Deadlines.“ In: *Computer Performance Evaluation. Modelling Techniques and Tools*. Ed. by P. Kemper and W. Sanders. Vol. 2794. Lecture Notes in Computer Science. Springer Berlin Heidelberg, pp. 169–181 (cit. on pp. 7, 293).

Zhong, H., S. Thummalapenta, T. Xie, L. Zhang, and Q. Wang (2010). „Mining API Mapping for Language Migration.“ In: *Proceedings of the 32Nd ACM/IEEE International Conference on Software Engineering - Volume 1*. ICSE '10. Cape Town, South Africa: ACM, pp. 195–204 (cit. on p. 285).

Zhu, L., A. Aurum, I. Gorton, and R. Jeffery (2005). „Tradeoff and Sensitivity Analysis in Software Architecture Evaluation Using Analytic Hierarchy Process.“ In: *Software Quality Journal* 13.4, pp. 357–375 (cit. on pp. 31, 113).

Zimmermann, T., A. Zeller, P. Weissgerber, and S. Diehl (2005). „Mining version histories to guide software changes.“ In: *IEEE Transactions on Software Engineering* 31.6, pp. 429–445 (cit. on p. 285).

## Online References

Compuware (2015). *Application Performance Management Survey*. URL: `http://www.cnetdirectintl.com/direct/compuware/Ovum_APM/APM_Survey_Report.pdf` (visited on 04/02/2015) (cit. on pp. 2, 7, 304, 306, 307).

Brekken, L. A. et al. (2008). *What is the n+1 selects issue?* URL: `http://stackoverflow.com/questions/97197/what-is-the-n1-selects-issue` (visited on 01/27/2015) (cit. on pp. 26, 121, 204).

Eclipse (2015). *Eclipse Modeling Framework (EMF)*. URL: `http://www.eclipse.org/modeling/emf/` (visited on 04/07/2015) (cit. on pp. 29, 349).

*EMFTrace* (2014). URL: `http://sourceforge.net/projects/emftrace/` (visited on 01/22/2015) (cit. on p. 300).

Goepel, K. D. (2014). *Multi-criteria decision making using the Analytic Hierarchy Process*. URL: `http://bpmsg.com/academic/ahp.php` (visited on 03/15/2015) (cit. on p. 210).

Google (2014). *Google Guava-Libraries*. URL: http://code.google.com/p/guava-libraries/ (visited on 03/10/2015) (cit. on p. 257).

Grabner, A. (2010). *Top 10 Performance Problems taken from Zappos, Monster, Thomson and Co*. URL: http://apmblog.dynatrace.com/2010/06/15/top-10-performance-problems-taken-from-zappos-monster-and-co/ (visited on 03/20/2015) (cit. on p. 204).

– (2012). *Top Performance Mistakes when moving from Test to Production: Excessive Logging*. URL: http://apmblog.dynatrace.com/2012/08/01/top-performance-mistakes-when-moving-from-test-to-production-excessive-logging/ (visited on 03/20/2015) (cit. on pp. 27, 204).

– (2013). *Top 8 Application Performance Landmines*. URL: http://apmblog.dynatrace.com/2013/04/10/top-8-application-performance-landmines/ (visited on 03/20/2015) (cit. on p. 204).

Haines, S. (2014). *Top 10 Most Common Java Performance Problems*. AppDynamics White Paper. URL: http://info.appdynamics.com/Top10JavaPerformanceProblems_eBook.html (visited on 01/02/2015) (cit. on pp. 26, 27, 159, 195, 204, 277).

Hirschauer, J. (2012). *Percentiles Made Easy*. URL: http://www.appdynamics.com/blog/apm/percentiles-made-easy/ (visited on 12/19/2014) (cit. on p. 63).

Kopp, M. (2012a). *Why Averages Suck and Percentiles are Great*. URL: http://insidetechtalk.com/why-averages-suck-and-percentiles-are-great/ (visited on 12/19/2014) (cit. on p. 63).

– (2012b). *Why Averages Suck and Percentiles are Great*. URL: http://apmblog.dynatrace.com/2012/11/14/why-averages-suck-and-percentiles-are-great/ (visited on 03/20/2015) (cit. on p. 209).

Krogh, J., P. Krogh, et al. (2012). *How to use EclipseLink Pagination*. URL: http://wiki.eclipse.org/EclipseLink/Examples/JPA/Pagination (visited on 01/29/2015) (cit. on p. 121).

Limburg, A. and L. Röwekamp (2013). *Was du später kannst besorgen: Lazy Loading in JPA 2.1*. URL: https://jaxenter.de/was-du-spater-kannst-besorgen-lazy-loading-in-jpa-2-1-2375 (visited on 02/20/2015) (cit. on pp. 121, 147, 204).

Linden, G. (2006). *Make Data Useful*. URL: https://sites.google.com/site/glinden/Home/StanfordDataMining.2006-11-28.ppt (visited on 04/02/2015) (cit. on p. 2).

LoadRunner (2014). *LoadRunner™*. URL: http://www8.hp.com/us/en/software-solutions/loadrunner-load-testing/ (visited on 01/02/2015) (cit. on p. 253).

Object Management Group (2011a). *Business Process Model and Notation (BPMN)*. URL: http://www.omg.org/spec/BPMN/2.0/ (visited on 04/12/2015) (cit. on p. 34).

– (2011b). *The UML Profile for MARTE: Modeling and Analysis of Real-Time and Embedded Systems*. URL: http://www.omgmarte.org/ (visited on 04/09/2015) (cit. on pp. 19, 34).

– (2012). *Architecture-Driven Modernization (ADM): Structured Metrics Meta-Model (SMM)*. version 1.0. URL: http://www.omg.org/spec/SMM/1.0/ (visited on 12/12/2014) (cit. on p. 55).

– (2014a). *Object Constraint Language (OCL)*. version 2.4. URL: http://www.omg.org/spec/OCL/2.4/ (visited on 12/29/2014) (cit. on p. 74).

– (2014b). *OMG Meta Object Facility (MOF) Core Specification, Version 2.4.2*. URL: http://www.omg.org/spec/MOF/2.4.2/ (visited on 04/07/2015) (cit. on p. 29).

OBrien, M., L. Rekadze, J. Sutherland, et al. (2012). *Optimizing the EclipseLink Application (ELUG)*. URL: http://wiki.eclipse.org/Optimizing_the_EclipseLink_Application_(ELUG) (visited on 02/20/2015) (cit. on p. 121).

Oracle (2013a). *Java Persistence API: XML Schemas*. URL: http://www.oracle.com/webfolder/technetwork/jsc/xml/ns/persistence/index.html (visited on 04/15/2015) (cit. on pp. 122, 349).

– (2013b). *Oracle® Fusion Middleware Solutions Guide for Oracle TopLink*. URL: http://docs.oracle.com/middleware/1212/toplink/TLADG/performance.htm#TLADG412 (visited on 02/20/2015) (cit. on p. 121).

– (2015). *Glassfish - World's first Java EE 7 Application Server*. URL: https://glassfish.java.net/ (visited on 02/20/2015) (cit. on pp. 121, 208).

Red Hat, Inc. (2015a). *Hibernate JavaDoc (4.3.8.Final*. URL: http://docs.jboss.org/hibernate/orm/4.3/javadocs/ (visited on 02/20/2015) (cit. on p. 24).

– (2015b). *Hibernate ORM: Idiomatic persistence for Java and relational databases*. URL: http://hibernate.org/orm/ (visited on 02/20/2015) (cit. on p. 24).

SAP SE (2015). *SAP HANA Cloud Documentation: Persistence Service*. URL: https://help.hana.ondemand.com/help/frameset.htm?

e7b3c275bb571014a910b3fb4329cf09.html (visited on 02/20/2015) (cit. on p. 121).

*SoGoSurvey* (2015). URL: http://www.sogosurvey.com/ (visited on 01/06/2015) (cit. on p. 167).

Still, A. (2013). *Category Archives: Performance Anti-Patterns*. URL: http://performance-patterns.com/category/performance-anti-patterns/ (visited on 12/08/2014) (cit. on p. 195).

Sutherland, J. (2010). *Batch fetching - optimizing object graph loading*. URL: http://java-persistence-performance.blogspot.de/2010/08/batch-fetching-optimizing-object-graph.html (visited on 02/20/2015) (cit. on p. 121).

Sutherland, J., R. Sapir, D. Clarke, et al. (2013). *EclipseLink/Examples/JPA/QueryOptimization*. URL: https://wiki.eclipse.org/EclipseLink/Examples/JPA/QueryOptimization (visited on 01/30/2015) (cit. on p. 121).

The Apache Software Foundation (2013). *Apache OpenJPA Project*. URL: http://openjpa.apache.org/ (visited on 02/20/2015) (cit. on p. 24).

– (2014). *Apache Derby*. URL: https://db.apache.org/derby/ (visited on 04/16/2015) (cit. on p. 208).

– (2015). *Apache JMeter™*. URL: http://jmeter.apache.org/ (visited on 03/15/2015) (cit. on pp. 203, 207).

The Eclipse Foundation (2013a). *EclipseLink 2.5.0, build 'v20130425-368d603' API Reference*. URL: http://www.eclipse.org/eclipselink/api/2.5/index.html (visited on 01/29/2015) (cit. on pp. 24, 121, 138).

– (2013b). *Understanding EclipseLink (Concepts Guide) 2.5*. URL: http://www.eclipse.org/eclipselink/documentation/2.5/concepts/ (visited on 02/16/2015) (cit. on pp. 121, 123, 136, 144).

– (2014). *Java Persistence API (JPA) Extension Reference for EclipseLink, Release 2.5*. URL: http://www.eclipse.org/eclipselink/documentation/2.5/jpa/extensions/ (visited on 01/30/2015) (cit. on pp. 121, 123, 131, 133).

– (2015). *EclipseLink Project*. URL: http://eclipse.org/eclipselink/ (visited on 02/20/2015) (cit. on pp. 24, 121, 208).

van Hoorn, A. (2014a). *Markov4JMeter - Probabilistic and Intensity-Varying Workload Generation for Session-Based Software Systems*. URL: https://www.se.informatik.uni-kiel.de/en/research/projects/markov4jmeter (visited on 04/16/2015) (cit. on p. 207).

W3C (2012a). *W3C XML Schema Definition Language (XSD) 1.1. Part 1: Structures*. URL: http://www.w3.org/TR/2012/REC-xmlschema11-1-20120405/ (visited on 04/12/2015) (cit. on p. 34).

– (2012b). *W3C XML Schema Definition Language (XSD) 1.1. Part 2: Datatypes*. URL: http://www.w3.org/TR/2012/REC-xmlschema11-2-20120405/ (visited on 04/12/2015) (cit. on p. 34).

Wert, A., C. Heger, R. Farahbod, D. Knöpfle, P. Merkert, M. Oehler, and H. Schulz (2015a). *DynamicSpotter*. URL: http://sopeco.github.io/DynamicSpotter/ (visited on 04/06/2015) (cit. on p. 310).

Wert, A., C. Heger, R. Farahbod, H. Schulz, and M. Oehler (2015b). *Adaptable Instrumentation and Monitoring*. URL: http://sopeco.github.io/AIM/ (visited on 04/24/2015) (cit. on p. 208).

Williams, L. G. and C. U. Smith (2002a). *Five Steps to Solving Software Performance Problems*. Software Engineering Research and Performance Engineering Services White Paper. URL: http://www.perfeng.com/papers/step5.pdf (visited on 01/02/2015) (cit. on pp. 3, 83, 87, 90, 104, 107, 159).

Winand, M. (2012a). *Nested Loops*. URL: http://use-the-index-luke.com/sql/join/nested-loops-join-n1-problem (visited on 01/27/2015) (cit. on pp. 26, 121, 204).

# List of Figures

# List of Tables

# A. Appendix

## A.1. Persistence Configuration Metamodel

Figure A.1 shows the persistence configuration schema (Oracle, 2013a) modeled with the Ecore metamodeling language (Eclipse 2015) as the persistence configuration metamodel in the form of a UML class diagram.

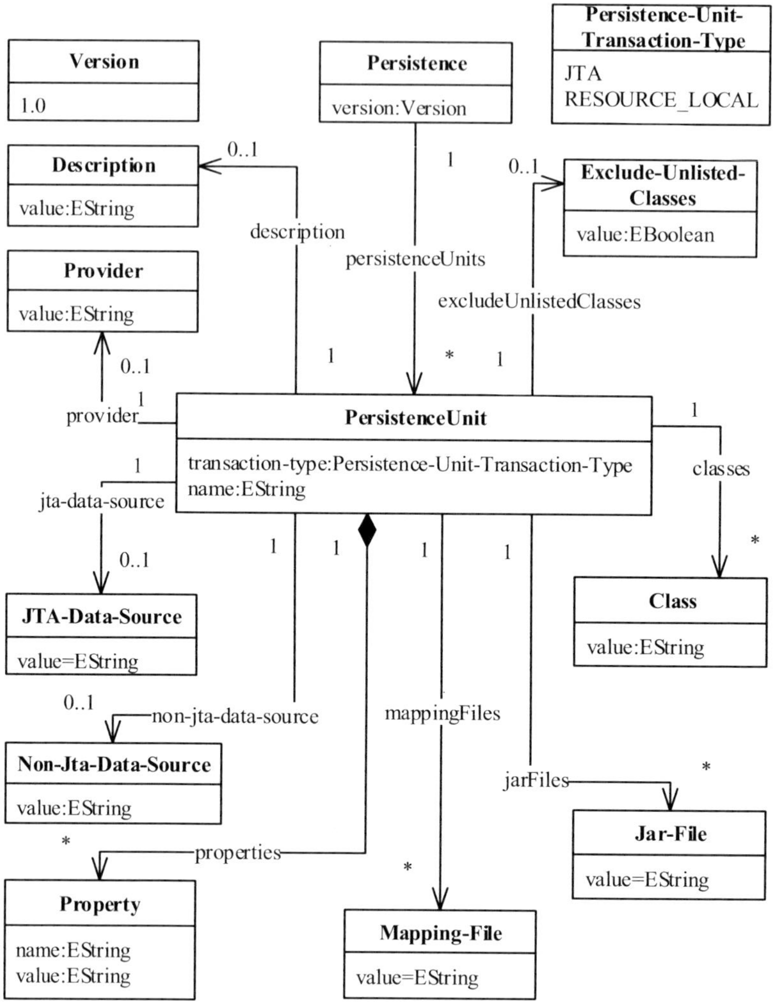


**Figure A.1.:** Persistence configuration metamodel

## A.2. Metamodel-dependent Change Types

Table A.1 shows a non-exhaustive list of metamodel-dependent change types for creating change plans.

**Table A.1.:** Metamodel-dependent change types

| Metamodel | Change type |
|---|---|
| JaMoPP Java | UpdateReference<br>UpdateReference<br>AddMethodCall<br>AddIdentifierReference<br>AddStringReference<br>UpdateAnnotationParameterList<br>AddAnnotationAttributeSetting<br>AddArrayInitializer<br>AddAnnotationInstance<br>AddAnnotationParameterList<br>UpdateElementAnnotations<br>AddInt<br>AddOrdinaryParameter<br>AddClassMethod<br>UpdateConcreteClassifier<br>AddReturn<br>AddMultiplicativeExpression<br>AddDivision<br>AddMultiplication<br>AddLocalVariableStatement<br>AddLocalVariable<br>AddNamespaceClassifierReference<br>AddClassifierReference<br>AddReflectiveClassReference<br>AddCastExpression<br>UpdateParametrizable<br>AddParameter<br>DeleteParameter |

## A.3. Online Survey Questionnaire

This section shows a digital print out of the online survey questionnaire.

| | |
|---|---|
| Persistence configuration | AddProperty<br>UpdateProperty<br>DeleteProperty<br>UpdatePersistenceUnit |

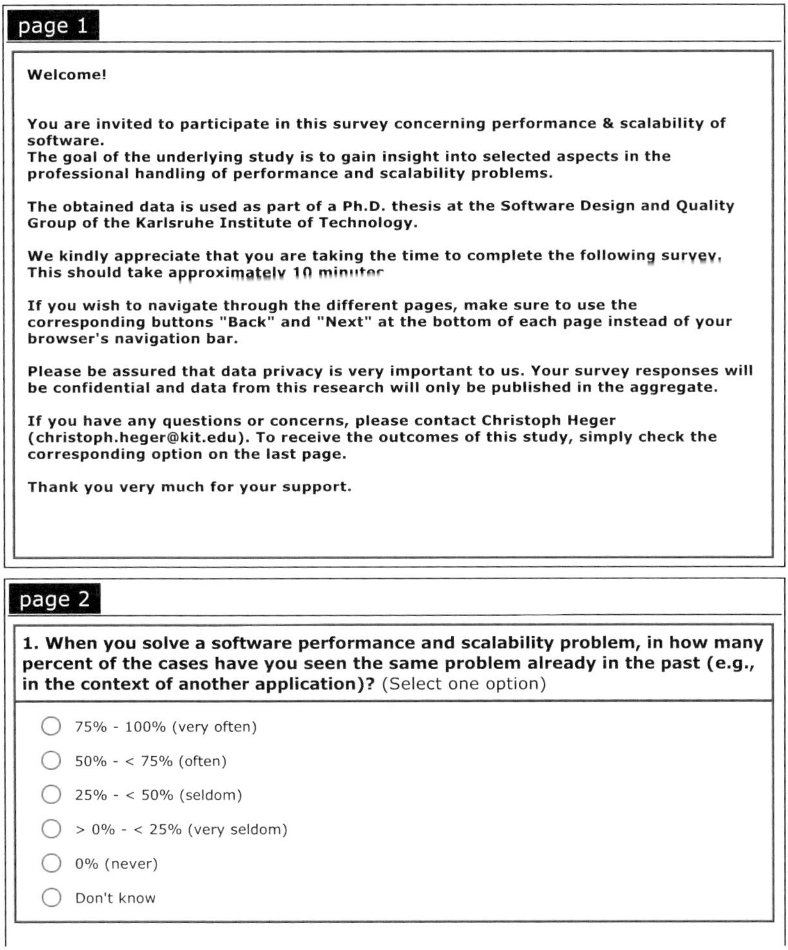

**page 1**

**Welcome!**

**You are invited to participate in this survey concerning performance & scalability of software.**
**The goal of the underlying study is to gain insight into selected aspects in the professional handling of performance and scalability problems.**

**The obtained data is used as part of a Ph.D. thesis at the Software Design and Quality Group of the Karlsruhe Institute of Technology.**

**We kindly appreciate that you are taking the time to complete the following survey. This should take approximately 10 minutes.**

**If you wish to navigate through the different pages, make sure to use the corresponding buttons "Back" and "Next" at the bottom of each page instead of your browser's navigation bar.**

**Please be assured that data privacy is very important to us. Your survey responses will be confidential and data from this research will only be published in the aggregate.**

**If you have any questions or concerns, please contact Christoph Heger (christoph.heger@kit.edu). To receive the outcomes of this study, simply check the corresponding option on the last page.**

**Thank you very much for your support.**

**page 2**

**1. When you solve a software performance and scalability problem, in how many percent of the cases have you seen the same problem already in the past (e.g., in the context of another application)?** (Select one option)

- 75% - 100% (very often)
- 50% - < 75% (often)
- 25% - < 50% (seldom)
- > 0% - < 25% (very seldom)
- 0% (never)
- Don't know

**Figure A.2.:** Online survey questionnaire for invited respondents

**2. When you recall software performance and scalability problems you have seen in the past 3 years, how many of them were new to you and how many of them did you already know?**

(a) percent of problems that were new to you

______________________________

**3. When you solve software performance and scalability problems, in how many percent of the cases do you apply solutions that you have already applied in the past (e.g., in the context of a different application or problem)?** (Select one option)

- ○ 75% - 100% (very often)
- ○ 50% - < 75% (often)
- ○ 25% - < 50% (seldom)
- ○ > 0% - < 25% (very seldom)
- ○ 0% (never)
- ○ Don't know

**4. When you solve software performance and scalability problems, in how many percent of the cases do you apply solutions that others have already applied in the past (e.g., a solution that you found in a book on software performance and scalability problems or a performance pattern)?** (Select one option)

- ○ 75% - 100% (very often)
- ○ 50% - < 75% (often)
- ○ 25% - < 50% (seldom)
- ○ > 0% - < 25% (very seldom)
- ○ 0% (never)
- ○ Don't know

**5. When you solve software performance & scalability problems, do you follow an established process that is also used by others or do you follow your own process?** (Select one option)

- ○ I have not solved any software performance and scalability problem in the past
- ○ I decide from case to case what I do
- ○ Established process
- ○ Don't know
- ○ Own process (Please describe) ____________

**page 3**

**Please distribute 100 points between the following periods of time according to how often you are busy with solving a software performance and scalability problem for that time span.**
**Example: Assuming that you solve 50% of all software performance and scalability problems in less than a few hours and you need more than a month for the other 50% of the problems, you give 50 points to the first and 50 points to the last time span. Accordingly, all other time spans receive 0 points.**

**How often takes you the solution of a software performance and scalability problem...**

**6. ...less than a few hours?** (Enter a value between 0 and 100)

**7. ...a few hours to a day?** (Enter a value between 0 and 100)

**8. ... more than a day to a week?** (Enter a value between 0 and 100)

**9. ...more than a week to a month?** (Enter a value between 0 and 100)

**10. ...more than a month?** (Enter a value between 0 and 100)

**page 4**

**When you think on software performance and scalability problems you have worked on in the past, in which of the following scenarios have you been how often? Please distribute 100 points between the following scenarios according to how often you have been in the described scenario in the past. Example: Assuming you are 75% of the cases in the one problem, one solution scenario, and 25% of the cases in the more than one problem, more than one possible solution for each problem scenario, you give 75 points to the first scenario and 25 points to the last scenario. Accordingly, all other scenarios receive 0 points.**

**11. One problem, one solution.** (Enter a value between 0 and 100)

**12. One Problem, more than one possible solution.** (Enter a value between 0 and 100)

**13. More than one problem, one possible solution for each problem.** (Enter a value between 0 and 100)

**14. More than one problem, more than one possible solution for each problem.** (Enter a value between 0 and 100)

page 5

**When you think of deciding on which solution of a software performance and scalability problem to implement, which decision criteria (e.g., performance improvement, implementation effort) do you consider in making the decision on which solution to implement?**

**15. Please list some of the decision criteria:**

**16. Do you agree with the following statement?**

**"The existing support for finding a solution for a detected software performance & scalability problem is insufficient." (Problem has been identified and root cause has been isolated)** (Select one option)

○ strongly agree ○ slightly agree ○ slightly disagree ○ strongly disagree ○ don't know

**17. If any: What kind of support do you currently have to solve a detected software performance and scalability problem?**

page 6

**Imagine you get a tool that supports you in solving software performance and scalability problems. Please distribute 100 points between the following support possibilities according to how important it is for you that the tool provides the following kind of support to you. Example: Assuming all listed support possibilities are equally important for you, you give 20 points to each support possibility.**

**How important is it for you that the tool...**

**18. ... proposes generic solution patterns completely automated to you that you have to transfer into the actual application and problem context, without the tool interacting with you (e.g., a generic solution pattern like to distribute functionality evenly among components).** (Enter a value between 0 and 100)

**19. ... proposes semi-automatically application and problem specific solutions while interacting with you (e.g., an application specific solution like WHICH functionality to move to WHICH component).** (Enter a value between 0 and 100)

**20. ... describes the implementation of solution proposals (e.g., describing the implementation with change activities, listing parts of the architecture, components, classes, and methods that are impacted by changes).** (Enter a value between 0 and 100)

**21. ... supports you in conducting performance evaluation experiments (e.g., what metric is to be analysed, where in the system and how the information is to be obtained).** (Enter a value between 0 and 100)

**22. ... supports you in making a decision about the solution to implement.** (Enter a value between 0 and 100)

**page 7**

**23. How long do you engage yourself in the context of solving software performance and scalability problems?** (Select one option)

- ○ < 1 year
- ○ > 1 - 3 years
- ○ > 3 - 5 years
- ○ > 5 - 10 years
- ○ > 10 years
- ○ Don't know

**24. In which environment do you work? (Multiple answers are possible)**

- ☐ University
- ☐ Industry
- ☐ Consulting
- ☐ Other (Please specify) ____________

**25. How many employees has the company you work for?** (Select one option)

- ○ < 100
- ○ > 100 - 500
- ○ > 500 - 5.000
- ○ > 5.000
- ○ Don't know

**26. What is your role in this environment? (Multiple answers are possible)**

- ☐ Manager
- ☐ Software Engineer/Developer
- ☐ Quality Engineer/Tester
- ☐ Researcher
- ☐ Designer
- ☐ Performance Engineer
- ☐ Architect
- ☐ Product Owner

☐ Consultant

☐ Other (Please specify) ______________

**27. Have you ever solved a software performance and scalability problem in an industrially used application?** (Select one option)

○ Yes

○ No

○ Don't know

**28. If you have answered the previous question with "Yes": Please describe at least one of the problems abstractly that you have solved in an industrially used application.**

______________________________________________

______________________________________________

**29. Please check one (or both) of the following options if you wish to receive the results of this study.**

☐ Send me the results to the same e-mail address as the invitation.

☐ Send me the results to the following mail address: ______________

**30. Do you have any additional comments?**

______________________________________________

______________________________________________

# The Karlsruhe Series on Software Design and Quality

Edited by Prof. Dr. Ralf Reussner // ISSN 1867-0067

Band 1 **Steffen Becker**
Coupled Model Transformations for QoS Enabled Component-Based Software Design.
ISBN 978-3-86644-271-9

Band 2 **Heiko Koziolek**
Parameter Dependencies for Reusable Performance Specifications of Software Components.
ISBN 978-3-86644-272-6

Band 3 **Jens Happe**
Predicting Software Performance in Symmetric Multi-core and Multiprocessor Environments.
ISBN 978-3-86644-381-5

Band 4 **Klaus Krogmann**
Reconstruction of Software Component Architectures and Behaviour Models using Static and Dynamic Analysis.
ISBN 978-3-86644-804-9

Band 5 **Michael Kuperberg**
Quantifying and Predicting the Influence of Execution Platform on Software Component Performance.
ISBN 978-3-86644-741-7

Band 6 **Thomas Goldschmidt**
View-Based Textual Modelling.
ISBN 978-3-86644-642-7

Band 7 **Anne Koziolek**
Automated Improvement of Software Architecture Models for Performance and Other Quality Attributes.
ISBN 978-3-86644-973-2

Band 8 **Lucia Happe**
Configurable Software Performance Completions through Higher-Order Model Transformations.
ISBN 978-3-86644-990-9

Band 9 **Franz Brosch**
Integrated Software Architecture-Based Reliability Prediction for IT Systems.
ISBN 978-3-86644-859-9

Band 10 **Christoph Rathfelder**
Modelling Event-Based Interactions in Component-Based Architectures for Quantitative System Evaluation.
ISBN 978-3-86644-969-5

Band 11 **Henning Groenda**
Certifying Software Component Performance Specifications.
ISBN 978-3-7315-0080-3

Band 12 **Dennis Westermann**
Deriving Goal-oriented Performance Models by Systematic Experimentation.
ISBN 978-3-7315-0165-7

Band 13 **Michael Hauck**
Automated Experiments for Deriving Performance-relevant Properties of Software Execution Environments.
ISBN 978-3-7315-0138-1

Band 14 **Zoya Durdik**
Architectural Design Decision Documentation through Reuse of Design Patterns.
ISBN 978-3-7315-0292-0

Band 15 **Erik Burger**
Flexible Views for View-based Model-driven Development.
ISBN 978-3-7315-0276-0

Band 16 **Benjamin Klatt**
Consolidation of Customized Product Copies into Software Product Lines.
ISBN 978-3-7315-0368-2

Band 17 **Andreas Rentschler**
Model Transformation Languages with Modular Information Hiding.
ISBN 978-3-7315-0346-0

Band 18 **Omar-Qais Noorshams**
Modeling and Prediction of I/O Performance in Virtualized Environments.
ISBN 978-3-7315-0359-0

Band 19 **Johannes Josef Stammel**
Architekturbasierte Bewertung und Planung von Änderungsanfragen.
ISBN 978-3-7315-0524-2

Band 20 **Alexander Wert**
Performance Problem Diagnostics by Systematic Experimentation.
ISBN 978-3-7315-0677-5

Band 21 **Christoph Heger**
An Approach for Guiding Developers to Performance and Scalability Solutions.
ISBN 978-3-7315-0698-0